101 Interventions Group Therapy

This newly revised and expanded second edition of *101 Interventions in Group Therapy* offers practitioners exactly what they are looking for: effective interventions in a clear and reader-friendly format. This comprehensive guide provides 101 short chapters by leading practitioners explaining step-by-step exactly what to do when challenging situations arise in group therapy. Featuring a wide selection of all new interventions with an added focus on working with diverse populations, this comprehensive volume is an invaluable resource for both early career practitioners as well as seasoned group leaders looking to expand their collection of therapeutic tools.

Scott Simon Fehr, Psy.D., CGP is a licensed psychologist, licensed mental health counselor, academician, international lecturer and author. Since 1993, Dr. Fehr has been a faculty member with the Master's Mental Health Counselor Program, the School Counselors Program and APA Doctorate Clinical Psychology Program in the Graduate College of Psychology at Nova Southeastern University in Fort Lauderdale, Florida, where he teaches Group Theory and Processes and Advanced Group Theory and Processes including supervising both Doctoral Directed Research Studies in group therapy and Master's and Doctoral Practicums.

101 Interventions in Group Therapy
Second Edition

Edited by Scott Simon Fehr

NEW YORK AND LONDON

Second edition published 2017
by Routledge
711 Third Avenue, New York, NY 10017
and by Routledge
2 Park Square, Milton Park, Abingdon, Oxon, OX14 4RN

Routledge is an imprint of the Taylor & Francis Group, an informa business

© 2017 Taylor & Francis

The right of the editor to be identified as the author of the editorial material, and of the authors for their individual chapters, has been asserted in accordance with sections 77 and 78 of the Copyright, Designs and Patents Act 1988.

All rights reserved. No part of this book may be reprinted or reproduced or utilized in any form or by any electronic, mechanical, or other means, now known or hereafter invented, including photocopying and recording, or in any information storage or retrieval system, without permission in writing from the publishers.

Trademark notice: Product or corporate names may be trademarks or registered trademarks, and are used only for identification and explanation without intent to infringe.

First edition published by The Haworth Press 2008

Library of Congress Cataloging in Publication Data
Names: Fehr, Scott Simon, editor.
Title: 101 interventions in group therapy / edited by Scott Simon Fehr.
Other titles: One hundred and one interventions in group therapy
Description: 2nd edition. | New York, NY : Routledge, 2016. | Includes bibliographical references and index.
Identifiers: LCCN 2016019707| ISBN 9781138100374 (hbk : alk. paper) | ISBN 9781138100381 (pbk : alk. paper) | ISBN 9781315657691 (ebk)
Subjects: LCSH: Group psychotherapy.
Classification: LCC RC488 .A32 2016 | DDC 616.89/152—dc23
LC record available at https://lccn.loc.gov/2016019707

ISBN: 978-1-138-10037-4 (hbk)
ISBN: 978-1-138-10038-1 (pbk)
ISBN: 978-1-315-65769-1 (ebk)

Typeset in Sabon
by Keystroke, Station Road, Codsall, Wolverhampton

Dedications

This book is dedicated to my Intrepid Colleagues who gave of themselves and their experiences. It, too, is dedicated to those who helped me put this book together and remained calm when I was not and to Christopher Teja of Routledge Press who started this ball rolling, which at times felt like it was rolling over me. It, also, is dedicated to my colleagues from the first edition, who now have passed away. You are missed.

Contents

About the Editor	xv
Foreword by J. Scott Rutan	xvii
Preface	xix

1. On Second Thought: Demonstrating Different Levels of Perception — 1
   TOBY BERMAN

2. Collateral Damage — 4
   JOSEPH SHAY

3. Lesbians Grieving Heterosexual Privilege by Creating a Loss Totem — 8
   KRIS DRUMM

4. A Culture of Nice in a Women's Group: It's Nice to be Nice — 12
   MELISSA BLACK

5. Countertransference in Groups With Severely Ill Inpatients — 15
   CARLA PENNA

6. The Use of Primal Scream to Facilitate Release in the African-American Male: Pain Demands to be Heard — 19
   MARVIN D. EVANS

7. Hiring a Group Coordinator Can Develop a Group Program — 22
   JOSHUA M. GROSS

8. Who Owes You an Apology? — 26
   ELLEN J. FEHR
   GARY L. SANDELIER

9. Not Just Talk: A Group Therapy Model Integrating Action Theory and Techniques — 29
   THOMAS TREADWELL

10	Anger: A Historical Account and an Ah Ha Moment KAREN TRAVIS	33
11	Battling the Alien: Working Through Self-Hatred in Group Therapy PATRICIA KYLE DENNIS	36
12	A Ritual for Termination MARVIN KAPHAN	39
13	Setting Group Culture Development in Motion AVRAHAM COHEN	43
14	Only the Lonely: Trauma and Group Identity RICHARD BECK	46
15	The Efficacy of Wedding Cognitive Behavior and Psychoanalytic Psychotherapies in Group Psychotherapy for Incarcerated Male Population URI AMIT	49
16	Sparking Connection: Increasing Awareness, Engagement and Relatedness CARLOS CANALES	53
17	Intercultural Group Therapy: Global Nomads, Expats and Lovepats MARIA VAN NOORT	57
18	Back to the Future: Attending to Detrimental Family Loyalties RUSSELL HOPFENBERG	61
19	The Undecided: Helping Clients Make Decisions KLIFTON SIMON FEHR	64
20	Degree of Action and Structure in Format to Facilitate Group Cohesion SHARAN L. SCHWARTZBERG	67
21	Attuning to Micro-Expressions in Group: A Relational Technique MARTHA GILMORE	71
22	The Group Therapist in the Making PRIYA KIRPALANI	74
23	Grounding: Coming into the "Here and Now" by Using Our Bodily Sensations MARGARET M. POSTLEWAITE	77

24	Post Traumatic Stress Disorder with Combat Veterans Using Cognitive Behavioral Group Therapy JUSTIN A. D'ARIENZO	80
25	The Group Sandwich Model for International Conflict Dialog Using Large Groups as a Social Developmental Space ROBI FRIEDMAN	83
26	A Five-Stage Technique to Enhance Termination in Group Therapy JERROLD LEE SHAPIRO	86
27	Mindfulness Practice: Interventions for Working with Young Children in Groups ELLEN DECKER REBECCA M. CORDISCO	90
28	A Relaxed Approach to Treating Phobia NORMAN CLARINGBULL	94
29	Building a Pathway to Success DARIUSH F. FATHI	98
30	Urge and Creativity in the Group Matrix: Applying Art Therapy Within Group Therapy TAL SCHWARTZ	102
31	"I Am Positive There is More to Me Than HIV" RACHEL L. KONNERTH	106
32	From Time to Time MARC G. SCHRAMM	110
33	Applying Expressive Therapies to Accelerate Cognitive Insight in Organizations BEN RIPPA	114
34	Treating Depression with a Dose of Anxiety RUSSELL HOPFENBERG	117
35	The Burden of Being Beautiful . . . Is 40 the End of the Road? KLIFTON SIMON FEHR SCOTT SIMON FEHR	121
36	Transforming Failures Into Honey LEYLA NAVARO	124
37	Humility in the Face of a Mistake MICHAEL P. FRANK	128

Contents

38 Promoting Communication and Interaction in a Group of Sub-Saharan Africa Immigrant Women — 131
CRISTINA MARTINEZ-TABOADA KUTZ
NEKANE OTERO

39 Letting Go of the Myth of Closure: One Practitioner's View — 135
DANIEL S. SCHOENWALD

40 The Shielded Name Tent — 138
TARA S. JUNGERSEN

41 Corrective Experiences in Intensive Group Psychotherapy — 141
RICK TIVERS

42 Mother–Daughter Interaction Through the Group's "Hall of Mirrors" — 144
SHOSHANA BEN-NOAM

43 Improving Emotional Processing With Group Psychotherapy — 148
DAVID CANTOR

44 Who's Responsible? Accepting and Integrating One is Not Always the Victim — 151
RACHEL L. KONNERTH
KLIFTON SIMON FEHR

45 Hot Air Balloon — 154
T. WING LO

46 Long-term Intergenerational Women's Psychotherapy Groups — 157
SHARI BARON

47 The Evolution of Gay Group Therapy — 160
LEWIS ZEN JORDAN

48 Group Therapy for Therapists — 163
TOBY ELLEN NEWMAN

49 Refilling and Repairing Your Glass: Insightful Exercise for Dually Diagnosed Clients — 166
IAN JACKSON

50 Am I Modeling or Muddling? Cranking Up a New Group — 170
SCOTT SIMON FEHR

51 Fireball — 173
BARNEY STRAUS

52	A Chair is Not a Chair is Not a Chair JOSEPH SHAY	176
53	The Masks We Wear CLAUDIA P. CALABRESE	180
54	Animal Assisted Therapy With a Group of Young Children With Social Problems STANLEY SCHNEIDER CHANA SCHNEIDER	183
55	"Am I My Mother's Daughter?" Eliciting Self-Awareness in the Transmission of Gender Roles Through Family Role Models LEYLA NAVARO	187
56	Living with Dying: How to Keep the Group Alive When the Members are Dying TOBY ELLEN NEWMAN	191
57	Bringing a New Member Into Group: Marking a New Place in the Cycle JOSHUA M. GROSS	195
58	The Crystal and the Stone: Use of Transitional Objects in Groups SHARI BARON	198
59	You Can Teach an Old Dog New Tricks! AVA J. KOTCH	201
60	Using Dreams in Group Therapy ROBI FRIEDMAN	204
61	The Group Therapist as Storyteller MARVIN KAPHAN	208
62	Using Primary Language to Access Primary Affect JERROLD LEE SHAPIRO	212
63	"What's so Funny?" The Group Leader's Use of Humor in Adolescent Groups SEAN GROVER	215
64	Using Grammar to Increase Immediacy and Affect MARTHA GILMORE	219
65	Group as a Place to Practice New Behaviors MYRNA L. FRANK	223

Contents

66 Counterresistance: Its Manifestation and Impact on Group Intervention and Management — 227
CARLA PENNA

67 "When Boundaries Breathe" — 231
RICHARD BECK

68 "What Do You Mean I Should Tell Her What I Think About Her?" Psychoeducation About Interpersonal Processes — 234
ANNE M. SLOCUM MCENEANEY

69 Advice Giving — 237
RUSSELL HOPFENBERG

70 Bridging as a Tool to Avoid Scapegoating — 240
MELISSA BLACK

71 The "I's" Have It! — 244
MARGARET M. POSTLEWAITE

72 Women's Empowerment Group Using Art Therapy — 248
TAL SCHWARTZ

73 From Silence to Frenzy: Resistance in the Face of Shame — 252
STEVEN L. SCHKLAR

74 "After The Group has Ended": Imagery to Vivify Termination — 257
MIRIAM IOSUPOVICI

75 Diminishing Dissociative Experiences for War Veterans in Group Therapy — 261
VIVIEN HENDERSON

76 I am Part of the Group Matrix — 265
BEN RIPPA

77 To Err is Human: Turning Our Mistakes Into Useful Interventions — 269
DAVE M. COOPERBERG

78 The Ability to Verbalize One's Needs Clearly in a Geriatric Population — 273
TOBY BERMAN

79 Norm Repair — 276
JOSEPH SHAY

80	Alchemy and Transformation: The Disturber in Group AVRAHAM COHEN	280
81	Family Member Association CAROL SCOTT DRURY	285
82	Building Self-Esteem Using Assertiveness Training and Props SHEILA SAZANT	288
83	Group Supervision Horseback Riding Workshop for Increasing Self-Awareness TAL-LI COHEN	291
84	Poetry as a Projective Technique and Springboard for Dialogue in Group Therapy SCOTT SIMON FEHR	295
85	Unexpected Consequences: Maintaining the Boundaries in a Therapy Group for Older Adults GEORGE MAX SAIGER	299
86	Creative Use of the Group Contract in Long-Term Psychotherapy Groups MELISSA BLACK	302
87	An Angry Outburst: Responding to Aggression ROBERT A. BERLEY	306
88	A Difficult Session MARVIN KAPHAN	311
89	The Nine Basic Steps for a Successful Group JOSHUA M. GROSS	315
90	Stress Inoculation Training for Trauma and Stress-Related Disorders JUSTIN A. D'ARIENZO	317
91	Using Metaphors and Stories to Resolve Impasses and Bridge Resistance JERROLD LEE SHAPIRO	321
92	Therapist Self-Disclosure as an Intervention Toward Normalizing and Eliciting Hope SCOTT SIMON FEHR	325
93	Directed Eye Contact: Nonverbal Communication as a Group Strengthening Tool SHARI BARON	329

Contents

94 "Remember Be Here Now"   332
ELLEN J. FEHR
GARY L. SANDELIER

95 Changing Chairs: Experiential Exercise for Exploration of Interpersonal Boundaries   336
PATRICIA KYLE DENNIS

96 Surfing an Unexpected Group's Tide   340
URI AMIT

97 Mindfulness in Group Therapy   343
MARK A. COHEN
DAVID CANTOR

98 Trauma Therapy as a Community Enterprise   347
NORMAN CLARINGBULL

99 Dealing with Anger in Two Different Phases of Group Psychotherapy   353
MICHAEL P. FRANK

100 The Fee: A Clinical Tool in Group Therapy   358
SHOSHANA BEN-NOAM

101 Installation of Hope in Bereavement Groups for the Elderly   361
MARK A. COHEN

Index   365

About the Editor

Scott Simon Fehr, Psy.D., CGP is a licensed Psychologist, licensed Mental Health Counselor, Academician, International Lecturer and Author. He was raised on a Quarter Horse Farm before going off to university. It was his responsibility to care for 120 horses, which probably was the foundation of him later finding that group psychotherapy would become his passion. He has been specializing in group therapy in his private practice since 1979. He was accepted as a student in the first Psy.D. class in the state of Florida. Since 1993, Dr. Fehr has been a Faculty Member with the Master's Mental Health Counselor Program, the School Counselors Program and APA Doctorate Clinical Psychology Program in the Graduate College of Psychology at Nova Southeastern University in Fort Lauderdale, Florida, where he teaches Group Theory and Processes and Advanced Group Theory and Processes including supervising both Doctoral Directed Research Studies in group therapy and Master's and Doctoral Practicums. He also supervises licensed eligible post-masters and post-doctorate interns.

Dr. Fehr is a member of the American Group Psychotherapy Association (of which he is the Past President of the Florida Affiliate) and a Certified Group Psychotherapist (CGP) and member of the International Association of Group Psychotherapy. His first book, *Introduction to Group Therapy: A Practical Guide*, second book, *Group Therapy in Independent Practice*, and his third book, *Introduction to Group Therapy: A Practical Guide* (2nd edition) were published by the Haworth Press, Inc., as was his fourth book *101 Interventions in Group Therapy*. Dr. Fehr's fifth book, *101 Interventions in Group Therapy* (revised edition) and his sixth book *101 Interventions in Group Therapy* (2nd edition) are published by Routledge. He has been a reviewer for numerous psychology books and journals and was the guest editor of the Special Edition on Group Therapy in the *Journal of Psychotherapy in Independent Practice* (both from Haworth Press, Inc.).

Dr. Fehr's formal education was in Behavioral Psychology but his personal 12-year analysis, both in individual and group, was Psychoanalytic. Dr. Fehr is an international lecturer in group psychotherapy and has led over 8000 psychotherapy groups at this time. He is an avid collector of eighteenth- and nineteenth-century antiques, and a student of the Spanish Language and the Jungian Tarot.

Foreword

The Spanish have a delightful tradition of serving "tapas," small portions of food which allow diners to sample a wide variety of tasty treats without being over-filled.

Scott Simon Fehr's newest volume can be considered the tapas of group therapy. Fehr has assembled an international cast of well-known authors who address important issues in group therapy in concise, brief chapters.

As with tapas, sometimes these chapters whet our appetites for more, and at other times the brief "taste" is sufficient to answer the questions that are addressed. This approach allows Fehr's authors to range far and wide, examining instances that occur regularly in groups but are sometimes not addressed.

At times the chapters focus on technique – for example, how a leader might modify a dysfunctional group norm that has been established – or tell stories, or the use of humor and animals in group therapy. Other chapters focus on working with varied clinical populations, such as pregnant women, war veterans, trauma survivors and individuals in the military. There are chapters devoted to tiny but very significant issues – if a member is absent or a group is not filled, should an empty chair be in the circle or should there only be as many chairs as there are expected members?

This is an entertaining as well as filling book. The reader can pick and choose topics of interest, or the reader can enjoy reading from cover to cover, knowing that the book can always be put down within a page or two and picked up at a later time.

Enjoy!

J. Scott Rutan
Senior Faculty, Boston Institute for Psychotherapy

Preface

It is with pleasure that I have been asked to edit the second edition of the *101 Interventions in Group Therapy* text. This remarkable book has had quite an illustrious history yet the joy, for me, has been the opportunity of working with many renowned group therapists who gave of their time and expertise to make this again an incredible read. Although the general readership of the first edition and revised edition felt the books were of great value in our developing profession, there were a few readers who felt certain changes needed to be made which would make the book more comfortable for them. The first discomfort, for some readers, was that similar themes should be clumped together and the book divided into thematic sections. This is quite understandable yet the book was not designed to be a text book per se but rather a text that could be picked up and put down for a later date, and spontaneously opened to any place and read what chapter arose. This was beautifully stated in Dr. Rutan's Foreword. He referred to the book as a tapas of group therapy information. Thus changing that format to thematic sections would be losing the essence of the concept of how the book was originally designed. The second discomfort came from readers who rigidly adhered to a particular paradigm and either felt there were not enough chapters related to their paradigm of practice or were downright hostile toward the many different types of paradigms our colleagues use in their practices. This is a book of creative interventions and perhaps the only book of its kind where colleagues talk about interventions in their work that they generally would not talk about due to the judgments of our colleagues. Without creativity our profession will not grow nor move forward but at a snail's pace. For many contributors, they had the professional courage to put into print: this is what I do and these have been the amazing results. Like snowflakes, people are uniquely different and one size does not fit all. It is my hope dear reader that you travel with these writers on a wonderful adventure in group psychotherapy.

Scott Simon Fehr
Hollywood, Florida

For free additional interventions from the first edition of *101 Interventions in Group Therapy*, please visit www.routledge.com/9781138100381

1 On Second Thought
Demonstrating Different Levels of Perception

Toby Berman

Introduction

How Perceived Individual Differences can Bring us Closer Together

It is truly amazing that people ever really understand each other. We all come from different histories and experiences, although some may seem comparable, besides we all have a different understanding of the use of language plus we differentiate in the personal understanding of the continuum of known vocabulary. These obvious separations in fact do just that. They separate individuals from each other. In order to bring people together in a healthy environment, we as therapists need to demonstrate that no matter what the differences may be we are all very much alike. We have the same hopes, dreams and concerns that generally the person next to us, whether in the street, bus, plane etc. is experiencing.

Another separation that keeps people apart is their cautiousness with perceived differences. This person may be of a different color, race, education, religion, finance or just plain physical appearance. This felt separation is simply a component of judgment. Most people prefer the ease of comfort within their homogenous population. The judgment being if you are not like me, you and I will not develop an interpersonal relationship or friendship. So how do we alleviate this historical judgment and the inhibition of moving out of one's comfort zone which in fact may have been handed down from generation to generation? We show that individual differences can truly be a remarkable component to being human with a profound opportunity of expanding our world.

Intervention

This intervention is really quite simple. We need to first show a group of people that part of what separates them is their different levels of perception of the same event. What is wonderful about the intervention is that there is no wrong or right answer thus eliminating competition and the fear of failure and not appearing intelligent thus demonstrating the uniqueness of each individual.

Procedure

1. Simply find a few sentences that can be interpreted multiple ways.
2. Write them on a board or hand out a sheet of paper with the sentences printed out.
3. Ask the clients what these sentences mean and reiterate there is no wrong or right answer.

Examples

1. He is a fine man. (What does that mean?)
2. My father was very strict. (What does that mean?)
3. Love is elusive. (What does that mean?)

As seen these sentences are generally not threatening sentences and can be interpreted in multiple ways. For example with sentence number 1, I have gotten responses such as "He is upstanding; He is responsible; He takes care of his family; He has a great ass, etc." For sentence number 2, I have gotten "He was very rigid; He was controlling; He made rules that had to be followed; He made me take out the garbage once a week, etc." For sentence number 3, I have gotten responses such as "I can never find love; Love requires a lot of work; People often say they love you but do not mean it; Love does not exist, etc."

With the many responses gathered from groups of people, it is interesting to observe two or more people from different cultures, races and education respond similarly and to watch the faces of these individuals hear what they interpreted said by someone whom they believed to be so very different than themselves. There are also those interpretations that are so foreign to the other members in the group that they become thoughtful and admiring by saying, "I would never have thought that."

These individual different interpretations begin to implement curiosity of the group members. They begin to want to learn more about the other people in their group. Interestingly, they start to seek components of each other's personalities that are similar to theirs. It is not uncommon for a straight guy to say to a gay guy, "You know I am having that same kind of issue with my wife that you are having with your partner," or an African American woman saying to a Caucasian woman, "Honey we are married to the same guy."

What is so remarkable about this intervention is the ultimate closeness that develops from people who, at one time, would never have even spoken to one another.

Client Responses

Most of the clients with whom we used this intervention very much enjoy it. It is not uncommon for them to ask if I have any more sentences that they can play with while they are in group together. It is also to be noted that many of the clients wish to develop, over time, more personal relationships with each other, i.e. having their respective families meet or go for coffee after group. Unlike a typical process group where we discourage outside socialization, in this particular group we encourage it as it builds bonds. Like a process group, we request that what is disclosed outside of the group during these events be brought back into the group for further discussion and in fact creates a role model or template for others to follow.

Conclusion and Contraindications

Individual differences make the world we live in interesting and unique. If used appropriately this intervention can not only show our differences but also our sameness. It would appear that it is easier to harm someone who is not like ourselves and yet with others like ourselves, in many cases, an inhibition curtails the action.

There have not been any experienced contraindications for the clients with this intervention. The only contraindication that may be found is within the therapist. If he or she lacks the sensitivity to the nuances of the responses, the therapist will miss many opportunities to provide a developing bond for the group members.

Toby Berman, Psy.D., is on staff at Mount Sinai Hospital in Miami Beach, Florida. Dr. Berman practices group and individual psychotherapy as well as psychological testing. She has written chapters and articles in many books and journals.

2 Collateral Damage

Joseph Shay

Theoretical Considerations

None of us wants to admit we cannot keep everyone safe in the room at all times. Readers, however, know there are unavoidable moments in group therapy that can be damaging to members. Given this reality, perhaps there are skillful ways to intervene to mitigate the damage.

My emphasis here is on what I call "collateral damage to another group member's process." By this I mean that the "damaging" member is actually engaged in acting out the very issues that brought him or her to group originally and is therefore engaged in a necessary reenactment which will thereby allow reflection and growth to occur. But *progress for one group member may come at the expense of another.*

Consider this clinical example familiar to readers (cf. Nitsun, 1996; Rutan, Stone, and Shay, 2014, chapter 14.) The group therapist asks Claire, a young woman in her first group session, "What are you feeling right now?" Claire replies, "I feel that people don't really want me here and that everyone is judging me which is what I always felt when I entered a new school when I was little." She continues, tearfully, "My parents never helped me integrate into the new school either." Bob, another group member, says Claire is whining and he assumes that she contributed to her lack of integration by her attitude. Claire, taken aback, exclaims, "What? What are you talking about?" The therapist asks Claire how she feels right now. Claire replies, "I feel misunderstood. I feel rejected. I feel unsafe." Bob says, "My parents never helped me adjust to school and I never complained. I got bullied by other kids and my father said, 'Deal with it, Bob.' I never whined." The group and the therapist know that Bob is so flooded by his history that his comments are infused with projection and transference and the attendant bitterness and rage. But Claire does not know this and she flees the room. The group is stunned.

For Bob, the resurgence and working through of such early wounds is essential to his ultimate progress. But his reactions—until they are understood and worked through—have the potential of damaging any member on the receiving end of his projections, in this case the new member, Claire. When members are so activated in the recipient role that they cannot tolerate their own affects, let alone begin to reflect on the experience, they have experienced damage, if temporary, in the group as a collateral effect of another member's necessary and inevitable group process.

Description of Group

This situation can occur in any group whether long-term, short-term, or theme-centered, that allows unstructured cross-talk and promotes open exchanges that can become affectively charged.

Intervention

The example above is a situation I have faced in different variations. The intervention described here was used in a long-term open-ended coed group, with the intervention made about three months into the life of the group.

In this group of eight, ages 25 to 50, members have begun to engage in deeper levels of sharing about their earlier lives and about their feelings in the room toward other group members. They are aware of the repetition in the group of childhood experiences and out-of-group interactions. Through exploration of these, the group is learning two things: first, the group is a petri dish for the appearance of earlier life experiences and second, the intensity of affect in the present is a marker that the affect is almost certainly fueled by experiences from the past.

Claire does return to the group session the day she flees but says, "I don't want to talk about this anymore," and for that moment, I agree. There are allusions to the experience in subsequent sessions. Three months later a similar situation arises.

Bob again accuses Claire of moaning and failing to admit fault, not realizing he is identifying with his aggressor father. Claire begins to weep and look toward the door. My intervention here is expressed in one paragraph though in actuality it is often broken into more bite-size comments across a session or several sessions. Rarely do I speak at such length but do so here for the sake of illustration.

In this intervention, because I am making a larger point to the group, I do not name Bob and Claire but I could just as easily have named them directly. The intervention has four parts: recognizing the process as having distortions within it; naming the potential benefit of the process; validating the feeling of being damaged during it; and expressing hope and belief that the group can tolerate and benefit from it.

Taken as a whole, I say, "There are a lot of really powerful feelings in the room, some of which did not originate here. That's how group therapy is and what I tried to explain when I met with each of you before you came to group. I know this is hard. Remember, *it's the very intensity of the feeling that can give you evidence that something else is at work here, before any of you met each other.* The beauty of group therapy is that you can get in touch with powerful feelings and express them but that doesn't mean that the comments that come from those feelings are accurate about the person they are expressed to. They may be or they may not be.

"This can be a very painful part of group because a comment can come your way that really hurts you, and you can even feel damaged by it because it hits you in a vulnerable spot. But our goal together is to reflect on what gets activated in us so we can learn from it. As I've expressed before, *group therapy is about action and reflection*, and that action can sometimes feel painful to you before the reflection happens. The group is strong enough, and I am hopeful that each of you is strong enough, to be able to tolerate this process and to return each week to understand what happened."

General Client Responses

In one such circumstance, a member who had been the one attacked replied, "Well, that sucks," suggesting the intervention was not helpful to her. Another rejoined, however, "Remember what we've been learning; it's not really about you. You don't have to own that." When group members really inhabit this idea—i.e., own what's yours and reject what's not yours—they are actually freed to own parts of the truth embedded in another member's distortion of them.

Conclusion

There is a deeply human wish on the part of all group therapists to shield wounded individuals from further wounds. Group therapy is not the place for that, however, because as safe as we wish it to be, it is in the very re-experiencing of these wounds that corrective experiences and healing can occur. Generally speaking, group members in successful groups learn that experiencing pain in group interactions is part of, not a failure of, the healing process. To prepare them for that in the screening phase makes it less likely they will be damaged by it.

Possible Contraindications

This type of intervention is rarely contraindicated except when, in the working through of the process, the member who is "damaging" feels too shamed by the suggestion of distortion or projection, or the member who is "damaged" feels too invalidated by the implication that his or her feelings are overpersonalized.

References

Nitsun, M. (1996). *The anti-group: Destructive forces in the group and their creative potential*. London: Routledge.

Rutan, J. S., Stone, W. N., & Shay, J. J. (2014). *Psychodynamic group psychotherapy* (5th ed.). New York: Guilford.

Joseph Shay, PhD, CGP, FAGPA, a psychologist in private practice in Cambridge, MA, has an affiliate position at the Harvard Medical School in the Department of Psychiatry, supervises at McLean and Massachusetts General Hospitals, and is on the faculty of the Psychoanalytic Couple and Family Institute of New England, the Northeastern Society for Group Psychotherapy, and the Massachusetts General Hospital Center for Psychodynamic Therapy and Research. Dr. Shay is the co-author of *Psychodynamic Group Psychotherapy* (4th and 5th editions) and the co-editor of *Odysseys in Psychotherapy* and *Complex Dilemmas in Group Therapy*.

3 Lesbians Grieving Heterosexual Privilege by Creating a Loss Totem

Kris Drumm

Introduction: Letting Go

Grieving unresolved loss is important for our emotional growth and capacity. As the nature of grief is pain, many of us avoid, repress, and deny the grief that accompanies letting go of people, situations, places, and other losses that are accumulated whenever a great change occurs. The result of this suppression and denial can be depression and/or anger (Whitfield, 1987). The intervention outlined in this chapter was used to assist lesbian clients in identifying and grieving losses incurred by "coming out," and living openly as a lesbian.

For LGBT people, there are losses that most of us must come to terms with when we acknowledge and make public our sexual orientation or gender identity. There are a myriad of possible losses, mostly rooted in the societal marginalization and stigmatization of homosexuality and gender variance (Herek, 1984; Cass, 1979). These losses may be extreme; as exile from family, church, community, or loss of employment.

Privilege is often assumed or unrecognized by those who have it (McIntosh, 2007). Often, it is only when we lose rights and protections that we realize not everyone enjoys the same freedoms. This article describes a process used in a group of lesbians to assist in identifying and coming to terms with the loss of heterosexual privilege that had protected them from rejection and marginalization.

Population

This intervention was used with a closed therapy group of 7 women who identify as lesbian and ranged in age from 30–60. The amount of time lived openly as lesbian varied from 6 months to 40 years. They had been meeting for several months, and had established substantial cohesion and rapport.

Intervention

One woman who had initially joined the group to obtain support as she began to admit her sexual orientation to herself and others shared her dismay at unexpected consequences this admission had for her. This sparked an in-depth discussion of the consequences of openly claiming one's same-sex sexual orientation. The loss totem was introduced at the next session to provide a concrete activity to facilitate reflection and identification of shared experiences of losses.

Directions

The facilitator procured and supplied group members with the following:

- Beading cord: One 12–18 inch piece to each participant.
- A plate of varied beads: Varied in color, size and shapes, obtained at craft and thrift stores.
  The plate was placed in the center of the group in a manner that was easily accessible by all participants. (Alternatively, members can be supplied with paper cups they fill with beads from the plate passed around the circle.)
- Paper and pen for participants to write down the losses as they string the beads to aid them in remembering the losses identified.

The group facilitator explained, "Totems are objects that have sacred and symbolic meanings, and we are going to create totems together to honor the losses that each participant has experienced as a result of claiming her lesbian identity. To be considered: any losses of dreams, expectations, rights, friends, family, or protections that you assumed. Different beads may seem to suit some losses better than others. Participants select beads and string them in silence." The beading process took approximately 15 minutes.

When the group was finished with the bead stringing process, the facilitator deconstructed the process by asking what it was like to create the totem, and then initiated a go around for each member to share her totem, and explain what each bead represented, and if that particular color and shape had any significance, followed by a discussion about the similarities and differences in the women's experiences. The facilitator asked members what they would like to do with their totems after the group, and members shared ideas.

Client Responses

The group became readily involved with the totem making exercise and, when sharing in the go around, there were tears as well as a few bouts of laughter as some of the losses identified were in retrospect seen as gains. For example, one woman spoke about the loss of respect she had experienced at her job, and the fear and shame she felt at the time, and then laughed as she reported that now, 15 years later, she occupied a high-ranking position at a much better company and had occasion to interact with the same people who treated her with homophobia and discrimination. One woman cried bitterly as she lamented the reaction of her daughter who would not allow her to come out to her grandchildren, or to bring her partner of 7 years to holiday or family celebrations.

A woman who had been out for over 20 years cried as she spoke about losing friendships and her church community, and expressed surprise about crying, saying, "I thought I had gotten over that a long time ago." One lesbian in the group used a blue crystal bead that she thought looked like a teardrop to symbolize the loss of freedom she experienced since feeling fearful to demonstrate any form of public affection at all to her lover. "I am grieving the loss of feeling safe in many ways," she said. This opened up an animated discussion between group members about the ways they feel less safe in the world since living openly as lesbians. The group began to recognize that the common thread, loss of approval, was strong for all of them. The woman who had been living openly as a lesbian the longest, affirming her same-sex attraction since third grade, said she did not relate to many of the losses, as she explained "I never had approval to begin with . . . so I never felt any loss." As the conversation unfolded, some participants began expressing anger as they listened to each other and considered the societal context of homophobia and heterosexism. Finally one woman exclaimed "But I would do it again tomorrow, and not wait so long!" To which all participants cheered in agreement.

When considering what to do with their totems, a couple of women decided to toss theirs into a river to symbolize letting go of the pain associated with them, and others chose to keep them as reminders of their resilience.

Conclusion

Creating a symbolic "loss totem" assisted the lesbians in this therapy group to identify and feel losses accompanying living openly as lesbian. The activity promoted a healing process of transformation, freeing participants to embrace the freedom, joy and power of living in alignment with Self. Sharing this process in a group amplified the therapeutic experience as participants came to understand that the marginalization they may be experiencing is societal, not personal.

Possible Contraindications

This author has used this intervention with groups to process losses incurred by aging, addiction, and bereavement with similar effectiveness. Ideally, groups have established substantial rapport and members have reasonable capacity for emotional regulation.

References

Cass, V. (1979). Homosexual identity formation: A theoretical model. *Journal of Homosexuality*, 4 (3), 219–235.

Herek, G. (1984). Beyond "homophobia": A social perspective on attitudes toward lesbian and gay men. *Journal of Homosexuality*, 10, 1–21.

Kitzinger, C., Wilkinson, S. (1995). Transitions from heterosexuality to lesbianism: The discursive production of lesbian identities. *Journal of Developmental Psychology*, 31 (4), 95–104.

McIntosh, P. (2007). White privilege: Unpacking the invisible knapsack. In M. L. Anderson and P. H. Collins (Eds.), *Race, Class, and Gender: An Anthology* (pp. 98–102). New York: Thomson Wadsworth.

Whitfield, Charles L. (1987). *Healing The Child Within*. Deerfield Beach FL: Health Communications, Inc.

Kris Drumm is a Licensed Clinical Social Worker, with advanced certification in Heart-Centered Hypnotherapy. Kris is in private practice and living in Wilton Manors, Florida.

4 A Culture of Nice in a Women's Group

It's Nice to be Nice

Melissa Black

Introduction

Social expectations and gender role conditioning have left many women socialized to "be nice" or "play nice". This quality of niceness, so often cultivated in girls and women, requires that they step away from their complete experience, negating the utility of genuine feelings when those feelings fall either on the negative side of the spectrum or when any emotions are felt too intensely. The outcome generally fosters superficial relationships in the service of being perceived as a Good Woman who is nurturing, caring and never angry. Being perpetually nice is a road block to self-knowledge and intimacy and ultimately may become a psychological defensive.

Nice women in the earliest stages of group can lend to cohesion and a feeling of safety, but this can quickly become stultifying and eventually destructive as "nice" does not make room for any emotional experience that is not approving, empathic, sympathetic or caring. The novice therapist may mistake the nice, caring and empathic group for one that is doing its work, but the collusion to exclude the direct expression of negative emotional experience often leads to the passive and potentially destructive expression of negative affect prevailing in the group.

Population

This intervention occurred in an open ended, psychodynamic, women's process group. All 7 members of the group have had or are in combined individual psychotherapy. Ages ranged from 37 to 76, with an average age of 48. Ethnicity was predominantly Caucasian, with 1 Hispanic and 1 Indian. Religion varied with 3 Christian, 1 atheist, 1 Hindu, 1 Jewish and 1 agnostic. All but one member had children and all had at least a bachelor's level education.

Intervention

The membership was down to 7, and will be at 6 when the next planned termination occurs in approximately 3 months. This session was the first for a new member who was brought in to start the rebuilding process. As this group session began, the soon-to-terminate member was quick to welcome the new member, giving the history of the group including the recent terminations and news of upcoming termination. As the new member began to speak of her own story, the group became dedicated to asking superficial and inane questions and becoming almost ridiculously "nice." This long-term group was not a group prone to superficiality and I found this odd.

General Client Responses

Due to this odd group as a whole response, I made a group as a whole interpretation, "I wonder if death can be avoided in 'nice groups'?"

The interpretation led to 2 different types of client responses. The first was a mobilization of the underlying frustration at the nice group. One member became agitated and said rather loudly, "My head is about to explode with all the niceness in the room. I don't really care if her dog is trained or if her garden grows vegetables." This loud vocalization in the aftermath of my "death interpretation" was met with resistance until one member finally stated, "I just wanted her to have all the time she needs to feel heard; I didn't want her to have to face something like you are doing right now. It's just not nice." At this emphatic statement, the group burst into laughter. The fallacy of nice had just revealed itself!

This led to the second type of client response. The soon-to-terminate member said, "I'm afraid if we aren't nice then she will leave. I won't be able to leave a dying group." Another member responded to this with, "There is nothing wrong with being nice if we can also be angry and afraid. But I understand what you mean; who knows, there may not be a group left soon." This was a more direct expression of the repressed anger toward me, as the therapist, for letting the group become fragile in its numbers. The group was able to explore the underlying fear directly and it was a theme that brought a great deal of richness into the room.

Conclusion

A women's group can be a very special therapeutic environment for exploration and stepping out of the societally imposed gender roles most women face. Awareness of the regression back into "niceness" is essential for the therapist as it is a place for women to hide from the more important and intimate affects of life. Just as anger and hostility can become a marker for a men's group to avoid loving and nurturing each other, being a nice group of women can be a marker for the therapist that the group is avoiding competition, anger and other less than angelic affects.

Possible Contraindications

A clear group contract stating the objective of experiencing and enhancing the complete range of emotional experience is a necessity for any psychodynamic process group. A thorough discussion with prospective members about the need and the importance of experiencing and expressing all emotions is ethically mandated to avoid the expectation of a support group when a client is entering a therapy group. In addition, cultural influences must be considered by the therapist and the client must be willing to discuss any of these influences that become inconsistent or are in conflict with the majority culture of the group.

Dr. Melissa Black is a licensed Clinical Psychologist and Certified Group Psychotherapist. She is in private practice as a member of the Group Analytic Practice of Dallas in Dallas, Texas, and is a Clinical Professor in Psychiatry at The University of Texas Southwestern Medical Center in Dallas, Texas.

5 Countertransference in Groups With Severely Ill Inpatients

Carla Penna

Introduction

Group Psychotherapy for severely ill or dying inpatients has been conducted in health care settings for decades. In the United States, a special report on group interventions for patients with cancer and HIV diseases provided relevant data about the topic revealing the efficacy of group work with this population (Bernard, 2004).

Groups for severely ill patients reduce patients' isolation, providing emotional support, sharing of information and experiences. In addition, they allow the development of psychological skills to cope with illness and the fear of death. Groups can also instill hope in life and in the future (Newman, 2008). The majority of reported group interventions with this population are conducted within interpersonal (Yalom, 1983), educational or supportive approaches (Marcus & Bernard, 2000). However, supported by the interventions under the group analytic frame of reference (Rice and Rutan, 1987; Mello Filho, 2000; Presberg and Kibel, 1994), I conducted analytic oriented psychotherapy groups with severely ill cardiac inpatients in a General Hospital in Brazil.

Countertransference and the Severely Ill Inpatients

The main difficulty in dealing with these groups is that the fear of death and the threat of death are always at stake. Moreover, as Skogstad (2001) observed in cardiac wards, sudden deaths may occur and a patient's condition may change rapidly, so the anxiety of not being able to keep someone alive is always an undeniable threat. In general, it is very difficult for staff, even in General Hospitals, to deal with the spectrum of death.

From the therapist's point of view a group with this population elicits deep countertransference issues, which *need* to be acknowledged and dealt with to the benefit of a 'good enough' group interaction. That is, working with severely ill patients, some off treatment conditions, the therapist needs to come to terms with his/her fantasies and fear of one's own mortality. It requires a good personal psychotherapeutic treatment as well as special ability to daily cope with dying people.

Description of Group and Client Population

The cardiac ward was composed of twenty-one beds, male and female rooms, facing a huge veranda. The ward's facilities did not offer a proper setting for groups, even though I conducted a weekly open group, for both genders in the ward's veranda. The group was composed of low-income inpatients, waiting for diagnosis, invasive procedures and pre- or post-heart surgery treatment. The majority of inpatients had severe coronary diseases, some with compromising comorbidities or already off treatment conditions. It was not possible to establish in advance the permanency of a patient's membership in the group. Some attended one or two sessions only, but some remained for more than three months. Many left the group due to hospital discharge, however some did not return from the intensive unit due to surgical complications or because they did not survive. The natural anxieties set off by patients' illness were increased by social deprivation and family difficulties.

Interventions and Countertransference

Step 1: Structure and Attendance

The structure of an inpatient group with severely ill inpatients requires flexibility because it is almost impossible to know in advance the group's composition. So, every week it is necessary to 'select' the group participants of the day's session. To accomplish the task, small investigations on the psychological and clinical conditions of the inpatients are required so as to know who is going to attend the group. Some patients are highly motivated, others refuse to participate. Some others are not allowed by their physicians to participate in the group due to their fragile health conditions. This 'weekly grouping stage' is the most exhaustive and self-demanding step of the whole endeavor. It elicits in the therapist feelings of dismay, avoidance and helplessness. However it is fundamental to survive this step and contain the huge amount of projective identifications coming from the inpatients, while developing skills to cope creatively with the inpatients and the ward's projected anxieties.

Step 2: Defrosting Feelings

Generally, the turnover of an inpatient group is high, so each session might be a 'box of surprises'. Sometimes in these situations some therapists protect themselves using a more structured approach. Under an analytic framework, the idea is to stimulate a free-floating discussion; however it was observed that in these settings a more active therapist's role is also required (Mello Filho, 2000). So, after the stimulation of a short self-introduction, the inpatients are able to discuss their hospitalization, their illness and expectations regarding their future. It was observed that the sessions warmed up quickly and the inpatients were able to communicate in a special way, providing their biography and the role of illness in their cycle of life. In this sense, an emphatic and fearless therapist's attitude allows the inpatients to 'defrost' and share inner feelings about life and illness.

Step 3: Talking About Death

Hospitalizations trigger in inpatients regression and deep anxieties associated with hopelessness and fear of death and even in hospital settings it is not easy to find people willing to discuss death. Nevertheless in a group composed of severely ill inpatients, the fear of death and the death of some of the members is a reality. Instead of avoiding the subject, the therapist's willingness to foster the discussion on this difficult topic is essential. The inpatients 'grasp' the therapist's availability and start to disclose his/her fears of life and death in the sessions. It is not an effortless task but the combination of the therapist self-awareness, and the understanding of his/her countertransference as well as a more active role in the group sessions, which allows the creation of a containing therapeutic space. It permits an emphatic and a deep contact with former unspeakable feelings.

Conclusions and Contraindications

Conducting group analytic psychotherapy with severely ill inpatients demands an accurate attention to countertransference issues and a daily internal negotiation with the therapist's willingness to cope with high levels of primitive anxieties and fears. This careful attitude might prevent therapists' re-traumatization and burnout syndrome (Marcus & Bernard, 2000). Reflection or support groups for the therapists might also be helpful. The awareness of the therapist's own limits is fundamental in this work, however its acceptance and recognition will be one's best tool in his/her group's interventions.

References

Bernard, H. (2004) Group interventions for patients with cancer and HIV disease. *International Journal of Group Psychotherapy*, 54 (1), 23–27.

Marcus, M. and Bernard, H. (2000) Group psychotherapy for psychological traumata of prolonged, severe and/or terminal illness. In Klein, R. and Schermer, V. (Eds) (2000) *Group Psychotherapy for Psychological Trauma*. New York: Guilford Press.

Mello Filho, J. (2000) (Ed.) *Grupo e corpo: Psicoterapia de grupo com pacientes somáticos*. Porto Alegre: Artmed.

Newman, T. E. (2008) Living with dying: How to keep the group alive when the members are dying. In Fehr, S. S. (ed.) (2008) *101 Interventions in Group Therapy*. New York: The Haworth Press.

Presberg, B. and Kibel, H. (1994) Confronting death: Group psychotherapy with terminally ill individuals. *Group*, 18 (1), 19–28.

Rice, C. and Rutan, S. (1987) *Inpatient Group Psychotherapy: A Psychodynamic Perspective*. New York: Macmillan.
Skogstad, W. (2001) Working in a world of bodies: A medical ward. In Hinshelwood, R. and Skogstad, W. (Eds) (2001) *Observing Organizations: Anxiety, Defence and Culture in Health Care*. London: Routledge.
Yalom, I. (1983) *Inpatients Group Psychotherapy*. New York: Basic Books.

Carla Penna, Ph.D., is a psychoanalyst and group analyst from Rio de Janeiro. She is past president of the Brazilian Group Psychotherapy Association and Group Analytic Psychotherapy Society of the State of Rio de Janeiro. She is a member of the Group Analytic Society International and works in private practice.

6 The Use of Primal Scream to Facilitate Release in the African-American Male
Pain Demands to be Heard

Marvin D. Evans

In the song "Inner City Blues," Marvin Gaye laments, "it [inner city blues] makes me wanna holler the way they do my life . . . makes me wanna holler and throw up both my hands." And in the seminal work *Black Rage*, authors William Grier and Price M. Cobbs (1968) write, "aggression leaps from wounds inflicted and ambitions spiked. It grows out of aggression and capricious cruelty."

The history of racism in America is replete with examples and anecdotes like those above. However, the impact of systemic and generational racism is no clearer reflected than in the lives and experiences of the African-American male. The generational impact of systemic racism continues to insert itself into the matrix of black life at all levels. The pernicious effects of systemic racism are coded into the DNA of all African-Americans. No black male in America is immune, whether he is President of the United States who is routinely slurred on social media, or the African-American infant whose mortality rate is more than twice that of non-Hispanic white infants owing to a number of factors, chief among them socioeconomic deprivation (www.cdc.gov/reproductivehealth).

As a male African-American psychotherapist, my interest and work has been in looking at how repressed pain as a function of racism shows up in the presenting issues of African-American men with whom I work. I am impressed the pain and despair that makes one want to literally and metaphorically "holler and throw up both my hands" continues to show up as neurotic and/or acting-out behaviors such as exaggerated aggression and impaired social skills; behaviors that I proffer ultimately emanate from a place of primal pain and unmet need. Moreover, in working with this population I find the efficacy of insight therapy compromised unless primal injury is first addressed. As Arthur Janov, the father of Primal Therapy, points out, the problem with talk therapy is that "we need to talk to a brain that doesn't talk—that feels." (YouTube—What is Primal Therapy by Dr. Arthur Janov).

The intervention I am presenting is a technique used in Primal Therapy known as the primal scream. It is essentially a technique that allows the client to relive traumatic events, often screaming or crying in order to achieve catharsis. I find this intervention particularly relevant, as the rage and despair many African-American men experience is a function of the repressed pain of systemic racism that has neither been addressed nor encountered visceral release. The primal scream allows the African-American male client to give voice and somatic expression to fixated energy attached to generational oppression.

It should be noted I am taking liberty to stretch the traditional definition of primal to extend beyond traumatic events experienced early in an individual's life, to include the body politic of African-American life as experienced in a hostile environment.

Population

Theoretically, this intervention could be applied to any African-American adult male living in the USA, as all have been adversely impacted by systemic racism whether conscious of it or not. However, I have found this intervention to be most effective for African-American men who present with issues related to the trauma of disenfranchisement or marginalization. In my experience these are men who have encountered the criminal justice system, or who have faced overt discrimination in the workplace or in other areas of socialization where there is substantial interface with the dominant culture, i.e., white Americans. And though this intervention might be apropos for African-American females, due to the politics of gender, sex, and patriarchy, I find the female African-American has encountered a less virulent version of racism than has her male counterpart and for that reason, my use of this intervention has not considered her circumstance.

Intervention

The intervention usually begins with an acknowledgment and reflection of the client's feelings and experiences of racism. "John, indeed racism is alive and well in America. You report experiencing it in very direct ways such as disparate treatment in the criminal justice system; and in subtle ways such as the way white women grab their purses as you pass or approach them." I proceed to explain how the imprint of racism rarely gets exorcised and shows up in displaced and neurotic ways such as addictions, physical illness, impaired relationships, etc. I share that for many men pain shows up as anger.

We discuss how the pain of racism shows up in the body as rigidity, exaggerated masculinity, depression, etc. I explain what the primal scream is and invite the client to give permission for his pain to come through, and to participate in an exercise where he yells, swears, and/or screams as loud as he can for as long as he can, but for no less than three minutes.

I explain the primal scream allows the client to give voice and form to repressed primal pain that is centuries old. I acknowledge that for the client the idea might seem ridiculous or awkward. I then interpret his possible inhibition to express himself as possible resistance. To counterbalance this inhibition for the client who remains self-conscious, I give him a whistle and encourage him to blow it as long and forcefully as he can, but for no less than three minutes. I find this alternate technique for the intervention usually takes about three minutes for the client to move out of his head and into his body.

General Client Response

I find this intervention beneficial for men able to move past their inhibitions. Catharsis evidenced by crying—sometimes uncontrollably so—figures prominently for many. The therapist should allow this and also become aware of a possible countertransference need to rescue. During the processing of the exercise clients report feelings of having a weight lifted off them; others report feeling drained. In subsequent sessions, I find the client presents with a more relaxed posture; has greater access to emotions; and is better able to engage cognitive restructuring.

Conclusion/Contraindications

The use of primal scream therapy is a powerful tool for therapists to use assisting the adult African-American male client who presents with angry or depressed affect attributable to his experience of racism. Successful engagement of the intervention results in a client who is less anxious and better able to engage talk therapy.

When implementing the primal scream intervention, the exercise should only be performed in an environment where the client is isolated from others unless he is part of a group intervention. A secluded office or outdoors space is the best environment to execute this technique. Finally, I do not recommend this intervention for children; nor do I recommend it for men who have a diagnosed history of physical or verbal abuse, as the experience of raging might enact previous trauma.

References

Grier, W. H. & Cobbs, P. M. (1968) *Black Rage*. NY: Harper & Row Publishers, Inc.
Nyx & Gaye, M. (1971) "Inner City Blues" [recorded by Marvin Gaye]. On *What's Going On* [album] Detroit: Motown (1971).
Primal Therapy (2008, August 8) What is Primal Therapy by Dr. Arthur Janov [video file]. Retrieved from www.youtube.com/watch?v=_bc003JICgY.

Marvin Evans is a Licensed Clinical Professional Counselor with a private practice in Chicago, Illinois. His area of specialization is in working with marginalized populations.

7 Hiring a Group Coordinator Can Develop a Group Program

Joshua M. Gross

Introduction

Group Therapy is commonly experienced as a difficult if not elusive intervention that is hard to initiate and maintain in mental health clinic settings. Nonetheless, in some settings group programs thrive and this is likely due to the presence of an individual with expertise in how to practice group therapy effectively. This intervention is about hiring a Group Coordinator and why this can make a difference in the culture of a clinic as well the economics of providing mental health care.

A single therapist will see people for therapeutic hours and will essentially have a 1:1 ratio of hour to session. A group therapist may meet with 7, 8 or 9 individuals for 90 minutes and spend a half hour in documentation. The group model can yield up to 9 individuals being seen in a 90-minute weekly session for the total clinic cost of 2 hours' group therapist time. If the clinic develops a model where some of the cases move out of individual treatment and into group, there are substantial opportunities for providing more care for less cost as a result of a developing economy of scale (Gross, 1997). If multiple therapists are offering group interventions the clinic may have the opportunity to meet the needs of a wide variety of individuals in the group program.

The Association for University and College Counseling Center Directors Annual Survey for 2013–14 (AUCCCD, 2014) showed that only 22.7% of their responding centers had a Group Coordinator, which is their term for the individual who is responsible for the oversight and direction of group programs. While most mental health professionals of all professions have proficiency in individual treatment, many have had no more than a single course on group in graduate training and may or may not have had much supervised internship or residency supervised practice to establish a base of expertise. Given the wide range of practice experience many clinics have no individual present with expertise in group therapy practice and thus struggle with the development of group programming.

Intervention

Group Coordinators commonly arise out of a clinic setting where an individual who has group expertise practices group work and others become aware of this. Administration often takes a supportive stance and encourages this individual to take a leadership role often called Group Coordinator. The presence of an individual with this expertise as well as an administrative mandate to practice, train, supervise and administer, the Group Coordinator can significantly change the Group Culture (Gross, 2015) which can be defined as the number of staff who do group divided by the total number of staff that results in a percentage. As the percentage of staff doing group increases the clinic experiences an economy of scale that allows for administration, training and clinical supervision of group work which increases referrals, choices of intervention and staff opportunity to do groups that interest them. It is easier to do group therapy where groups are commonly running than to do it on your own as the only group therapist.

Given this, the intervention of hiring an experienced group therapist with the necessary skills and interest in developing a group program may yield significant financial and programmatic benefits to the clinic and the population it serves.

General Client Responses

It is not uncommon for the person in individual treatment to respond poorly to the idea of referral to a treatment group. Issues of anxiety, shame, privacy and sometimes personal boundary are often aroused with the prospect of having to talk about personal issues in the presence of unknown others. Group Coordinators have skills and expertise that can assist those people as well as staff members unfamiliar with group work in developing strategies to assist both those in treatment as well as colleagues who may make referrals in understanding these fundamental group therapy issues and how to resolve them effectively and properly. Group therapists commonly deal with these issues of resistance and know well how to help people make sense of these emotions as a function of their ability to explain how the interventions work and why they can be so effective (AGPA, 2015a). Many people can benefit from group therapy and we see tremendous variation in how these services are offered as a function of service delivery models that have been developed in different clinic settings. We know that many different types of populations can achieve significant benefit from group therapy who may present with various clinical presentations and symptoms (AGPA, 2015b).

Conclusion

Administrators and directors of clinics that do not have group therapy occurring on a regular basis may be missing out on one of the more cost effective and treatment efficacious interventions in the mental health area. Combined group and individual treatment plans make sense in an environment where quality care and cost effectiveness need to coexist in a caring and responsive clinic environment. When these services are not available it is uniformly the result of the lack of expertise in group therapy services delivery. The savvy administrator who wants their clinic to offer group services when they are not available will do well to engage in a search for a competent and experienced Group Coordinator who will know how to develop services in any number of clinic settings where they presently do not exist.

Possible Contraindications

Group therapy does not work for all people at all times. Some people may need a course of individual treatment to prepare them for the necessary give and take that is inherent in the therapy group. Individuals who are unable to share and cooperate or are so disoriented or unable to control their behavior or affect may not be good candidates for group therapy. Experienced Group Coordinators know these caveats and are familiar with the Standards for Practice such as those outlined in *The Practice Guidelines for Group Psychotherapy* (AGPA, 2015a).

The hiring of a Group Coordinator may also have impact on the life and process of a well-established clinic staff that is accustomed to treating individuals in the one to one setting. Sometimes issues of anxiety, territoriality and difficulty with cooperation are experienced in the early stages of group program establishment. Experienced Group Coordinators are familiar with these issues and know well about the developmental stage of group culture and how to intervene in a manner consistent with the clinic's level of group culture development (Gross, 2015).

References

American Group Psychotherapy Association (2007) *Practice Guidelines for Group Psychotherapy*. Retrieved from www.agpa.org/home/practice-resources/practice-guidelines-for-group-psychotherapy.

AGPA (2015a) *The Practice Guidelines for Group Psychotherapy*. www.agpa.org/home/practice-resources/practice-guidelines-for-group-psychotherapy.

AGPA (2015b) Evidence Based Practice in Group Psychotherapy.www.agpa.org/home/practice-resources/evidence-based-practice-in-group-psychotherapy.

AUCCCD (2014) Association for University and College Counseling Center Directors www.aucccd.org/.

Association for University and College Counseling Center Directors. (n.d.) *Welcome to AUCCCD*. Retrieved from www.aucccd.org/.

Gross, J. M. (1997). Promoting group psychotherapy in managed care: Basic economic principles for the clinical practitioner. *International Journal of Group Psychotherapy*, 47, 499–507.

Gross, J. M. (2015) Group culture and its stages of development. In Alonso, J. (Chair), Bleiberg, J., Cox, J. Drapkin, R. G., Gross, J. M., Kirpalani, P. and MacNair-Semands, R. R. Group Coordinator's Workshop II: Building skills in group program development and leadership. All day theory and skills training event at The Annual Meeting of The American Group Psychotherapy Association, San Francisco, CA.

Joshua M. Gross, Ph.D., ABPP, CGP, FAGPA, is Director of Group Programs at the University Counseling Center at Florida State University and practices as a Group and Family Psychologist. He is a licensed psychologist, Certified Group Psychotherapist, Fellow of The American Academy of Group Psychology, Fellow of The American Group Psychotherapy Association and serves as Member of the International Board for The Certification of Group Psychotherapy.

8 Who Owes You an Apology?

Ellen J. Fehr
Gary L. Sandelier

UNFORGOTTEN HURT

It is quite realistic to believe that most sentient beings have had experiences in their lives where they have been either judged, abused, misunderstood, or in fact rejected for either real or imagined perceptions on the part of another person or persons. These types of experiences often have a profound effect on the recipient and can, if repeated, cause dramatic changes in the individual's personality and interpersonal relationships in the present and in the future. It was suggested (Fehr, 2003) that a simple intervention/technique could be used to generate, perhaps, information that might not necessarily come to light in a group therapy session that ultimately will have a profound effect on the client ultimately helping to restructure an individual's personality and current interpersonal relationships. This generated information can then offer avenues and roads for further exploration with possible conscious decision-making behaviors toward what one may choose to leave behind and thus no longer be burdened in his or her present nor in the future.

The Appropriate Population

For this intervention to be effective, the group population must have a certain degree of ego strength, the ability to be somewhat introspective, open to disclosure with a minimum of defensiveness, and be willing to re-experience previous emotional pain on the continuum of mild to perhaps intense.

An Intervention of Dialogue

This intervention could not be any easier for the group therapist. It is only two direct questions: one presented before the other with concomitant discussion and then subsequently the other with its concomitant discussion. It is not uncommon for this intervention to take two group sessions, if not longer, if the information disclosed brings forth multiple associations within the group members' lives. It is suggested that the two questions be kept separated and solely presented in a group session for which it has been designated.

The Two Questions
- Who owes you an apology?
- To whom do you owe an apology?

Surprising Client Responses

It is not uncommon, at all, to find that group members truly get into this intervention. For some initially, there may be trepidation but once the group members begin to disclose their previous experiences of hurt, a prolific dialogue ensues. Clients often identify not only with the events or experiences in another group member's life, and if not the experience, at least the feeling or the residual feeling which the client has been carrying around, in many cases, for many years.

Conclusion

This very simple intervention/technique will elicit a wealth of personal information on the part of the group members. They will often have the opportunity of experiencing the corrective emotional experience, because the group members are often very supportive and sympathetic to the disclosure, and they offer multiple identifications to the group member disclosing his or her feelings. This experience of multiple identifications with support and empathy helps the client to not feel alone or what Corsini and Rosenberg (1955) referred to as "universalization," which (Yalom, 1970) later referred to as "universality." Interestingly, when the question is posed, "To whom do you owe an apology?" a number of group members will say, "No one!" Thus we can introduce at this time how often many people are very sensitive to what has been done to them but are insensitive to what they have done to others. This often helps elicit, for some members, recollections of what, where, and when they have been less than sensitive in their relationships.

Contraindication

Although we have not found this intervention to have had any contraindications if explored with the appropriate population, it was suggested (Chew, 2006) that posing such questions without knowing the vulnerabilities of the group members and not having clinical tact and timing may place the clients in danger of unnecessary negative experiences. We do not disagree with that statement but feel the ethical and experienced group therapist is well aware of the ego strength of his or her group members.

References

Chew, J. (2006) Book review. *Introduction to Group Therapy: A Practical Guide* (second edition). *International Journal of Group Psychotherapy*, 56 (2), 251–253.

Corsini, R. J. & Rosenberg, B. (1955) Mechanisms of group psychotherapy: Processes and dynamics. *Journal of Abnormal and Social Psychology*, 5, 406–411.

Fehr, S. S. (2003) *Introduction to Group Therapy: A Practical Guide* (second edition). Binghamton, NY: The Haworth Press.

Yalom, I. D. (1970) *The Theory and Practice of Group Psychotherapy.* New York: Basic Books.

Ellen Joan Fehr, M.S., is a Licensed Mental Health Counselor who specializes in running groups related to Women's Issues. She is also a published author.

Gary L. Sandelier, M.S., is a Licensed Mental Health counselor who runs Men's Groups that focus on interpersonal issues and personal growth.

9 Not Just Talk
A Group Therapy Model Integrating Action Theory and Techniques

Thomas Treadwell

Introduction

This brief chapter combines Action and Cognitive Behavioral Techniques (CBT) in applied group settings. Although both CBT and Action models stress the discovery process through Socratic questioning, the use of certain structured CBT techniques (e.g., Automatic Thought Record) provides additional ways of stimulating the development of self-reflection and problem-solving skills. The group cognitive action therapy (GCAT) model focuses on identifying disturbing situations, activating moods, negative thoughts, balanced thoughts, and recognizing distortions in thinking initiating a negative interpretation of an event. With the increasing popularity of cognitive behavioral therapy techniques, especially those developed by Beck and his colleagues (see Beck J. S., 2011: Beck, A. T., Rush, Shaw, & Emery, 1979) and incorporating CBT techniques within an action-oriented environment produces persuasive results. Thus, the blending of the two models yields a complementary eclectic approach to multiple problem-solving strategies. The GCAT environment provides a supportive and safe climate to practice new thinking and behaviors (Treadwell, Kumar, & Wright, 2004).

Client/Patient Population

This particular intervention has proven to be effective with university students and patients diagnosed with mood, substance abuse, anxiety, and personality disorders.

General Guidelines and Intervention for Running a Group Therapy Model Integrating Action Theory and Techniques

In applying various CBT techniques within the context of psychodrama, it is important to devote the first two sessions (at least 3 hours each) to educating participants about the GCAT model to create a safe and secure environment in which individuals can share their concerns freely with group members.

The initial didactic sessions convey the notion that the group format is, foremost, a problem-solving approach for working through various interpersonal, occupational, educational, psychological, and health-related conflicts. At the outset, the therapist introduces the group members to the significance of completing the Beck Depression Inventory-II, the Beck Anxiety Inventory, or the PHQ-9 and Anxiety Inventory on a weekly basis. Diagnostic instruments are completed before the start of each session and stored in *personal folders* to serve as an ongoing gauge of their progress in the group.

In addition to the Beck inventories, group members complete Young's (Young, Klosko, & Weishaar, 2003; Young & Klasko, 1994) schema questionnaire(s), where therapists can obtain additional data on early maladaptive and dysfunctional schemas/core beliefs. The Social Network Inventory, similar to a genogram (Treadwell, Stein, & Leach, 1993), is utilized to map and quantify participants' relationships with family members, significant others, groups, and organizations. Informed consent and audio visual forms are distributed. The audiovisual recordings establish an ongoing record of group activities and serve as a source for feedback when needed

Applying CBT Interventions and Techniques to Psychodrama

Automatic Thought Record (ATR, Greenberger & Padaskey, 1995)

- Essential psychodrama techniques of role reversal, doubling, self-presentation, interview in role reversal, mirroring, future projection, surplus reality, empty chair techniques (Moreno, 1934; Blatner, 1996; Kellerman, 1992) can be applied directly to situations indicated in Automatic Thought Records (ATR). During the initial didactic sessions, it is extremely helpful to teach the group members how to complete an ATR. It is central to introduce the ATR as a self-reflection strategy to recognize automatic thoughts that occur within and outside therapy sessions. This is helpful for improving problem-solving and mood-regulation skills.

Automatic Thoughts (ATs)

- Automatic thoughts are instantaneous, habitual, unconscious, and affect a person's mood containing one or more *cognitive distortions*. The auxiliary egos and the therapist may help the protagonist discover possible cognitive distortion(s) in the protagonist's stated AT.

Downward Arrow Technique

- The downward arrow technique consists of challenging the protagonist by repeatedly asking the questions: "If that were true, why would it be so upsetting?" and "Being upset means what to you?" The technique can be used during any stage of psychodrama to explore a deeper understanding of the core beliefs/schemas underlying an AT.

The Case Conceptualization Technique

- This technique is applied as an ongoing therapeutic tool. Case conceptualization may help the group member reflect on various rules, conditional assumptions, beliefs, and means of coping. Additionally, Beck (2011) referred to such bias as the negative triad, viewing oneself ("I am worthless"), one's world ("Nothing is fair"), and one's future ("My life will never improve") in a negative manner. This view is usually distorted and the purpose of designing a case formulation is to challenge the patient's views of *self, the world,* and *the future.*

Client/Patient Responses

Once *taught* the basics of the automatic thought record participants realize this technique yields real life data that is not terribly threatening. They show signs of relief and begin to see that automatic thinking is what "we" all do. Further, recognizing "their" core-beliefs and schemas "all" people possess across the life span serves to *normalize* the action behavioral therapy process permitting group members to feel at ease.

Conclusion

Assimilating CBT with action techniques creates a powerful and effective group process enabling participants to address problematic situations with support of group members. Students and clinical populations respond well to CBT/Action techniques and find them helpful in becoming aware of their habitual dysfunctional thought patterns and belief systems that play an important role in mood regulation. The basic cognitive behavioral coupled with schema-focused techniques merge nicely within the psychodramatic framework. Group members begin to see the usefulness of structured CBT and Action techniques and adapt accordingly.

The GCAT is *data based* enabling group members to track dysfunctional thoughts, depression, and anxiety statistics week to week. The GCAT model integrates CBT and Action techniques to provide a balance between explorations of emotionally laden situations with the more concrete, data-based, problem-solving process.

Contraindications

It is recommended to avoid using action techniques during session one and focus on psycho-education. It appears the preferred size of a group is between 5 and 10 members with sessions lasting 2 to 3 hours. The following *exclusions* are recommended: (a) individuals with self-centered and aggressive disorders display strong resistance to group work—they tend to lack spontaneity and are rigid in their portrayals of significant others (that is, they either insulate or attempt to dominate others in the group); (b) rule out individuals with narcissistic, obsessive compulsive (severe), and antisocial personality disorders since individual therapy is more suitable for them; and (c) individuals with cluster A personality disorders and impulse control disorders have difficulty functioning in a group.

References

Beck, A. T., Rush, A. J., Shaw, B. F., & Emery, G. (1979) *Cognitive therapy of depression*. New York: The Guilford Press.

Beck, J. S. (2011) *Cognitive behavioral therapy: Basics and beyond* (2nd ed.). New York: The Guilford Press.

Blatner, A. (1996) *Acting-In* (3rd. ed.). New York: Springer.

Greenberger, H. & Padaskey, C. (1995) *Mind over mood: A cognitive therapy treatment manual for clients*. New York: The Guilford Press.

Kellerman, P. (1992) *Focus on psychodrama: The therapeutic aspects of psychodrama*. Philadelphia, PA: Jessica Kingsley.

Moreno, J. L. (1934) *Who shall survive? A new approach to the problem of human interrelations*. Washington, DC: Nervous & Mental Disease.

Treadwell, T., Kumar, V. K., & Stein, S. (1990) A review of psychodramatic action and closure techniques for adolescents and adults. *Journal of Group Psychotherapy, Psychodrama, and Sociometry*, 43 (3), 102–115.

Treadwell, T., Kumar, V. K., & Wright, J. (2004) Enriching psychodrama via the use of Cognitive Behavioral Therapy techniques. *Journal of Group Psychotherapy, Psychodrama, & Sociometry*, 55, 55–65.

Treadwell, T., Stein, S., & Leach, E. (1993) The social networks inventory: A diagnostic instrument measuring interpersonal relationships. *Journal of Small Group Research*, 24 (2), 155–178.

Young, J. E. & Klosko, J. S. (1994) *Reinventing your life*. New York: Plume.

Young, J. E., Klosko, J. S., & Weishaar, M. (2003) *Schema therapy: A practitioner's guide*. New York: The Guilford Press.

Dr. Thomas Treadwell is a licensed Psychologist, Trainer, Educator, Practitioner of Psychodrama and Certified Group Psychotherapist. He, too, is Clinical Associate at the Center for Cognitive Therapy, University of Pennsylvania and a Professor of Psychology at West Chester University where he teaches cognitive group therapy courses and high performance virtual teams in educational and organizational settings.

10 Anger

A Historical Account and an Ah Ha Moment

Karen Travis

Introduction

Anger is part of the human experience. Anger rises up when we feel threatened whether real or imagined, frustrated, or stressed. Anger is not bad; it is what "I" do with my anger that gives anger a bad name. I feel sorry for anger. It seems no one really wants to claim the emotion. Many people see anger as bad and rarely want to own it. You made me mad, you should or should not have, if you had not . . . are most often typical comments. The other oriented statements keep us away from owning our own thoughts, feelings and behavior. Some people act out their anger and/or turn the anger inward onto self without being fully aware of where their anger has originated. This is painful and destructive.

Although the subjective experience of anger is often unpleasant and humans often seek to decrease such negative internal states, anger when properly channeled can motivate persistence in the face of frustrating situations. At times, however, negative internal states can propel humans to behave in an impulsive or suboptimal manner (Gerhart et al., 2015).

I want group participants to understand the messages they received about anger, and learn what pushes their buttons. These two particular interventions seem to go hand in hand and have helped people gain greater understanding and awareness of their anger. In this awareness they begin to own their own feelings, unlock some of their blocks and allow them to harness their feelings of anger that they may feel they lost with others or self. It is hoped the client will learn 1. anger is universal, 2. preferable ways to process the emotion and 3. seek alternative and more effective skills in processing the emotion.

During these exercises and the sharing of information I am tuned to the group process as well as the here and now.

Population

I utilize this intervention in a psycho-educational anger group that I conduct at an Intensive Outpatient/Partial Hospital program (IOP/PHP) with higher functioning adult clients. The group meets once a week for 2 hours. I have also used it in my private practice while conducting a 6-week psychoeducational anger group, meeting once a week for 90 minutes. Both in the IOP/PHP and my office clients enter the group on a voluntary basis. The intervention could be incorporated into short-term or long-term process-oriented groups as well.

Intervention

Step 1. I introduce today's topic. Letting them know I am going to take them through a series of questions that they will answer silently. I explain the purpose is to work on the first goal of the group: becoming more aware of their anger. The other two goals we work toward are, understanding what anger does for or against them and learning ways to deal constructively with their anger. I ask members to recall the very first time they were angry. How old are they? Perhaps they did not use the word angry. Who is involved in the scene? What is the location—school, home, neighborhood? What are the surroundings like? What are the circumstances? What happened? Who got involved? What was told to them by an adult or parent? What message did they take away about anger?

Step 2. I ask them to take a sheet of paper and write down the highlights that stand out to them from this experience in about 3 minutes. I emphasize this is for them to keep and will not be collected. In a short- or long-term group some modification could be done here. Perhaps, bringing this to life for one group member and then of course everyone hears the question which would ignite sharing and feedback.

Step 3. I ask who would like to share their experience. Time rarely permits for everyone to share in detail.

Step 4. Current anger beliefs and expression of the emotion along with the first time they recall being angry are explored. I begin to bridge the past with their current life, empowering them to see how early learning may still be connected to their present life. All group members are invited to give feedback and give voice to their past messages about anger.

General Client Responses

Initially when asked to recall the first time they were angry, many will say "I cannot think that far back", but with some prompts I have not had someone unable to do the exercise. This exercise can create much emotion and intimate knowledge of themselves. They can begin to recall shame, embarrassment, humiliation, and even punishment for their feelings of anger. Some of the most common things to arise are: not being understood or listened to, the sense of unfairness, and being bad for having angry feelings and expressing them overtly.

Conclusions and Contraindications

In the IOP/PHP setting the group can change from day to day and week to week. The leader would understand who is new to the group and anything that may be more pressing for the members on any given day. This intervention needs to be taken seriously as it can evoke much emotion. It is important the leader has some skill and experience to process, knowing how to bring some closure to the group and utilize the intervention in the way that would be organic to his or her style of therapy and client population. I give my report to a clinical staff member so that the next group therapist knows of the significant happenings in the group with any or all members.

Overall, I have found this intervention to be highly effective and lend itself to many types of groups and populations. Therapeutic factors of universality, instillation of hope and imparting of information can certainly be seen as change agents (Yalom and Leszcz, 2005).

It is hoped through continued work in the IOP/PHP program they can arrive at what Rutan and Stone (2001) call the working through process that allows the patient to become accepting of his/her defensive structure, to recognize that it served a valid function in history even if it has become too burdensome in the present.

When a human being can further understand self, it becomes beneficial to self and their interpersonal relationships. When the client begins to own their feelings and understand the development of their anger, this understanding gives them new domain over their own life.

In understanding what pushes their anger buttons it helps them clarify their values and be better prepared in dealing with others. I am privileged to see the light bulb go on, no matter (what) the wattage size.

References

Gerhart, G., Holman, K., Seymour, B., Dinges, B. and Ronan, G. (2015). Group Process as a Mechanism of Change in the Group Treatment of Anger and Aggression. *International Journal of Group Psychotherapy*, 65 (2), 181–208.

Rutan, S. and Stone, W. (2001). *Psychodynamic Group Psychotherapy*. New York: The Guilford Press.

Yalom, I. D. and Leszcz, M. (2005). *The Theory and Practice of Group Psychotherapy* (5th ed.). New York: Basic Books.

Karen Travis, LCSW-BACS, BCD, CGP, FAGPA, is in Private Practice, a contract group therapist at Jefferson Oaks Behavioral Health, is on the faculty at the LSU-OLOL Psychiatry Residency Program where she co-leads short-term groups with psychiatric residents in training, and supervises post masters social workers for licensure in Baton Rouge, LA. She has held governance positions with the Louisiana Group Psychotherapy Society and the American Group Psychotherapy Association; currently she is in-coming chair to the Group Foundation for Advancing Mental Health.

11 Battling the Alien
Working Through Self-Hatred in Group Therapy

Patricia Kyle Dennis

Introduction

At the beginning of a group therapy session, Shannon asked for help from the other members. She reported feeling intense self-hatred after her mother ignored her birthday once again. There was an empty hole inside her that she could never fill. She tried filling it with food, but that only gave her temporary relief. Lately the hole was full of horrible feelings. Brianna picked up on Shannon's description with one of her own. "It's like the movie *Alien* [Scott, R., 1979]. This awful monster is living in it and I'm battling it, but I can't get it out. The Alien is my self-hatred. It's interfering with my life."

This seemed to strike a chord for everyone in the group. Their focus became "battling the Alien." They uncovered awareness and rage about ways they had internalized and identified with their parents' self-hatred. This was followed by grief about their parents' failures to love and care for them. As a result of their work in the group, they began to disavow the self-hatred they had carried for years.

Population

Watching the movie *Alien* may feel like a journey into psychosis, but the phenomenon described above can occur for healthier individuals. Growing up in a family whose parents projected self-hatred into the children interferes with the development of healthy self-esteem in adulthood. A dysfunctional family history is so pervasive among the general clinical population that it is worth considering the relevance of the intervention described below to all therapy groups.

Groups often come together over the shared experience of addiction to a particular substance or activity. The addiction substitutes for love. On the other hand, the negative effects of addiction exacerbate the very self-hatred that the patient wants to conquer. This intervention might be especially useful for people who suffer from addictions.

Intervention

When Brianna associated to the Alien, I was reminded of a phenomenon described by psychoanalytic object relations theorists called the *introjected bad object* (Armstrong-Perlman, 1991). The dynamic begins when the child feels frustrated and unloved by her parent. Rather than attacking the parent, she attacks the self, thus saving the relationship with her parent. She internalizes the parent's projected self-hatred. She starts to believe that the faults are her own. The resulting lack of self-esteem becomes entrenched.

I made an interpretation to the group: "The Alien is hatred that gets inside of you—you believe it is about a part of you—but it is really about a part of your parent." At first, the group reacted with curiosity and confusion. But as they dissected this idea, it sounded logical and relevant to everyone's experiences.

Coming to this awareness marks the beginning of an intervention that the group therapist can make to assist members in undoing damage to their self-esteem. They need to understand, feel, and sort through what parts of them belong to self and other. They must accept the hopelessness of their wish to be loved and accepted by the parent. They must mourn the loss and acknowledge the good in the relationship. Ultimately, they must feel hope for the self (Armstrong-Perlman, 1991).

Group therapy has much to offer in this process (Ganzarain, 2008). Some of the group members' early experiences of introjection will be recreated in the group interactions. These may be explored and related to similar childhood experiences. Members search for ways to respond to primitive fears while preserving both the relationship and the self. A positive experience in group can foster a belief and trust in love prevailing over badness.

The group therapist's role (Tuttman, 1992) is to facilitate an atmosphere that encourages increased openness to exploring feelings and fantasies. Primarily, she provides a holding container by using empathy, mirroring, and interpretation. She is ever watchful for what appears to be projective processes among members. The therapist values whatever is expressed. She conveys an appreciation of the patient's experiences and feelings while allowing archaic fantasies, internalized object representations, and projections to emerge.

General Client Responses

In Shannon and Brianna's group, members frequently expressed appreciation for the work, putting it as a priority over other obligations. They used the group as a laboratory and support system by experimenting with claiming their place in the group and articulating their feelings. They focused on shame associated with hated parts of themselves, its connection with their ongoing rage, and grief about selfish and negligent parents. They helped each other recognize strengths and needs while practicing new ways of relating. This was not without a great deal of struggle and angst. Sometimes the grief felt unbearable.

Conclusion

For the therapist, the depth of this kind of work in group therapy is both challenging and gratifying. Tuttman (1992) says that the group leader must feel and show optimism while finding enjoyment and meaning in the work. Managing countertransference reactions requires ongoing supervision and psychotherapy.

For patients who are highly motivated to heal from their hurtful childhood experiences, exploration and working through the phenomenon of the introjected bad object should be considered. The group therapy modality offers benefits and support to help see participants through times of suffering and despair. The process of free association leads them to recognize their shared experience of introjection of the bad object and join with each other and the group leader in battling the Alien.

Possible Contraindications

One member seemed unable to progress. She offered much to the discussion by articulating her despair and seemed to have an intellectual understanding what was going wrong. But when she was overcome by her emotions, her defenses were so strong that nobody seemed to be able to help.

When a patient is unable to tolerate this intervention, it might be tempting to suspect a borderline or psychotic personality organization. However, contributing factors to low self-esteem are idiosyncratic and therefore unpredictable. The group therapist must be alert to the struggle of each member, her capacity to deal with it, and its effects on group process. The group experience is no longer therapeutic when one member sets out to destroy it. Support of more fragile members through individual therapy is necessary, and at times, a mutual decision to end that person's group therapy is beneficial to all.

References

Armstrong-Perlman, E. M. (1991). The allure of the bad object. *Free Associations*, 2: 343–356.

Ganzarain, R. (2008). Introduction to object relations group psychotherapy. In G. Saiger, S. Rubenfeld and M. D. Dluhy (Eds.) *Windows into today's group therapy: The National Group Psychotherapy Institute of the Washington School of Psychiatry* (pp. 97–111). New York: Routledge/Taylor & Francis Group.

Scott, Ridley (Director). (1979). *Alien*.

Tuttman, S. (1992). The role of the therapist from an object relations perspective. In R. H. Klein, H. S. Bernard and D. L. Singer (Eds.), *Handbook of contemporary group psychotherapy: Contributions from object relations, self psychology, and social systems theories* (pp. 241–277). Madison, CT: International Universities Press, Inc.

Dr. Patricia Kyle Dennis, LCSW, CGP, specializes in eating disorders in private practice. She leads psychotherapy groups for women who present with the problems of overeating and gaining weight.

12 A Ritual for Termination

Marvin Kaphan

> Only in the agony of parting do we look into the depths of love.
> (George Eliot, 1866)

Introduction and Theoretical Considerations

The Practice Guidelines for Group Psychotherapy published by the American Group Psychotherapy Association (Science to Service Task Force 2007) points out the lack of attention that has been paid to the crucial termination phase of psychotherapy. The document states that "the end stage and the various aspects of the termination process can crystallize individual gains and promote the internalization of the therapy experience." Their literature review (AGPA, 2007) concluded that three goals were necessary for the termination process:

1. Review and reinforcement of change which has taken place in the course of treatment
2. Resolution of relationships with therapist and group members
3. The use of the tools of therapy to prepare for future life difficulties.

Termination is a change of status. From my own experiences, living over eight decades, ritual has always been accepted as a rite of passage that marks a person's transition from one status to another, including birth, coming-of-age, marriage, and death. The hunger, either conscious or unconscious, for an experience of closure at the time of separation becomes so great that group members often create some form of ritual (Shapiro, 2002). These may be helpful toward the group goals, or simply ease the anxiety of separation.

Since my childhood, I have recognized the power and emotional impact of the funeral scene from the novel *The Adventures of Tom Sawyer* (Twain, 1996), where the protagonist has the opportunity to observe his own eulogy. We see in that situation, how members of the community become more aware of the strength of their ties to the "missing" boys, and the boys are forced to hear praise of which they had not previously been aware.

Description of the Groups

All six of my groups were open-ended, having continued for over fifty years. Patients leave based on their needs and growth. New patients enter when openings are available. The groups were all heterogeneous psychodynamic groups, with, wherever possible, a family-like configuration of younger men, older men, younger women and older women. Since these were all private patients, the groups all tend to be more or less high functioning, but each group seems to develop a distinct personality.

Intervention

The Group Agreement that each new group member signs, includes the understanding that when the group member is ready to leave the group, he or she will give the group a month's notice. This period is used to focus on the member's reasons and readiness for leaving.

Toward the end of the last session of the notice period, the group performs a ritual I have named "The Funeral". In this ritual, the patient is asked to stretch out on the floor, silently, with eyes closed, while the group gathers around and talks at length about what this patient has meant to them.

Next, the group is encouraged to talk about how this group is going to be different next week, without this patient. One interesting consequence is that, almost always, each group member will see something different that will be missing. Almost invariably, in later sessions, that member tends to provide the piece he or she feared would be missing in the group.

After the procedure is complete, the patient is invited to "Re-awaken" and respond as he or she wishes.

General Client Responses

In over fifty years of performing this ritual, these ritual sessions have been the most deeply emotional and powerful of each patient's group experience. Every member of the group is surprised at the profundity of the perceptions revealed. In my opinion, it very effectively achieves the termination goals listed in the afore-cited AGPA Guidelines. Also surprising, is the light-hearted and joyous atmosphere that accompanies the deep emotional responses.

Almost always, the problems the group members have been addressing during their course of treatment include some aspect of attachment, of fear of intimacy and of self-esteem. This ritual seems to underline, very vividly, what the patient has achieved, especially in these areas.

Reactions to the Title

From time to time, patients who have never experienced the ritual demonstrate some nervousness or concern in reaction to the title, but more experienced members of the group have always succeeded in reassuring them. When

I mention the ritual to colleagues, they are sometimes repelled by the name, but usually become interested in the technique when they hear it described. The initial reaction may be connected with a tendency in our culture to deny death, as evidenced by a growing tendency to replace the term Funeral with "Celebration of Life".

In one of my groups, a patient who had had great discomfort with the concept of death had managed to "accidentally" miss a series of these rituals. This led to a fascinating series of sessions focused on existential issues. Eventually, that patient's fears were resolved, and he now joins in these rituals enthusiastically.

Possible Contraindications

It is possible that in the outpouring of emotion that takes place in this farewell ceremony, any unresolved issues might burst forth, leading to very painful or destructive situations. In the years I have used this procedure, this has never happened, probably due to the fact that part of preparing for ending is a focus on unresolved issues. If some have not been completely resolved, I think that would become clear during the notice period.

Conclusions

Although some practitioners feel that there is a particular value in the ritual being developed by the group itself (Shapiro, 2002), I believe that these are more likely to fall short of the desired goals. A quite complete survey of termination rituals in college counseling center groups (Terry, 2011) seems to produce nothing similar to this intervention. In view of the fact that this intervention directly achieves the goals recommended by AGPA and the apparent lack of contraindications, I am happy to suggest this intervention to other colleagues.

References

Eliot, George (1866). *Felix Holt the Radical*. Chapter 44. New York: John B Aldon Publishing Company.
Practice Guidelines for Group Psychotherapy (2007). New York: American Group Psychotherapy Association Press. http://209.190.242.22/guidelines/termination.html.
Shapiro, E. L. (2002, April). Parting Gifts. *International Journal of Group Psychotherapy*, 52: 319–36.
Terry, L. (2011, April). Semi-Structured Termination Exercises. American Psychological Association Society of Group Psychology and Group Psychotherapy Division 49 [Newsletter] 7(3), 25–30.
Twain, Mark (1996). *The Adventures of Tom Sawyer*. New York: Oxford University Press.

42 Marvin Kaphan

Marvin Kaphan, MSW, LFAGPA, CGP, BCD, is a former president of the Group Psychotherapy Association of Southern California. He has engaged in the fulltime private practice of psychotherapy since 1960. He has maintained six ongoing groups for over fifty years, and has given lectures and demonstrations throughout the United States and Canada, including two at the American Psychiatric Association.

13 Setting Group Culture Development in Motion

Avraham Cohen

Introduction

> The art of peace is to fulfill that which is lacking.
> (O Sensei—Morihei Ueshiba, founder of aikido)

I take it as axiomatic that the goal of counseling is human growth and development (Schneider, 2004). Moreover, I see suffering as a signal for growth-oriented change (Brazier, 1997, 2001). Group counseling offers special opportunities for growth. A culture of support, insight, and growth, personally and interpersonally can develop.

The leader (as an 'elder') has a special opportunity, as a model. This chapter explicates an initiatory practice for growth-oriented culture development.

Population

The group culture dimensions exist in any group and is a powerful influence on the group and its process, development, and ability to move toward achievement of its identified task(s) (Cohen, 2009/2015). The question to be addressed is how group culture can be addressed from the outset so that it is coordinated with these tasks. Specifically, this form of intervention is recommended for psychotherapy groups, and for counselor and psychotherapy education groups.

Intervention

Any action that disrupts the automaticity of our life patterns can be called "intervention." Group itself can become a powerful intervention in that committed group members create a culture of change. It is the responsibility of the leader to initiate this culture. The group leader most crucially demonstrates with his or her very being, that he or she is conscious/self-aware of inner world experience, and that he or she works with this content to further personal and relational development (Cohen et al., 2013). This can be shown by manner, use of language, honesty about themselves, directness, and care in their interactions with group members. This is not a technique. It is an outcome of ongoing personal work that will likely include some reflective practice, and an extensive experience of personal therapy.

There are specific kinds of statements that, when sufficiently coordinated with an authentic way of being, convey a strong message about group culture, values, and practices. For instance, it is important for group members to hear that I am an advocate for therapy and that I have availed myself of this process with some fine therapists over many years, and that I see this as an integral part of my own personal and professional growth, and well-being. As well, I will as merited mention various life-style practices that I work with for my own enjoyment and development. This latter is in the service of setting a tone of self-care along with specific suggestions about these practices and the associated philosophy.

Statements about particular values using carefully crafted language along with in-the-moment authenticity offers a message that indicates personal agency, responsibility, awareness, and most importantly suggests values and processes about the group culture. Here is a sample of a statement that a leader can make to a group from the outset and repeat in various forms over time:

> I am aware that I am feeling a little vulnerable at this moment. These are our first moments together as a group and I am aware that a lot of eyes are on me. [Pause.] I am suddenly remembering the first time I was asked to read out loud in class. I was 'hit' by a wave of feeling associated with the silence after the teacher asked me to read. I was afraid to even look around my class. I did have a strong sense of 'being looked at.' I was seven years old.

What was happening here? I might be seen as 'rambling on' about myself. There was of course a deeper message being conveyed that was very important for the group and its aim to help participants look into themselves in the service of becoming more whole and secure as human beings. The very first statement models awareness, disclosure, and vulnerability. The second statement acknowledges the presence of the group members and their effect on a human being. In this case the human being is the group's leader. The leader is suggesting by a way of being that being open and vulnerable as a human being is acceptable.

The next statement is about a memory of the past. The memory is related to the current moment. The leader is modeling inner world awareness, relationship between the past and the present, and feelings from the past that are connected to the present. The leader goes on to acknowledge the effect of others on inner experience. This is a relational reference; namely, others have an effect on us. The tone and manner will convey that this is not a pathology indicator. The leader mentions his age at the time of the memory. This suggests that a part of a person that is apparently an adult can also still be much younger and that the past is related to the present.

Much more could be said about these few sentences. Through this personal sharing the group leader is setting some cultural value possibilities for the group, values (Cohen, 2010) that will be important if the group is to realize its potential to facilitate work that will support the group members in their quest for more fulfilling lives. I have made such comments in therapy groups and in counselor education groups. I have also made such statements at the outset of workshops and academic conference presentations. In response, I have invariably noted absorption and engagement by whoever is present.

General Client Responses

Clients and students in counselor education programs have invariably commented that this early modeling of the leader is inspirational and safety creating. Absences tend to be minimal. Clients and students report life-changing experience in themselves and in their relationships.

Conclusion

The importance of a leader modeling the values of the group is central from the outset. Increased feelings of agency and the development of inner security are associated with this intervention.

Contraindications

- A leader who has limited experience of personal work.
- A group that exists within a context that 'prohibits' inner work.

References

Brazier, D. (1997, 2001). *The feeling Buddha: A Buddhist psychology of character, adversity and passion*. New York: Palgrave.
Cohen, A. (2010). Nurturing the community development dimension in groups as a pre-emptive intervention. In S. Fehr (Ed.), *101 interventions in group therapy* (pp. 509–513). New York: Haworth.
Cohen, A. (2015). *Becoming fully human within educational environments: Inner life, relationship, and learning* (2nd ed.). Vancouver, BC: Writeroom. (Original work published 2009.)
Cohen, A., Fiorini, K., Culham., T., & Bai, H. (2013). The circle of leadership integrity within business organizations. In W. Amann & A. Stachowicz-Stanusch (Eds.), *Integrity in organizations: Building the foundations for humanistic management*. London: Palgrave Macmillan.
Schneider, K. (2004). *Rediscovery of awe: Splendor, mystery, and the fluid center of life*. St. Paul, MN: Paragon House.

Dr. Avraham Cohen, recipient of numerous academic and professional awards, is a Professor at City University of Seattle (Vancouver, Canada site) where he is also the director for the full-time Master in Counseling program. He has been in private practice as a psychotherapist for 28 years, has presented his work at national and international conferences, and is author and co-author of many publications.

14 Only the Lonely
Trauma and Group Identity

Richard Beck

Introduction

Many therapists lead groups at conferences locally, nationally or internationally. This intervention addresses the complexity of group leadership when culture, language, and trauma intersect in one dimension of human experience, namely, "loneliness." The author was privileged, as Chair of the Task Force for Disaster/Trauma Management of the International Association of Group Psychotherapy and Group Processes, to be the only American invited to give a lecture and lead a small group at a conference in Sarajevo, Bosnia-Herzegovina. To understand different cultural perspectives, I asked, through personal correspondence, international colleagues, "What would you inform people about if you had a minute to speak?" I incorporated the following paraphrased suggestions into my lecture and group leadership.

The Suggestions of International Colleagues

In Rome, observing my description of a group at a supervisory session, they said, they remind me of the Elvis Presley song, "Only the Lonely." (Correction: It was a Roy Orbison song.)

A member in Kiev offered, there is sadness, hurt, depression, anger, fear, but most of all loneliness.

A colleague from Spain suggested the presence of silence in the communications in families and societies with those conflicts. I would describe how silence is an efficient mechanism of transmission of trauma, and also indiscriminate transmission to children, to offspring, by traumatized people without taking in account their capacity of assimilating.

I would see/listen and share with those who have suffered. To recognize their pain, their despair, and their stories, in order to remember and to learn what could be done in the future to restore what has been destroyed if ever possible. This was from another colleague from Spain.

From the United States a colleague suggested that, with dedication and persistence, our Japanese colleagues relentlessly continue their outreach work to help the victims and families that were/are affected by the tsunami and nuclear fallout. Sometimes support can be achieved through the concept of "walk with them."

A United Kingdom contribution was when you feel overwhelmed with helplessness, when you haven't a clue what words, method or strategy could possibly address the amount of unspeakable pain in front of you, get up off your chair, stand in front of the speaker and open your arms. Hold the person. Say nothing.

An Israeli colleague offered that when pain is overwhelming holding, using words, is a comforting solution.

I might say that it is very deeply shattering when we experience just how terrible human beings can behave toward each other—killing, raping and maiming—without any apparent reasons or qualms of conscience. This not only traumatizes individuals but can also disrupt the whole fabric of society. It is necessary to be there for the suffering victims to work toward repairing a sense of justice—something that can often take many years, even generations, but that it is a fight that we must not give up on. This is from a colleague in Austria.

Again from Spain, a colleague suggested that those of us raised and educated as Catholics are instructed to grow with a sense of guilt due to what was explained as the Original Sin. [I] never understood why, or what it was about. As I grew older, [I] understood that guilt makes us accept punishment without even asking why since punishment is the only way to erase guilt and the uncomfortable feelings related to it.

Where there is life, there is hope, suggested a colleague from the United Kingdom, and where there is hope, there is life. By hope, I mean the ability and willingness to exercise the transcendent imagination. However, I think that it is important to understand the symbolism of the conception of Jesus by God's word through Mary's ear. Relational listening and hearing, and conveying that the traumatized have been heard, are vital for our work. It is hard not to sound trivial and pretentious in the context of so much despair in while in the comfort of one's home within fairly stable democratic societies.

Our small group consisted of members from Sarajevo and Tuzla. Most were Muslim, and most were psychiatrists. English was their second or third language. Some group members knew each other and others did not. During the conference, the group met six times in addition to attending presentations.

The concept of loneliness needed to be introduced when the group and its members would be open to it. I waited patiently throughout the sessions, allowing the group to go where they needed to, allowing the group to supervise *me*. In the fourth meeting, after a heated interaction between members, it felt like the right time to formally introduce the concept of loneliness.

I took a deep breath and asked, "How do each of you experience loneliness, both in this group and in life?" There was silence, and I felt a wave of sadness. The members looked at me for guidance. Finally, one woman spoke. She described being a teenager during the Siege of Sarajevo, described playing piano by candlelight as a way to soothe herself from harsh conditions—no food, no electricity, and no water.

48 *Richard Beck*

Group members followed suit, speaking about love lost, lives lost and life alone. After each person had shared, I asked how it felt to express those feelings with the group. The following poem, shared in a large group setting, describes those feelings:

"Silence"

Silence speaks louder than words.
Silence screams louder than noise
Opens windows and doors
Breaks
Jazz.
Blues.

The base.

The base of the world.
Silence is poetry
And it says:
"I don't know what to say,
All is said,
But we can pray."
    Jasmina Mulaosmanović

Client Responses

In general, the group members expressed their feelings about loneliness when given the opportunity. For group members to express their feelings, the leader needed to establish trust and safety before an intervention could take place. To establish trust, the leader must listen patiently during preliminary sessions, allowing each member to go where they needed to go, not where the leader wanted them to go. Thus, an intervention needs to be timed when the group is cohesive and ready.

Conclusion

There were two interventions demonstrated in this paper: first, asking trusted colleagues how they would intervene; and second, allowing for the group members' responses to unfold as the group saw fit. Loneliness is a universal phenomenon, as demonstrated by the group members in Sarajevo. If group leaders are present at the right time, under the right circumstances and with the right leadership, we can melt away the loneliness.

Richard Beck is a therapist specializing in psychological trauma and its treatment in group practice. Richard teaches at Columbia University, and writes and lectures about trauma both nationally and internationally.

15 The Efficacy of Wedding Cognitive Behavior and Psychoanalytic Psychotherapies in Group Psychotherapy for Incarcerated Male Population

Uri Amit

Introduction

An assemblage of men falling on the schizoid-paranoid spectrum (Klein, 1984) poses a years-long challenge to therapists to keep them sufficiently curious about the process, motivate regular attendance and awake the nascent basic human tendency to unfold and self-enhance (Rogers, 1951).

General analytic comments about the group's dysfunction alone will asphyxiate the inherent desire to unfold. Members will further regress within the schizoid-paranoid spectrum and are likely to flee as the fear of remembered annihilation would be recalled. Nonetheless, group processes' psychoanalytical maps drawn by Bion (1961), Turquet (1974), Lawrence et al. (1996) and others (Hopper, 1997; Weinberg, 2007) are not to be disregarded, but are to be visually presented, in a here-and-now language described and with an inclusion of known personal histories. The goal is to unearth the forces that promoted erroneous thinking that steered the men toward maladaptive behaviors and realize their present aliveness.

To wed the two approaches is to reduce the likelihood for falsification of change. A necessary condition is the ability of the therapist(s) to remain attuned to the process despite the "borderlinish attacks on linking" (Bion, 2013), and provide the space in which the members can consider the impact of the past-in-the-present.

Population

Adult males committed to a forensic facility dedicated to treatment and assessment of their dangerousness. Dangerousness is attributed to a "mental abnormality" or "personality disorder" reflected in their criminal history and odious sexual offenses in particular. Via a specific statute, the commitment follows a completed criminal sentence.

Individually and as a whole, the men in this group organize themselves around early traumatogenic experiences and "chosen glories" (Weinberg, 2007) of undetected unlawful behaviors, *outré monde* sexual attempts to suppress despondency (Winnicott's manic defense [1935]) and perspicaciously sidestepping institutional rules. This group of men is also infamously known for both resistance to treatment and its ability to use clinical lingo, and sound convincing to unaccustomed listeners.

Of no less importance is the men's belief they are victims of social injustice and political prisoners and must, therefore, unite against the dangerous system and its agents, correction officers and clinicians. The clinicians who have access to explicit and implicit primitive fantasies and carefully couched thoughts have the power, as the myth goes, to prolong their life-long miseries with a stroke of a pen.

Interventions

Groups meet for 90 minutes, some are psychoeducational in format and others are psychotherapy groups. The latter convene thrice weekly and tend to begin with silence that creates discomfort that often discharges with complaints. For example, "I am tired of this hell hole," or "When will I get the f—ing report," or "Where is the form you told me you will bring me?" Or objections to the conditions of confinement, or criticism of the (free) medical/dental care and so on (*me-ness* [Lawrence et al., 1996]).

An expressed grievance by one is often enough to create an agreeing choir of few while others either minimize the misery, or remain unresponsive, or rush to offer a solution and later wonder aloud why they were shunned by others (*massification/aggregation* [Hopper, 1997]). During "bitch time," it is not unusual that a member or more will demand that the co-leaders "do something about it" (*dependency, fight-flight* [Bion, 1961]; *one-ness* [Turquet, 1974]).

Here I may either point to parallel experiences such as with a grossly inattentive parent(s), or to the need to rationalize parental disregard, or to a flight into silence to avoid parental sadistic scapegoating, or to siblings' rivalry, or to alliances within families and to whatever other experiences I am able to recall during the process. I tend to also invite the group to consider evoked feelings and, once expressed, to note that the feelings may not be "strange," but rather familiar given the reported personal histories and offense dynamics (e.g., what was said and done during offending).

At other times, written assignments given in psychoeducational classes are presented in group therapy for input (*dependency* [Bion, 1961]). Family news are also reported on in order to receive advice on how to manage related problems, or describe a dispute with another resident or a correction officer. Feedback follows, for it pays, so the men believe, to offer it as it may look good on reports and eventually expedite release, as well as to discharge induced anxiety and appear sound thus refuting the belief they suffer from "mental abnormality" (a condition for civil commitment).

The feedback tends to be deadening for it often amounts to talking at others rather than encourage unearthing the etiology of corrupted thinking. To abort intellectualization, I often step up to the board, draw caricatures using the intellectualizers' names, echo what I heard using as many as possible of the words uttered and ask, "Might you, X, have feelings about these [pointing to two or three caricatures] exchanges?" Or ask X, "Might there be another way to respond so that Y [pointing to the figure] could hear you?"

Role-playing follows instantaneously. A seemingly monotonous presentation affords for an examination of life's experiences that culminated in indeterminate forced containment that may also help to free the human spirit.

Conclusion

Flawed cognitive processes and maladaptive behaviors are not questioned so as to not further defensiveness and the self-protective shell. Instead, bridging between the men and engaging the visual and auditory senses are utilized and seem to provide a safe environment in which the self-protective shell tends to crack, albeit very slowly.

My contact with group members extends beyond the scheduled sessions for I pass by them on my way to and from the treatment area. I often stop to stand or sit by them in a table for four to just say hello and enquire about their families. With time, these brief stopovers help to create *transitional spaces* (Winnicott, 1953) as evidenced in shorter "bitch time" and work intensity once the course was set.

Contraindications

At this point after multiple experiences with this intervention, there do not appear to be any contraindications.

References

Bion, W.R. (1961). *Experiences in group and other papers*. London: Tavistock.
Bion, W.R. (2013). Attacks on linking. *International Journal of Psychoanalysis*, 40, 308–315.
Hopper, E. (1997). The fourth basic assumption. *Group Analysis*, 30, 439–470.
Klein, M. (1984). *Envy and gratitude and other works 1946–1963*. London: Hogarth.
Lawrence, W.G., Bain, A. and Gould, L.J. (1996). The fifth basic assumption. *Free Associations*, 6 (37), 28–55.
Rogers, C. (1951). *Client-centered therapy: Its current practice, implications and theory*. London: Constable.
Turquet, P.M. (1974). Leadership: The individual and the group. In Gibbard, G.S. et al., eds. *The large group: Therapy and dynamics*. San Francisco, CA and London: Jossey Bass.
Weinberg, H. (2007). So what is the social unconscious anyway? *Group Analysis*, 40 (1), 319–334.
Winnicott, D.W. (1935). *The manic defence; through pediatrics to psychoanalysis: Collected papers*, 1958; New York: Basic Books, Inc.

Winnicott, D.W. (1953). Transitional objects and transitional phenomena. *International Journal of Psycho-Analysis*, 34, 89–97.

Dr. Uri Amit has held senior clinical positions in forensic facilities for over thirty years, is a psychology faculty member at a large public research university and is a private practitioner. He is affiliated with a psychoanalytical institute in a metropolitan city, a Diplomate of the American College of Forensic Examiners and a Certified Group Psychotherapist by the American Group Psychotherapy Association.

16 Sparking Connection
Increasing Awareness, Engagement and Relatedness

Carlos Canales

Introduction

The beginning of every meeting is an important marker for the development of each group session. It sets the foundation for subsequent interactions, often serving as a basic sample of the work ahead. People non-consciously orient themselves toward their environment, and make bonding efforts toward one another. Sometimes these efforts are in-sync with their needs for affiliation, and other times they are contrary to their explicit intention for building relationships.

At the start of each group session, I frequently state an open-ended ritual that suggests my overarching aim for a process group: to raise intrapsychic and interpersonal awareness; increase contact and engagement; and, maximize bond-building or important emotional linkages between members and the group-as-whole. In the words of Diana Fosha (2000), I want to facilitate so that the implicit may become explicit; the explicit may develop into the experiential; and, the experiential may live relationally. My general belief is that when we move out of our heads as a guiding strategy to navigate life or relationships, we increasingly gain more access to our bodies, sensations, emotions, instincts, and present environment in a fluent manner; securely interrelating back and forth moment-to-moment.

Population

This intervention is applicable for all therapy modalities as well as presentations and workshops. Interestingly, running several groups with undocumented folks, Latinas, gay men, or other identified minorities at a university counseling center has shown me the increased richness of this intervention because of its specific orienting and bonding effect. In nature, all animals look for those who are like them and who first recognize them; particularly when threatened. I believe this organismic predisposition empowers the intervention poignantly; specifically, when establishing safety, offering support, and encouraging risk.

Intervention

After shutting the door in the group room, I typically take my seat and begin group by uttering variations of the following message:

> Welcome! Take a moment and let yourself arrive. Notice how you are in this moment, how you allow yourself to be in your own particular way . . . sense into how your body supports your experience. Use all of your senses and just become aware through them. Notice if you prefer to look inside, discerning your feelings or whether your attention goes outside toward your environment or peers. Let your eyes wander, and see if you can register what they see and how it feels to just let your eyes guide you as you make contact with your group. When ready, feel free to share as you feel comfortable, but also notice what is uncomfortable, what you would not want others to know about you in this moment.

I sometimes share with my group the image of a squirrel posturing erect and looking right and left for what is out there, registering safety or threat, niceness or blah-ness, what is yummy or not. As the group matures and settles over months of work, additions to this basic prompt can be added. If I sense that the group knows the difference between lobby chatting vs. entering the therapy space, I may add something like:

> Give yourself a moment to let yourself be with your experience. Notice how you make contact with yourself and with others. Feel! Know how you feel and what desires and wants come about with this feeling. Who would you want to tell about this feeling? Notice who you might miss as you notice your internal experience right now. Stay curious about your own forming process. [Welcome the session!]

In a group of six to eight members, this intervention typically takes about three to five minutes at the most. Sometimes members become curious about their experiences or the changes in their awareness over time. Sometimes they will choose to carry their insights further into the session.

General Client Responses

People frequently function with little awareness of their bodily sensations or their feelings, and instead they organize by to-dos or logical, conscious goals (Fosha, Siegel, & Solomon, 2009). This experiential exercise prompts group members to integrate sensations and emotions right away, implicitly inviting and reinforcing a more integrated way of relating. The intervention slows people down and differentiates between inner and outer awareness thereby, increasing our sense of how we form inside and how others may affect that organization.

During first meetings, members report things such as: "I feel calmer now that I slowed down," or "I noticed anxiety because I typically don't share with a group of people." Regardless, they are more present and available for the session. If a member has something pressing to share, I have found that the exercise does not prevent them from jumping in with their desired goal. However, the therapist has the option to help this member notice how they approach others when in need, or when eagerness is more prominent.

Interestingly, in one of my Latina groups, members recurrently shared variations of feeling at home; having found their people; not needing to perform; having a sense of being accepted because the other member is just like them; and, an awareness of being a minority everywhere else and the cost of such vigilance. This type of sharing was useful as it maximized bonding right away and increased supported risk-taking.

Watching for non-verbal responses is also very important while tracking group members' reactions. Some members close their eyes as they look inside. Others lock their eyes on the therapist. Some look around at all group members, while others look away from the group orienting toward the trees outside of my office. All information is grist for the metaphoric mill.

Conclusion

If self-awareness, connecting, and bonding are desired factors to increase group cohesion and interpersonal contact in group therapy, why not use interventions right from the start that encourage it (Billow, 2003)? This intervention is simple and malleable. It naturally scaffolds for future work. I believe that when therapists develop their own language in presenting this intervention while attuned to their group, the results will enhance the life of the group.

Possible Contraindications

While I believe the model is applicable to all groups, sometimes there are extraordinary occurrences where an individual can become too reactive and can step outside of his or her emotional windows of tolerance. This can happen by either a present crisis that needs immediate attention or by traumatic reactivity. Looking inside or looking at others may simply be too much. Even though these are very atypical cases, I can think of two occurrences in over twelve years of practice. It is important to attune to your clients first before deciding on an intervention. If the therapist notices that someone becomes too dysregulated, my recommendation is to shift to a relaxation exercise or a mindful breathing practice.

References

Billow, R. (2003). Bonding in Group: The Therapist Contribution. *International Journal of Group Psychotherapy*, 53 (1), 83–110.

Fosha, D. (2000). *The Transforming Power of Affect: A Model for Accelerated Change*. New York: Basic Books.

Fosha, D., Siegel, D., & Solomon, M. (Eds.). (2009). *The Healing Power of Emotions—Affective Neuroscience, Development, and Clinical Practice.* New York: W.W. Norton & Company.

Dr. Carlos Canales is a licensed Clinical Psychologist and Certified Group Psychotherapist. He works in private practice at the West Des Moines Center for Psychotherapy.

17 Intercultural Group Therapy
Global Nomads, Expats and Lovepats

Maria van Noort

Introduction

Since there are also people in need among the 180 different nationalities living in Amsterdam and surroundings, I decided in 2005 to start an English-speaking intercultural group. It meets every other week for two hours. People come to this group for diverse reasons: experiencing isolation; trouble integrating into society; and feeling torn between different cultures. But all the members wish to have better contact and interactions in private as well as in public life.

Client Population

Most clients are referred by general practitioners or mental health organizations and some have previously been in individual treatment with me. Their diagnoses include depression, anxiety disorder, identity problems and a lot of acculturation stress. They all arrived in The Netherlands as voluntary immigrants and came here for study, work or because of love.

Cultural Shock

Culture shock is the physical and emotional discomfort one suffers when one decides to live in another country with other social codes than one's place of origin. Anxiety arises as a result of losing all familiar signs/symbols of social interaction. Cultural shock can produce numerous symptoms. A colleague of mine grouped responses of immigrants by Stressors. The development of emotional, behavioral and physical symptoms is a response to different stressors which can be grouped together in a diagnostic system of categories such as: Primary support group; Social environment; Educational problems; Occupational problems; Housing problems; Access to health care services; Problems related to interaction with legal system; and other Psychosocial problems such as disasters, elections, hostilities in the country of origin. It is notable that non-immigrant patients usually have two stressors, while immigrants have between five and eight stressors.

Third Individuation Process

According to Salman Akhtar immigration is a complex psychosocial process that can lead to a hybrid identity. He describes four lines of psychological development toward this identity (Akhtar 1995). These four dimensions are:

- Drives and affects—experiencing feelings of love, hatred and ambivalence toward the country of origin or the new country
- Interpersonal and psychic space—how far or near is the distance to dear ones in the country they left and finding out acceptable limits of interpersonal space in the new country
- Temporality—dealing with the uncertainty of staying temporarily or forever in the new country
- Social affiliations—making deeper levels within the new society's social networks, clubs, etc.

The experiences immigrants go through when they start to live in another country and culture is comparable to what adolescents go through in terms of separation and individuation phenomena. Immigration can be called a third individuation phase.

It is true that immigrants in this group are adult when they enter, but the combination of cultural shock and many losses in important domains of life form a heavy load. One could view this as an adult reorganization of identity.

Situation Before the Intervention

In 2012 I started my third intercultural group; this one group consists of six people from different regions of the world. They meet every other week. Half of the group members are native English speakers and half are not. It was surprising to observe and experience how group members individually touched upon and worked through the four above-mentioned developmental lines.

The beginning phases of all three groups were characterized by much sharing about differences in culture. In particular negative experiences with Dutch culture and the Dutch people were expressed. This exchange expanded to comparing ideas behind rituals and habits in each person's culture.

In this type of group I learned to ask more contextual questions like "What role and position do you have in your family of origin and culture and how is that played out in the culture of this group?" This type of questioning sometimes sets off an exploration of memorial days and special celebrations and their meaning in a specific culture as well as what they meant in this group.

Intervention

After one and half years of Group Therapy, the group has survived the forming and storming phases of group development and now engages in more intimate sharing. This is how it happens: one group member (A) starts to talk about a part of her identity and others join in and exchange input about this subject (van Noort, 2010).

A: I so enjoy much speaking English in this group—especially about the Australian part of me: school, landscape, atmosphere. Well F, what about your Austrian part?

F (smiles awkwardly but picks up the question and shares enthusiastically about her Austrian friends): I was bullied and that was not so nice but they also found me exotic because I came from a Mediterranean country. Actually I did not know what to do in order to belong.

A AND F (asking B): What about your African part, which you never wanted to talk about?

B (there is a long silence before she shares an impressive story): I strongly disliked being there. I felt ashamed about apartheid and feared being judged for being white.

B lived for a while with one parent in a society where there was great mistrust toward white people. She then experienced great anxiety and exclusion. Now she trusts the group enough to share this part of her identity. The whole group listens intensively and empathizes with her how awful that must have been for her. The group gives a deep compassionate sigh.

This exchange resembles the card game of Quartet where you ask for and give away cards that belong together in order to make suits. In this case the suit or topic is multicultural identity and the different parts that it makes up. Within the group therapy this playful game becomes serious but reinforces the sense of identity.

General Client Responses

The group members have become closer with each other. Further exploration of their part identities and how to manage clashes and pitfalls has taken place. In the following sessions the term "multi-faceted identity" was viewed less as a stigma or sign of being a misfit. Having a multi-faceted identity came to be experienced as a challenge, something worthwhile to work on and share with others.

Conclusion

A group approach where one transitions between individual psychodynamic, group dynamic and cultural aspects seems to build up constructive relations with and between immigrants. Useful concepts and adaptation of familiar frames and methods can help to overcome gaps between cultures.

Contraindications

Placing involuntary immigrated clients in this type of group is not suggested. A specialised treatment focused on trauma is first required for them. Take time for a good diagnosis. Many have been diagnosed as borderline patients. A cultural shock and acculturation stress symptoms can produce a blurry view of what is going on. A client's English does not have to be perfect or even very fluent. Basic understanding and speaking proficiency is all that is necessary.

References

Aktar, S. (1995) A third Individuation: Immigration, identity and the psychoanalytic process, *Journal of the American Psychoanalytic Association*, 43, 1051–1084.

van Noort, M. (2010) Interculturele Groepstherapie. *Tijdschrift voor Psychotherapie*, 36, 332–346.

Maria van Noort Drs, Psy.D., is a psychotherapist in private practice for individuals, couples and groups in Amsterdam, The Netherlands. She is also a supervisor and training analyst.

18 Back to the Future
Attending to Detrimental Family Loyalties

Russell Hopfenberg

Stuck in the Past

Many times, group members express an awareness of their struggles and that problematic behavioral patterns are connected to their family histories. However, members are often unaware that enacting their difficulties may serve to maintain a deep emotional connection to their families of origin. The anxiety associated with making a change is due in part to the reality that doing something different will sever this particular family connection and lead to feelings of loss and abandonment.

Sometimes, the avoidance of self-activation toward making a change includes a fantasy that "a new and improved parent in the past" would serve to maintain a parental connection while allowing the patient to engage in behavior that runs counter to original parental teachings. However, since this wish is a fantasy, it does not usually translate into real changes that help the patient meet their current needs. The intervention described here highlights and normalizes group members' wishes for having had a different experience when they were growing up, and enables members to make behavioral changes. It also facilitates group resonance and support around the feelings of loss and abandonment that result from making changes, changes that break old family loyalties.

Patient Population

The intervention described below is used in a psychodynamically oriented therapy group. It should work well in a group that has already demonstrated cohesiveness and in which members have revealed their presenting difficulties, some of their relevant history and an ability to tolerate the use of humor and analogy. If you decide to use it, those members who have not seen the film *Back to the Future* (Zemeckis et al., 1985) should be given "a spoiler alert."

Intervention

This intervention has three steps:

- Preparation: Evaluate the group discussion and notice a theme of pre-determined difficulty. Statements that contain phrases such as "I can't" or

"I've never been able to . . ." combined with current or prior discussion of parallel behavior by one or both parents may be good indicators that group members are reacting with patterns learned in their families that maintain a family connection, rather than responding to the current reality.
- Comment: Verbalize the wish that our parents would have been different, and describe the movie scenes.
- Process: Facilitate the group integrating the intervention into the group culture, and the members' resonance with and support for one another.

Preparation—Case Example

Anne was a lawyer who had success working in a corporate environment. Upon moving to her own practice, she reported that she was doing a good job with her clients but had a great deal of difficulty procuring new business. At times she talked about her experience of her father's manufacturing company. Anne would talk about how her father "could operate and troubleshoot every piece of machinery." However, her father's company eventually went under as he had difficulty with marketing and finances.

Ben was a mechanical engineer who had an extremely impoverished social life. He was in his mid-30s and had never been in a romantic relationship. During his time in the group, Ben recounted a variety of ways that neither of his parents took the time to attend to him. For example, if he had difficulty with homework, they would hire a tutor rather than help him themselves. When his doctor said that he needed to exercise more, they hired a personal trainer.

Catherine, a mother of two boys, lost custody of her older son to his father as she was convicted of a felony and has a substance dependence. She has been in recovery but has had relapses. Catherine's mother abandoned the family when she was four and she was raised by her father and eventually her step-mother. Her father provided for Catherine but was emotionally unavailable to her as he favored her two brothers.

During this particular group meeting, Catherine described difficulties in her marriage. She said she feels like she has to do everything, even though she and her husband have domestic help and she is at home full time. She discussed her husband as being unsympathetic with how difficult it is to take care of her infant son all day. At this point, Ben discussed his difficulty "just attending to himself, let alone, a child." He then noted the connection between his discomfort being invited out after work and his having been a loner when he was growing up. He said that he related to Catherine because his parents emotionally abandoned him and that he "was raised by nannies." Catherine commented that she can see how Ben would have difficulty socializing because he "probably feels like nobody would want to spend time with him because his parents didn't." Anne said she wished that her father had done better in his career and had given her a better feel for business.

Comment—Case Example

With Anne making a direct connection between her experience and history, the therapist can comment: "It's true that things might be much easier now if our parents had been different, but I've only heard of one person who has ever made this happen—Marty McFly. If you remember, near the beginning of the movie *Back to the Future*, Marty's girlfriend tries to convince him to send his audition tape to the record company. Marty replies: "What if I send it and they don't like it. I just don't think I can take that kind of rejection." When he goes back in time, Marty finds out that his father (George) writes science fiction stories. He asks George if he can read one but George says: "Oh no, I never let anybody read my stories. What if they didn't like 'em, I couldn't take that kind of rejection." A little while later they have a similar exchange about George asking Marty's mother Lorraine to the dance. Now, we all know what happens. George knocks Biff out, and he and Lorraine go to the dance together. When Marty gets back to the future, his parents are successful, his brother is off to work at the office, and his sister has boys calling her. And it's implied that Marty will send his tape into the record company. But for us, since we don't have a DeLorean, we have to activate ourselves to take the risks necessary to attend to our needs.

Process—Case Example

Members discussed the things they learned in their families, both useful and problematic. Ben described feeling angry and guilty about continuing his patterns of behavior for so long. He and the group explored ways that he might make changes. Catherine had difficulty making the connection between her behavior and that of her mother. She said that she could see how someone might see it that way but she's "trying to do the opposite" of what her mother did. This led to deeper discussion regarding similarities and opposites vs. separation and autonomy. Anne resolved to work on expanding her business, rather than only attending to plying her craft.

Contraindications

This intervention is intended for use in a group that has shown cohesiveness and support, as well as an understanding of the connection between modeled parental behavior and their own difficulties. It is contraindicated if members have had experiences of unresolved parental abuse.

References

Zemeckis, R. (Author & Director), Gale, B. (Author) & Spielberg, S. (Producer). (1985) *Back to the Future* [Motion picture]. USA: Universal Pictures.

Russell Hopfenberg, Ph.D., CGP, FAGPA, is a Consulting Associate Faculty member in Medical Psychology at Duke University where he teaches courses in group psychotherapy. He is a past president of the Carolinas Group Psychotherapy Society, a past Board Member of AGPA, and maintains a private practice in Raleigh, NC.

19 The Undecided
Helping Clients Make Decisions
Klifton Simon Fehr

Introduction

Many of the clients come to see us for various reasons. One that seems to be less initially discussed is their conflict with decision making. They generally do not come into our consultation rooms with the insight that decision making often is a conflictual burden for them, but rather will talk around the concept which slowly reveals itself as they speak about their lives. Very often they are not aware of how much this conflict affects their experiences. Repetitive behaviors that offered some degree of comfort and some success are generally used when making a decision for these people. Thus, they also limit their world and growth and it almost appears to be a repetitive compulsion.

For some, the decision difficulty runs the continuum of the simplest, i.e. pondering a menu which elicits anxiety to some especially when the other dinner guests begin to become annoyed, and some of the most profound decisions, which can lead to panic attacks, i.e. who do I want to marry or should I change my profession etc., which holds control over one's life direction.

How does one know if he or she is making a good decision? Some decisions are frivolous whereas others are profound affecting one's future. Do we make the future decisions from our gut or our mind? Ideally, using both would be the direction to implement but that is not so easy.

The gut gives one the feeling that it is the right decision because it feels right. Yet that can be a slippery slope. How many things in your life did you feel "this is right," but later felt it turned out wrong? The mind, on the other hand, can give us facts, research and maturity in thinking. But like the gut it too can be wrong and not a good route to go as facts, research and maturity of thinking can also turn out to be distorted.

So some people become immobilized in making changes. As a group leader it becomes one of our many responsibilities to guide them into feeling more comfortable with decision making. Let the group members know that many decisions can be changed, if they are not set in stone, and when an individual makes a decision he or she comes out of conflict. Yet, the individual's level of neuroticism can make a decision more painful than the conflict leading up to it.

Intervention

Oddly the beginning part of this intervention appears to be the most difficult, and that is helping clients become aware of the fact that a lot of their anxiety is due to their difficulty with making decisions. It requires them to be able to move into abstract thought and be introspective. Guide them to realize that beneath many of their complaints is the pressure of a decision that has to be made about something or some things.

Once the client(s) become aware or cognizant of this, the therapist can move to the second phase which seems, for some, a bit difficult because the group's focus is on them without the group members discussing themselves. We put three chairs in a sort of triangle. One of the chairs represents the positive outcome of the decision to do something where the client discloses all kinds of positive variables and the group members help to add positive variables. Then the client relocates to another chair and begins to disclose all the negative variables of making the decision to go in a particular direction and the group members again help with presenting negative variables that they could foresee happening. These first two chairs represent the cognitive conflict that exists in the client's mind about his or her decision. The client then moves to the third chair and speaks from his or her gut feelings about his or her decision. The group members again help by projecting their feelings onto what has been the conflict.

Client Responses

Generally the clients' responses have been quite favorable to this intervention. For one it helps them become aware of the many factors that have been in operation within their personalities, which in the past has been the cause for great confusion. Learning how to discriminate one's thoughts and emotions is of great help. It too has been disclosed by the group members sitting outside and providing help that in some way it has helped them with some of the decisions they have been pondering for quite a while.

Conclusion and Contraindications

This rather simple intervention can be quite effective with helping clients compartmentalize the many extraneous variables affecting their conflicts in making a decision. It is also a nice intervention for a new group leader who wants to introduce a rather safe intervention. It, too, sets the tone for future group sessions in the sense that it is this author's belief that behind almost every decision lies an unknown need that is pushing for gratification. This can be seen quite clearly when one person says to another, "You make the decision." Quite possibly a dependency is in operation as is the need to not take responsibility but a discussion of the correlation between decision making and needs will be saved for another chapter at another time.

There have not been any contraindications seen in this intervention. The only behavioral manifestation that seems to have caused some discomfort is for those clients who do not like to be the center of attention, but they appear to transcend this discomfort rather quickly.

Klifton Simon Fehr, M.S., is a Mental Health Counselor whose professional experiences lie within the populations of addictions, HIV gay clients and Men's Group within the Penal System. He is in the process of developing a private practice with a focus on group psychotherapy.

20 Degree of Action and Structure in Format to Facilitate Group Cohesion

Sharan L. Schwartzberg

Introduction

A practitioner's first exposure to group therapy becomes a template from which future practice is derived. In particular, the group format and the degree of structure imposed by the leader on the process are imprinted in the leader's clinical reasoning. Group therapies are commonly categorized as psychodynamic, interpersonal, cognitive, and behavioral. Each of these conceptual frameworks indicates the group's composition, leader role, and intervention principles. By carefully considering the degree of structure imposed, rather than follow implicit knowledge of past experience, the leader can more consciously shape group outcomes.

I propose a rehabilitation paradigm, the Functional Group Model (Schwartzberg & Barnes, 2012, 2014; Schwartzberg, Howe, & Barnes, 2008) as a theoretical basis for determining the degree of structure as a component of the group design.

The assumption underlying the model is that by changing the degree of structure a leader can facilitate outcomes such as group cohesion. The processes used in the group have a direct bearing on the group outcomes and former aims both tacitly perceived and empirically known to be of a value. In a functional group the group and tasks are structured to achieve maximal involvement of members through group-centered action, spontaneous involvement, member support and feedback, maximal sense of individual and group identity, and a "flow experience" where the challenges for action are balanced with the members' capabilities and cultural orientation.

Population

I will use a process group in a graduate program in a University professional program for certification in occupational therapy as an example of how a leader can structure the format to influence outcome.

Intervention

Action Components of a Functional Group (Schwartzberg, Howe, & Barnes, 2008)

There are four types of action that the leader uses as a guide in structuring the group format in consideration of the group's maturity or phase of development. These are the distinguishing features of a functional group.

- *Purposeful Action*—structure activities, action or inaction, that individuals and the group perceive as congruent with their needs and goals
- *Self-initiated Action*—structure activities, action or inaction, that supports exploratory behavior of individuals and task involvement
- *Spontaneous Here and Now Action*—structure activities, action or inaction, that encourages expression of thoughts and feelings related to the here and now
- *Group Centered Action*—structure activities, action or inaction, that yields leadership emerging from the group membership and interdependent action through consensus.

When creating a new group I first assess the members' capability for self-direction around the group's task and then design the group experience to match member ability. I am concerned with a group member's ability to communicate, problem solve, have insight, and generalize from the experience. I rely upon the types of action as a schema to grade the level of expectation and processes. The sessions follow four steps to structuring the group process: (1) orient the group to the design, (2) explain the procedures to the group, (3) set up the task or activity, and (4) follow up time to assess the experience (Schwartzberg, Howe, & Barnes, 2008).

These steps are shared among members and the leader. This is determined by two factors: (1) the social-emotional, cognitive, and physical capacity of group members, and (2) the group's phase of development. For several years my co-instructor and I structured the process groups so that students co-leading groups in the community had a chance to try out activities with their peers. The students decide upon the week's activity, which co-leader pair will facilitate, and when. The structure of the group impacts the outcomes. The group's phase of development also influences the type of structure and degree of success in facilitating member alliances, empathy, and cohesion.

I find that it is very important to build in rituals to enhance feelings of safety early in the group. The beginning of any group requires more structure to provide a sense of boundaries and safety. I make sure there is the exact number of chairs and a clear agreement to maintain safety, confidentiality, clear expectations and health boundaries.

General Client Responses

Inevitably we found ourselves bored with one tedious activity after another. The activities selected were parallel tasks, rather than ones that would facilitate group exploration and interaction. Upon self-reflection, the leaders came to realize they were co-constructing the passivity in the group. We examined reasons we may have been avoiding exploring the resistance to member initiative for fear of student backlash, anger, and increased anxiety in the beginning of the program or around exam time, to name a few considerations. Our co-leadership issues around competition, vacation schedules, differences in seniority, may have also been at play as we colluded with group members' silence in an underground reaction to authority.

Conclusion

I encourage leaders to examine their theoretical model and identify how the structure influences desired group outcomes. Each of the models mentioned in the introduction have indications and contraindications regarding the type of structure to impose on member selection, group size, composition, and group processes. Inevitably group format influences the degree of activity and inactivity of the leader. Conscious attention to both verbal and nonverbal expectations of activity or inactivity in the group warrants leader consideration.

Possible Contraindications

A precautionary note is given about how much structure is sufficient and when it becomes stifling to individuals and the group as a whole. As a general rule, I would offer as little structure as necessary. If the leader takes on too much responsibility for the group task, supporting members' emotional needs, it is likely the group remains dependent. On the other hand, if there is too little structure the members are likely to feel anxious, unclear of the group's purpose, and dissatisfied with the climate of the group. When the group is contained early on in a supportive, caring and successful experience it is likely members will be able to tolerate the conflicts, personal disclosures, strong attachments and ending of the experience.

References

Schwartzberg, S. L., & Barnes, M. A. (2014). Functional group model: An occupational therapy approach. *Israeli Journal of Occupational Therapy*, 23(2), E7–E26.

Schwartzberg, S. L., & Barnes, M. A. (2012). Functional group model. In Kleinberg, J. (ed.). The *Wiley-Blackwell Handbook of Group Psychotherapy*, pp. 139–167. Chichester, West Sussex UK: Wiley-Blackwell.

Schwartzberg, S. L., Howe, M. C., & Barnes, M. A. (2008). *Groups: Applying the functional group model*. Philadelphia, PA: FA Davis.

Dr. Sharan L. Schwartzberg is a Professor of Occupational Therapy at Tufts University where she teaches group process in the Graduate School of Arts and Sciences and is a Certified Group Psychotherapist. She holds secondary appointments in the School of Medicine in the Department of Public Health and Community Medicine and the Department of Psychiatry.

21 Attuning to Micro-Expressions in Group
A Relational Technique

Martha Gilmore

Introduction

Much of the substance of what happens in group lives in the subtle, non-verbal interactions between people—the micro-expressions that are all too easy to miss. Paying close attention yields important clues to material that exists only in "the unthought known" that powerfully influences our lives. These unformulated experiences are not easily available for verbal processing and can remain segregated and unmentalized in our less conscious self-states. Working from a relational and attachment-based framework, I find that focusing on micro-expressions and the reenactments they uncover can provide life-changing opportunities for growth.

The Group Members/Population

While I work primarily with a fairly sophisticated and educated population, I believe this technique is likely to be useful with almost any population. What I am focusing on is the subtle nuances of behavior, mostly non-verbal, which do not require any particular level of psychological or intellectual functioning to occur. This technique is especially useful for accessing more primitive self-states (Gilmore, 2012) that are not readily conscious or available for more adult or "rational" processing.

Intervention

This technique requires paying the therapist to pay close attention to the non-verbal interactions in the group and then allowing her/himself to comment, develop, enhance, and explore the interactions. It requires the group therapist to keep an evenly hovering attention that does not overly focus on the content of the interactions or the themes within the group. The process of noticing the interaction, choosing which ones to highlight, and pursuing the exploration, requires the development of a skill set that is highly attuned to the group and to the particular patient being addressed. Wallin (2007) provides a thorough explanation of the use of non-verbal experience in individual therapy to work with early attachment wounding. The group provides many more opportunities for relational issues to be evoked and available for working through.

Example one: In her second session in an established group, Karen revealed a childhood experience of abuse that her mother covered up out of shame. Consciously invested in Karen building more of a connection with the other group members, the therapist, Nancy, made a linking comment to other members. Members joined in sharing feelings of shame about their own families. After a few minutes, Nancy noticed that Karen looked somewhat vacant and inquired about her experience. She could only say she was fine and interested in what other members had to say. Another member, Diane, became tearful and shared that she imagined Karen felt Nancy reacted to her disclosure (linking to other members rather than responding directly) in a way that felt similar to her mother's reaction. Karen was surprised by this thought but was intrigued. The group took up the issue and Nancy endorsed the idea of such a reenactment. The next session Karen returned expressing gratitude and exploring her tendency to notice interpersonal injuries but not be able to name them without this kind of help.

Example two: In a mature co-led therapy group, "Mark" worked consistently with the male therapist, John, on issues regarding his conflictual relationship with his abusive, rejecting father. He rarely mentioned his mother beyond blandly saying that she was a good mother. One day, discussing this issue yet again, he answered a question from Nancy, the female therapist, and looked at her with such longing it took her breath away. John didn't notice and followed up with another statement, pulling Mark's attention back. After a few moments, Nancy followed up on her hunch that Mark's longing look was an opening to a new type of experience that could provide an important opportunity. She interrupted the flow and asked Mark what he experienced a moment ago when he looked at her. He looked back and said he hadn't noticed anything. Nancy summarized the interaction, saying, "I asked you how you felt after you had a fight with your dad and when you said 'lonely' you had such a look on your face." Mark looked startled at first, then longingly, and then started to cry. Nancy just kept eye contact with him warmly, tearing up a bit herself. Soon Mark was able to talk about how surprised and touched he was that she noticed and mirrored his feelings. Somewhat later he was able to access material about how much he had needed his mother to notice his pain and respond to him in a genuine way. As time went on, this experience of being met emotionally by Nancy seemed an important part of healing some of Mark's deep emotional wounds.

There are innumerable micro-expressions available for examination in any interaction and choosing which to highlight and explore can be a complicated process. I find it most useful to focus on attachment behaviors including proximity-seeking, avoiding, and self-regulating ones. Numerous techniques can be used to highlight and explore micro-expressions. From a gestalt tradition, one can simply ask that the group member exaggerate the expression and report what he/she experiences. Ormont's (1990) bridging technique can be used as in, "Diane, what do you think Karen is experiencing right now?" This happened spontaneously in the first example above. The judicious use of self-disclosure can be helpful. For example, in the second example, Nancy might have followed up with a disclosure of her concordant projective identification with Mark by saying, "I felt such loneliness when you looked that way at me." It is important to help the group member stay in the self-state that was evoked and to avoid intellectualizing about what is going on.

Typical Responses

As seen in the examples above, it is common for group members to be startled and confused when asked about their non-verbal behavior, especially if it is subtle and outside of their awareness. Members often dismiss the importance of such seemingly insignificant experiences until this type of intervention has become a norm for the group. The therapist may need to count on those mirror neurons and trust that her/his attunement and intuition are valid. Over time, I have found that groups become quite alert and excited when they experience this kind of attunement and have the chance to explore what lies beneath.

Conclusions and Contraindications

I have found a focus on micro-expressions in group to be a powerful intervention that helps the group explore new territory and moves it deeper into the here-and-now and away from an intellectualized "talking heads" therapy. Caution must be used to avoid eliciting humiliation and the feeling of being scrutinized by the therapist. Group members with a strong sense of shame or paranoia will need to be approached particularly delicately.

References

Gilmore, M. (2012). Working with primitive defenses in group. In J.L. Kleinberg (Ed.), *The Wiley-Blackwell handbook of group psychotherapy*. Chichester, West Sussex, UK: John Wiley & Sons, Ltd.
Ormont, L.R. (1990). The craft of bridging. *International Journal of Group Psychotherapy*, 40, 3–17.
Wallin, D.J. (2007). *Attachment in psychotherapy*. New York: The Guilford Press.

Martha Gilmore, PhD, CGP, FAGPA, is a licensed psychologist and certified group psychotherapist with the Sacramento Center for Psychotherapy in Davis and Sacramento, California. She is a Fellow of the American Group Psychotherapy Association and Clinical Professor at the UC Davis Medical School, Department of Psychiatry.

22 The Group Therapist in the Making

Priya Kirpalani

Introduction

The Inner Dialogue

"It's been like 10 minutes. Say something. Just say something. He just said what I was going to say. Ugh. On the bright side, I guess at least I'm on the right track. So, now say something else. Hurry up—before he says what you are thinking again. But what if I don't say it as eloquently or well thought out as he does. OK, maybe I should wait to see if we are still on the same page. Wow, it's been like 30 minutes now and I haven't said a word. What is wrong with me? Just do it already. At this point, people probably think that I am mute or something. Now, when I do speak, I'm sure everyone is going to turn their heads to look at me. How awkward! But I guess that's normal though—people looking at you when you speak. That's mannerly, right? Oh my gosh, stop already! What is taking me so long? SAY SOMETHING!"

This was basically my first experience as a group facilitator during my internship year. At the time, I would have never imagined writing this chapter, let alone leading another group again (outside of the internship requirement, that is). However, after discovering the power of the group process with the help of a few *very* influential supervisors, I was hooked! Since then, based on my own supervisory experiences (both as a supervisee and supervisor), I have found the following intervention to be quite effective in facilitating the training of the beginning group therapist.

Population

This intervention is recommended to draw out the developing group therapist who is in "his or her head." Typical traits of this type of therapist in the making include anxiety, perfectionist tendencies, and a preference for structure. These qualities (while useful in some ways) can often be roadblocks to the novice group clinician. However, the following intervention can assist in removing these obstacles and facilitating growth.

Intervention

For the Trainee

1. *Get out of your head.* While it may seem simple, this is actually quite difficult, particularly if you have a tough time dealing with ambiguity. Regardless, challenge yourself and set a "say something" goal. Once you meet that goal and are able to recognize that you will not be booed in response, add to it. Just remember to set small goals. While admirable, lofty goals can often cause you to stumble because you are trying to attend to too much too quickly.
2. *Trust your gut.* While most graduate programs initially (or let's be honest, sometimes always) encourage students to quiet their internal responses to clients and focus on scholarly research and evidence-based treatments, your best tool is often the use of instinct. Chances are if you are reacting this way to a client, others in the group are as well. Listen to your gut response, then look for group interactions to corroborate it, and finally check it out with the group.
3. *Say what you feel and think.* Similar to any other exchange you have on a daily basis, feelings and thoughts come up when interacting with group members. Instead of habitually ignoring these reactions and trying to execute some fancy intervention technique you learned about in a class or textbook, simply share what's going on for you and ask group members if they can relate in some way. Chances are at least one group member will be able to connect to your feedback. In the same vein, you are also modeling this ability for the group and moving the process into the here-and-now.
4. *Be yourself.* While easier said than done, just be yourself! There is no need to adopt a fancy, yet false therapist persona. First off, it's exhausting and secondly, it's disingenuous. If you are asking group members to be genuine and in the moment, why not model that behavior yourself? It is actually quite liberating once you take the risk and realize the impact of simply being who you are!

For the Supervisor

1. *Normalize anxiety.* Trainees typically think they are on an island when it comes to their self-evaluation of their own anxiety. Dispel that myth by normalizing the fear that is associated with acquiring a new skill, such as learning how to ride a bike or drive a car. If you are feeling ambitious, perhaps share about your own apprehensions as a group therapist.
2. *Share about your first group experience.* More often than not, trainees assume that their first group experience is uncharacteristic. If applicable, share about your first group experience or if it does not apply in your case, refer to the introduction of this chapter or those similar to it. Much

like in group, recognizing that you are not alone in your experience can be a powerful motivating factor in promoting growth and change.
3. ***Acknowledge your blind spots and/or growth areas.*** In my experience, trainees often place supervisors on a pedestal and assume that they are perfect. While flattering and a great self-esteem booster, my recommendation is to knock yourself off that pedestal and acknowledge your own blind spots and/or growth areas. Let's be honest, as supervisors we are not perfect and we do not have it all figured out either. While this would require making yourself vulnerable, it can be quite powerful in humanizing you and making you more approachable as a supervisor.
4. ***Model being a group therapist.*** In my opinion, the best way to teach is to do. When providing feedback to a trainee, make sure that you are following your own advice as well. In that regard, supervising a trainee on how to be a group therapist is an effective means to stop and check in with yourself as well. Should you feel motivated, share about this process. When appropriate, share about what you have learned from the trainee as well.

Typical Response

In my experience, these interventions are quite effective. The typical response is usually a "deer in headlights" blank stare as most trainees are not accustomed to using themselves as vehicles for change or hearing about their supervisors' less than perfect selves and/or experiences. However, after the initial shock wears off, I have found these recommendations to be consistently effective in drawing out the anxious, novice group therapist.

Conclusion and Contraindications

While this intervention is intended to encourage the trainee who is in "his or her head," it tends not to be as successful with the so-called "Stepford" trainee, who is supposedly perfect in every way and does not have the ability to acknowledge his or her shortcomings. Similarly, this intervention is contraindicated for the over-functioning novice group therapist, who says too much too quickly and needs to get back in his or her head and be more intentional about his or her role as a group therapist.

Dr. Priya Kirpalani is a licensed Clinical Psychologist and Certified Group Psychotherapist, who currently works as a University Psychologist and Group Therapy Coordinator at Florida International University Counseling and Psychological Services in Miami. She also works in private practice at the Center for Psychological Fitness in Cooper City, FL.

23 Grounding
Coming Into the "Here and Now" by Using Our Bodily Sensations

Margaret M. Postlewaite

Introduction

When I started a new therapy group five years ago, I was aware that several of the members were "talkers," highly activated individuals whose way of relating required them to entertain and/or command attention. I began the group using a mindfulness-based exercise, in an attempt to promote greater reflection and enhanced listening. It worked. First, it provided a reference point for anyone in the group to use. Second, it served to settle the group into a more reflective state. And frequently, it opened up areas of exploration that brought us more directly into the here-and-now. As I began Somatic Experiencing® training (SE™) and I learned more about the power of settling the nervous system, I refined the intervention to focus on grounding, using our bodily sensations to come into the moment and center ourselves. Within the SE literature, my "grounding" may be closer to "orienting," noticing what the energy is there, without changing it, as opposed to sending energy into the ground.

Population

This intervention can be used with any group to enhance the reflective capacity of its members. I have used it in a shortened form as part of my introduction to lectures and workshops—my goal being to increase the participants' capacity to listen, to focus and to bring online their cognitive functions. I encourage group and individual clients to "ground" as they face difficult tasks—doing taxes or bill payments, phone calls or conversations—including highly activating moments in the group process. By settling our nervous systems, even a little, we have more of ourselves available to process, remember, learn, share, and problem-solve (Levine, 1997).

Intervention

As the group begins, particularly if there has been a break in the continuity due to vacation or holiday, I invite the group to arrive in a different way. I utilize the simple directive, adapted from SE work, to *ground oneself*, that is, to bring oneself into the present moment. I acknowledge that we have all been "elsewhere"—coming from work/driving/conversations in the waiting room—and I encourage members to enter into the present moment as fully as they can. To assist this, I invite them to:

> focus on the bodily sensations that arise when you bring your attention to your back against the chair . . . your rear-end on the seat cushion . . . noticing your feet on the floor . . . and then become aware of your breath. Do not change it. Just notice it.
>
> As we shift from outer to inner, notice what happens in your body—where are you carrying tension or activation? Notice this . . . And now let's shift our attention to a part of our body that is most comfortable in this moment. It does not have to be big, just notice a place that is less-tense, less-activated, perhaps neutral if not comfortable. What happens as you shift your attention there? Notice it. And then, taking a moment, watch what happens as you shift your attention back to the place of discomfort, and then bring it back to the place of greater comfort . . . As you pause, notice what sensations happen throughout your body. When you are ready, allow yourself to come back into the room and out of your body . . . Look around, orient to this space—you have been in another place—and then notice what happens as you look at the other members present.

Then the group session continues with whatever arises next.

Client Responses

Many clients report that this SE intervention has been enormously useful to them in bringing them into the moment, away from the frenetic thoughts and obsessive concerns about the future or past, and in valuing the groundedness that they achieve. Some report a "love–hate relationship" with the intervention: hating the idea of doing it, of looking more deeply into their bodies, and yet find it "totally settling," increasing their ability to let things go, and describing the "sacred space" that can ensue.

Outside the group, some use the technique to manage their difficult temper or other emotions, some as they begin to teach a class, some with insomnia struggles, some with significant bodily pain. They learn that this intervention can be done internally in 30 seconds, and can help to regain balance. They have discovered that the goal of this experience is not relaxation; rather it is to develop a heightened awareness of their bodily sensations in *this* moment. As they come into a grounded present, they bring a different sensibility. They can approach experiences with a greater awareness of self and other.

There is an aspect of SE Grounding that parallels Mindfulness, in that the invitation is to approach one's experience of the moment without judgment, and with curiosity and openness. This grounding adds the usefulness of bodily sensations to track activation and places of quiet in one's nervous system.

Conclusion

Often when we are in pain or discomfort, we can only focus on pain. Learning that we can actually shift our attention to a pain-free, or at least neutral, place can be a powerful discovery. The effect of this intervention allows for a deepening of experience with one another, a shifting from reporting events or happenings, particularly after a break, to an increased focus on the issues and concerns that emerge as members come together to work. In my SE training, I have learned to appreciate that when members become activated (aroused), particularly with anger or frustration, they lose their capacity to process information or feedback. They can no longer engage in real dialogue. By grounding themselves, members have more resilience and greater openness to learning in the moment.

Contraindications

Given the large variety of places that this technique has been used, I see no argument against using it; however, the practitioner needs to practice this first and develop a comfort with the intervention. When a client has particular difficulty tracking sensation, I introduce other methods suggested by Levine (2010) to help them develop this capacity.

Another variation is to ground standing up, focusing on your feet, noticing your body's gentle movements, attending to the workings of your toes and heel, following how your feet are connected to the floor, the floor to the foundation, and the foundation to the earth—truly a way to be grounded! This can be the first step in trauma healing work, assisting someone to discover a solid, safe place within their bodies—a place that can be available at any time.

References

Levine, P. (1997) *Waking the tiger—Healing trauma: The innate capacity to transform overwhelming experiences.* Berkeley, California: North Atlantic Books.
Levine, P. (2010) *In an unspoken voice: How the body releases trauma and restores goodness.* Berkeley, California: North Atlantic Books.
Somatic Experiencing®Trauma Institute (SETI), www.traumahealing.org

Margaret M. Postlewaite, PhD, CGP, FAGPA, maintains a full-time private practice of individual and group psychotherapy, psychoanalysis and supervision in White Plains, NY. In addition to offering workshops and presentations at conferences, she consults on group and individual therapy for agencies and organizations.

24 Post Traumatic Stress Disorder with Combat Veterans Using Cognitive Behavioral Group Therapy

Justin A. D'Arienzo

Introduction

My psychology career began as an active duty Navy psychologist from 2003 to 2008. I was stationed in Virginia, Florida, Cuba, and aboard the USS *Kitty Hawk* Aircraft Carrier once ported in Japan. While serving, I trained in several psychotherapeutic modalities to treat Post Traumatic Stress Disorder (PTSD) to include cognitive behavioral therapy (CBT), exposure therapy, group therapy, and eye movement desensitization and reprocessing therapy (EMDR). After fulfilling my obligation, I began a private practice initially treating veterans with PTSD based on the numerous Iraq and Afghanistan war veterans returning home with this disabling condition and the military treatment facilities being overwhelmed in providing this care.

Those with PTSD often require a great deal of support in comparison to typical therapy patients. Effectively treating this population requires frequent appointments, immediate symptom reduction, and multiple interventions. Addressing these specific needs, 12 of my most severely impaired combat trauma patients were offered the opportunity to participate in a one-hour weekly PTSD Cognitive Behavioral Group meeting for six months in addition to each member participating in weekly individual therapy sessions in addition to their medication management appointments. Ten agreed to participate, but only eight participated for the duration.

Population

Participants were active duty members from the U.S. Navy, U.S. Marine Corps and U.S. Army. Most of the participants were being medically discharged for PTSD and other combat-related injuries. There were two officers and eight enlisted. The majority had served multiple combat tours in Iraq and Afghanistan, and two had been involved in piracy operations near Somalia. All were formally diagnosed with PTSD at a Military Treatment Facility prior to their referral to my office. Additionally, I had treated all the patients on an individual basis for at least two months prior to group commencing. All were male, one was Hispanic, one was African-American, and the others were Caucasians. Ages ranged from 20 to 38.

Intervention

The method of treatment was an integration of cognitive behavioral therapy, processing and support. Cognitive therapy was utilized in reframing traumas with the group's help. The intent was for the individuals to gain rational and balanced interpretations of traumatic events, and to facilitate the discovery of purpose and meaning as a result of these experiences. Second, regarding the behavioral component, desensitization of traumatic memories and related triggers were targeted. Members had been trained in relaxation skills individually with diaphragmatic breathing, biofeedback, progressive muscle relaxation, and mindfulness. Through verbal repetition of these events in group, the participants practiced self-regulation whether the topic was theirs or one in which they identified. Further, the group was a place of support and security simulating trusted military units in which they had belonged. The "supportive unit" served as a normalizing agent regarding their prolonged stress reactions to traumatic events as well as to provide support and accountability in taking risks to psychologically expose themselves to "real world" triggers in between sessions.

General Client Responses

Client response was positive, although two of the ten did drop from group and individual therapy during the duration. The remaining members had a significant reduction in symptoms and an improvement in their ability to cope with their remaining symptoms. All members were very anxious about their initial participation. Realizing they all suffered from the same malady, and reluctance and anxiety about participating or disclosing, the group quickly coalesced. Further, each member had a successful military career but possessed preconceived notions that other prospective participants did not truly have PTSD and were "gaming" the system. Once realizing the other members had also once been successful military members, and similarly legitimately suffered from PTSD, the members quickly united. Moreover, the fact that the individuals maintained contact after group treatment ended suggests that group cohesion had been gained.

The group became a valuable resource in understanding how the medical board and military discharge process worked, what services were available within the veteran community, and most importantly, how to access these services. As a resource and given that each member was at a different place along the path of the medical board process, the group served to dramatically resolve uncertainty about the process. Uncertainty had greatly fueled their PTSD symptoms.

The group did become a normalizing agent for the members where they realized that other members were experiencing similar fears in seemingly benign social situations as compared to their past combat experiences. They now feared or avoided situations like public speaking, attending school and work meetings, hunting, sporting events, sending children to school, attending parties, or having their partners leave their sight. Anxiety regarding these and other events became less shameful, embarrassing, and distressing as they learned their fears and anxieties were linked to their PTSD and were "normal" based on their experiences.

The group did serve as a rallying point where they encouraged others to confront fears and recount experiences in group. One member mustered the courage to challenge his wife's affair and then divorce her. Another had a 75-mile commute to base each day and was unable to access other services he needed due to his sense of obligation not to leave his Marine unit. The group pushed him to communicate his needs to his command. Due to his committed track record, his command gladly transferred him to a unit closer to his home, which then facilitated his access to resources that he needed prior to discharging from the service.

Finally, the group encouraged the youngest member to seek substance abuse treatment for his alcohol problem. This sailor's father was a Vietnam veteran and alcoholic who had recently suicided. The sailor, a corpsman having deployed with three separate Marine units, drank alcohol to cope with his night terrors, suicidal ideations, guilt, intrusive thoughts, and constant state of severe anxiety. The group challenged him to address his problem and identified that he was following in his father's footsteps. The sailor did attend treatment, maintained sobriety following the group's completion, matriculated into college, and found a stable job prior to his medical discharge.

Conclusion

Cognitive Behavioral Group Therapy is an effective modality in treating combat veterans with post-traumatic stress disorder. Creating a unified group mirrors a tightly knit combat unit where members are willing to take risks together. By infusing Cognitive Behavioral Therapy into the group process, individuals cognitively reprocess events in a healthier manner, improve their willingness and courage to seek help, and develop new behaviors that improve their functionality and decrease their symptomatology.

Possible Contraindications

Given the military culture of never showing weakness, there was resistance in gaining participation. Further, I found that many of those that would not participate lacked time based on other medical appointments or due to work restraints. Two nonparticipating individuals refused to participate as their anxiety was so impairing that they were too agitated or too paranoid to sit in a closed room with a group of people whom they did not know.

Surprisingly the two officers maintained their participation. Two enlisted corpsmen did drop out for unknown reasons.

Dr. Justin A. D'Arienzo is a Board Certified Clinical Psychologist in private practice in Jacksonville, Florida, specializing in Clinical, Forensic, Business, and Military Psychology.

25 The Group Sandwich Model[1] for International Conflict Dialog Using Large Groups as a Social Developmental Space

Robi Friedman

Introduction

The Sandwich model is designed to cope with conflictual situations in disturbed communities. It combines the relative security of small groups with the social character of large groups. Using the opportunities large groups can offer as the setting which offers the maximum face-to-face encounter possible (80–300 and even more, conducted right) participants can establish a unique social dialogue. Such powerful verbal and especially non-verbal experience exposes the participants to the views of others, as well as enables the ability to voice one's own view. The Large Group (LG) interaction, sandwiched between two Small Group (SG) sessions may have a unique potential to transform hate into co-existence and stop violence. The magic of seeing and feeling each other together with the development of a dialogue seems especially important after the failure of social media to cope with conflict.

Humans, being predominantly social, are deeply motivated by inclusion, exclusion and rejection dynamics. The different interpersonal settings, from dyads to small and large groups, are potential spaces which provide for differential coping necessities in relations. Moving to SGs, which unconsciously still hold the familiar promise of defending against exclusion or rejection, may give participants the possibility to feel secure while starting to voice conflicts. Then the LG, with its completely different atmosphere, may well provide for a unique opportunity to voice conflict and have a dialogue in the less secure social group. If it is possible to facilitate the LG to air questions of positions inside the group, or rejection and possible expulsion from the group and extermination, together with other, more specific anxieties and hate—it will be a start for the working through of the conflict. Moving back from the LG to a short SG, the Sandwich model provides for a further opportunity to understand and cope with social dynamics of splitting and hating.

Selfless attitudes, together with societal and authoritarian dominance, can be elaborated. The LG, this uncanny space, surrounded by the relative personal intimate security of the SG may be the optimal place to dialog with extremism and fanaticism. We need a FaceLOOK, in which violence-inhibiting mechanisms like guilt, shame and empathy can operate, contrary to the FaceBOOK, where virtual emotional distance makes endless fights possible. Finding a voice and the right tone in the presence of the threatening 'mass' and learning in the LG to move from a boundary-less chaos to a dialogue with mass and authority are developmental achievements.

The Population

The model has been applied to both professionals and laymen in conflicts, e.g. in Ukraine during the war, in Northern Ireland, with politicians and leaders of the civil society and in German–Jewish dialogues. In schools, in whole villages and kibbutzim, non-professional participants learned the SG model and especially the LG 'tweeting' language. Participants' minimum age may be lower than we think—right now as my experience is with no less than individuals of 15 years old.

The Intervention

When the dozen conductors arrived in the village about a hundred participants were waiting for us. For a while they were on the verge of violence following a dispute over accepting former enemies to live amongst them.

In the Introduction (15 minutes) the Sandwich model and its advantages and difficulties were explained to participants and encouraged a commitment to a 'working alliance' to the program. The SG as a preparation for the LG was explained, together with the aims of the LG and possible anxieties: to communicate freely worries and aims in short tweets, which aim to a dialog.

SGs (1 hour) helped the participants find their voice and a kind of preliminary openness to diverging opinions.

After that an LG (1 hour and 10 minutes) of all 11 groups, together with their conductors, was formed. In this LG many of the community's socio-political positions were voiced in a very personal, emotional tone. This experience aroused both very strong feelings together with the awareness of differing and similar views and the danger of acting-out angry and opposing feelings.

After a pause (20 minutes) a very short SG session (30 minutes) had the function of calming down those who felt threatened by the LG. It also provided for an additional space in which to voice yet unspoken issues. A closure session of 15 minutes, in which attempts of voicing more significant contributions seemed possible, thus finished the intervention.

Groups were led by highly professional conductors toward thinking and digesting some of the main problems in the village. They were encouraged to 'tweet' instead of monologing. All conductors shared the group analytic approach that LGs are not necessarily potentially psychotic and may be facilitated to constructive and honest dialog. In some interventions the SGs are led by trained members of the organization, who learn to provide a secure space for airing conflicts in the community.

General Client Responses

The vast majority of the participants of such Sandwich model intervention wrote surprisingly favorable feedback. While many felt at first overwhelmed by the massive 'groupishness' of the evening and especially by the LG, unknown to the general population, many wrote about their awareness of the community's conflict and rifts. The developmental process ignited by the Sandwich model continued in the following days and weeks. I think it takes sometimes months to understand the power of the Sandwich model intervention. The most important feedback was that violence did not return for at least a year.

Conclusion

Legal accords (like High Court rulings or the 'Good Friday agreement') still leave communities, who have to live with 'others,' vulnerable to their traditional enmities, difficult stereotypes and tendencies to split and reject. In order to cope with the 'unfinished business' the Sandwich model may be a very good solution if adopted as an ongoing process to be applied in the community.

Contraindications

The LG is a complicated interaction for the participants and has to be led accordingly by professional conductors who have a constructive approach to the LG. Although the individual's acquaintance with masses seems natural, for many participants the loss of intimate security in the LG is either unpleasant or threatening. Conductors have to see also the developmental opportunities LGs provide. Resistances are part of the work until participants grow more familiar and less anxious with the LG, even if already from the start many of the participants agree that the LG provides for an optimal practice space for the political and the social.

A changed facilitation of the LG toward considering it a developmental space for dialog makes the LG fascinating and rich in variations, not necessarily having it as the exposure to its aggressive sides. Approaching the LG with the belief that it is only full of aggression rather elicits more than investigates violence. The LG dark side, by being a mass, does not need stimulation or over-interpretation to appear.

Note

1 Temporary and affectionate name.

Robi Friedman (PhD) is a clinical psychologist and group analyst in private practice and an instructor at Haifa University. He is currently the President of the International Group Analytic Society and a co-founder of the Israel Institute for Group Analysis.

26 A Five-Stage Technique to Enhance Termination in Group Therapy

Jerrold Lee Shapiro

In my six-decade career teaching group therapy and serving as a group therapist, I have concluded that the three biggest errors made by novice group therapists are: 1) poor, or absent screening; 2) premature therapeutic interventions; and 3) ineffective termination. The last failure is akin to building a beautiful house and neglecting to include doors.

For therapy to have maximum impact, considerable amount of time is mandatory to manage group termination. Termination contains two essential tasks for group members (Shapiro, Peltz and Bernadett-Shapiro, 1998): 1) Saying goodbye—and facing loss; and 2) Transfer of training.

Saying Goodbye

Goodbyes are often difficult. Whereas "hello" represents the opening of possibilities, "goodbye" offers a loss, an ending, and to existential therapists like myself, an opportunity to address ultimate endings (mortality) (Shapiro, 2016). There can be several obstacles to effective termination including: 1) group leaders' personal resistance; 2) leaders' needs for reassurance; and 3) lack of training in closing. Because of these personal and pragmatic issues, training programs often avoid teaching termination. I recently queried 50 advanced graduate students in a practice-oriented program about their training. They were beginning internships in which there was an expectation of their leading short-term counseling groups with regular terminations. Although the average number of initial sessions was approximately 18, the modal number of terminations they had experienced was zero.

Transfer of Training

A crucial aspect of any therapeutic endeavor involves the clients' abilities to take what was learned in group and to incorporate those into their back home worlds. In general, symptom-oriented groups are more inclined to focus on this, although what clients learn in group therapy and the powerful internal shifts that often occur, are not solely encompassed in symptom-alteration or new behaviors. In what Bugental (1987) called "life-changing" therapy, transfer-of-training involves far more complex and meaningful internal shifts.

Description of Population

I work almost exclusively with carefully-screened, time-limited, closed, clinical and growth, process-oriented groups. In these groups, the termination phase does not unfold organically in process as do the preceding phases (Introduction, Transition and Treatment/Working). Termination occurs when the time for group meetings is elapsing. The timing can seem inconvenient, insensitive, intrusive and unnatural. The technique described here is designed to bridge somewhat that gap in the time-limited closed group. However, these techniques may be readily modified to work in an ongoing open-ended group. Indeed, as members regularly leave an open group, increasing experience and comfort with both aspects of termination may well be beneficial. The approach is definitely viable to groups of children, adolescents and adults.

Description of Intervention

The termination process commonly spans several sessions (i.e., three sessions in a closed 12-week group), and involves several stages and techniques to enhance dealing with both crucial tasks. Our procedure has five stages:

1) **Leader announces imminent ending of group** (or planned leaving of one or more members). Characteristically, the group does not respond initially to the leader's announcement. Usually, group therapists have to become increasingly insistent that members focus on feelings about the ending, the loss of group support, concerns about other losses in life and initial questioning about how to transition with the new learning and experience of group into "real life," outside of the cultural island of the group.

2) **Invitation to work.** Many group leaders refer to this as asking members to deal with "unfinished business" before time runs out. "This is the time to bring up whatever is left unfinished." Often, the quieter members will use this time to discuss issues that previously had been unspoken.

3) **Trust boost**—to better encourage members to deal with their back home worlds after group support has ended, a technique to both boost intra-group trust and to refocus on the world outside of group is often quite helpful. This is particularly powerful if the group ambiance has been powerfully supportive and focused more on the here-and-now. My personal favorite is to go around the group and ask each member "tell the group something important about yourself, that there's been no reason to bring up before." Sometimes, responses have been very surprising and significant:

A very dour middle-aged man reported that he was known for his humor and had actually had a brief career with an improvisational comedy troupe.

In another group, a young man reported that he was a Roman Catholic priest. He claimed that if others had known, it would color how they responded to him. Faster than an "Amen" to a particularly inspiring prayer, another member of the group underscored the concern by querying, "How could you think that, *Father?*"

More ominously, a woman in the group revealed that she had been contemplating suicide for several months.

A shy 35-year-old man in the group who had been struggling with issues of loneliness, revealed that he had tried an online dating site and had gone out twice—a revelation that was met with group applause.

The sharing of these "shadow" aspects of life both filled out the individual personas to other members, and brought the outside world more directly into group discussion—an opening to address transfer-of-training more specifically.

4) **Transfer of training**—Going around the room again, the leader asks each member "what have you learned new in the group and how could that be used in your life outside of group?" Often this can be time consuming and frequently there is considerable role-playing that accompanies the plans. In one group, a man reported he had learned to be more honest with his emotions and to share those. He planned to do so with his boss and co-workers at his (emotion-unfriendly) job-site. After several role-play "takes," he wisely revised his plan to share his feelings more with his long-time partner, a few friends and his teenaged daughter. Had he just gone onto the job and begun emoting, he might have fared poorly.

5) **Saying goodbye**—The final stages of termination may involve useful feedback for members, rituals (preferred by some group leaders), saying goodbyes and making any follow-up plans that may be appropriate.[1]

Conclusions

Termination, the final phase of therapy, offers opportunities for members to consolidate changes in their lives and to face the loss of what has hopefully been a supportive experience. Unless group therapists encourage clients to face both issues, much of the therapeutic benefit of the group may be diminished. The technique described here is one method to enhance the positive impact of the group therapy experience.

Contraindications

Like all techniques, termination processes must be adjusted to the nature of the group and to members' ego strength. In an open group with frequently changing membership, this becomes more of an individual than group exercise. If some members are likely to feel deserted and angry at the loss of a particular member, the technique may encourage them to be critical and angry at the leaving member and treat her or him more as a deserter, than a graduate. This is particularly common with clients who have personality disorders. In addition, leaders must be able to handle and process their personal levels of discomfort to avoid unconsciously avoiding termination or using the process to extend the life of the therapy.

References

Bugental, J.F.T. (1987) *The art of the psychotherapist.* New York: W.W. Norton.
Shapiro, J.L. (2016) *Pragmatic existential counseling and psychotherapy: Intimacy, intuition and the search for meaning.* Thousand Oaks, CA: Sage Publishing.
Shapiro, J.L., Peltz, L.S., and Bernadett-Shapiro, S.T. (1998) *Brief group treatment: Practical training for therapists and counselors.* Monterey, CA: Brooks/Cole.

Note

1 Not infrequently, members meet without the therapists in more social environs, after the group has ended.

Jerrold Lee Shapiro, Ph.D., is Professor of Counseling Psychology at Santa Clara University, a licensed Clinical Psychologist and a Fellow of the American Psychological Association. In addition to over 200 papers and journal publications, he has written 13 books, including, *Pragmatic existential counseling and psychotherapy: Intimacy, intuition and the search for meaning* (2016). He has been doing groups and teaching process group therapy since the mid-1960s.

27 Mindfulness Practice
Interventions for Working with Young Children in Groups

Ellen Decker
Rebecca M. Cordisco

Introduction

With the increased popularity in the practice of mindfulness for adults, it has become clear that it is equally important to examine the benefits of introducing mindfulness practices to children (Thompson & Gauntlett-Gilbert, 2008). Burke (2010) provides a review of the current research with regard to mindfulness-based approaches for children. She suggests that further empirical evidence is needed to determine the clinical efficacy of a mindfulness approach in improving concentration and attention and in the alleviation of anxiety, depression and stress in children.

According to Semple & Lee (2011) there are a distinctly different set of considerations when utilizing mindfulness practices with children as compared to adults. When designing mindfulness interventions for children, it is important to keep in mind developmental differences related to emotional and cognitive maturity, and to develop techniques accordingly. For our purposes, mindfulness will be defined as the awareness, openness and concentration on the present moment. As Burdick (2014, p. 20) describes, "Mindfulness is paying attention to what is going on right here, right now, inside of us and outside of us." We suggest keeping things as simple and fun as possible. In our experience, children respond best when the leader models an environment of acceptance and awareness.

Population

These interventions are designed to work with elementary students, but can easily be adapted for children of all ages. Interventions can be used in a variety of settings, including schools, private practices, and agencies.

Interventions

Introductory Activity: "Listening to the Bell"

Welcome the group and invite them to sit comfortably in a circle. Explain to the children the purpose of the group. Begin by saying: "We are going to spend some time today paying attention to what is going on right now—inside and outside of us. This will help us calm down and relax and do our best in school."

Show the children the chime bell and instruct them to take a deep breath. Model the breathing with them. Tell the children that you are going to ring the bell, and that you want them to listen carefully and raise their hands quietly when they can no longer hear the sound of the bell. Model quiet listening and raise your hand as well. When all hands are raised, have the children take another deep breath.

Go around the circle and ask the group members to tell the group every sound they notice. This is fun for children and helps them connect to the present and to their own senses. We find that the children love this part of the activity. End the intervention with another deep breath and congratulate the students for learning and practicing mindfulness!

Main Mindfulness Activities

Bubble Meditation

Have each group member sit in a circle in a comfortable position. Bring out a jar of bubbles and gently blow some in the circle. Tell the children that sometimes our thoughts are like bubbles, and that it can be helpful if we learn to just "let the thoughts go" if they are bothering us. Put the jar of bubbles away and make sure that all bubbles have dissipated. Ask group members to close their eyes and imagine a bubble rising up in front of them. Ask them to imagine that the bubble contains a thought, feeling, or perception. Encourage them to watch the bubble rise up and float away. Say "hi and bye" to the bubble as it floats away. Encourage members not to judge, evaluate or think. Then, imagine another bubble and watch it float away. End the session by having the group take a deep breath. Process with the students their experience of the intervention.

Sitting Still Like a Frog (Snel, 2013)

Have each group member sit in a circle in a comfortable position. Ask members to describe a time when they have observed a frog sitting. Remind them that a frog can jump, but is also capable of sitting very still for long periods. If you have a small frog toy it can be fun to have it out for the children to see. Explain that you would like them to try to sit still and breathe like a frog for a little while. Read the following script: "The frog sits still and breathes, preserving its energy instead of getting carried away by all the ideas that keep popping into its head. The frog sits still, very still, while it breathes. Its front tummy rises a bit and falls again. It rises and falls. Anything a frog can do, you can do, too. All you need is mindful attention. Attention to the breath. Attention to peace and quiet" (Snel, 2013, p. 24).

Smell and Tell

Have each group member sit in a circle in a comfortable position. Pass around something fragrant to the children, such as an orange, a lemon, or a sprig of a fragrant flower or plant. Ask them to close their eyes and breathe in the scent. Encourage them to focus only on the scent. After all have had a chance to smell the object, process their feelings with regard to relaxation and mindfulness.

Breathing Buddy Exercise

Have each group member sit in a circle in a comfortable position. Hand out a small stuffed animal to each group member. If you have enough room, children can lie on the floor and place the stuffed animal on their belly. Students may laugh and play at first, but encourage them to become mindful of their breathing. Students should breathe in silence for one minute. Encourage them to notice their breathing buddy moving up and down. Students enjoy this exercise, and it helps them to see that mindfulness can be fun.

"Calm Place" Intervention

Have each group member sit in a circle in a comfortable position. Ask the students to close their eyes. Help them to imagine a calm and safe place. Tell them this could be the ocean, a park, a lake, their room—anywhere they feel safe and comfortable. Ask them to imagine the sights and smells. Tell them that this is their "special place" where they can go in their minds if they feel overwhelmed, down, or under stress.

General Client Response

Children generally love these exercises! In our experience, the response of the children is directly related to the leader's style of presentation. Use "kid friendly" language and have fun! Smile frequently, show enthusiasm, and provide positive reinforcement for the children in their attempts at mindfulness practice.

Conclusion

Mindfulness is a valuable skill that has been taught for thousands of years. Taught in a fun and relaxing manner, mindfulness can be a very valuable skill to help children clear their minds and manage their emotions. There are many resources describing other mindfulness interventions for children.

Possible Contraindication

Children who are actively psychotic or in crisis are not good candidates for these interventions.

References

Burdick, D. (2014). *Mindfulness skills for kids and teens.* Eau Claire, WI: PESI Publishing & Media, PESI Inc.

Burke, C.A. (2010). Mindfulness-based approaches with children and adolescents: A preliminary review of current research in an emergent field. *Journal of Children & Family Studies.* 19:133–144.

Semple, R.J. & Lee, J. (2011). *Mindfulness-based cognitive therapy for anxious children: A manual for treating childhood anxiety.* Oakland, CA: New Harbinger Publications, Inc.

Snel, E. (2013). *Sitting still like a frog.* Boston, MA: Shambhala Publications, Inc.

Thompson, M. & Gauntlett-Gilbert, J. (2008). Mindfulness with children and adolescents: Effective clinical application. *Clinical Child Psychology and Psychiatry.* 13:395.

Ellen Decker, Psy.D., is a Certified School Counselor and has worked with children for over 35 years. She has a private practice specializing in issues important to women.

Rebecca M. Cordisco, M.S., is an Elementary School Counselor in Hillsborough, NJ. Her professional interests include grandparents raising grandchildren with regard to the role of the school counselor.

28 A Relaxed Approach to Treating Phobia

Norman Claringbull

Introduction and Theoretical Considerations

Is Cognitive Behavioural Therapy (CBT) 'proper' psychotherapy? If it is, does it have a place in group therapy? The debate goes ever on (see Whitfield 2010, House & Loewenthal 2008, and many others). For me, however, its resolution is simple: 'Whatever works, works!'

I have long been a 'practice-based evidence' centered psychotherapist; one who is comfortable with trial-and-error treatment planning. This therapeutic stance has underpinned my development of a particular CBT/Integrative Therapy mix targeted at helping group therapy clients presenting with debilitating anxiety conditions. For these client groups, my preferred CBT method is Relaxation Therapy (RT). This is a powerful therapeutic technique useful as either as a stand-alone symptom management tool or as part of a Systemic Desensitization program (Wolpe 1958).

RT involves teaching clients how to purposefully calm themselves and then to use that calm to manage their anxieties. My approach to RT is based on Erickson's theories (see Havens 2005 for a comprehensive review). Clients are shown how to employ a series of muscle and breathing exercises to achieve a state of total physical and mental relaxation. If practiced on a daily basis, this self-administered therapeutic tool is a valuable means of lowering anxiety base-levels generally. It is also an effective self-management technique for attenuating adverse/excessive anxiety responses to stressful stimuli.

Some might argue that acquiring RT skills is more akin to psycho-education than psychotherapy. That is why all my group RT programs include facilitated time for mutual reflection and sharing.

Client Population

Anxiety affects everybody, everywhere. Because CBT in general, and RT in particular, is a flexible, non-threatening, therapeutic modality, it is applicable to anybody anywhere.

Intervention

The client group was undifferentiated demographically. However, all had been psychologically traumatized by car crashes. Subsequently, they had all developed severe phobic reactions (panic) to even the idea of car travel, let alone the reality.

Session 1: We began with explanations of anxiety and its causes, Relaxation Therapy, and Systemic Desensitization (see Claringbull 2011, pp. 78–98). As with all the ensuing sessions, the group members then had an opportunity to share their hopes and fears about themselves and the therapeutic process. Finally, they were tasked with going home and preparing written accounts of their car crashes for the next session (personal debriefings).

Session 2: The group shared highlights from their personal accounts (group debriefing), and were reminded of the basics of RT.

Session 3: The group members were collectively led through a series of muscle-relaxing and breathing exercises that were 'tweaked' individually as necessary. All achieved excellent levels of physical and mental calm. Finally, after the usual facilitated sharing period, the group was instructed to practice RT daily.

Session 4: After a communal RT deepening exercise, the group members were asked to use their personal stories derived after Session 1 to work on constructing a group 'anxiety-response ladder'.

Anxiety ladders depend on the assumption that excessive anxiety does not surge into being when a critical event is actually encountered but that it evolves over a preceding 'build-up' period. Initially emerging at a low level, the anxiety intensifies as a stepped series of event nodes, or 'ladder rungs', are reached. As the ladder is 'climbed', anxiety levels increase and eventually becomes unmanageable. This group's collective anxiety ladder looked like the one below.

Rung	Event	% anxious
1	Informed of a need to drive somewhere in 2 days' time	1
2	Aware that a car journey is planned for tomorrow	5
3	Wake up and remember 'today's the day'	10
4	Late morning—it's getting closer	20
5	Only an hour to go	30
6	It's time	45
7	Getting ready	65
8	Opening front door	80
9	Walk to the car	95
10	Open car door	100—Panic

Session 5: The group members were again placed in a state of deep relaxation. They were then encouraged to imagine that they were at Rung 1. Members

who experienced real-time anxiety in response to this imaginary activity were shown how to use breathing techniques to reduce/eliminate their symptoms. This process was repeated for Rung 2, then Rung 3 and so on.

Sessions 6 & 7: It took a further two group sessions before everybody could imagine themselves reaching Rung 10 without panicking.

Session 8: The group members were instructed to independently re-acclimatize themselves to real-life car travel in four stages spread out over at least four days. On each occasion, RT was to be used as a preparatory 'emotional prophylactic'. Additionally, they were taught a short-form RT method also developed by me—the '3-second method'. This is a 'quick-fix', do it anywhere, anxiety management tool.

Stage 1: Leave the house and stand by the car
Stage 2: Sit in it
Stage 3: Start the engine and drive a few yards
Stage 4: Drive a mile or two on quiet roads

General Client Responses

All of the clients, except one, were soon able to drive short distances and upon follow-up three months later all had become comfortable with car travel. The unresponsive client was referred on to a PTSD service.

During the follow-up session, those who had continued to regularly practice RT reported additional benefits. They had found that by maintaining lower base-line anxiety levels they were freeing themselves to re-assess their interpersonal and intrapersonal relationships. Some had referred themselves to ongoing psychotherapy in order to properly reflect on these changes.

Conclusion

RT can be a useful tool in group therapy. However, modern integrative/eclectic therapists will be aware of the dangers of exclusively relying on RT, on CBT generally or indeed on any other single psychotherapeutic modality. Therefore, as ever in the psychotherapeutic world, flexibility and adaptability is the name of the game.

Contraindications

RT is usually targeted at enabling clients to regain control of the chaotic areas of their psychological being. Therefore, psychological disorders for which the treatment modalities tend to be based on encouraging acceptance (obsessions, compulsions, thought disorders, etc.), may not respond to RT and may even be worsened.

Additionally, RT (and CBT generally), is not indicated for clients who are unable or unwilling to accept its principles or who are reluctant to do their 'homework'.

References

Claringbull, N. (2011), *Mental Health in Counselling and Psychotherapy*, Exeter UK, Learning Matters (Sage Publishing)

Havens, R. (2005), *The Wisdom of Milton H Erickson*, Carmarthen, Wales, UK, Crown House

House, R. & Loewenthal, D. (2008), *Against and for CBT: Towards a Constructive Dialogue*, Monmouth UK, PCCS Books

Whitfield, G. (2010), Group CBT for Anxiety and Depression, *Advances in Psychiatric Treatment*, 16, (3), 219–227

Wolpe, J. (1958), *Psychotherapy by Reciprocal Inhibition*, Stanford CA, Stanford University Press

Dr Norman Claringbull is a UK Senior Accredited Psychotherapist and Licensed Trauma Therapist. Formerly the Head of Counselling and Psychotherapy Studies at the University of Southampton, he currently maintains an extensive private consultancy practice.

29 Building a Pathway to Success
Dariush F. Fathi

Breaking Down Goals into Small Attainable Steps: An Introduction

Clients who are new to group may have little idea how group therapy works or how it can be helpful to them. It is important to explain the group process, rules, and expectations of group therapy; however, many clients still have difficulty grasping how group therapy can help them achieve their psychotherapeutic or personal goals. Even "seasoned" or "veteran" group members can become complacent in group by reverting back to unhealthy patterns of behavior and losing sight of their reasons for attending group.

The analogy of "building a pathway toward success" can assist group therapy clients with understanding how group can be helpful, while simultaneously encouraging clients with identifying, setting, and articulating what their current goals are. The analogy of "building a pathway toward success" implies that brick by brick, or step by step, we can take small, achievable steps toward our long-term goals.

The Goals

The goals of this intervention are:

- To encourage clients to both articulate, share and give voice to their goals
- To help clients become action oriented toward their goals (today, or this week)
- To break down large goals into a series of smaller, achievable "steps"
- To assist group process and flow through eliciting member support and feedback
- Vicarious learning—group members learn by hearing others describe, share, and break down their goals into small, achievable steps.

Population

This intervention has wide ranging applicability with different client populations and presenting problems. It has been used with adolescents, young adults, and adults presenting with a wide range of clinical diagnoses and severity ranging from mood, thought, and substance use disorders to general relationship and lifestyle problems.

Intervention

This intervention is implemented by a series of questions posed by the group therapist to the group members to facilitate understanding of the "Building a pathway toward success" concept, and generate dialogue among group members. The goal of the intervention is to assist clients with articulating their goals to the group, discuss small steps they have or can begin implementing to achieve those goals, and to elicit support and feedback from other group members. The questions are asked in a round-robin fashion to each participant in the group.

The group therapist (*Modify the dialogue as it pertains to the population and type of group*).

Introduction to Intervention

As individual group members you have many differences but you are all here for the same reason: to reach personal goals. You could be here to achieve mental health goals like feeling less depressed or a personal goal such as to make more friends or find a job. Regardless of your goals, group therapy and process can help you get there. Progress toward goals always occurs in a series of small steps. Brick by brick, or step by step, you can build a pathway toward achieving your goals.

Questions to ask Group Members after the Introduction

1. What are your goals, and how do you think this group can help?
The group therapist should provide clarification as to how group can be helpful if the client does not know. The group therapist may also elicit feedback from group members to answer the question—i.e., What do other group members think regarding James' question? How can group help him/her achieve this goal?

2. What have you been doing to build a pathway toward achieving your goals?
If the client responds "nothing," the group leader (or preferably group members) can ask: "What's been getting in the way?"

3. What small steps can you take this week to build a pathway toward your goals?
The therapist and preferably the other group members should explore current obstacles and collaboratively encourage the client to identify small, attainable steps.

4. What steps can you take today?
This question is important to begin to motivate the client to make changes in their life today and throughout the week, rather than say "I will start tomorrow, next week, or when this or that happens first."

Goals clients have declared to the group can be revisited in future sessions by other group members or the group leader. In my experience, the use of this intervention helps group members tend to keep each other accountable toward pursuing their individual goals by asking for status updates, providing encouragement and support, and assistance with problem solving barriers and setbacks. The ways in which the other group members hold each other accountable tend to be consistent with the stages of the group process.

General Client Responses

Most clients are generally open and receptive to identifying and articulating their goals for treatment. If a group member is having difficulty identifying goals, skip them and go to the next group member. Hearing other group members share goals can assist clients with identifying goals for themselves and may help ease anxiety and demonstrate effective ways of articulating one's goals. It is important for the group leader to answer group member questions and explain how group can be helpful toward their goals (or how it cannot, if applicable).

Questions Generated by Clients Include

How can group therapy help me cope with schizophrenia, depression (or other diagnoses)? How will group therapy help me make more friends?

Group member questions should be answered *honestly* by the group leader, while also eliciting feedback from other group members (particularly more experienced group members, if possible) to help newer clients gain an understanding of and add credibility to the effectiveness of group therapy.

Conclusion and Contraindications

This intervention can assist both new and old clients with becoming oriented toward group therapy and process, providing answers and clarification about the nature of group therapy, and encourage clients to "get to work" on their goals. It elicits group members to be both action oriented and supportive of each other in pursuit of successful outcomes for all.

At this time there have not been any contraindications implementing this intervention. Clients work at a comfortable pace in a successive approximation format thus lessening the anxiety of change.

Dr. Dariush F. Fathi is a post-doctoral resident at Community Health Centers Inc., where he is completing a residency training program in integrated behavioral health. He has worked with a wide variety of clients and clinical presentations. He holds a strong interest in individual, couple, and group therapy and is a graduate of Nova Southeastern University's Clinical Psychology Program.

30 Urge and Creativity in the Group Matrix
Applying Art Therapy within Group Therapy

Tal Schwartz

Introduction

Foulkes (1964), the founding father of group analysis, described the individual as a starting point in the group network—the "matrix". The matrix is a hypothetical network of communication and reciprocation, created and developed in the group; it is the common ground, which determines the meaning and importance of all of the group proceedings. The term receives a visual facet when the group process merges two approaches—therapeutic group analysis and art therapy. The combination of these approaches produces non-verbal communication and encounters with unconscious feelings.

For this, we may first use a squiggling technique. When a patient uses the squiggle technique with closed eyes, they squiggle intertwined lines, without direction or control. Squiggle drawing, supposedly a meaningless behavior, actually fulfills the role of both physical and symbolic venting. Sort of a "release net" to understand the unconscious substance of the individual and the group. Winnicott, who used squiggle technique, lent his unconscious in order to connect with the patient's unconscious (Winnicott, 1971).

Client Population

The squiggling technique is used as a web of lines, first representing a personal fabric to the individual and, through a process, becoming a group fabric. The patient's image is meaningful to understanding of the group's inner world. Winnicott (1971) presented the squiggling technique in his diagnostic interviews complemented each other's drawings.

Intervention Guidelines

Presented below are the different stages in the process of working with squiggling, constructing a personal fabric and having it become a group tapestry.

Stage One: Creating the Squiggle

Each participant receives a pencil and a blank piece of paper. Before starting the squiggle on the page, participants practice by drawing small and large circles and figure eights in the air. They also trace the exterior of the page with their hand, in order to internalize the space of the page. Participants are then requested to close their eyes and create a squiggle on the paper.

Stage Two: Finding an Image

Following the squiggling stage, participants are requested to find a concrete image to work on. The lines of the squiggle are like a net thrown into the "sea", which uses "bait" to raise images from the unconscious. The patient pulls the net in from the unconscious, through it, raising visual images. These images will contribute to the collective group unconscious, the unconscious basis of the group process.

Stage Three: The Image Fleshes Out

The patient colors only the images that float above the net, so they stand out and can be seen clearly. They may add details and color to the image, if these are needed to strengthen the power of the image.

Stage Four: Self-Presentation of the Image

In the fourth stage, the fleshed out image presents itself to the patient—the patient uses a projection technique, and allows the image to "speak" in first person. For example: "I am a question mark, I can tell you about myself . . .", and so on.

This stage happens between the patient and their self, through a process of writing. It is the phase that connects to the patient's unconscious inner representation, a sort of "key" to the hidden door leading into the patient's unconscious world, which later on will construct a network of insights.

Stage Five: Completing the Personal Tapestry

The group participants' worldview completes itself through the group fabric, with every participant marking two words, which have significance to them, out of a list of sentences put forth by the image. They pass these words, written on paper, alternately to the participant on their right, and then to the participant on their left. These people write free associations for the chosen words. The images in the group create fertile ground, with the associations supplying a significant contribution, as they highlight and strengthen the squiggle drawing and the personal and group creativity derived from them. The content of the words may also supply suggestions and messages regarding the personal and group unconscious material. The process creates a joint dialogue between the individual who created the image and the image; and between the image and the members of the group. Relating to the content arising from the squiggle drawing, the group participants facilitate the understanding of the hidden meanings—the creator, and the entire group's.

Stage Six: "I"

In this stage, group members are requested to add the word I to the beginning of each sentence. Now the projection is connected directly to the patient. This is the moment of intimate contact with the self and internal resonances of insights, especially in view of the group work with the image. Sometimes the net raises images whose "innocence" quickly dissipates, giving way to the "shadow" in the patient's personality (Jung, 1963); the hidden parts of the personality, the guilty and inferior.

Short Case Examples

During a group meeting, one of the participants exhibited the image of a snake in her net. Initially, she looked at it amiably, and commented that the "snake looks sweet". When we got to the part in which the image (the snake) introduces and presents itself, she suddenly recoiled from it. The snake spoke of itself, and relayed messages that were hard for her to hear and contain. The outer upper part of the snake's body was drawn in blue, which represented calmness and quiet to the patient; while from within, the body included color, which in the world of nature is used as a warning color such as animals warn those that threaten them that they are poisonous. The "sweet" snake was now a snake with aggressive capabilities, and its fangs threatened those in its vicinity. The associations to two words she chose, resonated by the group, related to the poisonous capabilities of the image: poison, which became representative of the group's unspoken aggressiveness, and of the underlying power struggles between the group members.

Conclusion

The Shadow is a concept welcome in therapy, so that the patient confronts processes, integrates and becomes conscious of an element in our lives completing the self and our worldview. There is an approach which sees the matrix as a "hoop" encircling the group. The net, which the patient creates during the squiggle, uses and holds the parts of the patient's self and creates meetings between their repressed parts and those of the whole group. The constructed matrix is used to create an enveloping and secure feeling. The imagery is usually very significant and the group, echoing and resonating the images arising in it, allows the process of observation and insight, and even makes the image more bearable. Like a fisherman, the patient can fix the holes in their net in order to keep their inner representations; occasionally, when they are incapable of doing so, the group may fix the net for them, during the analytical part of the meeting.

References

Foulkes, S. H. (1964). *Therapeutic Group Analysis*. New York: International University Press.

Jung, C. (1963). *Memories, Dreams, Reflections*. London: Routledge & Kegan Paul.
Winnicott, D. W. (1971). *Mirror Role of Mother and Family in Child Development. Playing and Reality*, pp. 130–138. Middlesex: Penguin Books.
Winnicott, D. W. (2003). *Play and Reality*. Harmondsworth: Penguin.

Dr. Tal Schwartz is a licensed Art Therapist and Family and Couple Psychotherapist. She is in private practice and a professor at Ben-Gurion University where she teaches art therapy and group therapy in the Graduate School of the Center for Social Workers and Art Therapist Studies.

31 "I am Positive There is More to Me Than HIV"

Rachel L. Konnerth

The worst loneliness is to not be comfortable with yourself.

(Mark Twain)

More than a Disease—Rewriting your Story

In Acceptance and Commitment Therapy (ACT), theorists explain that one of the core processes that lead to human suffering is being attached to the conceptualized self, which is a progressive story consisting of formulations of the past and predictions for the future based on experiences that have occurred in one's life (Luoma, Hayes, & Walser, 2007). Furthermore, this concept of ACT also reveals that "by the time a client comes in for therapy, this process has woven a spider's web of categories, interpretations, evaluations, and expectations regarding the self" (Luoma, Hayes, & Walser, 2007, p. 16).

As therapists, we must realize that clients will enter our offices with their own construction of a story that describes who they are, most of the time those stories being a negative interpretation of the self that highlights weaknesses and insecurities. It has been my experience that a client with a negative story has difficulty in creating positive self-talk, the confidence to change ineffective and harmful behaviors, and the ability to develop healthy relationships.

I have worked with many clients who are HIV+, a chronic virus that continues to be stigmatized in many communities. The majority of my clients seek mental health treatment due to feeling isolated from social support and having difficulty establishing healthy interpersonal relationships. They often talk about the shame and guilt they feel for being HIV+ and how they will suffer from their medical condition for the rest of their lives.

When individuals are diagnosed with a life threatening or chronic disorder, they often begin to self-identify with that disorder. For example, "I am HIV+", "I am a drug addict", or "I have cancer". This creates a concrete, established set of ideas about the self that fuses the person with the condition that they are facing, rather than a set of complex ideas that make up an entire human being. The latter provides a feeling of empowerment within the individual to change the story and have more control over their behaviors and thought processes.

Being self-focused and centered around the disorder, the individual is inhibited from feeling that they have control or power over themselves and their thoughts, feelings, and emotions. By changing the story to, "I am a human being who has learned that using methamphetamines to cope with life has been unsuccessful; I feel scared that I have a chronic condition; or I feel that I will always be lonely because I am HIV+," these statements allow the individual to diffuse from identifying with their struggles and leaves room to go through a grieving process rather than feeling like they are forever suffering from a disease.

Population/Group Participants

This intervention has been used in open-ended, process groups focused on same gender loving minority men ages 18–30 that are HIV+. It could work with any population dealing with a chronic, potentially life-threatening disease and also with those who struggle with substance abuse. This technique is applicable for anyone who is seeking to create a new sense of self and who would benefit from identifying and highlighting positive aspects of their personality. It is important as a therapist to assist individuals coming to therapy in dealing with their grief and assisting them in bringing awareness to their strengths so that they recognize they are able to overcome their suffering.

"I Am Me" Poem

Materials

The most basic materials needed to complete this intervention are paper and a pen or pencil. To promote more creativity with the participants, markers and crayons can be used in addition to other art supplies like glue, magazines, scissors, and glitter.

Step 1

Explain the idea of a conceptualized self and how individuals construct a story about the self based on past experiences and what they believe will happen in the future. Discuss insecurities (i.e. being HIV+, struggling with substance abuse, having cancer, etc.) and how we have constructed a story about the self that is centered around specific vulnerabilities.

Step 2

Pass out materials to participants and discuss the development of a new story by writing an "I Am Me" poem. The body of the poem will be a series of statements that read "I am _____" and "I feel _____." The blank represents positive aspects of the self, accomplishments that promote healthy self-talk and confidence, and feelings that encourage acceptance and power. For example, "I am a father to 2 beautiful, young boys," "I am a high-school graduate," or "I feel like I have difficulty talking to my partner about my status."

Step 3

Instruct the group members to write the poem on the piece of paper that was passed out. If applicable, decorate around the sides of the poem in order to make it more visually appealing for hanging somewhere that is seen often.

Step 4

Share the poem with the other group participants and receive feedback from social support.

Client Responses

It has been my experience that a majority of my clients who are HIV+ or battling drug and alcohol addiction have never heard the words, "I am proud of you and you deserve a better life." They perceive the world as a critical and hostile place with little to no hope for a better future. The feedback and responses to the "I Am Me" poem have been overwhelmingly positive and helpful in realizing that there are more aspects of the self than what they have constructed. Many of my clients realize that they are still a partner, a son, a friend, a co-worker, and a person with many accomplishments.

Helping individuals to see the bigger picture and the value that they have as a person in society can help them to stay away from falling victim to their medical condition or personal struggles. Recognizing personal strengths and accepting what has happened, can assist clients in grieving their past and accepting a new future. Acknowledging that support is available and knowing how to reach out to others can help an individual not to feel alone and to feel a sense of empowerment over their own body.

Conclusions and Contraindications

As therapists, we are inclined to help our clients in recognizing the full person that embodies every human being, not solely our weaknesses or insecurities. To have the ability to focus on positive traits and additional aspects of the self is often a new, uncomfortable exercise for many clients. One possible contraindication I have for this intervention is that a minimal amount of education regarding the client's condition is needed for this technique, both for the client and the therapist. When a client is still unsure about what is happening with the physical body, it is difficult to get out of the suffering stage and into the grieving stage. In addition, this intervention may be useful for other chronic medical or psychological conditions and can help those who are stuck in a victim role to transform into a more empowered role by creating a new conceptualized self.

References

Luoma, J.B., Hayes, S.C., & Walser, R.D. (2007) *Learning ACT: An Acceptance & Commitment Therapy Skills-Training Manual for Therapists*. Oakland, CA: New Harbinger Publications, Inc.

Rachel L. Konnerth is a licensed Mental Health Counselor in Fort Lauderdale, Florida, who conducts individual and group psychotherapy in community, residential treatment, and private practice settings. She has worked with diverse populations including HIV+, LGBTQ, homelessness, incarcerated, minority, and substance abuse.

32 From Time to Time

Marc G. Schramm

Introduction

I wish I could remember where the idea of this intervention came from. I do not even remember the first time I used it. In rare moments of reverie, I imagine that it was bestowed on my younger self by an older me yet-to-be. That is a befitting fantasy: the intervention is meant to stimulate an orientation to the future so as to provide help for the future's past, which is to say, the present.

The literature on personal identity over time starts not with a researcher, but with the philosopher Derek Parfit (1984), who proposed that a person's "psychological connectedness" between current and future self reflects the degree of their sense of overlap in beliefs and values of those selves. Bartels and Urminsky (2010) report that when such psychological connectedness is reduced, people make impatient choices. Hershfield (2011) reviewed the growing literature on how perceptions of the self over time can dramatically affect decision making, finding that people with psychological connectedness that is realistically positive are more willing to make choices today that may benefit them at some point in the years to come.

Van Gelder, Hershfield, & Nordgren (2013) note that the failure to think through the delayed consequences of behavior is one of the strongest individual-level correlates of delinquency, and found that by strengthening the vividness of the future self, adolescent involvement in delinquency can be reduced.

Subjects who wrote a letter *to* their future self were less inclined to make delinquent choices. Kress, Hoffman, and Thomas (2008) describe their use of therapeutic letter writing, including letters *from* one's future self, in their work with survivors of sexual abuse. I have found no articles on using this sort of letter in group work, however.

Population

This intervention is appropriate for most any population, and I believe that in a mixed adult group the variety of perspectives adds additional layers that are not available in a group of narrow age range.

Intervention

Typically I have used the intervention sparingly, and in the context of a session in which many members feel stuck in therapy and life. Sometimes the group recognizes this commonality on their own, and sometimes through my own observation of it.

I ask each of them to imagine and share what their future self twenty years from now (the time span is variable) might, if they could, communicate to them. (For older adults, whether in a seniors' group or as members of a mixed group, I offer the alternative of imagining what they would communicate to an earlier self at some time in the past.) On occasion a member or members has chosen to take on the task as a homework assignment, expanding the imagined communication into a longer letter.

General Client Responses

"Stock tips!"

Actually, this sort of response has been surprisingly rare, and has never been a resistance to the task. Responses have fallen into three general categories. The first is lack of a real sense of what the message would be. This has always been resolvable in group therapy. While this intervention can be done in individual therapy, I have rarely found the work produced as rich as in group, where there is more interactive cross-fertilization and co-construction, much as with dream-work in group. Thus, those who are initially stuck are often helped by hearing the answers and suggestions of other group members. This first style of response thus has so far always resolved into one of the other two.

The second sort of response has been imagining specific advice for not staying stuck and for overcoming avoidant anxieties, with the reassurance that this will work out better than the alternative of staying stuck. I had expected most responses would be along those lines.

To my surprise, a third category has proven more common than the first two combined. The advice in these cases may be the same as in the second category, but with a distinct difference: the most frequent message people project from their future selves is that everything will work out, that they will get where they want and need to go in therapy and in life. This response is less frequent in individual therapy, and I think this speaks to the greater success of group therapy in the installation of hope.

Conclusion

The value of an orientation to one's own future is of established value (Bartels & Urminsky, 2010; Hershfield, 2011; Sadeh & Karniol, 2012; Van Gelder, Hershfield, & Nordgren, 2013). My experience suggests that group therapy can enhance this through empathy, instillation of hope, modeling, and social facilitation.

Possible Contraindications

Kress, Hoffman, and Thomas (2008), in their use of written letters with survivors of sexual abuse, suggest contraindications such as active homicidal or suicidal ideation, severe substance abuse, and strong narcissistic or borderline personality features. I have had some mild to moderate substance abusers do well on the verbal exercise, as well as some with narcissistic or borderline personality features, and wonder if the group context and dynamics make a difference, providing a greater degree of modeling, engagement, and empathy.

As noted earlier, in work with older adults, I allow a shorter time-span as appropriate, or sometimes suggest they think what they might communicate back in time to an earlier self. I would be very cautious about using this intervention for those with terminal illness or greatly advanced age. A truncated time-span, say five years instead of twenty, might too easily be poorly received by any such patient for whom hope may be difficult to muster. I might not do the exercise at all lest the comparison with the imagined future of others be too isolating. Much depends on the individual in question, and whether there is a fellow-group member also facing more imminent mortality.

Advanced age and terminal illness are not the only sources for a lack of hope about the future. The one other concern I have always had, but have never yet had to deal with, is depressive hopelessness. I can too easily imagine a group member responding to the exercise with a despondent message from his or her future self that things will turn out badly, that there is no hope. Yet—so far—even from my most depressed patients struggling with suicidal feelings, this sort of response has never been forthcoming. Is this due to the power of group to instill hope? Yes, I think, but I believe the mechanism of this goes back to the situation in which I have offered the exercise: the collective experience of being stuck. Shared feelings of hopelessness have the power to transform despair into hope of a better future.

References

Bartels, D. & Urminsky, O. (2010). Impatience as Intertemporal Egoism. Proceedings of the 32d Annual Meeting of the Cognitive Science Society.

Hershfield, H. E. (2011). Future self-continuity: How conceptions of the future self transform intertemporal choice. *Annals of the New York Academy of Sciences*, 1235: 30–43.

Kress, V. E., Hoffman, R., & Thomas, A. M. (2008). Letters from the future: The use of therapeutic letter writing in counseling sexual abuse survivors. *Journal of Creativity in Mental Health*, 3: 105–118.

Parfit, D. (1984). *Reasons and Persons*. Oxford: Oxford University Press.

Sadeh, N., & Karniol, R. (2012). The sense of self-continuity as a resource in adaptive coping with job loss. *Journal of Vocational Behavior*, 80: 93–99.
Van Gelder, J. L., Hershfield, H. E., & Nordgren. L. (2013). Vividness of the future self predicts delinquency. *Psychological Science*, 24: 974–980.

Dr. Schramm is a fellow of the American Group Psychotherapy Association, and twice past-president of the Tri-State Group Psychotherapy Society.

33 Applying Expressive Therapies to Accelerate Cognitive Insight in Organizations

Ben Rippa

Introduction

The Human Resources Consultant of an insurance company invited me to find an effective intervention to improve a positive communication between the seven Executive Directors. He related that the regular meetings were a battlefield of individual fighting for honor and glory producing a split between their Departments creating a destructive Anti-Group organizational atmosphere of mistrust, failure of communication, interpersonal disturbance, aggression, hatred and envy (Nitsun, 1996).

The collective work was difficult as the cognitive discussions among the directors became a vicious circle of blame and accusations. At that time, I was teaching at the Kivunim School of Psychodrama, becoming acquainted with artistic expressions that could accelerate a transformation process and the quality of communication. Among the various Expressive Therapies, we decided to implement the drawing technique as that seemed to be the most appropriate for the Directors.

Population

The Executive Directors were: The Chairman General Director, who years ago had been a theater player; The Treasurer; The Director of a small insurance company added recently, and four directors of the Administrative Departments: Basic Insurance; The Director in Contact with the Insurance Agents; Special Projects; and Computation. All seven were middle-aged men, highly-qualified Counters and Economists.

Intervention

My intervention began by meeting the seven participants separately in a one-hour session to check our mutual expectations. I explained the idea to improve the organizational atmosphere and informed them that the program would begin with a one-day Marathon to start a warm up in a free open "artistic setting." This would be followed by three 90-minute meetings after the Marathon. No one expressed any enthusiastic hope. The general response was: "Try, but it is a 'mission impossible.'"

I was especially impressed by the lack of interest of the Director in contact with the Agents who, looking at me, expressed, in verbal and non-verbal communication, his competitive attitude toward his colleagues. In spite of the negative atmosphere, the HR Director and I decided to move ahead. The good and correct relationship that I had with him was a good model behavior for the Directors.

We scheduled a one long Thursday (10 hours—two breaks). We had a special Hall in a well-located Tel Aviv Hotel. After a short welcome introduction, I spread out large white sheets of paper and markers of different shapes and colors. My instructions were very short: everyone will express in one sheet what came out of his mind, using the markers. Quietly and silent, encouraged by the Chairman's positive attitude, they concentrated on the requested task and starting drawing. Everyone drew at his own personal pace.

They then went around, looking at what their colleagues were achieving, making observations on the quality of everybody's artistic creativity. Some were connected to the first sheet and continued working on it. Others changed sheets to express a new idea. I concluded the drawing activity 90 minutes before the end of the Marathon. We then sat in a circle around the pictures. Each person had the opportunity, without my guidelines or interpretations, to explain his picture and tell his feelings. Some were personal reactions, expressions of satisfaction, hope for a better future. But, others expressed confusion and lack of security. It is interesting to note that the time ran quickly in a calm atmosphere.

As planned, one week after the Marathon, I met the seven Executive Directors once a week for three times for 90 minutes at the Company's Central Office Meeting Room. Opening the first session I explained that everyone was free to talk about their pattern of communication or any issue concerning the working style of this Executive. I conducted these sessions as a dynamic group, in an Organizational environment, meaning: concentrating on the interpersonal communication and avoiding individual analytical observations. The Chairman, who was positively satisfied from the flow of the Marathon, opened the session with an outlook of the Company. The Director of the Agents stressed their lack of interest from these employees. He said that the desire of the other executives to develop direct contacts with the clients has a negative impact on the company as it may cause the disappointed Agents, who are the most important communication channel with the clients, to switch to competing companies.

This hard statement aroused hidden feelings and competitive aggression, changing the setting from a dialog group to a setting of monologs. The Accountant Director said, in a monotonic way, that his work is very important but he does not expect a special appreciation from anybody. The director of Basic Insurance emphasized the success of the Direct Insurance program, of which his Department is in charge.

At the middle of the second meeting I had a feeling that there was time to express my thoughts. I related that I feel like we are in a battlefield, and everyone is fighting with his own artillery, without joining his efforts with other colleagues, like a personal fight to be an individual winner. After my short intervention, there was a silent pause. The last session was more like a friendly social small talk. The atmosphere was of a warm relationship, which now included me.

General Client Responses

The dynamics of the flow of the Directors' participation became slowly more cooperative. By the end of the third session they were also more open and confident in me.

Conclusion and Contraindications

The use of Expressive Therapies could help when verbal encounters are not effective in changing a rigid pattern of communication. Expressive Therapy allows applying at different times different styles of conducting the group according to the specific situation. For example: During the Marathon I was very active in organizing the session, talking and explaining the task, plus observing that everyone is working on his picture and helping to explain the drawings. My style of intervention was different during the sessions after the Marathon: I let the flow of feelings, including mine, go on. At this time, I do not foresee any contraindications to this methodology.

References

Nitsun, M. (1996). *The Anti-Group, Destructive Forces in the Group and Their Creative Potential*. London: Routledge.

Ben Rippa, born in 1930, received his PhD in 1982 from the University of Maryland, U.S.A. Ben is an honorary member of the IAGP, and an honorary member of the Israeli Institute of Group Analysis. In recent years his main interests include a client-oriented approach, applying aspects of Group Analysis to organizational consultancy and the junction of different practices to form effective intervention techniques.

34 Treating Depression with a Dose of Anxiety

Russell Hopfenberg

Emotional Symptoms, Enabling Behaviors

Among the most common presenting difficulties in group therapy are depression and anxiety. Although these are diagnosable psychiatric disorders, many times the behaviors that enable and maintain these painful feelings serve important but undiscovered functions. Addressing these enabling behaviors may bring to the fore their role, and facilitate alternative choices.

In the group meeting, it is often the case that the topic of anxiety and depression lead members to engage in a robust discussion of the symptoms themselves. They may describe the medications that they have tried, books that they have read, family histories of their symptoms, etc. Although the group members gain interpersonal support and connection with each other through these discussions, another result may be an endorsement of passivity regarding their difficulties. When this move toward passivity becomes apparent, a useful intervention would serve to maintain the group members' interpersonal connection yet help the group adopt a more active stance regarding attending to their difficulties.

Patient Population

The intervention described below is used in a psychodynamically oriented therapy group. Patients treated in this modality characteristically have the cognitive ability to be introspective and integrate abstract concepts.

Intervention

This intervention has three steps.

- Preparation: Evaluate the group discussion and notice an avoidance of self-activation "due to anxiety" and the resulting depressed and defeated feelings. If this occurs . . .
- Comment: Verbalize the connection between anxiety and depression.
- Process: Facilitate the group integrating the intervention into the group culture, including clarification of the historical context of the group members' difficulties.

Preparation—Case Example

Aaron began the meeting by saying that "nothing's changed." He had been a member of the group for eight months and joined with a complaint of severe depression and anxiety following losing his job as a high-level manager. Since that time, he has found it increasingly difficult to function. He went from procrastinating about looking for a job to avoiding it altogether. He then began having difficulty leaving the house and interacting with family members. Betty, who was struggling with anxiety regarding taking steps toward developing a more robust social life and creating an online dating profile, expressed her resonance with Aaron's feelings of anxiety. She discussed feeling lonely and that she often feels depressed. Cathy struggled with marital and family issues. Regarding her marital issues, she would often avoid voicing her concerns with her husband until, at some point she would get angry and yell, then apologize and feel depressed.

The meeting followed a typical pattern, with members offering suggestions to one another regarding their difficulties. For example, Cathy recommended that Aaron accompany his wife grocery shopping. To this he replied that he is too anxious to even think about going on a shopping trip. He said that it takes a lot for him to come to the group meetings even though he feels relatively safe here.

As the meeting progressed members responded to suggestions with comments like "I get too anxious" or "I'll try but my anxiety makes the thought of it overwhelming." The conversation then turns to medications that they have tried, especially antidepressants, and also recommendations and interventions that they have experienced in individual therapy. While discussing the medications, they often described feeling depressed and hopeless.

Comment—Case Example

At this point, the therapist can say something along the following lines: "You've all been clear that the prospect of taking action is anxiety provoking. Yet without taking the risks that you recommend to one another, you've made it clear that you are left feeling depressed and disheartened. Now, as you all know, anxiety and depression are typically viewed as being psychiatric disorders. But the way it sounds to me, the group is pointing out that these are actually your only choices. You can hold yourself back and feel depressed or activate yourself and feel anxious. I'm sorry to say, I haven't found door number three."

It is important that the intervention end with a little respectful light-heartedness, otherwise the therapist would be siding with depression, as humor is actually connected to the toleration and alleviation of anxiety.

You can further describe the two sides of the dilemma in the following manner: "Although both of these options seem pretty bad, the words themselves do indicate possible outcomes. Anxiety has a couple of different meanings. You can be anxious meaning fearful, or you can be anxious meaning eager and excited. I don't think there is another meaning for depression. Also, the kind of anxiety that you've been discussing is almost always anticipatory. So activating yourself to go out, or address issues in your relationships, or write a dating profile, even though very anxiety provoking, can lead to feeling eager and excited. But it seems that holding yourself back leads to depression and nowhere else."

Process—Case Example

Betty said that, even though she's not as anxious as Aaron, the anxiety she feels makes her "draw a blank" when trying to write a dating profile. Members then began talking about ways that they could take steps in the direction of their goals. Betty said that she might be able to write something even if wasn't specifically related to her goal. I asked Betty her hypothesis about why it's so difficult for her to write about herself. She discussed her experience of her mother and ways that mother "was the star of the show." Members expressed having a better understanding of why she found it so difficult to write about herself in a personal manner as she was always supposed to be invisible. Members then discussed more of their own histories and its connection to the anxiety that they feel regarding self-activation.

Patients' Responses to the Intervention

By elucidating the dilemma with which the group is struggling, members typically respond to the intervention by exploring ways that they can activate themselves. They resonate with one another's difficulties and help each other explore the connection of their anxiety to their histories. In their early life experiences, this avoidance was endorsed in the culture of their families. As the group moves toward experimenting with a different culture, one that endorses self-activation, it is important for the therapist to understand some of the subtle changes that members may make. For example, in a later session, Aaron said that his wife wanted him to accompany her to the pool. He told her that he didn't want to go because he doesn't want to burn and also doesn't like getting in the water. I noted that his reasons were not "I'm too anxious." Aaron agreed and said that he actually offered that he and his wife take a walk together in the evening instead.

Conclusion and Contraindication

Many times, a therapy group can be caught in a dilemma. If this causes the group interaction to take on a stereotypic pattern or move toward a passive stance, it is important for the therapist to facilitate the group's development toward personal exploration and interpersonal support. There are no specific contraindications regarding this intervention. However, it is important to carefully word or modify the intervention so that members who may have a powerful investment in their diagnoses do not feel shamed.

Russell Hopfenberg, Ph.D., CGP, FAGPA, is a Consulting Associate Faculty member in Medical Psychology at Duke University where he teaches courses in group psychotherapy. He is a past president of the Carolinas Group Psychotherapy Society, a past Board Member of AGPA, and maintains a private practice in Raleigh, NC.

35 The Burden of being Beautiful... Is 40 the End of the Road?

Klifton Simon Fehr
Scott Simon Fehr

Introduction

As you are aware, we live in a superficial society that embraces youth, beauty and economic status above intelligence, accomplishment and kindness of heart. We as a society are bombarded with all kinds of stimuli that reinforce the belief one has to be young and beautiful to be desired and being desired translates into being accepted and thus ultimately one is felt loved whether real or imaginary.

The prevalence of this belief is strongly reflected in the community of gay men. Sadly though the transition to middle age begins the decline of being desired. For those men who developed other characteristics or accomplishments during their youth and beauty stage, the transition to getting older appears to be somewhat easier. For example, those men who continued on with their educations or found a profession which has served them to provide for themselves and therefore lessened their economic dependency on others fared more effectively as this helps with the transition to middle age and beyond.

For those who did not look to the future while still young, the transition to beginning middle age is often painfully sad. As seen, the increase of alcohol, drugs, dangerous sexual liaisons and hours in the gym briefly counterbalance the light once shone upon them which was the light of being desired by other men.

Generally in contradiction to the heterosexual community where being over 40, for a man, can be advantageous, being over 40 in the gay community is not. Those familiar with the concept of continuous reinforcement (Ferster and Skinner, 1957) are aware that when continuous reinforcement of a behavior declines so does the behavior. The behavior is then extinguished. In this case of the maturing gay male, the initial continuous reinforced behavior of sexual, happy, playful and narcissistic is now replaced with a strong neediness in relation to being desired and wanted. In fact, it is paradoxical and the behaviors to be desired begins to increase.

Theodore Reik's (1963) famous book titled *The Need to be Loved* illustrates too the need to be desired. Yet, the need to be desired and having been continuously desired can become a form of addiction and like any addiction when taken away the individual manifests stages of withdrawal and will do all sorts of unhealthy behaviors to recapture the old feeling. When one is young it seems as if everything including youth and beauty will last forever as well as life.

Population

The population of this group are gay gentlemen over the age of 40. These men sought psychotherapy, in particular group, as a venue to help reduce their developing depression and anxiety. It seems to be that 8 group members, (Fehr, 2003) is a relatively good size as too many more, the group becomes less effective and less than 8, for example such as 5, often turns into individual psychotherapy if the therapist is remiss in bridging the members together. These men are selected especially due to their lament of how when they were younger a sense of a red carpet treatment was laid before their feet which is no longer there.

Initial Phase

The group design is ongoing with members coming and going. It is seen that the members who have been in the group longest tend to bring the new members along a lot faster than when the initial 8 members began together, (Fehr, 2003). Although the men went into the group because of distress, the beginning few groups tend to have a sexual and seductive inter-relatedness of the members. A recapturing of all the men they have had in their lives and how each ultimately disappointed them seems to be an initial theme. As the group levels off and a sense of comradeship with the other members begins to develop the sexualizing and seductive remarks diminish as the men begin to bond. Some members related that they had had a lingering thought, on entering the group, that perhaps they would find "Mr. Right" here in therapy.

The Intervention—of Loss and Gain

The intervention for this particular group focuses on the experiences of loss and gain. The guys came to this group due to feelings of loss thus requiring the therapist to help turn that concept around and begin to focus on gain. For example: Although you are now over 40 and have felt this tremendous loss in your life, what have been some of the gains you feel you have obtained with having more life experience, greater awareness of others and more solidly developing your career goals?

After some of the guys said nothing was gained, others interestingly came up with issues that had in the past burdened them which no longer do. Such as, on an interpersonal level that is not correlated with romance or sex, some of the guys realized that the world does not have to always like them or in fact love them. They too have become more careful with their spending and in some cases have become more responsible adults. It also was brought up that it is becoming easier for them to build friendships with people of their age instead of their previous transitory encounters and they are developing friendships in the heterosexual community rather than the majority of their social life being exclusively within the gay community.

Conclusion

Helping people especially in this case requires that a therapist be able to find positives where only negatives have existed.

Contraindications

There really are not any contraindications for the group members but rather the contraindications are more a part of the therapist's experience. He or she must be able to be comfortable with sexuality in its many creative forms and also, at times, a lot of hostility not only directed to the therapist but to the individual group members. This is not a hand-holding group but one that often requires a reality approach. Saying to a client in this group, you poor dear look what you have gone through, is not generally in the client's interest. Building the client's ego strength and self-esteem unrelated to physical attractiveness needs to be the goal of the group therapist.

References

Ferster, C.B. & Skinner, B.F. (1957). *Schedules of Reinforcement*. New York: Prentice Hall.
Fehr, S.S. (2003). *Introduction to Group Therapy: A practical guide* (2nd ed.). Haworth Press: New York.
Reik, T. (1963). *The Need to be Loved*. New York: Farrar, Straus and Company.

Klifton Simon Fehr, M.S., is a Mental Health Counselor whose professional experiences lie within the populations of addictions, HIV gay clients and Men's Group within the Penal System. He is in the process of developing a private practice with a focus on group psychotherapy.

Dr. Scott Simon Fehr is a licensed Clinical Psychologist and a Certified Group Therapist. He is on the graduate faculty of Nova Southeastern University's School of Psychology. He has written and edited several books and has a son who is following in his professional footsteps.

36 Transforming Failures Into Honey

Leyla Navaro

Everything started with the famous Spanish poet Antonio Machado's poem,

> Last night as I was sleeping,
> I dreamt—marvelous error!—
> that I had a beehive
> here inside my heart.
> And the golden bees
> were making white combs
> and sweet honey
> from my old failures.

Introduction

This is an intensive weekend workshop. The aim of the work is about reviewing our failures, errors, so-called wrongs while reassessing them in the group to finally transform them into growth and learning experiences. The metaphor of Kintsugi is purposefully used to illuminate the experience. Kintsugi (Japanese: golden repair) is the art of repairing broken pottery with gold or silver dusted lacker. According to this philosophy, breakage and repair should not be disguised but enhanced since they make part of the history of an object. People are more valuable with their shortcomings, errors and failures, because they have learned from their experiences and grew out of them. Along with verbal communication, art therapy and movement enhanced the work. A rich material of colors, crayons, acrylic painting, paper, glue, and of course pottery was used for the purpose.

Intervention

The group worked during three days for a total of 16 hours: four sessions of group-as-a-whole (twelve participants) and four sessions of small 'home' groups (six participants each). Four co-leaders facilitated the group as a whole and each 'home group' worked with two co-leaders during the small group sessions. The group was formed of twelve women, ages between

28 to 60, all professionals, urban, and educated, voluntarily registered to the workshop.

First Day: Trials and Errors

Helping the group to share why they choose to participate in this particular workshop.

Warm-up exercise (dyads): "Choose a person you know less in the group and communicate silently on a piece of paper using your left hand" (or right for leftists). Beyond warm-up, the purpose of this exercise is to use the less capable hand which is bound to eventual failures. After this silent communication, the dyads were instructed to share verbally their experience. Back to the whole group, the experience was commonly shared: How was it to use your less capable hand? How was it to communicate non-verbally? How did it feel?

The group is instructed to illustrate or paint their experiences.
Sharing in 'home groups' (1.5 hours)

Second Day: Catharsis

Whole group: Each member is asked to write a failure, error or wrong on a piece of paper and then throw it in a basket that stands in the middle of the group. Then the group is asked to stand up in a circle around the basket. Each member picks up one 'confession' from the basket and reads it aloud. Then the whole group in chorus repeats the confession aloud three times in a row. When all nameless confessions have been read, the group shares the experience. How was it to write a 'wrong' and to hear it repeated aloud? A participant reported: "At the first reading I felt shame, at the second the shame dimmed, at the third it was already acceptable."

Each member is given a clay pot. The instruction is to break it and then write or paint about the feelings that the breaking evokes in her. The sharing is done in their home groups where lot of tears and pain come up. The catharsis of the breaking is powerful as it affects both the 'victim' and the 'persecutor' sides of the experiences. There is a lot of intimate sharing and containment.

In the afternoon, the visit of Sagalassos is scheduled. Sagalassos is an archeological site with remains of Hellenistic and Roman period. Half-broken columns, armless ancient statues, amphitheater remains are visited. The metaphoric parallel is with broken pieces that carry so much value as to visit them. Feelings, thoughts and emotions are painted on the site. A whole group sharing follows.

Third day: Reparation

Each member is asked to work with her broken pot parts, to either repair or create new forms. The sharing follows in their home groups. Some healing messages are being voiced out. A young member who suffers from chronic epilepsy had already shared her despair and loss of hope during the first 'home group' meeting. She shares that the act of breaking and then collecting the broken parts provides her with new strength to face her disease. She has painted the inside of her broken pot parts with bright colors while sparkling them with golden dust. She talks about hope and forcefulness to face her disease.

A woman in her fifties who is going through a painful post-divorce period talks about her resistance to mourn her lost relationship. She cries a lot during the second 'home group' session following the breaking of the pot. She confesses that she has never allowed herself to cry, neither to mourn her divorce. The group contains her pain and legitimizes her mourning. During the repair session, she has wrapped a broken pot piece in black paper and thrown the other broken pieces in the waste basket. She intends to take this black wrapped broken piece to her home. Incidentally she wears on that day a black T-shirt and black trousers. The group mentions that she must unconsciously be in her mourning period. She seems more relieved and much less tense than her starting point.

Two members refuse to break their pots. One declares that it is too scary for her, feeling angry toward those who went to break them without hesitation. She shares that she already felt like a broken pot, thus does not wish to reiterate such breakage. She is in continuous therapy with one of the leaders. Another member chooses to keep her pot intact while painting on its outside the names of all her family members.

Final Session, Whole group

A bowl of honey with small pieces of bread rests in the middle of the group. The members are instructed to take some honey and either eat it themselves or offer it to someone in the group, while sharing the reason of the offer. It is a meaningful and funny sharing with lots of laughter and emotional connectedness.

Conclusion and Possible Contraindications

The use of art material and pottery has accelerated the processing of conscious and unconscious thoughts and feelings regarding wrongs and failures. The concept of failure or wrong is mainly cognitive and only verbal communication could evolve rather in the cognitive. Art material enhances the expression of emotions, accessing more rapidly to the unconscious. The breaking of the pottery followed by intended repair or change are powerful cathartic interventions. They provide some immediate healing material which can be processed further on.

Most of the participants are already in therapy, therefore apt to work out this powerful weekend workshop during their following sessions.

The mourning member as well as the young member with chronic disease declared their wish to continue further personal work.

It would be unfair, moreover dangerous to apply the above format to unknown group members. The forcefulness of the catharsis may provoke unwanted personality schisms and create personal crises that might not be controlled. It is important that prospect applicants to such a workshop be known, followed or previously interviewed.

Note: This workshop has been created and applied together with Solmaz Havuz, Deniz Yucelen, and Sereda Gultekin.

Leyla Navaro, M.A., is an Individual, Couple and Group Psychotherapist, Adjunct Faculty and Supervisor at Boğaziçi University, Istanbul, and author of several books on gender, competition, passion and power.

37 Humility in the Face of a Mistake

Michael P. Frank

Introduction

Mistakes in therapy are inevitable. If you are not making mistakes you are not growing as a therapist. Some mistakes are just small slips or momentary lapses in attention. Others, however, are more fundamentally tied to our assumptions about how we should do our work, or to limitations in our training, experience, or, dare I say, our personality. Embarrassingly, the mistake I will discuss here was of the latter type.

So if the question is not whether, but when, we will make a mistake, it is important to consider how we deal with mistakes when they occur. In group work, therapist mistakes are public and affect everyone in the group. This adds to our experience of chagrin, regret, fear, and most importantly, shame. We have to overcome the impulse to defensively avoid, hide, blame, downplay, or explain away our errors. One way or another, we have to deal with them as forthrightly as possible with a degree of humility.

Population and Situation

I was teaching a ten-week class on group therapy to about 40 therapist interns at a community counseling center. The idea was to introduce them to what I consider to be good interpersonal/psychodynamically based long-term group psychotherapy. Each 110-minute class meeting included some didactic presentation, discussion, and a "fishbowl" demonstration group. Each week, I would introduce a way of working and demonstrate it with the group. So as to give as many of the attendees as possible an *in vivo* group experience, and because I thought that ten weeks was too long a time to ask volunteers to commit to being in the demonstration group, I had the group form itself anew each week. Part of what I was teaching was the developmental phases of group, so I had some concern about whether these would manifest in the group. It turns out they did.

The main ways of working that I wanted to demonstrate were interpersonal, intrapsychic, group-as-a-whole, and the therapist–group member relationship. I would limit my interventions to only the one that I had presented that week. I believed that this would provide the clearest understanding of each of these modes. All went well until I got to the group-as-a-whole presentation.

Intervention (The Problem)

I had presented on the topic of intervening at the whole-group level many times and it had always gone well, so I set into it this time with all the complacency of someone who has never had a crash at a particular blind intersection, so he approaches it without due caution. This was my first mistake.

I gave my usual call for volunteers and six attendees rolled their chairs into the center of the room to form the group. I began, as is usual for me, with silence, curious to see how this group would begin. Rosemary looked around the group, took a breath, and said, "Well, I might as well start." She then launched into a tale of how someone close to her had been brutally raped and murdered by two men.

The group sat in shocked silence.
Rosemary then recounted how, for years, she had harbored fantasies of revenge and how this had burdened her life.

The group continued to sit in silence.
I had not expected to have to deal with anything like this and I just was not fully "in gear". I found myself on the horns of a dilemma. Clearly the group was having difficulty dealing with this story and Rosemary's intensity as she told it. I wanted to make a whole-group comment about this, but I was afraid that doing so would shame, and potentially harm, Rosemary.

So I sat in silence.
Rosemary, by now, was flooded with emotion and continued to recount how she had found the perpetrators, who were in prison, and ultimately confronted them. When she learned where they had come from in their lives, including extremely abusive childhoods, she said that she found her way to some compassion and forgiveness. The trauma, however, was still with her—and was now also with the group, including the observers.

Somehow, the group finished its time, the class meeting ended, and we went our separate ways.
I knew I had not responded adequately to the situation and was feeling ashamed, inadequate, and afraid of the effects that this experience may have had on all of the attendees. It was not an easy week. I ruminated over how I would address this in the next class. A part of me really wanted to just show up and continue as if nothing untoward had happened. Maybe no one would say anything and I would not have to face it. The better part of me, though, understood that this was not an option—that I needed to bring it up, make some sense of it, and allow for reactions. Since I was putting myself out as a good model, I would need to invite discussion of my poor handling of this event in the hope of all of us learning something of value.

The following week I acknowledged my error and talked about why I thought it had happened and what I had learned from it. I shared my own difficult feelings and what it was like for me to deal with them. To not have done so would have been to invite a huge elephant to enter and make itself comfortable in the middle of the room. It also served as a model for therapist transparency and humility.

General Client Responses

It seems that this incident was the thing that everyone remembered from the class. Many of them came up to me later—even months later—to express appreciation for how I dealt with the situation and how it showed that our humanity is an important part of our professional persona.

Conclusion

Mistakes are not only inevitable, they are important. They show our humanity, our willingness to take risks to achieve good ends, and our own commitment to growth and positive change. But these good things do not occur unless we are able to acknowledge errors nondefensively and invite others to participate in looking at and learning from them.

So how did this mistake happen?

By design, I had limited myself to only one mode of intervention. Normally, I would have engaged with Rosemary directly to help her contain her emotions and take that responsibility off the shoulders of the newly formed group. In my hubris, I put myself at a disadvantage from which I was unable to recover. I think that this is a trap many therapists can find themselves in, particularly early in our careers. In our insecurity and need to appear effective we latch onto a particular theory or method that we convince ourselves is sufficient to handle any issue. Then we rigidly adhere to it, convinced of our rectitude, and are rendered powerless to adapt more creatively to difficult situations. If allowed, the therapist's ego needs can be detrimental. Presenting ourselves as human can do more for client growth than being brilliant and always right.

Possible Contraindications

Early in the life of a group, the members will likely have a need to idealize the leader, so one has to be more careful about transparency than with a more developed group.

Michael P. Frank is a licensed Marriage and Family Therapist, a Certified Group Psychotherapist, and a Life Fellow of the American Group Psychotherapy Association. He maintains a private practice in Los Angeles, and is the Clinical Supervisor and Coordinator of the Group Therapy Program at the Maple Counseling Center in Beverly Hills, California.

38 Promoting Communication and Interaction in a Group of Sub-Saharan Africa Immigrant Women

Cristina Martinez-Taboada Kutz
Nekane Otero

Introduction

The aim of this is to show the relevance of therapeutic programs and support groups with women with high cultural distance from the host country. Promoting empowerment, communication and interaction in a group of immigrant Sub-Saharan Africa women has special needs. They come from a very complex social system with many languages and cultural groups. Migration opens to these women doors to a new world of values specifically those regarding gender. At first, there is not only more gender equality, less oppression and discrimination in the new society (Spain) but also more feelings of uncertainty and insecurity. Those women are from a collectivistic culture. They usually take care of the house and children and they are expected to be submissive to family needs so they do not look for individual recognition but they search for safety and support.

When they apply to be part of an empowerment program led by the Red Cross they also expressed their interest in knowing more of the host country and to improve language and life. Dynamics were developed to expand self-esteem and strength group identification. However, from the very first moment there was persistent social contrast between them, setting limits on communication through a paradox, the degree of use of English and not Spanish that was a shared goal and potential common language for all of them.

Comparison is always both enhancing and threatening to personal and social self-esteem. Even if they had been part of the same situation, they showed little identification and a lot of hostilities between ethnic subgroups even if they came from the same area of Africa. To go over it we developed a no oral dynamic showing clearly personal diversity and group similarities by using images, written words and body expression. Subsequently, empathy, genuine intimacy and identification increased inside the group as a whole so they could go far beyond.

Population

Twelve immigrant women from Sub-Saharan Africa composed the group. They had very traditional beliefs and behaviors. They felt culture shock, status deprivation, and downward mobility. They sought to improve their psychosocial situation and their families needed them to work. They also needed to maintain a positive self-concept and to develop new skills. Sharing problems and competencies with other women who have a similar situation seemed like the right direction for creating this particular group. They would be part of a psychosocial therapeutic group in which interaction was an essential process.

Group Intervention

Group intervention was carried out at the Red Cross in the north of Spain within an empowerment program supported with public funds. Migration of these women is considered as an example of the world nowadays. They had an interview to acquire some information on their life story and on their reasons and expectations of migration. We evaluated their attitudes and emotions during the process and looked at the insight they had into their current situation. Our final assessment was whether they were eligible to participate in the program.

Intervention

Initially the purpose focused on creating a setting of trust between the women and the therapists through positive interaction. Individual presentation was facilitated so language difficulties emerged and were associated to the ethical and cultural diversity. Tension arose among the women rather quickly. A subgroup insisted on speaking English although it was not their native language. The potential common language was Spanish.

Thus we designed a workshop frame explicitly leaving oral language aside. Therefore in its place diverse pictures were offered. Those images were of women doing their housework, being with family, images of domestic threat or violence, and images of well-off or harmonious feelings.

They were required to:

- Identify images in which they felt reflected and stack them on one side of the wall.
- Identify images in which they didn't feel mirrored at all because they considered the situations were not identifiable. They had to stack them on the other side of the wall.

Following on, they were asked to put under each photograph a word that identified the location of the image (house, street, country), also the emotions they felt, i.e. joy, fear, anger, satisfaction, sadness, rage, etc. The process had to be carried out silently. Later on, they made categories on the basis of what they fear, what they enjoyed, what they wanted to be like or would not like to be.

In the following session, women constructed sentences on images on which they had previously worked. In case they required assistance there were dictionaries available to seek accurate words or phrases. Sentences made were transcribed, and they were asked to vote on the phrase that best reflected their reality. The phrases were placed on the floor and each participant placed herself near the phrase she had chosen. If someone showed something negative she could suggest a modification. However if representations were positive, they could signify with a specific title.

Clients' Responses

In general the women's responses were positive after those sessions. The group overcame the difficulties they had with oral communication and then chose to speak the common language and tried more effectively to communicate to each other. On one hand, there appeared the shared perception of migration mourning in which the loss of extended family, friends, language, culture, social status and common ethnicity had been taken from them. Yet on the other hand, it was observed that when shown the images unrelated to their present emotional state, their emotional affect was diminished as they could not mirror the emotionality of the presented stimuli. Women participants reported higher state self-esteem and more empathy with peers. The emergence of similar social situations, emotions and shared meanings by those women allowed genuine dialogue beyond ethnic and oral language into a more intimate and trusting communication.

Conclusion and Contraindications

Women moving to a new country are exposed to new ideas and social norms that can promote their rights but enable them to participate in society because of feelings of inability and social distance to the host society. Sometimes it is easier for them to find support and equality among other African women.

The program for effective assimilation was designed to promote social skills, gender equality and mutual support, to develop fuller awareness of linguistic and cultural traditions and to inspire mutual empathy based on dialogue, understanding and tolerance. But it was necessary to approach diversity and develop a group representation of similarities including difficulties by gender.

This might suggest a way of dealing with inter-group ethnic conflict situations that can incite resentment, fear and mistrust. At first, Sub-Saharan Africa women were aware of themselves as ethnic subgroups. They lacked the control necessary to deactivate this arising struggle and to reaffirm themselves. So finally promoting symbolic interaction allowed them to respect themselves, the others, to share troubles and efforts, and support each other from their own genuineness as immigrant African women.

There are no contraindications in this intervention but rather an open opportunity for ethnic subgroups living the same experience of migration to learn attitudes and face inner discernment as they can see outside discrimination in their passage to hope.

Dr. Cristina Martinez-Taboada Kutz is a professor of University of Basque Country in Spain at the Department of Social Psychology where she teaches and researches groups. She is past president of the Spanish Society of Group Psychotherapy and Group Techniques, SEPTG. She is a Board member of the International Association of Group Psychotherapy and Group Processes, IAGP, and a senior member of the Psychoanalytic Association of Group Analysis, APAG.

Nekane Otero is in charge of Community Integration Programs for the Red Cross (Gipuzkoa, Spain). She is a researcher who specializes in immigration, women and values.

39 Letting Go of the Myth of Closure
One Practitioner's View

Daniel S. Schoenwald

Introduction

For those seeking the aid of interpersonal process group therapy, as opposed to symptom-based or situational-focused groups, an individual's goal often lies within his/her desire to heal from a rejected relationship and to learn how to form more rewarding ones in the future. For both therapists and the population at large, the first half of that equation is often associated with the term "closure," a term with as diverse a set of meanings as there are individuals. Clients may have a fantasy of having a final communicative or physical encounter that will allow them to leave the old relationship behind with more positive feelings than which they are currently experiencing. However, regardless of the goal for each individual, I have come to view its search as "overrated," for its fruition tends to be elusive and rarely satisfying. Closure, as a concept, is more often a myth than a reality.

Why? Final conversations rarely unfold in vivo as they do in the client's mind, a perfectly orchestrated scene. A pre-planned speech often fails to have the eloquence or desired effect when faced with the emotionality of the encounter. Furthermore, as one cannot control the actions of another, the fantasized returned communication usually fails to meet expectations. As a result, one therapeutic goal is to help the client psychologically grasp the concept of closure as a myth and teach him/her to let go of the neurotic need.

Population

Members of all groups and genders can be candidates for this type of intervention, as the experience of feeling unfulfilled following rejection in a relationship is practically universal, especially among clinical populations. While the intervention can be delivered in individual formats, its strength is increased by the group setting. However, because of the emotional complexity of adult relationships, this topic is not recommended for adolescent groups where the developmental level has not reached a mature stage.

Intervention

At the heart of understanding a client's need for "closure" is the exploration of what the individual is actually seeking, for this need varies. In my experience, at the core of the desire, one of three fantasies is most common. The first is an apology/validation. In this fantasy, the rejected individual wishes an expression of sorrow from the former partner for actions in the relationship, possibly with an explanation, thereby validating the client's sense that he/she was not at fault for the failure. A second is a clarification of feeling, whereby the client has a prepared expression that will elevate his/her standing by the rejected individual and further clarify one's strength. Third, an individual maintains a reunion fantasy as a result of some combination of the previous two.

Effective interventions with this material hinges on the exposure of these fantasies as myth while teaching the client to "let go" of unlikely outcomes they would bring, as well as the invitation of increased frustration. At the center of these exposures is the notion that the proposed interaction does not change what either party already believes was the reason behind the termination of the relationship; minds are rarely changed in these scenarios.

We must teach clients that, just like group therapy sessions, not every relationship can end with positive feelings, and we must have some sense for that tolerance. The questions remain how best to deliver this information, and the benefit of a group intervention as opposed to one from the individual therapist. While interventions from an individual therapist can have significant positive effects, there is a potentiation effect (to borrow a medical term) of having multiple members of a group express therapeutic messages.

Returning to the initial issue of what the client in question is seeking behind the need for closure (the fantasy), a useful tool is for the group therapist to pose that question to the group members (group as a whole intervention). As ideas are proposed, clarification ensues regarding the specific nature of that fantasy as the client acknowledges the connection to those hypotheses. At that point, further feedback is sought from the group as the therapist asks the other members to express their feelings about the fantasy, often exposing the various distortions that a client may be telling him/herself about a potential closure-oriented meeting (i.e., reunion fantasy). In this sense, the intervention, as many group interventions are, is an interactive mechanism between the client, the group, and the therapist as opposed to less useful individual (but within group) interventions.

Additionally, as the client is often seeking validation from the estranged former partner, a more healthy manner of receiving honest feedback in a safe environment is through the dynamics of the group. The therapist may utilize this opportunity to ask the various members their experience of the client in question, which will likely be a combination of both his/her positive attributes as well as various challenges that can be addressed in subsequent sessions. Additional feedback may also communicate how members experienced the client's relationship overall, possibly shedding light on unhealthy patterns within that dynamic and encourage the client to find a more suitable partner.

The parallels of this intervention with the concept of "letting go" of obsessions are quite apparent, especially for those with extremely hurt feelings following the termination of a relationship. These clients are prone to obsessive thoughts. However, just as with obsessive thinking, engaging in a compulsive behavior (in this sense, attempting to communicate with a former partner) tends to strengthen the obsessive thought through a process of reinforcement. Having experienced members in an existing group is an added benefit as they will often be able to communicate this in digestible terms to the client.

General Client Responses

Several client responses can be anticipated as a result of this particular intervention. Most commonly, I have encountered the client who feels a sense of relief, for he/she had never considered the theory of closure as being "overrated," and after an initial pause, often acknowledges that the concept makes sense and can move forward in a healthy direction. A smaller proportion reports feeling unsure, and states the need to think about the theory for some time before making a final decision. A third, and also smaller group, disagrees with the idea, and continues with the expression of finding a communicative closure as necessary

Conclusion

"Closure is overrated" has long been a therapeutic theory that I have postulated and communicated to my clients through a variety of interventions. Needing a final communication with a rejecting partner to feel he/she can move forward in relational life is often a neurotic desire which leads one to feel unfulfilled and emotionally stuck. Exploring the underlying need behind the closure fantasy within the context of group therapy will often lead to more sustaining growth and healthier relationships in the future.

Dr. Daniel S. Schoenwald is a licensed clinical psychologist working at Denver Health Medical Center, where he treats adults in the outpatient clinics of a large city-based hospital. He facilitates a men's therapy group at the hospital and also maintains a small private practice in the area.

40 The Shielded Name Tent

Tara S. Jungersen

That Which is Hidden

Group member anxiety is prevalent during the group orientation and formation process. Member insecurities, indecision about self-disclosure, and apprehension about the novelty of the group modality permeate this process, allowing the opportunity for calculated risk-taking (Yalom & Lescyk, 2005). Practically speaking, anxiety can inhibit one of the most basic tasks during the formation process: committing to memory all of the group members' names. While both group leaders and group members alike may benefit from a memory aid to promote member name recognition, the simple act of introductions can also allow for deeper self-exploration, and become a normative process for the expected level of disclosure in the group. This exercise explores both manifest and latent content of group member introductions.

The Appropriate Population

This intervention requires members to have the ability to self-reflect, be willing to self-disclose, and be comfortable with both verbal and non-verbal tasks. I have used this technique with both adults and adolescents in treatment and non-treatment focused groups. Additionally, this intervention allows culturally diverse group members to explore some of their own backgrounds and influences, which Gladding (2016) notes is a basic component of ethical group practice.

Guidelines for Intervention

Each group member uses an individual piece of standard-sized paper, folded in half, to create a name tent that will stand upright in front of her chair. Using pens, colored pencils, or markers, each member writes his or her name on the side of the tent that will face outward. Members are then asked to decorate this side of the name tent with words and/or images that represent that which is outwardly known and visible to the world (e.g., "I'm a pilot", "I like popcorn", "I'm married"). Next, group members are asked to open up the hidden, underside of the tent, and to draw or write out representations of that which is hidden or shielded from the world (e.g., "I'm insecure about my weight", "I'm gay", "I'm getting a divorce", "I hate my career choice").

The group leader then prompts for volunteers to introduce themselves, and to describe the contents of both the outer and inner portions of their tents. Group members then leave the tents in place for one or two sessions to aid with name retrieval. The tents can be temporarily reinstituted in future sessions with the addition of new group members to aid in introductions.

Typical Responses

Group members really enjoy the chance to go beyond the typical superficial or contrived introduction icebreakers. The introduction of this technique in the beginning of the group allows members immediate vicarious learning about levels of self-disclosure, as well as universality about common similarities and insecurities (Yalom & Lescyk, 2005). Additionally, members experience first-hand feedback about their level of self-disclosure, allowing exploration of emotional intimacy and defenses. Many members report immediate insight that they typically adopt a 'wait and see' approach to new relationships, allowing others to 'make the first move' for fear of being rejected or viewed as abnormal. Powerful insights about assertiveness, boundaries, trust, and secrets are typical, as are references to the disclosed information throughout the life of the group. Group leaders may also utilize the level of self-disclosure undertaken in this exercise to adapt future interventions based on group length and purpose, and may consider a follow-up exercise to repeat this intervention as part of a group termination activity to track member changes across time.

Conclusions and Contraindication

As the first group meeting session may be used for general structuring and practical tasks, this intervention may be more appropriate for the second or third group meeting in order to capitalize on the balance between anxiety and self-disclosure in the forming stage of the group. This technique would not be indicated for involuntary or coerced group members, due to the required self-disclosure of the shielded portion of the tent, though this portion of the exercise could be delayed until rapport is established. Also, the risk exists that group members could experience negative emotions should they self-disclose too soon or do not yet feel safe in discussing their inner worlds; however, the experienced group leader can mitigate these emotions through support and linking. Additionally, if time constraints are a consideration, the creation of the tent may be assigned as a homework task in order to allow for more in-group time for processing.

References

Gladding, S. T. (2016). *Group work: A counseling specialty* (7th ed.). New York: Pearson.

Yalom, I. D., & Leszcz, M. (2005). *The theory and practice of group psychotherapy* (5th ed.). New York: Basic Books.

Dr. Tara S. Jungersen is a Licensed Clinical Mental Health Counselor and National Certified Counselor. She is an Associate Professor at Nova Southeastern University where she teaches group, community mental health, substance abuse, and counseling techniques in the Department of Counseling.

41 Corrective Experiences in Intensive Group Psychotherapy

Rick Tivers

Introduction

People come to therapy for a multitude of reasons. These include: symptom removal or reduction, repairing of internal emotional wounds, and interpersonal relationship repair. Many of the issues clients experience stem from their family of origin. Clients may have felt unseen, unnoticed or highly intruded upon and violated. The process of group therapy of mirroring family has the potential to heal past wounds, hurt, and shame (Yalom & Leszcz, 2005). These feelings are often felt in the clients' day-to-day lives. Clients may appreciate insight from either their therapist or other group members, yet insight alone does not create emotional shifting within the client. Clients shift when going through corrective experiences by changing the outcomes of various interactions, both with the therapist and fellow group members (Corey, Corey & Corey, 2014). The population this serves is for adolescence and adults who are open to an interactional group process.

Intervention

Some corrective interventions with clients whose significant authority figures were intrusive include the following.

1. The therapist asks for permission to provide feedback and is overly conscious about boundaries with that client.
2. The therapist acknowledges the client's need for space, which could represent safety that the individual who has been intruded upon needs.
3. The therapist can talk for the client with permission and then ask the client if it was accurate. If the therapist was accurate the client may acknowledge the feeling, while boundaries were respected.
    Temporary merger occurs and helpful regression can be explored at a later date. If the therapist was inaccurate about the feedback, the client can have a corrective experience by sharing his/her experience with the therapist. The corrective experience comes when the client begins developing a sense of self when talking about his/her truth. The corrective experience is completed when the therapist honors the client

for being true to him/herself, as opposed to playing an ingrained "family pleaser" role.

The therapist then shares his/her reactions to the client. Further corrective experiences emerge as other clients notice their own desire to please those in authority. It is crucial that the therapist acknowledge in a highly affirming way that the client is taking a healthy, positive stance toward using his/her own internal authority.

4. The therapist asks the client to pick another group member to represent a mirror. The therapists ask the first client to say the following line, "I'm sorry for (being overly critical, being self-shaming, etc.)." He/she will repeat the line(s) to the other group members. The deeper corrective experience occurs when the therapist intervenes and suggests changing the line to "I will work on becoming sorry."

The therapeutic value empowers the client for sharing his/her authentic truth (Fehr, 2003). The therapist will process this with the "mirror" and the rest of the group about what it was like for them and what feelings emerged.

Although many therapists' style is to be less directive, if it is the intention to create significant healing experiences, then I believe it is useful to take therapeutic risks with our clients. I refer to this as active reparenting.

These interventions are highly useful for individuals who intellectualize as an avoidance of confronting painful or uncomfortable feelings. Any client whose major treatment focus is on shame reduction or repair can make use of these active interventions.

Client Responses to Intervention

Clients respond to these types of active treatment interventions in that they report feeling seen, understood and that shame is reduced. They also report that treatment helps them to develop a stronger, more powerful sense of self.

Conclusion and Contraindications

Action-oriented techniques for a population of adolescence or adults can be highly effective when the treatment goal is shame reduction. The therapist's main focus should be on the therapeutic relationship and the techniques are only used to enhance the healing nature of that relationship

This type of treatment would not be clinically appropriate for clients with severe personality disorders and /or lower emotional functioning. This type of treatment is highly useful for clients with adjustment disorders, anxiety, or who have traits of personality disorders, but are higher functioning.

References

Corey, M., Corey, G. & Corey, C. (2014). Groups Process and Practice (9th ed.). Belmont, CA: Brooks/Cole.

Fehr, S.S. (2003). Introduction To Group Therapy: A Practical Guide (2nd ed.). Binghamton, NY: The Haworth Press.
Yalom, I.D. & Leszcz, M. (2005). The Theory & Practice of Group Therapy (5th ed.). New York: Basic Books.

Rick Tivers, LCSW, CGP, is a psychotherapist in private practice in Chicago, Illinois. He teaches Group Therapy and Humanistic Psychotherapy, in addition to Training and Development at the Chicago School of Professional Psychology.

42 Mother–Daughter Interaction Through the Group's 'Hall of Mirrors'

Shoshana Ben-Noam

Mother–Daughter: An Ambivalent Relationship

Mother–daughter relationship sets the foundation for a woman's relational self. It affects the daughter's emotional, interpersonal and professional journey, particularly during transitional stages such as entering college or getting married.

Daughters are commonly ambivalent toward their mothers, at times loving and at other times resentful and critical. When the positive experience predominates, it enhances the daughter's sense of self and confidence, opening the opportunities for either modeling the mother's choices, or exploring new horizons, whereas daughters who are mostly enraged and preoccupied with 'mother blaming' may often compromise their personal and professional growth by modeling their mothers to avoid guilt and conflicts about surpassing them (Bernardez, 1996; Brenner, 2002; Caplan, 2000; Fuller & Plum, 2010).

In all-women groups focused on mother–daughter relationship issues daughters need to understand 'mother blaming' attitudes and learn to accept mothers as human and imperfect. This may lead to crossing their barriers to a fulfilled life journey.

An Insightful Group Population

All-women psychodynamic groups, with female group therapists, are most appropriate for obtaining insight into the mother-daughter relationship. These groups are suitable for exploring and working through negative and/or conflicted feelings, and for identifying with caring/empathic and assertive women. Members need to be self-reflective adults, capable of accepting feedback and modeling others' behaviors. Adolescent girls may not be ready for this therapeutic work. The more insightful members will benefit the most from these groups.

Interventions

The female group therapist is the most prominent maternal authority in this type of group. Often some of the members also exhibit this authority.

In a safe/cohesive 'here and now' group, both positive and negative feelings such as anger, frustration and envy are elicited, explored and worked through. Painful experiences with abusive or unprotective mothers as well as daughters' unfulfilled longings are shared and reflected upon. Often mothers are depicted as emotionally unavailable, or ineffective in instilling self-confidence. Mothers are then blamed for daughters' unsuccessful or compromised personal and/or professional lives.

To explore members' painful mother–daughter experiences and facilitate the understanding of 'mother blaming', the group therapist needs to be empathic, emotionally responsive and assertive. Identifying with assertive behavior may help members let go of powerlessness and become more self-empowered:

Diane (a 28-year-old member in my group): I am a pleaser. I try to please everybody. My boss gave me an extra project. I barely handle the projects I have. I work ten or eleven hours a day but I couldn't say no. My mother was an alcoholic. If I argued with her about anything when she was drunk, she beat me up really hard.

Sandra: You are always agreeable here too. I never know what you think. I don't really know who you are.

Me: Is it scary to speak your mind here?

Diane: Yes.

Me: Who may beat you up here?

Diane (laughing): No one. I always watch Sandra as she gets mad when someone interrupts her talking. I can't do it.

Sandra: Can you try?

Weeks later Sara interrupted Diane while she was talking. Diane then said: "Wait, I am in the middle of the sentence." The group applauded.

Here's the dialogue from a different session:

Mary (a 36-year-old woman): I keep dating the wrong men. Jerry broke up with me. We had problems. I thought we can work it out. Maybe I am not meant to get married. My mother got divorced twice.

Karen: My mother wanted me to get married since I was 19. I am 29 years old now and still didn't find Mr. Right.

Jennifer (responding to Karen): You're beautiful, smart, perceptive, I bet many guys want to date you.

Karen: Yes, but I am not sure I want to get married. My mother never encouraged my career. She got married at 19 and was always a home maker. She isn't interested in my professional successes. I feel

	guilty about these successes since my mother never had these opportunities even though she is a smart, talented woman.
Mary:	I am proud of you for heading the international department in your company. I am also trying to get promoted. Is it possible your mother wanted you to get married young rather than focus on a career because she is from a different generation?
Karen:	I know she loves me but it hurts that she doesn't support me.
Me (to Karen):	You're hurt and angry she hasn't supported your career. Did you ever tell her?
Karen:	No. I can't get angry with my mother.
Me:	What about getting angry with someone in our group?
Karen:	I get scared when Kathrine gets angry. I don't think I can do it.
Kathrine:	Is it possible you have been taking out the anger on your mother by defying her wish that you get married, especially at a young age?
Karen:	Ha, I never thought about it.
Mary:	Maybe I keep dating the wrong men because my mother got divorced twice?

And the work continues . . .

Conclusion

An all-women safe, hard-working and reflective group, focused on mother–daughter relationships, may help members work through intense negative feelings towards their mothers, and decrease or eliminate 'mother blaming'. The therapist's interventions plus the group's 'hall of mirrors' may contribute to members' enhanced personal, interpersonal and professional satisfaction.

Contraindications

This type of group isn't indicated for borderline, highly aggressive or narcissistic women who may not be able to explore and reflect on the mother–daughter intense relationship. In addition, group therapists who are highly conflicted in the relationship with their mothers and/or are 'mother blaming' may not be suitable to lead these groups.

References

Bernardez, T. (1996). Conflicts with anger and power in women's groups. In DeCant, B. (Ed.) *Women and Group Psychotherapy*. New York: The Guilford Press.

Brenner, J.R. (2002). Mothers and daughters in Israel—only human: A group experience. In Brenner, J.R., Savran, B. & Singer, I. (Eds) *Women in the Therapy Space*. Jerusalem, Israel: The Counseling Center for Women.
Caplan, P.J. (2000). *The New Don't Blame Mother: Mending the Mother–Daughter Relationship*. New York: Routledge.
Fuller, C. & Plum, A. (2010). *Mother–Daughter Duet*. Colorado Springs, CO: Multnomah Books.

Shoshana Ben-Noam, PsyD, is a Clinical Psychologist, Certified Group Psychotherapist and a Life Fellow of the American Group Psychotherapy Association. She is also an Adjunct Professor at Pace University Doctoral Psychology Program and maintains a private practice in New York City.

43 Improving Emotional Processing With Group Psychotherapy

David Cantor

Introduction

Frequently when people enter into psychotherapy they are unable to access and express their feelings. This inability to process one's feelings interferes with self-soothing and with creating an emotional connection to others. These in turn are psychological factors in depression, anxiety, and relationship problems. Because the group functions as a microcosm of the external world, each group member will manifest their particular emotional style in relating to the other members and to the group as a whole. How they block and numb their feelings in the real world will reveal itself in group therapy. The experience of group psychotherapy, with its emphasis on how one relates and emotes, can highlight this inability to process one's feelings.

Many people come into group psychotherapy with specific blocks to processing their feelings. When there are emotional blocks then there are specific internalized rules that interfere with emotional processing. These blocks mirror the specific emotional and interpersonal rules which the person has internalized over the course of their life. These rules are reflected in the person's internal dialogue or in the things that they tell themselves about feelings/relationships and what to do with them. This internal dialogue can be understood as a relationship between the person and him/herself.

When a person has trouble processing feelings, then it is likely that their internal dialogue consists of prohibitions against this process. These prohibitions against feeling are usually harsh and judgmental. In addition, these prohibitions are often resistant to change. They serve to shut down the person emotionally and to create distance interpersonally. Because the group is an arena for emotional and interpersonal learning these prohibitions are more easily identified than in individual psychotherapy. Once these blocks are identified and corrected the person is more able to access and express their feelings and thus they experience more satisfying interpersonal relationships and also experience less emotional distress.

Population

This intervention has been used in adult outpatient psychotherapy groups. As a whole, the group members tend to function fairly well in love and work, though with difficulties. They tend to have intact reality testing, satisfactory verbal skills, have at least average intelligence, and have workable introspective abilities especially toward emotions, beliefs, internal dialogue, and interpersonal relationships. It is best used in a group that has been together for a while and has a certain level of trust and cohesion.

Intervention

The intervention is applied when the group therapist or the group becomes aware that a member is shutting down, blocking, or numbing their feelings. This blocking can be identified by the lack of emotional richness in their communication and by their verbalizing a lack of feeling. At this point the group member is asked if they are aware that they are shutting down emotionally. The group member can usually verbalize that they are shutting down emotionally once their attention is brought to it. The therapist and the group members then ask about their internal dialogue concerning feelings.

This group member's inner dialogue is usually negative and serves the purpose of decreasing awareness and the experience of feelings. The most common examples of this emotion limiting internal dialogue include "there is no point in feeling because it would not do any good", "shut up, you don't have any reason to cry" and "it's your fault, you don't have a right to feel anything". The contexts that are routinely discussed in group include a group member's inability to express their feelings toward a parent, a friend, or a spouse.

The intervention consists of several steps. First, a group member begins by discussing an emotionally important interpersonal issue. While listening to this group member, the group therapist and the other group members make note of their internal reactions in order to see if they feel an emotional connection to what is being said. This information is then presented to the group member as a hypothesis, not as a judgment. This allows the group member the space to process it without feeling controlled. The group then asks about what the person is saying to themselves about this issue.

Once the negative internal dialogue has been clarified the group member is asked to verbalize these negative remarks out loud. The group member is then asked to direct these negative remarks toward another group member. That other group member is then asked to respond to these negative remarks with the opposite reaction. For example, if the first group member says "It's your fault, you don't have a right to feel anything" then the latter group member can respond by saying "No, it is not my fault and I do have a right to feel whatever I feel." It can be useful to have the group member direct the negative remarks to a fellow group member who treats him/herself in a similar fashion. This technique highlights for both members how emotionally limiting it is to speak to oneself in this manner.

General Client Responses

This can be a very powerful intervention for group members because it makes manifest and observable the attitude and dialogue that closes them down emotionally. When this negative attitude toward feeling is seen by the group member they usually react with a renewed effort to be kinder toward themselves. They become more willing to feel and to express what they feel. The other group members through identification also tend to respond with greater emotional awareness and expression.

Contraindication

This particular intervention has not been used in an inpatient setting and is not suitable for patients who lack the ability to differentiate between reality and fantasy. It is also not appropriate for individuals who cannot clearly differentiate between themselves and others. After the role play, each group member must be able to return emotionally to the room and to who they are. This intervention would likely not be effective with individuals who cannot do this. Finally, this intervention is not suitable for newly formed groups that lack trust and cohesion.

Conclusion

In conclusion, patients often enter into group psychotherapy experiencing difficulties in emotional processing. These difficulties are a reflection of internalized rules which manifest in how and what they tell themselves about feeling. This internal dialogue is often negative, and the emotional impact is often out of the patient's awareness. This intervention is useful in creating awareness of these rules along with the consequences of rigidly following them. This awareness, along with real time practicing in the group, helps improve the person's emotional processing. It is a useful technique in an outpatient setting with patients who have reasonably intact reality testing and satisfactory introspective abilities.

Dr. David Cantor is a licensed clinical psychologist in private practice and has led over 2000 hours of group psychotherapy. He has previously taught several classes as an adjunct faculty at East Tennessee State University.

44 Who's Responsible?
Accepting and Integrating One is Not Always the Victim

Rachel L. Konnerth
Klifton Simon Fehr

Introduction

Any erudite or at least aware individual will come to see and feel that the concept of responsibility is often placed on the other person. Our society has developed into a continuous theme of, "It is not me, it is the other person." Obviously there are events that occur that are in fact the responsibility of the other person, i.e. a car accident if you were abiding by the laws of driving, unprovoked molestations, crimes, etc.

Yet if one watches the news or listens to the radio, it will be seen that many reports indicate that everyone is a victim and few people have any part of the responsibility of the event that had befallen them. We do not have to go any further than our own personal lives to observe people with whom we work with, play with, or just plain interact. From the person at the supermarket who gives you the wrong change and blames you for not telling this individual you did not tell him or her you gave them a twenty dollar bill or to many young individuals who do not have any conception that they may have caused an event.

Sadly, hit and run accidents are on an exponential rise here in Florida. It seems people do not acknowledge responsibility. Of course responsibility can generate wonderful consequences and it can also generate painful consequences.

In almost every relationship that we have counseled, over these many years, it is always the other person who has been the cause of the difficulty. If only the other person would change, life would be so much better. Trying to help clients realize that they have their part in the tension and conflict can often turn you, the therapist, into the enemy of life and love.

Population

In the learning to take responsibility group, it is necessary that the group comprises individuals who can easily go into abstract thought and have the ability to be introspective. The group itself comprises adults 25–65 years of age who are in an interpersonal relationship with either someone of the opposite sex or the same sex. Their initial presenting problem is the difficulties they are having in their relationships. Group, by its very nature of mirroring, is the logical choice for therapeutic intervention as it allows the client to see him/herself in the person of another. This particular group was comprised of eight individuals: five men and three women.

Intervention

Before an actual intervention can take place, it is first necessary to allow all the clients to complain about their significant others. This in itself creates a bonding through identification and also helps the clients not feel alone in their distress. When everyone has gotten out their feelings about their significant other we can begin to work toward the direction of what their responsibility is in causing the conflict. Sometimes it can take two to three groups before everyone gets out the ongoing anger they have toward their partners. This is a very necessary component of the therapy as the client needs to be heard which is often one of the most common complaints the clients have toward their significant other.

Once the group has rallied together in the sense that they feel empathy and identification with the other group members, we introduce the concept of "Did you ever consider that perhaps you may have a part in the conflict and difficulty?" This part can be a bit tricky as you may become, in the eyes of the clients, an individual who was warm, supportive and understanding to the virtual surrogate of their significant other who is always blaming them for the tension in the relationship.

It then becomes necessary to give a little psychology lesson about transference and what feelings it can elicit and the concept that during emotional turmoil, it can be quite difficult to be aware of our own personal behaviors.

Clients' Responses to Intervention

Initially, for many of the clients, the entire blame of the conflictual relationship is due to their partner. Moving them away from that belief, and perhaps in some cases it may be true, is like walking a fine line. Some clients feel that you are now taking the side of their partner and can get quite angry and confrontive which we as therapists must allow and deal with that escalation of emotion toward us effectively. We cannot retaliate because of some unresolved issue within us. Some clients disclose that they feel deceived by the group leader or hurt that the group leader did not really understand the pain and unhappiness they had been experiencing.

Some clients disclose that yes they had considered that they were part of the problem but their partner pushes certain buttons and this awfulness comes out of them for which later they are sorry. Others agree with the client who stated that they felt they had a part in the conflict but they were not about to relate that to their partner as they felt their partner would use it against them at a future date.

Conclusion and Contraindications

Helping clients become more responsible not only in their relationships but, too, in their individual lives can be not only quite a challenge but also a gratifying experience. To watch a client attenuate his or her defenses and open their minds and grow is wonderful.

This intervention may come with some contraindications. Foremost in its ideal situation, it is fortuitous to have the partner in another group going through the same therapeutic process in order that you do not come to be perceived as the enemy who agrees with your client. It is not uncommon for a client to return home and disclose that the therapist agrees with him or her. Another issue may arise that in fact these two people basically should not be together and the possibility of a divorce or termination of the relationship will ensue. This intervention should not be undertaken by a therapist who has the need to be consistently liked by his or her clients as these groups elicit a lot of anger. Some of this anger is toward the partner, other group members and to the group leader. If the group leader is an individual who needs to be always liked and admired by his or her clients, this intervention is not suggested.

Rachel L. Konnerth is a licensed Mental Health Counselor in Fort Lauderdale, Florida, who conducts individual and group psychotherapy in community, residential treatment, and private practice settings. She has worked with diverse populations including HIV+, LGBTQ, homelessness, incarcerated, minority, and substance abuse.

Klifton Simon Fehr, M.S., is a Mental Health Counselor whose professional experiences lie within the populations of addictions, HIV gay clients and Men's Group within the Penal System. He is in the process of developing a private practice with a focus on group psychotherapy.

45 Hot Air Balloon

T. Wing Lo

Introduction

Hot Air Balloon is a group therapeutic exercise invented by the author to facilitate the therapist and the group to assess clients' relationships with other people, especially their significant others. It can also be used to assess the clients' life goals. This group exercise is applied with one key client at a time, with other group members participating in the role play. It is normally applied in the early stage of group intervention when members are not very familiar with each other. When used in the group context, members will be led to understand each other's relationship problems or life goals in a dramatic form through their active participation. The exercise can also help group members to review and reformulate their relationship problems or life goals, enabling them to face their concerns directly and immediately.

Population

As the exercise is exploratory in nature, there is no particular requirement on the nature of clients' problems. However, the number of group members in the role play should correspond to the number of significant others or life goals named by the key client. Since the client will be asked to push someone off a hot air balloon, the exercise is not suitable for children.

Intervention

Exercise 1: Assessment of Human Relationships

1. The therapist narrates the scenario, "Mary won a lottery that provides a free trip to Africa. Mary is allowed to invite 5 to 7 significant others to go with her in this trip."
2. After Mary picks the significant others, the therapist announces that this time they are not travelling by plane, and are instead taking the hot air balloon.
3. Chairs are arranged into a circle, and the client, Mary, stands in the middle.

4. The therapist invites group members to play the roles of Mary's significant others. They stand on the chairs while facing outside (with their backs to Mary).
5. The therapist continues to narrate the scenario, "In the middle of the ocean, the hot air balloon runs out of gas, and is sinking . . ."
6. The therapist asks Mary to make a decision to throw one of her significant others off the hot air balloon, so as to save the others.
7. Mary picks one person to push off the hot air balloon, and the therapist asks her to lightly push that person off the chair.
8. The therapist then asks Mary to explain her reason for picking that person. Mary answers ". . ." The therapist has to ensure that Mary pushes the person off the hot air balloon before asking her to explain [because client's talk does not necessarily represent action].
9. After Mary explained, the therapist invites the "victim" to tell Mary and the group his/her feeling of being pushed off of the balloon.
10. Afterwards, group members are invited to ask Mary questions regarding her decisions. They can ask in the shoes of the characters in which they played a role, or they could ask questions in the shoes of Mary's group members.
11. The therapist invites Mary to respond to the victim's expression and other group members' comments, especially when some negative issues are involved or identified.
12. The therapist continues with the story about the African trip, and soon Mary is asked to push the second person off the hot air balloon. After Mary pushed one of the group members off the chair, the therapist asks Mary to explain her decision. The session continues with the therapist asking Mary to push the third, fourth . . . person off the hot air balloon.
13. Each time when a member is being pushed off, he/she will be invited to disclose his/her feelings after listening to Mary's explanation, and then group members are invited to give comments.
14. During the process, Mary is not allowed to choose to jump off the balloon herself.
15. One of the questions the therapist and group members can ask is whether Mary has regretted any of her decisions during the exercise. Mary replies ". . ."
16. Each group member can take turns in being the client. After all members finish their turns, group discussion regarding everyone's decision will follow.
17. After the group discussion, the therapist makes a conclusion and provides encouragement and support to all members.

Exercise 2: Assessment of Life Goals

This exercise is used to assess priorities in life. Instead of asking Mary to name her significant others, Mary is invited to name her life goals.

1. The therapist begins the exercise by narrating the scenario, "Mary won a lottery that provides a free trip to Africa. Mary is allowed to bring 8 to 10 friends to go with her in this trip. The friends would be "family," "leisure," "religion," "career," "further study," "romance," "political participation," "service to the underprivileged," "academic achievement" and "friendship."
2. Chairs are arranged into a circle and Mary stands in the middle.
3. The therapist invites group members to be the life goals suggested by Mary. The group members sit on the chairs while facing outside (with their back facing Mary).
4. The therapist continues to narrate the scenario, "In the middle of the ocean, the hot air balloon runs out of gas, and is sinking . . ."
5. The therapist asks Mary to make a decision to throw one of her life goals off the hot air balloon, so as to save the others.
6. Mary picks one person to push off the hot air balloon, and the therapist asks her to lightly push that person off the chair.
7. The therapist then asks Mary to explain her reason for picking that person. Mary answers ". . ."
8. After Mary explained, the therapist invites group members to ask Mary questions regarding her decisions.
9. Repeat steps 11 to 17 in Exercise 1. The therapist asks Mary to forgo the above-mentioned life goals one by one.

General Client Responses

The exercise aims to explore clients' relationship problems or life goals. However, when they decide to push someone off the balloon, they may be experiencing some personal issues or recall some happy and unhappy scenarios in life, and thus they are likely to be confronted with the issues. Being the audience, group members are involved and may go through the same psychological journey as the key client. Touching on human relationships, some clients could be very emotional. A few may be shocked by being asked to push someone off the balloon. Other group members, who have encountered similar problems, may express similar negative feelings.

Conclusion and Possible Contraindications

The therapist has to provide constant encouragement, empathy, and support to the key client and all other participants throughout the process, especially when emotional scenes emerge. If the therapist decides that Mary's case requires immediate treatment (e.g. in view of her emotional outburst), the subsequent part of the group session will focus on handling Mary's issues. Group members should be mobilized to provide mutual support before the end of the session.

Professor T. Wing Lo, a Hong Kong registered social worker, is head and professor at the Department of Applied Social Sciences, City University of Hong Kong, where he teaches group counseling and therapy.

46 Long-term Intergenerational Women's Psychotherapy Groups

Shari Baron

> Women in groups, like women in life, often tend to play the role of the "second sex" (de Beauvoir, 1952)—that is, they subtly subvert themselves to the men around them. This dynamic is largely unconscious to both men and women, and both sexes play a part in creating it.
>
> (Holmes, 2002)

Introduction

Intergenerational women's psychotherapy groups provide an environment where women see themselves as automatically "first class" without needing to struggle with an impulse to subvert themselves to the men who are around them. These groups also provide a safe place for women to explore their feelings about the milestones of the female life cycle that they would find difficult to discuss in front of men: menstruation; fertility concerns and disappointments; pregnancy; new motherhood; nursing a baby; peri-menopause; menopause; and, dealing with aging and loss of parents.

The stresses on women during these highly demanding life passages are rarely discussed in mixed-gender groups; intergenerational women's groups provide the opportunity to explore feelings about these stresses with other women who may have already experienced similar concerns. In addition, many women will discuss sexuality concerns with other women when they would not bring these issues up if men were in the room.

Finally, one cannot ignore the importance of a safe women's group for the working through of childhood sexual abuse or sexual assault at any age.

Population and Client Histories

Julia, age 29, was sexually abused by an older brother as a young child. She has been in group for two years, frequently exploring her sadness about the isolation she felt in her family of origin and the pain and disappointment she feels about her parents' rejection when she told them of her abuse experience. Julia has been estranged from her parents for a few years, and she feels close to the older women in group as she adjusts to marriage and parenthood without family. Julia is now pregnant with her third child. Sally is 56 and her somewhat rejecting daughter-in-law is pregnant with what will be Sally's first grandchild. Julia and Sally are able to use their relationship with each other to explore their feelings about family bonds, disappointments and expectations while experiencing pregnancy and childbirth. Mary, in the same group, is very close with her aging mother, and her strong negative reaction to Julia's rejection of her mother provides an opportunity for all three women to investigate their assumptions and feelings about family obligations and desires.

Betty, age 42, remains dependent on her parents while she struggles to develop a career. Her parents are emotionally rejecting and critical, even as they continue to support her financially. She lives in an apartment they helped purchase, they give her an allowance to supplement her meager income and are regularly sarcastic and condemning of her lifestyle. Anne, age 68, and her husband are comfortable financially, travel extensively and are very generous with their two adult daughters. The younger daughter, Susan, is 38, lives three states away in a house her parents bought, works part time in a drug store and travels with a rock band whenever she can. Anne is struggling to define some boundaries with Susan to encourage her sense of responsibility, and she is often reactive to Betty's criticism of her parents. Together, they explore from opposite perspectives how their similar families have dealt with similar issues, and their honesty with each other help each of them to see her situation more clearly.

Both Jane and Kim are very overweight, and both have explored what their obesity means to them in their relationships outside of the group. Jane is 58, a business executive, single and maintaining a long-term affair with a married man. Kim, 39, is a housewife, married to a man who has become uninterested in sex with her and uses online sites and phone sex for satisfaction. Despite their apparent differences, both Jane and Kim are able to use their relationship with each other to explore what sexuality means to them as obese women, and to examine how their fears and expectations have colored their life choices. Jean, 35, also in the same group, has recently come out as a lesbian, and Kim finds herself attracted to Jean and the idea of what it would be like to be gay. Because the group provides a safe environment to explore difficult topics, all three of these women are able to discuss what would otherwise be "taboo" subjects, and they are able to look at their fears and excitements without worry that they will be judged or rejected.

Kathy, age 28, joined the group to learn more about her social anxiety and her fears about relationships. After two years in the group, she learns that her younger brother is a drug addict, and much of her work begins to focus on her fears and frustrations with her mother who continues to be codependent with him. Maria, age 49, is in the same group which she joined as she was in the process of separating from her husband. She is struggling with her 22-year-old son who is addicted to heroin. Maria loves her son and allows him to stay at her house, admits that she has driven him into a "bad" neighborhood to make a drug buy, and yet is fearful for his health and life. Maria worries about how to break the cycle she is in with her son and finds Kathy's anger at her mother to be illuminating. Both women develop close feelings for one another as they struggle from different angles with similar issues.

Intervention

Long-term intergenerational women's groups provide a cocoon of safety where multiple transferences develop and are explored and the members use their reactions with each other and the therapist to examine their personal experiences in "real life" family, career and friendship relationships. Women age 25–85 have participated in groups led by the author, and the impact on their lives has been impressive. Members use their relationships with each other to explore emotional reactions to topics they would find difficult to bring up in a mixed-gender group.

Conclusion and Contraindications

With men present, women risk becoming the "second sex"; in a women-only group, women relate to each other more honestly and openly. Because women may be decades apart in age, their different perspectives enrich the culture of the group and allow for unexpected emotional discoveries. The group becomes a safe cocoon with the therapist as the "mother" (even though she may be years younger than some of the members) who guides the discussion and explorations into territory the members would not otherwise feel safe enough to explore, that of the transferences that develop among the members of the group.

As of this writing, the author has not found any contraindications.

References

Ellison, C.R. (2000). *Women's Sexualities: Generations of Women Share Intimate Secrets of Sexual Self-Acceptance*. Oakland, CA: New Harbinger Publications, Inc.

Holmes, L. (2002). Women in Group and Women's Groups. *International Journal of Group Psychotherapy*, 52(2), 171–188.

Shari Baron is a licensed Clinical Nurse Specialist and a Certified Group Psychotherapist who maintains a private psychotherapy practice in suburban Philadelphia. She also teaches group process and group therapy to psychiatric residents at the University of Pennsylvania.

47 The Evolution of Gay Group Therapy

Lewis Zen Jordan

Introduction

Group therapy serves as a tool for gay men to learn from and help one another through their needs, boundaries, roles and deprogram themselves from abusive and harmful beliefs about who they are, both as individual men and in relationship to each other.

In my own practice, gay men present their own specific issues surrounding self-love, sexuality, masculinity and self-definition in one's own life, relationships and society. The seemingly changing social attitudes and beliefs about male sexuality and masculinity are leading the pace with reduction of personal shame and feelings of guilt.

Shame and guilt have played strong roles in programming poor self-image and self-love for many gay men, often leading to extreme difficulty with intimacy and healthy boundaries, both with inner personal relationships and their own bodies. Despite social changes in attitude, negative sentiment toward gay men remains ever present, even from childhood with the inability of parents to relate to gay children.

The results of these negative sentiments lead to intimacy problems, relating to a feeling of not being enough, complete or whole, either as a man or sexual being. Codependencies and dependencies therefore run rampant for gay men in the gay community as seen in having drugs and alcohol dependencies. The escalation of other dependencies could be even more staggering if food, gambling, spending, sex and relational dependencies would be considered.

Although discrimination, prejudice abuse, and bullying are present for most gay men, this is not actually the core problem. Gay men tend to take on these abusive beliefs toward themselves as part of their own identification and therefore they do not complete the process of self-identification as a whole man, leaving them incapable of real intimacy. This remains their greatest source of pain and best place to start to self-empower in group therapy.

An obvious, yet often overlooked, foundational problem happens in the rearing of a gay child by straight parents, who do not know how to teach or model an intimate relationship with the same sex for a gay child. Additionally, straight parents fail to teach gay children how to identify into self-loving sex and gender roles that are healthy and intimate, undermining the possibility of having a healthy relationship with the self as a sexual being. This author has heard from patients that their early experiences are often directed toward competing physically [often through sports] with other boys, and in doing so are often called such things as "fag" or "pussy" when showing intimacy toward another boy with whom they may have an attraction. Many gay men only see relationship roles of the opposite sex, which further confuse and shame the child, impeding their development of the skills for close intimate connections with other men. This also affects their ability to have a healthy relationship that does not involve some stereotypical male and/or female role that undermines truly intimate connections, as such relationships cannot happen when one is playing a role that while understood, is not genuine and creates a duality in the personality that is at odds with itself.

Population

Gay men from ages 18 to 80, hand selected with some form of dependency as the main focus, specifically codependency, intimacy and sexual addiction, are best suited for group therapy. Access to insurance and the ability to pay for health care is favorable. Also men with functional dependencies work well in these group settings, whereby nonfunctioning patients belong in individual sessions.

Intervention

Since the main strategy of the group is to empower the individual to challenge his core beliefs about who he is as a man, sexual being and person (the self), the key is helping each patient to take responsibility for self-identification, therefore letting go of the foundational belief patterns that set up the adult to have poor boundaries and the need for dependencies. Each member, once aware of their own negative belief systems, starts to hold themselves and others accountable for defining the self in positive loving ways that encourage self-acceptance and love from themselves and others in the group.

The therapist in this type of group encourages the patient to take on the responsibility of their own emotions, manage them and not be a victim to them. He or she too encourages the patient to take on the responsibility of the thoughts they think and not be a victim to them, rather the creator of them. Helping the patient understand how to establish and maintain these healthy boundaries in interpersonal relationships is very important and not be the victim to them. Hopefully, this helps the patient understand that they are loved and respected for who they are and that they are capable of creating their own solutions to their own problems.

These strategies work together with the same goal of creating personal responsibility, meaning that one moves away from the role of victim into being the creator of one's own beliefs about who they are and who they want to be in relation to others rather than creating unrealistic fantasies.

Client Responses

Lower levels of depression, anxiety, chemical behavior and relational dependencies have been seen by this author in these types of groups. Individual response times and degree of healthy self-image vary depending on the patients' specific issues and willing participation in the group.

Conclusion

Group therapy empowers gay men to have healthy intimate relationships as self-defined whole men, as sexual beings. Group sessions encourage gay men to connect on an emotionally intimate level with other men, sometimes for the first time in their lives. When gay men start to self-define positively, their need to reach for dependencies such as sex, drugs, alcohol or codependencies abate.

As personally observed there are huge shifts currently happening in the gay community—shifts that are laying the way for a better foundation for self-loving gay men. Furthermore, with the recent legalization of gay marriage, gay men generally feel a new sense of socialized ease and the freedom to be themselves, empowering them even more to be real, authentic and have a better sense of self.

Possible Contraindications

Individuals who are not well suited for these types of groups are those who may be unable to participate in group therapy, for a number of reasons, and could be disruptive members. Other noncompliant members are those who cannot speak in front of a group, clients with traumatic brain injuries or clients with forms of severe personality disorders.

Dr. Lewis Zen Jordan, a graduate of University of Maryland and Nova Southeastern University Center for Psychological Studies, is a certified group therapist and has been leading groups since 2005. Currently "Dr. Zen" is a private practice therapist, author and speaker, conducting individual, couples and group therapy.

48 Group Therapy for Therapists

Toby Ellen Newman

Introduction

Therapists come together in groups for many reasons. Many therapists initially learn about group therapy in academic settings within classrooms. They may learn group techniques via lectures from a professor, or, if they are more fortunate, they may learn about groups from actually doing or observing groups within the classroom setting. Therapists also come together in groups during educational workshops, where they may get to participate in or observe structured sessions, often using fish-bowl techniques, where the mental health professionals in the audience watch the mental health participants within the staged, but often very therapeutic, training group. Therapists come together for supervision of cases and difficult situations, utilizing one another for consultation and discussion. Therapists come together in groups for support, often after working in traumatic situations; and, therapists come together in groups for their own group therapy.

Population

Therapy groups are typically composed of people with some like-minded characteristic, such as groups for people with addictions, behavior issues, relationship dysfunctions, or people facing life-changing situations such as illness (their own or family members) or grief and loss (including such issues as divorce or death). Therapy groups are also specifically useful for self-exploration and personal growth. Individual participants should be somewhat psychologically minded, have reasonably good ego-strength, and be able to make commitments as to participation, confidentiality, attendance, and finances.

In a therapy group of therapists, the issues of openness to participation and the utmost adherence to keeping confidentiality are of great importance. The participants are allowing themselves to be clients while wearing therapist coats. Therapists may have a professional self-image that may be in conflict with the fear of weaknesses being exposed which could lead to judgment from peers. The professional facilitator must be experienced and skillful in both general individual and group therapeutic interventions, as well as specifically in working with other mental health professionals. The facilitator must understand the boundaries of professional interactions and engender trust and safety within the group setting.

Intervention

The primary intervention is the facilitator's ability to listen, to observe, to recognize commonality, and to make comments in order to enhance connections among the group members. The facilitator maintains an awareness of group memory and history, and utilizes the "here and now" activity of the current session along with the information about past emotions and interactions in order to enhance individual functioning and group connections. The intervention involves stopping and thinking more than doing. The intervention is in doing less rather than more.

General Client Responses

Oftentimes, the client/therapists are hungry for a forum in which they can unburden themselves of the emotions they often need to contain. The client/therapists want to be seen and heard, and many react negatively to a facilitator who does not provide adequate mirroring and individual feedback. By absorbing and containing these negative emotions, the facilitator enables the client/therapists to have something to push against, and, in the midst of that struggle to be seen and heard, the group members can re-direct their energies within themselves. It appears to be a very successful intervention for the facilitator to "get out of the way" of skilled participants doing therapeutic work. It is almost magical when the facilitator points out common themes, struggles and successful adaptations and outcomes.

Conclusion

Individuals come to therapy with their own visions of themselves and others, and mental health professionals do so as well. Sometimes outside family or client issues and stories enter into the therapy room. Sometimes these outside issues are not relevant within the group therapy process and other times they completely take over the individuals' emotional and cognitive points of view. Therapist group members may put on their professional persona and try to utilize the group time for case discussions. Therapist group members may also deflect their group responses to one another by attributing psychological interpretations of meaning, as if they were working with clients.

The facilitator needs great skill in observation and reflection, and the ability to challenge the individual group members and the group as a whole in meeting its stated group tasks. The facilitator's greatest skill is in the observation of the individuals in the group and their interactions in the "here and now" of the group, while being attuned to the larger picture of the entire group process. The facilitator's greatest gift is the ability to do that observation, quietly, sometimes almost silently, to be able to use those observations to find similarities and common ground, in order to facilitate emotional connections among group members.

Possible Contraindications

The first possible contraindication is with the therapists who comprise the group membership. An individual therapist may be insecure in his/her abilities and may wish to use the group as a way to show off their perceived wisdom or superiority. Or, conversely, an insecure therapist group member may want to be the focus of attention of multiple professionals. The second, and most important, contraindication is in the person of the facilitator. The facilitator may want to utilize this type of group for self-gratification and adulation as the ultimate "super" therapist who can "fix" other therapists. The group members may have chosen this type of facilitator for those same reasons—a famous person leading their group may signify the group members' special importance and, therefore, their need for a superior leader. This often works for a while, but for the group to do long-term work together, the group members and the facilitator must all be sufficiently psychologically-minded, open, aware and attuned to the tasks of therapy and the challenges of being joined in exploring their sometimes imperfect selves.

Toby Ellen Newman is a Licensed Clinical Social Worker and Supervisor, and Certified Group Psychotherapist. She is in private practice in Houston, Texas, where she has been involved in a group for therapists for over a decade.

49 Refilling and Repairing Your Glass

Insightful Exercise for Dually Diagnosed Clients

Ian Jackson

Creating Insight About Sources of Distress

As a therapist working with clients in a residential setting who have co-occurring disorders, I have found it to be necessary to treat both the mental illness and substance disorder as interrelated issues rather than completely separate conditions. When counseling clients who are dually diagnosed, it is important to develop a correlation between the client's addictions and mental health, and to identify behaviors that affect both. This means assisting the client in recognizing the specific sources and factors that create perpetual negative consequences, which are often seen as a result of poor mental health and substance abuse.

Clients frequently come into therapy with a limited viewpoint and are able to see the factors to their problems more clearly when they take a step back and gain a comprehensive view of why they are experiencing so much distress. Therapists can apply appropriate interventions to the client's treatment that aims at bringing awareness to the manner in which someone exerts and receives energy through particular behaviors. Especially in clients with dual diagnoses, much energy is seen wasted on unproductive behavior and actions that are incongruent with their treatment goals.

Client Population

This intervention can be used with clients who are dually diagnosed, as well as, those suffering solely from a mental illness or substance disorder. This exercise requires the clients to utilize abstract thinking and conceptualize different behaviors and aspects of one's life. I have only used this technique with adults, but it may be useful for older adolescents who are able to understand complex ideas. The intervention has been successfully conducted in residential treatment settings and in psychoeducational and process groups.

Guidelines for Intervention

The facilitator completes steps one and two before the group begins and steps three, four and five during the group session. After the first two steps

Exercise for Dually Diagnosed Clients 167

are followed once, the group therapist can make photocopies and will not have to create the templates again.

Step One

Facilitator illustrates on a sheet of plain paper, a glass cup filled with liquid that has a hole in the bottom of the glass, demonstrating a leak (i.e. a puddle). Next, draw stick figures above the glass with drinking straws coming from inside the glass.

Step Two

Take a second sheet of paper and divide it into four equal sections by drawing two crossing lines across the entire paper (one horizontal, one vertical). Label the top left section "Entities that give/take energy", label the top right section "Reasons for my leak", label the bottom left section "Ways to mend the leak—Positive/Negative", and label the bottom right section "Ways to refill my glass—Positive/Negative".

Step Three

Hand out the first sheet of paper with the glass illustration to each client and describe the purpose of the exercise as being for the group members to gain insight and awareness regarding the origin and destination of their energy and effect of negative behaviors on their life. Indicate that the glass represents the person and the liquid represents one's energy. Describe the people with straws as representations of the various entities that are present in a client's life, who both drain and give energy to one's life; some examples could include family members, a boss, friends, a partner, and commitments. Next, define the leak as negative experiences, feelings, or behaviors that deplete energy from a person's life; some examples could include shame, guilt, depression, anxiety, substance abuse, and trauma.

Step Four

Hand out the second sheet of paper with the lines and ask clients to answer the questions in each box. Encourage clients to be thorough and detail-oriented when completing this step.

Step Five

Depending on the amount of time available for the group and the cohesiveness of the members, there are two ways in which you can process this intervention with your clients.

1. Have clients process their responses together, either in a round-robin style or random sequence, while encouraging group feedback and dialogue

(this works well when group members are comfortable with each other, feel safe within the group, and more than an hour is available).
2. Ask for a few volunteers to share their responses and encourage those who do not share to keep the papers with them in order to reflect and process the responses on their own, with an individual therapist, or with a sponsor/mentor.

Typical Client Responses

This exercise helps clients to visualize how much their negative behaviors are affecting their lives and it highlights ways they can create more positive and productive energy. The response from many of my clients has been that this is a unique and insightful way to illustrate the effects of poor mental health and substance abuse. Generally, there will be clients who realize that they can relate to one another through their experiences and are not alone in their struggles.

I have had several clients admit to selfishness when they are able to see how many people in their life they were draining energy from and neglecting. When clients list the negative ways that they refill their glass and mend their leaks, they become cognizant as to why their unwanted consequences continue to persist. Many clients have stated that this exercise helps them to view the "bigger picture" regarding the negative effects of their behaviors, identify aspects of the self they wish to improve, and feel empowered to begin behavior change. This exercise has also been proven to help clients develop empathy when they realize that they themselves are a massive source of depleting energy from many of the significant people in their lives.

Conclusion and Contraindications

When dealing with dually diagnosed clients, it is important to help a client gain insight to the correlation between one's mental illness and substance disorder. This exercise can be highly effective in having clients take responsibility for the ways they choose to cope with life. Clients who are open and honest about their behaviors are usually very successful in completing this intervention. Clients who are still in denial about their substance use or mental illness may have difficulty completing this exercise and see it as ineffective due to their lack of insight into the sources of their problems. It is important to encourage each client to keep the completed intervention papers for future reflection and to use them to help track one's progress in holding themselves accountable regarding desired behavior change.

A possible contraindication for this exercise could be if the group members do not feel secure disclosing past negative behaviors in a group setting and if they have difficulty with conceptual thinking. When conducting this exercise in a "round-robin style," it is important for the group therapist to utilize good time management skills because this intervention could take up to two sessions to complete depending on the size of the group.

Ian Jackson, LMHC, is a licensed Mental Health Counselor who specializes in substance abuse, specifically those who chronically relapse. He conducts group and individual psychotherapy in both residential treatment and private practice settings.

50 Am I Modeling or Muddling? Cranking Up a New Group

Scott Simon Fehr

Introduction

For the novice clinician and, at times, for the seasoned group therapist, starting off a new group can be quite challenging. This becomes especially true if you are working at an agency or facility where you do not have any input into who is going to be assigned into your group. A process group is by theory an unstructured event although preparation for it is very structured (Fehr, 2003). When that initial organizing structure, for a process group, is not available, the clinician is not given the most efficacious opportunity to create something wonderful and therapeutic. This is not to suggest that therapeutic growth cannot be obtained from random placements into the group but rather growth develops at a much slower pace due to tremendous distrust between the group members and toward the group leader. This distrust is due to everyone, including the group leader, being a stranger and in many cases both the members and the group leader are required to attend and not of their own volition.

The following intervention is related to creating a group from one's practice and how to crank it up in order that the members begin to speak or find their voice in this new environment. These particular members may be chosen due to a similar complaint or disturbance in their lives or due to the uniqueness of their individual personalities thus helping the other group members reduce their judgments toward people who are not similar to themselves.

Client Population

For this particular group, the client population of 4 men and 4 women between the ages of 25–50 is initially chosen from the clinician's private practice. They are all well educated and functioning individuals who manifest varying degrees of anxiety, stress and social discomfort. The clinician's choice is based on the belief that group, at this time, is the logical therapeutic next step for further growth and development for these specific group members. Although we may try to be all things ethically to our clients, we cannot be all transferential surrogates within a timely therapeutic experience unless our clients are committed to therapy for many years.

Group allows the clients the opportunity to form multiple transferences in which to work through many of their previous difficulties and conflicts. It also allows us, the clinicians, to observe how our clients interact and relate to others in an interpersonal environment.

Intervention

Most of us have been trained to speak as little as possible in both individual and group therapy. We, too, are warned against disclosing anything that could be construed as personal information as we want our clients to project their thoughts, fantasies and misbeliefs about us. Yet, in this intervention in order to crank the group up and encourage clients to speak, it is advantageous for the group if the group leader models self-disclosing behavior. This self-disclosing behavior, on the part of the therapist, can have a normalizing effect on the group especially if the therapist discloses information that the group members may be able to relate to in their individual lives (Fehr, 2010). As previously written (Fehr, 2010) the disclosure must be in service for the client and not for the therapist. Since the group is composed of clients from the therapist's practice, he or she is the keeper of knowledge of the individual clients. Therefore, the clients' disclosure(s) can be selected from the universal information that the therapist has from their previous individual sessions. Some examples from gestalting previous related client information of their interpersonal relationships may be that the therapist may wish to disclose some of his or her experiences for example: 1. "that my first night in group, as a client, was really an anxious experience for me. I thought everyone was going to be smarter, more successful and I would say stupid things and they would not like me, 2. I was so shy that I had a difficult time even saying my name without my voice cracking, 3. I had all these fantasies before coming to the group and while in the group that these people may be a bunch of weirdos and 4. My favorite self-statement during that first night was I am not coming back."

Typical Client Responses

The typical responses of the clients have been an affirmative response with identification to what the group leader initially felt as a client. Their sense of aloneness, at least, in this situation was attenuated. A male client once said looking straight at me, "If you can do it, I can do it." Although an obviously competitive statement, it was a great start.

Conclusion and Contraindications

As can be seen, the therapist's self-disclosures are both personal and non-personal. The statements are related to an experience the therapist had as a group member and possibly the experience these new group members are experiencing in their first group thus normalizing their thoughts and feelings. I have not had any contraindication using this intervention but once, in over 3 decades of running groups, a client related that my disclosure caused her discomfort because she wanted to see me as perfect. Yet, that was a fine springboard to elicit a discussion on the need to be perfect. A colleague of mine who works in an agency was once discussing the difficulty he had initiating dialogue in his groups. He tried this intervention and said, "Although it did not have an active effect on the group, 3 of the women who previously did not speak spoke a little about their feelings of being in the group." The one glaring contraindication that could be hypocritical is if the group leader presents him or herself as having been a group member and in fact never was.

References

Fehr, S.S. (2003). *Introduction to Group Therapy: A Practical Guide (Second edition)*. Binghamton, NY: The Haworth Press.

Fehr, S.S. (2010). *101 Interventions in Group Therapy (Revised edition)*. New York: Routledge.

Dr. Scott Simon Fehr is a licensed Clinical Psychologist and a Certified Group Therapist. He is on the graduate faculty of Nova Southeastern University's School of Psychology. He has written and edited several books and has a son who is following in his professional footsteps.

51 Fireball

Barney Straus

Introduction

Fireball is derived from a Native American game. It gives group members an opportunity to explore themes such as accountability, interpretation of rules, and self-perception. The intervention begins as a simple ball-tossing activity. It evolves into an opportunity for group members to reflect on their judgments of themselves and each other, and also provides an opportunity for people to increase their integrity, a key tenet of recovery from addiction overall, but particularly relevant to Step 10 of AA's 12 Steps thus "To take a daily inventory, and when we were wrong, promptly admitted it" (AA World Service, 1952). When the activity is working well, good conversations about judging others, self-regulation, and rule following may occur.

Population

I use this game with people who are recovering from addiction to drugs and alcohol and/or compulsive behaviors. I use a series of activities to exemplify the 12 Steps developed by Alcoholics Anonymous. While 12-Step programs are attended by millions of people, to many people who struggle with addiction, the idea of embracing God is anathema, so I use physical activities whereby the group becomes a de facto Higher Power. Cultivating a belief in a benevolent "power greater than ourselves" is an integral part of the 12-Step approach to recovery. I use Fireball as a means of initiating 10th Step reflection.

Intervention

You will need a ball for this activity. A large, squishy rubber ball works well. Begin by asking the group members to stand in a circle and start tossing the ball to one another. If you are working with a newer group, feel free to ask people to say the name of the person they are throwing the ball. This builds shared familiarity with group members' names.

Once the group has grown comfortable tossing the ball, explain that you are going to introduce a few stipulations. If a group member violates any of the guidelines, he/she is to step back away from the circle. The rules are as follows:

- First, no one except you, the group leader, is permitted to make any verbal noise. If a group member makes any extraneous noise, he/she is out for the round.
- Also, anyone who makes either a bad catch or a bad throw is out.
- Each person monitors his/her own behavior.
- Play a round until about half the group members have pulled themselves out.

Invite everyone back into the circle and explain that you are now going to add another criterion for expulsion from the round:

- If anyone makes a critical judgment, they are out.

So this time, extraneous noise, a bad catch or throw, or a negative judgment results in withdrawal from the round. Again, play until about half the group members have stepped away from the circle.

Invite everyone back into the circle, and ask how the last rule was interpreted, and what kinds of judgments people pulled themselves out for expressing.

Explain that for the final round, all of the aforementioned rules apply, and in addition, if you (the group leader) point to someone, they must take themselves out. Usually the leader points to random people. Again, stop the round when there are just a few people left. This final criterion highlights the difference between self-perception and others' perceptions of us. This is a highly transferable dynamic, and depending upon the needs of the group, can lead to some very rich discussion.

General Client Responses

This activity can lead to some very meaningful self-reflection and conversation. Some questions you might consider asking are as follows:

1. Do we tend to judge ourselves more harshly than we judge other people? Likewise, do others seem to have a more favorable impression of us than we have of ourselves? Why might this be so, and what are the implications? For many of us, this is certainly true. In a game like this, the criteria are obvious. What are some examples of less overt ways of succeeding or failing at something? How we look? Our sexual behavior? Can you think of a time when you judged yourself for having performed poorly, but someone else said that you did just fine?
2. Has the opposite ever been true for you, where you felt that you performed well but someone else found fault in you? Can you share an example when this happened?

3. Whether you tend to judge yourself more harshly or more easily than others, why do you think you have this tendency? Is this something that you would like to change about yourself? How might doing so be helpful to you?
4. How honest are we with ourselves in terms of how we judge ourselves and/or our fellow human beings? Was it difficult to admit to yourself and the rest of the group that you judged another group member?
5. Compare the experience of having taken yourself out of the circle versus having the group leader point at you. Was it easier to accept your own evaluation of yourself or an authority figure's judgment of you? In what other circumstances has this dynamic come into play? From a psychodynamic point of view, this issue has important ramifications. Did we take in others' opinions of us when we were young, rather than rely on our lived experience? In what ways were we impacted by this, if it happened? If the group leader pointed to people randomly, the difference between self-perception and others' perception of us is highlighted, and invites the question: "Which do we listen to more attentively—our own intuition or others' judgments of us?"

Possible Contraindications

Fireball is not for every group and it runs the risk of creating conversations and emotions that can be hard for some groups to deal with emotionally. Generally, though, people who are well into working the 12 Steps will be prepared to talk about concepts such as self-criticalness, judgmentalism, and hubris. Also, do not use a hard ball that can result in physical injury.

Conclusion

Integrity is crucial to long-term recovery. Many people initially come to treatment based on another person's judgment of them. Usually this is a loved one or boss. But in order for long-term recovery to be successful, people need to determine for themselves that they are better off without the addictive behavior in their lives. Only each of us really knows whether we have taken a drink or been active in our addictive behavior. In this sense, our own opinions are more meaningful than those imposed on us by others.

Note: I learned this activity from Frank Palmisano, Jr, who learned it from Brian Brolin. The activity has been passed along verbally. I am not aware of a written version.

References

Alcoholics Anonymous World Service (1952). Twelve Steps and Twelve Traditions, p. 88. New York: Alcoholics Anonymous World Service.

Barney Straus is a therapist in private practice in Chicago, IL. He is also an adjunct faculty member at Loyola University Chicago, School of Social Work, and at Roosevelt University, Department of Psychology.

52 A Chair is Not a Chair is Not a Chair

Joseph Shay

Theoretical Considerations

So here you are, standing in a large room with many chairs scattered around. You are about to have your first meeting of a new group. You have told all the members during the screening that the maximum membership of the group will be eight members. Since you do not yet have the eight, you are beginning the group with the five members you do have. One of them calls early in the day to say he is out of town on a two-week business trip so he will not be attending this week or next. For tonight then, you have four members, assuming they all show up. So, it is time to set up the chairs for tonight.

Do you set up eight chairs to reflect the maximum group size? Five chairs because you have five members (you hope)? Or four chairs because four members are expected tonight? Unsure, you turn to the introductory group therapy literature about how to run groups and find either *no advice at all* (Brabender, Fallon, & Smolar, 2004; Friedman, 1994; Pinney, 1970) or *confusing* advice (Rutan & Stone, 2001).

Brabender et al. (2004), for example, have a separate section on spatial characteristics of the group, and even mention the "configuration of the chairs" (p. 79) so everyone can see everyone else—but not a word about how to decide the *number* of chairs.

Yalom (with Leszcz, 2005) says "If members are absent, most therapists prefer to remove the empty chairs and form a tighter circle" (p. 282), implying that the number of chairs *can vary each week* since chairs for any session should match the attendance for that particular meeting. Rutan and Stone (2001) speak to this issue as well, and present two alternatives. In the first, the therapist sets up chairs for all current and potential members of the group, emphasizing that members are absent, that new members will be coming, and that members who have terminated can be remembered and mourned. In the second, just as Yalom does, as well as Fehr (2003), the therapist sets up chairs only for those expected for a particular meeting. They conclude, "The general principle in either approach is consistency" (Rutan & Stone, 2001, p. 180).

It is not until their fourth edition (Rutan, Stone, & Shay, 2007), that they add this approach: "A third approach, and perhaps the most common, is for chairs to be placed for the number of current members of the group, whether expected to be present for a particular session or not" (p. 194). This setup means that the number of chairs remains the same, week to week, and match the actual number enrolled in the group.

So What is the Group Therapist to Do?

I am going to present a vignette of a group therapist who has selected one approach—placing eight chairs to represent all potential members of the group—but then decides, based on reading the following argument for another approach—to change the arrangement after discussing it with the group members. Among the various models, I will argue for this one:

Model 1: The number of chairs should equal the number of actual members of the group—not the number of maximum members, and not the number of members coming to any particular meeting.

Drawbacks for Models 2 and 3:
Model 2: The number of chairs should equal the number of actual participants in any given meeting. Drawbacks include:

- interruption of consistency and predictability of seating arrangement from week to week;
- inability to know until the last moment how many chairs to set up;
- confusion should someone expected to be missing arrive unannounced; and
- less of a sense that missing members are actually still part of the group even when absent.

Model 3: The number of chairs should equal the maximum number of participants, current and anticipated, in the group. Drawbacks include:

- weekly reminder of participating in an incomplete experience;
- constant attention directed to the failure of the leader to fill the group;
- diminished sense that *we are the group* since new members have their chairs awaiting them; and
- shame in the group therapist who essentially makes a weekly admission that he or she does not have a complete group.

Assume then, that you are persuaded by Model I (knowing it too has drawbacks, primarily occurring when a member terminates the group and the chair is removed, making it seem more like a "death" without a symbolic reminder of this loss). How then do you make this change in your group, midstream?

Description of the Groups

Generally speaking, the nature of the chair arrangement from week to week—with respect to the number of chairs—has a greater effect on groups that are either ongoing, open-membership, and psychodynamically inclined, or time-limited with a closed membership. For groups in which the membership in its nature varies from week to week, for example, drop-in groups or support groups, or groups larger than, say, twelve, the number of chairs is important in that there be sufficient chairs for all, so that late-comers do not feel embarrassed, uncomfortable, or unwelcome.

Intervention

Although I have not used this intervention for precisely this problem, I have used it successfully numerous times for similar situations in which I have felt I have made a structural decision that warrants modification.

1. I arrange the room as I always have before.
2. At the beginning of the session, I say, "I've been thinking a lot about the way I set up the chairs in the room, and I would like to make a change in the arrangement, beginning in three weeks. I currently set up eight chairs to represent the maximum number of group members. In thinking about it, while this seems to have worked for the group, I've come to think there is a better way. I want to set up the chairs to match the actual number of you in the group currently. This will give us all a clearer sense of exactly who comprises the group at this point, so week to week, the group in its entirety equals all of you. Of course, I will add chairs when new members join and remove them when members terminate. I'm glad to hear your thoughts and feeling in reaction to this, and to answer questions you might have."
3. I then create a space for reactions, encouraging verbalization of all of them.

Typical Responses

The therapist can expect a host of responses, the most typical being a wish to retain the status quo. Some members may state that they have never actually felt comfortable with all the empty chairs because it suggested to them that they were not in a well-functioning group. Others may say they are glad because when they miss a meeting, they want their presence represented in the form of a chair. It is highly unlikely that a group member will fight vehemently to keep the status quo.

Conclusion and Contraindications

It is noteworthy that something as fundamental as setting up the therapy room is given so little direct attention in the literature, presumably because the answer seems obvious. It is not so clear. My primary motivation for arguing for the model I have discussed (chairs for all enrolled members, no more, no less) is that it helps the group therapist avoid the shame that I think is present in many group therapists when they have to signify, week after week, that they do not have a complete group. Second, using this model, the group members will have a consistent and continuous sense of who is in the group as an active member, whether they are present or not for any particular meeting.

The model is contraindicated if the group therapist is genuinely comfortable with his or her chair arrangement, and if the group is able to profit from exploring this aspect of the group therapeutically. "If the chair is not broke, don't fix it."

References

Brabender, V. A., Fallon, A. E., & Smolar, A. I. (2004). *Essentials of group therapy*. Hoboken, NJ: Wiley.

Fehr, S. S. (2003). *Introduction to group therapy* (Second edition). Binghamton, NY: The Haworth Press.

Friedman, W. H. (1994). *How to do groups* (Second edition). Northvale, NJ: Jason Aronson.

Pinney, Jr., E. (1970). *A first group psychotherapy book*. Springfield, IL: C.C. Thomas.

Rutan, J. S., & Stone, W. N. (2001). *Psychodynamic group psychotherapy* (Third edition). New York: Guilford.

Rutan, J. S., Stone, W. N., & Shay, J. J. (2007). *Psychodynamic group psychotherapy* (Fourth edition). New York: Guilford.

Yalom, I. D., & Leszcz, M. (2005). *The theory and practice of group psychotherapy*, (Fifth edition). New York: Basic Books.

Joseph Shay, PhD, CGP, FAGPA, a psychologist in private practice in Cambridge, MA, has an affiliate position at the Harvard Medical School in the Department of Psychiatry, supervises at McLean and Massachusetts General Hospitals, and is on the faculty of the Psychoanalytic Couple and Family Institute of New England, the Northeastern Society for Group Psychotherapy, and the Massachusetts General Hospital Center for Psychodynamic Therapy and Research. Dr. Shay is the co-author of *Psychodynamic Group Psychotherapy* (4th and 5th editions) and the co-editor of *Odysseys in Psychotherapy* and *Complex Dilemmas in Group Therapy*.

53 The Masks We Wear

Claudia P. Calabrese

Using the Concept of the Persona/Mask

Psychosocial theory poses that human development across the life span requires the resolution of a series of "psychosocial crises" in order for the person to be able to move on to the next set of developmental tasks (Erikson, 1968; Newman & Newman, 1998). In adolescence, identity development is the central task (Erikson, 1968) and biological, psychological, and societal factors come together to help shape and define personality. Identity and personality ultimately define who we are and how we relate to the world we live in, even how satisfied we are with our lives (Costa & McCrae, 1980). Therefore, in therapeutic work with adolescents, it is of paramount importance that interventions focus on supporting the process of identity formation and challenging them to avoid the allure of negative identity formation. This group exercise allows the participants to examine the idea of the mask as a role they take on—with peers, parents, in public—that prevents them from fully experiencing and interacting with the world around them.

An Adolescent Population

This group activity is ideal for adolescents because they have an intrinsic understanding of Shakespeare's idea that "All the world's a stage . . ." as proposed by Elkind (1967) because of their egocentric perception of the world that is magnified through the lens of an imaginary audience. The premise of the exercise is easy for adolescents to comprehend and they readily examine the roles they play in their lives. This author has also used this exercise in substance abuse and anger management groups.

Intervention

Materials

No materials are needed, although it is helpful to present a picture of the "tragicomedy" mask for reference. The picture then serves as an introduction to the concept of "the mask." Other materials that can be used with this exercise include paper and markers to draw masks.

Introduction

The group starts with a brief discussion of the masks and what they represent. Usually I will introduce the idea of how the masks were used in ancient Greek theater to distinguish between different characters. An actor would change his or her mask to represent characters that were either tragic (sad or pained expressions on the mask) or comic (smiling or leering). I then use the quote, "All the world's a stage/And all the men and women merely players." (Shakespeare's *As You Like It* [II, vii, 139–143]) to begin the discussion of how each of us plays different roles depending on our "audience." How we act and talk with our friends is different than how we speak to authority figures and how we act in different social settings.

Initial Discussion

I ask the participants to think about different roles they play in their lives. Going around the room, I ask participants to share how they act and talk when out with friends versus how they act when they are with their parents. I finish this segment by asking the participants to discuss how these different roles are helpful to them and to think about in which ways they may be destructive.

Central Discussion

Now that the participants are comfortable with the concept of the persona, (the roles we adapt to interact with people in different situations), I present the traditional idea of the mask: something used to hide one's identity. I now ask the group to think about one mask they use as a way of hiding their identity from the world. At this point, participants can draw their "mask" and present it to the group, act out their mask or simply describe it to the group. If the group is in the later stages of development, this is where the facilitator can lead a process discussion between group members about how they "present" to each other. Finally, I ask the group to discuss how their mask has prevented them from getting close to others in the past.

Closing Remarks

I find it helpful to end the session by wrapping up with the idea that masks can be useful for us in dealing with society and its pressures or that they can be counterproductive by preventing us from getting close to others. I use the participants' own words to describe this duality and I finish by asking the members to consider "putting down their mask" next time, instead of automatically reaching for it when they do not want to share their real feelings.

Client Responses

It has always been my experience that given the opportunity, adolescents love to talk about themselves. A therapist that approaches them with unconditional positive regard, but who is also able to challenge their assumptions will not find it difficult to work with adolescents. Most adolescents readily participate in this exercise and intrinsically understand the concept of the mask. Often, insights discovered in group are often brought up in subsequent groups ("You're wearing your angry mask again"), and serve as a relational tool in individual sessions. A group of clients in recovery from substance abuse related the mask to the role they play as addicts and the addictive behaviors that led to relapse. This was fertile ground for introspection and at the end of the session, most participants claim they are ready to begin to "put down their masks," and start relating to people in more intimate ways.

Contraindications

This activity works best in the middle or later phases of the group. Once group members know one another and have interacted for a few group sessions, they will be better able to use the process of the group to support deeper insights and greater self-awareness. I do not recommend this activity for a group whose members are just beginning to work together

References

Costa, P. T. & McCrae, R. R. (1980). The influence of extroversion and neuroticism on subjective well-being: Happy and unhappy people. *Journal of Personality and Social Psychology, 38,* 668–678.
Elkind, D. (1967). Egocentrism in adolescence. *Child Development, 38,* 1025–1034.
Erikson, E. H. (1968). *Identity: Youth and crisis.* New York: Norton.
Erikson, E. H. (1968). *Identity and the life cycle* (reissue). New York: Norton.
Newman, B. M & Newman, P. R. (1998). *Development through life: A psychosocial approach* (Seventh edition). Belmont, CA: Wadsworth Publishing.
Shakespeare, W. (1997). *As you like it.* In B. Mowat & P. Werstin (Eds.). *Folger Shakespeare Library.* New York: Washington Square Press. (Original work published 1600.)

Claudia P. Calabrese, LCSW, is a social worker practicing in Hollywood, Florida and is an Adjunct Professor in the MSW program at Barry University. She works with a culturally diverse population of adolescents and their families, focusing on substance abuse, juvenile delinquency and behavioral issues. Her experience in this field includes work with addiction disorders, severe mental illness, and dually diagnosed populations.

54 Animal Assisted Therapy with a Group of Young Children with Social Problems

Stanley Schneider
Chana Schneider

> We may describe as "social" the emotions which are determined by showing consideration for another person . . .
> (Freud, 1913, p. 72)

> So there grows up in the troop of children a communal or group feeling . . .
> (Freud, 1921, p. 120)

Introduction

Group therapy is an excellent medium for children with social withdrawal issues (Slavson, 1940) and shyness (Schaefer & Millman, 1994). Groups are natural settings for children (family, school, peers), and, therefore, well-structured therapeutic groups can be most beneficial for children who have difficulty expressing their individuality and consequently have difficulties with envy, competition, and normal feelings of anger. The group serves as a holding environment, allowing group members the possibility of regressing within clearly defined and protective boundaries (Schneider, 1990).

Since the pioneering work of Boris Levinson (1964, 1969), with his dog Jingles, and his coining of the phrase: "Pet Therapy," animal assisted therapy has become an important adjunct to our therapeutic repertoire. Although animals are used therapeutically in individual (Prothmann, Bienert & Ettrich, 2006; Fine, 2000), milieu (Holcomb & Meacham, 1989; Fine, 2000), and family (Sussman, 1985) contexts, structured group therapy with children utilizing animals and creative activities as a therapeutic medium, is a rarer phenomenon.

Client Population

This is a highly structured therapy group that utilizes animals and creative activities as a means to help five young children, ages four to six, who have social difficulties. The group meets for eight sessions. All the children are in group settings in schools (nursery/kindergarten), and the presenting issue is to help them with social readiness skills so they can integrate better in their educational and social contexts.

Therapists

The "therapists" included a family of chinchillas (mother, father, and three baby chinchillas) and a therapist trained in a three-year animal assisted therapy course of study at the Hebrew University in Jerusalem.

Description of Intervention

Task at Hand: Becoming Part of a Peer Group Culture and Learning How to Make Friends

Chinchillas are jumpy animals and react very instinctively to the emotional output of the handler, which is transmitted via smell and level of anxiety. They become "trained," and sensitized to the touch of a specific individual. As the child becomes more able to give of himself or herself, the chinchillas respond warmly. The children watch how the chinchillas interact as a family and how the mother and father watch over their young and carefully monitor strangers. The group members observe how the chinchillas have sibling rivalry and how they learn to share.

Step One

In order to prepare the group members to work with these animals, the chinchillas are touched and fed while they are still in their large cage. As the children begin to see that chinchillas do not bite and respond by approach-avoidance behavior, the group members are willing to risk and be more outgoing, and, most importantly, to watch and learn from their peers.

Step Two

The chinchillas are taken out of their cage and are placed in a large enclosed compound where they run freely and the children sit as a group. The group facilitator puts a chinchilla in a child's lap. The chinchilla is passed from child to child, and the chinchilla responds to the warmth and interest of each child. The group members learn sharing and how to take turns.

Step Three

The children learn by their own trial and error as well as watching how the other children respond. As the chinchillas interact and "fight" for food and attention, group members learn problem-solving behavior by discussing how to reduce conflict among the siblings and how to resolve conflict: giving more food, separate the fighters, giving more attention, etc.

We begin to notice how each child helps the other with his or her experience of success. This also increases each child's feelings of independence, and sense of responsibility (feeding the animals, cleaning the cage, giving the chinchillas a bath in their special sand, etc).

Step Four
Parallel to the work with the chinchillas, the children then work in the expressive medium, and this reinforces what the chinchilla "therapists" have taught them.

The group members are offered various creative projects that enable them to express what they have learned. Some examples: making toys and games for the chinchillas, and drawing/writing a story as a group collage/activity. These projects allow the group members to see one another's feelings, and work together on joint projects, which encourages group interaction, camaraderie, and helps develop a safe peer culture.

Client Responses

In the initial stages, group members get caught up in their own narcissistic needs. As the group progresses, they move into sharing, learning from one another and, more importantly, how to utilize the group to move themselves forward.

The group facilitator needs to maintain clear boundaries, with a judicious sense of empathy and acceptance. The chinchillas, instinctively, know how to do this.

Contraindications

This therapeutic intervention is contraindicated for use with very aggressive children. Chinchillas are sensitive to touch and can be harmed by being held/squeezed aggressively. Those children who are withdrawn and shy can benefit greatly from this intervention.

References

Fine, A. (2000). "Animals and Therapists: Incorporating Animals in Outpatient Psychotherapy." In A. Fine (Ed.), *Handbook on Animal-Assisted Therapy* (pp. 179–211). New York: Academic Press.

Freud, S. (1913). "Totem and Taboo." In *Standard Edition*, Volume 13. London: Hogarth Press, 1981.

Freud, S. (1921). "Group Psychology and the Analysis of the Ego." In *Standard Edition*, Volume 18. London: Hogarth Press, 1981.

Holcomb, R. & Meacham, M. (1989). "Effectiveness of an Animal-Assisted Therapy Program in an Inpatient Psychiatric Unit." *Anthrozoös*, 2:259–264.

Levinson, B. (1964). "Pets: A Special Technique in Child Psychotherapy." *Mental Hygiene*, 48:243–248.

Levinson, B. (1969). *Pet-Oriented Child Psychotherapy*. Springfield, IL: Charles C. Thomas.

Prothmann, A., Bienert, M. & Ettrich, C. (2006). "Dogs in Child Psychotherapy: Effects on State of Mind." *Anthrozoös*, 19:265–284.

Schaefer, C.E. & Millman, H.L. (1994). *How to Help Children with Common Problems*. Northvale, NJ: Jason Aronson.

Schneider, S. (1990). "Transitional Objects, the Holding Environment and Empathy." In S. Schneider & C. Deutsch (Eds.), *Boundaries in Adolescence*. Jerusalem: Summit Institute (Hebrew).

Slavson, S.R. (1940). "Foundations of Group Therapy with Children." In S. Slavson, *Dynamics of Group Psychotherapy* (pp. 523–537). New York: Jason Aronson.

Sussman, M. (Ed.). (1985). *Pets and the Family*. Binghamton, NY: The Haworth Press.

Stanley Schneider, Ph.D., is a Supervising and Training Psychoanalyst, and Group Analyst. Dr. Schneider is Chairman and Professor at the Integrative Psychotherapy Program, Hebrew University in Jerusalem.

Chana Schneider, B.Ed., B.S. and Teaching Certificate all in Special Education including a Certificate in Therapeutic Interventions in Animal Assisted Therapy, is in private practice with individuals and groups, Jerusalem, Israel.

55 "Am I My Mother's Daughter?"
Eliciting Self-Awareness in the Transmission of Gender Roles Through Family Role Models

Leyla Navaro

Influence of the Family Role Model

Family role models influence our conscious and unconscious attitudes, behaviors, and styles in which we relate in both our closest relationships and our relationships in general. We acquire them from our parents by simply living together, observing, or unconsciously copying them. Some are deliberately chosen and willingly followed, whereas many are unconsciously acquired. Group work helps to raise consciousness of these relationship styles through the processes of reflecting, inquiring, or mirroring.

Group Participants

This is a time-limited, psychoeducational group (twenty weeks) that has agreed to work around the transmission of gender roles by exploring family role models. The use of art material (colors, crayons, collage, etc.) is effectively applied to help accelerate latent unconscious material, which may not be elicited through mere cognition.

The group consists of eight women in their forties. Each is highly educated, socioeconomically comfortable, and is or has been professionally active in her career. Of the eight members, four are professionally active, two have taken early retirement, having left high-paid positions, and two are young mothers. Most are married with children, two divorced, one is single. Six members have had long-term group experiences and two are new to the group therapy experience. All members have gone to or are continuing individual therapy, at the same time as their group experience. Thus psychological insight and maturity is expected.

Intervention Description

A Four-Stage Approach

This intervention is introduced once cohesion and trust is sufficiently built in the group (more or less in the eighth week) to contain increased affect and allow for deeper emotional sharing.

Stage 1

Each participant has to represent her mother in a painting or collage. Various art materials are available in the room (papers, crayons, colors, collage material, etc.). Thirty minutes are given to work personally on the subject. Each painting or work bears the name of the Mother that is represented.

Stage 2

When finished, each participant is asked to present her mother to the group. Who is this woman? What kind of a life did she have? How was she when younger? What was her childhood? How was she as a person, a wife or partner?

It is suggested that all the participants speak in the first person, stating the Mother's name, as if the speaker were her own mother. For example, "My name is . . . (Mother's name). I am sixty-five-years old. My life has been . . . when I was a young girl. . . ." It was not uncommon for a few participants to speak in the third person and the therapist did not interfere. Yet the resistance was registered for further introspection.

Stage 3

Group interaction is encouraged, such as questions, requests for clarification, remarks, and feedback.

Stage 4

When each and all participants have completed this exercise the group reflects on the experience which it has shared. The therapist inquires, "What did we learn? Which parallels did you perceive between yourselves and your own mothers? Which similarities? Which differences? How do those realizations affect you in your personal lives at this time?"

Participant Responses

One of the most striking outcomes of this exercise is the realization of similarities in the mother/daughter dyad. Especially the realization of unwanted and unwished-for similarities, thus providing opportunities for striking self-awareness.

Examples of Participants' Responses

Jane, who was very critical of her mother, shared how displeased with herself she became when realizing that her own angered reactions were as aggressive and harsh as her mother's. This realization helped her to review her own angry behaviors and eventually try to modify them. At the same time, her self-awareness provided a decrease in her own feelings of anger toward her mother. Jane stated feeling a greater empathy toward her mother, after the exercise, with more understanding and acceptance.

Pat reported how saddened she felt about her mother's unsatisfied life. She realized that this sadness was unconsciously hindering her own pleasure and feelings of happiness in her own life. By identifying with her mother, Pat was not allowing herself nor her family to enjoy more in life.

Alicia reported that after this exercise her anger and rejection of her mother had diminished. She reported feeling more loving and admiring of her mother. Her resistance to her mother's remarks was less acute. The group's empathy and understanding helped Alicia to become aware of her mother's life struggles and helped to enlarge her limited perspective.

At the beginning, Julie had presented her mother as a selfish, ego-centered person, sparing more time for her own interests than for her family, an attitude always resented by both Julie and her sister. However, with the group's questions and remarks, an important reframing occurred in June's perception. She reported that now she could better understand her mother's joy and passion for life, and her refusal to comply with the traditional motherly roles. This understanding helped Julie to review her own compulsive motherly duties. She realized that as a reaction to her mother, she had adopted an overprotective mothering style which was quite frustrating and negatively affecting her existence. Julie decided to allow herself more time and space for her own interest areas.

Conclusion and Contraindication

This intervention aims to actively work on issues of separation/individuation in the mother/daughter relationship. "A daughter's identification with her mother contributes to a gender identity based on nondifferentiation and intimacy rather than differentiation and separation" (Chodorow, 1978, p. 109). As in the example of refusal of differentiation (Pat) separation, and individuation within the mother/daughter interaction is mostly an unconscious "oath of fidelity" in the girl's development (Lerner, 1988).

Examining a Mother's whole life span while presenting her to a group of strangers is a powerful tool in the objectification of the relationship. The internalized Mother figure, or the self-object (Kohut, 1977) becomes a "real" person with her assets, liabilities, strengths, and vulnerabilities. This opportunity and potential for awareness as the shift from subjectivity to objectivity is profoundly provided through the group interaction.

This intervention has limited contraindications but, this kind of exercise and intervention works most effectively in a mature group where participants have already acquired a certain degree of psychological growth and have been previously prepared for this kind of introspection. It is not advisable nor recommended for use in a clinical setting with borderline or psychotic patients.

References

Chodorow, N. (1978). *The Reproduction of Mothering*. Berkeley: University of California Press.
Kohut, H. (1977). *The Restoration of the Self*. New York: International Universities Press.
Lerner, H. G. (1988). *Women in Therapy*. New York: Harper & Row.

Leyla Navaro, M.A., is an Individual, Couple and Group Psychotherapist, Adjunct Faculty and Supervisor at Bogaziçi University, Istanbul, and author of several books on gender, competition, passion and power.

56 Living With Dying
How to Keep the Group Alive When the Members Are Dying

Toby Ellen Newman

Introduction

Groups for people with catastrophic illness come together for many reasons: to gain support, to reduce isolation, increase social contact, access information, improve problem solving, and find hope and motivation to cope with the illness and its treatment (McKusick, 1992).

Therapy involves finding the balance between providing accurate information that may or may not be positive, trying to instill hope for the future, and acknowledging the possibility of a lack of future.

Description of Group and Client Population

The following paragraphs are based on the author's experience of fifteen years of facilitating groups with people with HIV/AIDS and ten years in facilitating groups of people with cancer. The interventions should be universal in any psychotherapeutic support group that assists people in dealing with potentially life-threatening illnesses.

These groups can be held in an outpatient therapy practice setting or in a medical facility. It is probably best, under most circumstances, to have patients together with other patients, or family members together with other families, and try not to mix patients and family members within the same group. While it is sometimes required by the setting to have mixed groups, this therapist has found that, oftentimes, both patients and families try to "protect" their loved ones; fully honest communication is not always possible within a mixed patient/family group.

This author prefers to have a mixture of newly diagnosed patients together with longer-term survivors, but this could be a variable left to each therapist. Some settings divide patients by specific disease, e.g., only breast cancer patients, while in other situations, there may be a more general grouping.

The Four-Stage Intervention

The first intervention occurs before the patients even arrive and involves the therapist paying attention to the medical comfort needs of the patients.

Patients with compromised immune systems may need to have bottled water available. Patients on multiple medications may need to have snacks to take medication during the group time, and they may need to have a convenient bathroom easily available. Patients may not be able to walk stairs or navigate large parking garages.

In the *second intervention*, the therapist sets the safety parameters by outlining that the group will be addressing difficult issues and personal stories. Confidentiality will be expected and individual members and their stories will be respected. Sometimes a written confidentiality contract will be signed by the patients. In addition, the therapist also needs to pledge to respond honestly to situations. For example, if dementia or a loss of cognitive functioning is a possible outcome of the disease or the treatments, the therapist needs to be the one person who agrees to discuss honestly what he or she observes and not surrender to platitudes like "everything is fine." Establishing safety and trust are of paramount importance in working with this population.

The *third intervention* involves having the clients introduce themselves, their diagnoses, and give some medical information or update, and psychosocial history, almost every session. It is important to have clients state their diagnoses and some understanding of what is involved with that diagnosis, whether it is considered treatable or not. For many group members, this is the only place they can talk openly, without shame or blame (if they have HIV/AIDS, or lung cancer), without embarrassment (if they have prostate or anal cancer), and without "helpful" family members trying to insert their own comments.

The *fourth intervention* is active listening, reflecting back to the patients what they are saying and how they are feeling. The therapist should be nonjudgmental, open and accepting. The therapist should help members find a sense of belonging and connection. The leader should be able to guide the process of disclosure, be somewhat knowledgeable about the disease and treatment, and most importantly, be able to shift the discussion from the factual content of the disease and its treatments to the process of living and perhaps dying, with all the attendant emotions.

Patient Responses to Intervention

Patients come into the room wanting to talk about their situation. These groups tend to start in the middle phase of expected group development because there is the sense of limited time in which to get things said and work done. Patients are frightened; they may feel alone, with their known world turned upside down. The therapist's calm demeanor and lack of fear in allowing the unspoken to be verbalized provides a calming frame for the work of living with dying to take place. Clients process the shame and fear, and most come out at end of the group and disease process with a greater sense of wholeness about their inner selves.

Conclusion

Illnesses that are considered medically critical, with the possibility of being terminal, take the patient to the point of perceiving the inevitability of the end of his or her life (Frank, 1991). Experiencing this realization, in relation to your patient, impacts not only on the patient but also on the therapist as well. This realization of the end of life is a concept that can become a focal therapeutic issue, because it can elicit a reevaluation of the purpose and value of one's life. Group members may feel alive but removed from previous everyday tasks of living. They now have the opportunity to reflect on the life they had lived and how they would like their future to be, if in fact a future would be available to them. From his experiences and research, Frank (1991) writes that "illness takes away parts of your life, but in doing so it gives you the opportunity to choose the life you will lead, as opposed to living out the one you have simply accumulated over the years" (p. 1).

Working with this patient population allows you to help your clients (and yourself) see the choices ahead in their lives. Dealing honestly with the issues of grief and death can allow some people the freedom to live more openly and to feel more completely alive.

The group members may or may not be sufficiently motivated to listen and hear and want to grow to find meaning in their life. They may feel too physically ill or be suffering from major depression, and be unable to fully participate with all their heart and soul. Or, one strong group member intent on returning to his or her former life just the way he or she left it may dominate the entire group discussion.

The group leader has to decide with the members how to handle termination issues, such as notification of deaths of group members, how much medical information to give, and whether to bring up the question of attending funerals. Each death diminishes the group as a physical loss, but also as a reflection of the coming loss of the self. At the same time, each remembrance reassures the other group members they will also be remembered.

Contraindications

The predominant contraindication is in the person of the therapist. There are situations that require self-knowledge accessible on short notice. A member may discuss suicide or the cessation of active treatment. This can certainly cause discomfort, fear, and even anger for some of the group members who are focused only on survival. The therapist needs to examine his or her own beliefs, values, and ethics, in responding to this difficult, but vitally important group exploration. Keeping calm, buying time, assessing whether or not there is a viable plan are necessary while within the group. Therapist consultation is almost always indicated. Knowing enough about the critical illness at hand is not necessarily a discussion between choosing life versus death, but rather, at times, control of when or how the patient is going to die.

References

Frank, A. (1991). *At the Will of the Body: Reflections on Illness*. Boston, MA: Mariner Books.

McKusick, L. (1992). Earlier Intervention, Earlier Care: The Role of Support Groups. *HIV Frontline*, 7, 4.

Toby Ellen Newman is a Licensed Clinical Social Worker and Supervisor, and Certified Group Psychotherapist. She is in private practice in Houston, Texas, where she has been involved in a group for therapists for over a decade.

57 Bringing a New Member Into Group
Marking a New Place in the Cycle

Joshua M. Gross

Regression as a Normal Group Process

Process-based psychotherapy groups that last for any extended period of time are inevitably confronted with the problem of people leaving which presents us with the issue of bringing in new members. This is a normal developmental event in the life of a group and its implementation can significantly impact the quality of experience for both the new member as well as the existing group members. Group developmental stage theory tells us that groups will go through a series of developmental stages over time and that any changes in the group's membership will most often result in a regression in group developmental functioning.

Group Developmental Stages: Tuckman's (1965) four stages of group development tell us that we can expect a group to progress through a series of stages as members engage in interpersonal discourse and interaction. The initial stage of *Norming* describes the group's overall press to establish the necessary community standards that allow for organized and predictable social interaction. Through the development of community standards members become increasingly aware of their individual differences and are said to be *Storming*. As group members become accustomed to their differences, opportunities emerge for new social roles, described as *Borning*. When group members prepare to leave they are said to be *Adjourning* as they engage with others through a process of termination. The life cycle of a group involves an ongoing series of cycles through these developmental milestones. Bringing in a new member most often regresses the group back into the initial stage of Norming.

Population

Process-based psychotherapy groups are most often focused on the discussion of experiences and perspectives of the individuals in the group. Open-ended process groups may run for many years with an ever-evolving membership as people complete their treatment and others come into the group. The addition of a new member is a common event in an ongoing process group due to the natural attrition in members over time.

Significant or Negative Intervention

The leader can have a significant positive or negative impact on the overall functioning of the existing group and the new member's introduction by providing useful structure. The selection of a new member for an existing group is a matter of finding a good fit that is based upon the clinical judgment of the leader. This intervention goes further by considering the fact that the group will be regressed back to a new starting point with the addition of a new member. When we are faced with the task of bringing a new member into an existing psychotherapy group we have the opportunity to assist the existing group and the new member in making a transition that is consistent with the developmental status of the group.

Even in the case of a group that has existed for many years with a solid core of well-experienced members, the group composition is changed with the loss of an experienced member and the introduction of a new one. This point of time is at least temporarily marked by a change in relationships between members as well as the overall group-as-a-whole experience. By taking the time to prepare the existing group, and assisting them to deal with the impact of a loss, they are better prepared to engage in the many accommodations demanded by this transition. By preparing the new member as to what to expect and the group rituals they will be joining, the leader ensures that the transition will be less likely to cause distraction or resistance in the course of the work of the therapy group.

The intervention is best described as a two-point approach:

- The first point is that which is directed at the existing group. Upon coming to the point of being ready to incorporate a new member the group is best informed as to how this process will occur. Usually the therapist is in the position of making the selection of the new member and informing the group of the upcoming addition. The group will do well to be advised that this change will have an impact on how the group may feel to members and that it is reasonable to have mixed feelings about the transition. Group members who have been through this previously are likely to know what to expect and can offer their opinions about the upcoming transition.
- The new member should be known to the therapist and the preparatory process for joining a group is best carried out in one or more preparatory interviews. The new members should be apprised of the group rules and agree to abide by them. The therapists can assist the new member to feel less anxiety by telling them what to expect in the course of the initial meeting and what will likely be discussed at that time. By preparing the new member in this way it is more likely that he or she will be able to interact with existing group members in ways that will facilitate a positive initial experience.

At the start of the group meeting the therapist should acknowledge to the group and new member(s) that we have new people in the room and that this is an opportunity to review our rules. Upon completion of this discussion the group and the new member need to all once again agree to the rules and this gives everyone an equal basis for entering together into the work of the group. Process groups do best to focus on the experiences and perspectives of the individuals involved and as such it is often useful to ask the group members to say a little about who they are, what they are working on, and how they feel about the group. This ritual is often comforting in this period of transition and assists both the existing members and the new member to work through their anxiety and address the work of the group, mainly, to talk about their experiences and perspectives.

Effective or Contraindicated

The major concern about termination and adding of new members is the impact on the working therapy group. The leader can anticipate that this is a regressive situation (Fehr, 2003) and avert resistance by preparing the group and the new member. The leader who does not make these preparations, or is unclear as to the impact of such a transition, is less likely to be able to maintain the safety and structure of the group intervention through transitions of membership.

References

Fehr, S.S. (2003). *Introduction to Group Therapy: A Practical Guide* (2nd ed.) New York: Haworth Press.

Tuckman, B.W. (1965) Developmental sequence in small groups. *Psychological Bulletin*, 63, 384–399.

Joshua M. Gross, Ph.D., ABPP, CGP, FAGPA, is Director of Group Programs at the University Counseling Center at Florida State University and practices as a Group and Family Psychologist. He is a licensed psychologist, Certified Group Psychotherapist, Fellow of The American Academy of Group Psychology, Fellow of The American Group Psychotherapy Association and serves as Member of the International Board for The Certification of Group Psychotherapy.

58 The Crystal and the Stone
Use of Transitional Objects in Groups

Shari Baron

> The identity of the group and the individual is often symbolized by a totem...
>
> (Henderson, 1964)

The Transitional Object

The concept of transitional objects to reinforce object constancy has been a long established precedent in the study of child development and the psychodynamic model of psychotherapy (Baldwin, 1967; Stone & Church, 1973; Rutan & Stone, 2001). Yalom (1985) posited that, in group psychotherapy, the individual client and/or the group as a whole might view the therapist as a transitional object. In my groups, I often utilize a small, inanimate object to serve as a transitional object that ties the client to the group when he or she is dealing with a particularly difficult situation outside of group. This object encourages the group member, as he or she goes through the days between group meetings, to remember the support and attachment he or she feels from and toward the group. This intervention helps and supports him or her through the tough times in the real world.

Client Population

This technique has been used successfully in several different types of groups. Specifically, I maintain two ongoing insight oriented women's psychotherapy groups in my private practice where this transitional object concept was developed. I also facilitate mixed gender weekly support groups with cancer survivors at The Wellness Community of Philadelphia, a center serving adults with cancer and their families, and I have utilized this concept there as well with significant success.

Guidelines for Intervention

The group uses a glass crystal or small stone as a totem or transitional object. The item belongs to the group and, periodically, is passed around the room and then sent home with a group member who is feeling a particular need for support or encouragement as he or she faces the week ahead.

The genesis of this concept in my practice occurred over 25 years ago:

> Pat was crying, chokingly describing to the group her anxiety about her upcoming visit to her parental home in a mid-western state. Pat had experienced cruel physical and mental abuse in that home, and although she had done significant work in therapy and felt prepared to deal with the issues she might face once she was there, she admitted to feeling significant anxiety about leaving behind all of her support systems in Philadelphia. She was particularly upset about not having the support of her group for the two weeks she would be away. Just then, another group member dove into her large handbag and pulled out an old chandelier crystal. She offered it to Pat as a token of the group that she could carry with her on her journey. The group decided that, to make the crystal have even more power, we would pass it around the room and each member would hold it, symbolically putting positive energy into the crystal for Pat. Pat took the crystal with her on her trip and reported back to the group that having the crystal in her pocket helped her as she faced the old fears in her childhood home. The crystal then returned as the property of the group to be used again by others as needed.

After several years of using this and other crystals as transitional objects in that group, we also began a practice of giving a small glass crystal to each member as she leaves group. This technique has also been used with a great deal of success in support groups with adults dealing with cancer:

> Fred had been doing quite well, with his cancer officially in remission for quite some time. Lately, he had been having some pain in his abdomen, and he was beginning to feel worried that something might be seriously wrong. He called his doctor who ordered tests and a follow-up office appointment. Fred came to group a few days before the tests, openly expressing his fear and anxiety about a possible recurrence of his cancer. The group offered him, in this case, the group stone that had lived in this group for many years, serving the transitional object purpose. Group members passed the stone around, each person holding it for several minutes to pray, symbolically give it energy, or whatever form of supportive thoughts or feelings that member felt appropriate. Fred then took the stone with him when he had his tests and doctor's appointment, reporting later that the stone helped him remember all the others in group who had dealt with similar scenarios with success.

Typical Responses to this Intervention

While the group clearly uses the crystal as a transitional object, there is little discussion or analysis of the psychodynamic reasons for this practice. I have found that it is somehow safer for the group members to use the object when they do not think about the unconscious process that is in play. Most group members respond positively to the suggestion that they accept the caring of the group in this manner, and most report that having the crystal or stone in their possession somehow made their particular trials easier to handle.

Conclusions and Contraindications

The use of an inanimate object as a transitional object in group can have a powerful impact on the group as a whole and on individual members who may be experiencing particularly stressful out-of-group events. The character of the object matters little; what is most important is the symbolic nature of the process by which a crystal or stone (or any small object) may become a support to a group member who is in distress.

Some members who are particularly concrete in their thinking or severely depressed have difficulty experiencing the supportive nature of the transitional object, and these members may report that the token was not helpful. The therapist might encourage this client to have a goal of being able to report to the group his or her disinterest in the crystal or stone. When he or she is feeling comfortable enough with the group to be honest about this disinterest, this client might actually benefit from refusing to accept the token.

References

Baldwin, A. L. (1967). *Theories of Child Development.* New York: John Wiley & Sons.

Henderson, J. L. (1964). Ancient Myths and Modern Man. In Jung, C. G. (Ed.) *Man and His Symbols* (p. 120). New York: Dell Publishing Company.

Rutan, S. & Stone, W. N. (2001). *Psychodynamic Group Psychotherapy* (3rd ed.). New York: Guilford Press.

Stone, L. J. & Church, J. (1973). *Childhood & Adolescence: A Psychology of the Growing Person.* New York: Random House.

Yalom, I. (1985). *The Theory and Practice of Group Psychotherapy* (3rd ed.). New York: Basic Books.

Shari Baron is a licensed Clinical Nurse Specialist and a Certified Group Psychotherapist who maintains a private psychotherapy practice in suburban Philadelphia. She also teaches group process and group therapy to psychiatric residents at the University of Pennsylvania.

59 You Can Teach an Old Dog New Tricks!

Ava J. Kotch

Cognitive behavior group therapy emphasizes learning and conscious cognition and the adaptation of newly acquired behavioral techniques. It is well-suited for mood disturbances and has been researched and evaluated in terms of effectiveness in generative group therapy (Thompson, Gantz, & Florsheim, 1991). The group process includes identifying dysfunctional attitudes and distortions in thinking that create and exacerbate depression. Techniques utilized include but are not limited to:

- Helping patients identify their reactions and work toward understanding them in specific situations.
- Confronting and correcting distortions by reframing and realigning the meanings made by the individual.
- Determining the basic assumptions, and predetermined themes that underlie these reactions.
- Practicing alternative cognitive and behavioral responses to events that patient anticipates as stressors.
- Achieving mastery and maintenance of positive affects that help to create alternative and more appropriate and healthier objective assumptions (Rush, 1983). Depersonalizing, reducing dichotomous thinking, reframing, and focusing attention on partial positive outcomes as a way to counter cognition distortions exemplify this approach (Thompson, Gantz, & Florsheim, 1991).

Geriatric Major Depression Group Population

The group under study is open ended. The patients' ages range from seventy to eighty-five. All participants meet criteria for major depression and are on antidepressant medications.

Intervention

Most of my interventions are based on statements coming from the patients. One of my goals in group therapy is to lead the patient toward understanding that his or her faulty cognitions are in fact simply a very negative cognition set which has caused the attenuation of self-esteem and underlying depression.

Verbatim Patient Disclosure

Patient: I've left two messages for my daughter . . . she doesn't call me back. I'm not surprised . . . I was at a dinner party and the seat next to me remained empty . . . no one likes me and it is always like that.

Therapist: Can you share with us why this means that no one likes you and why you generally feel that no one likes you?

Patient: That's just how I feel. When I don't get a call back it means no one likes me—it's what I think.

Multiple questions and statements are then asked and given by other patients in the group. My focus is toward guiding the patient to understand that he, (in this case), has an overriding negative belief system and that changing negative thinking into more positive thoughts will facilitate the recovery process. Following are examples of the types of questions posed:

- Why do you say nobody likes you? Can you name people who do like you?
- Can you think of other reasons why the seat next to you was empty?
- Could you have any other explanation as to why your daughter did not return your calls?
- Does your daughter ever do nice things for you?
- Do you ever miss returning a call?
- Your expectations of others are always very high . . . I think you set the bar so high so then you can be disappointed.
- You tend to set things up so you can be disappointed again . . . like a self-fulfilling prophecy of doom.
- Can you possibly reinterpret these events and say how you feel if you put a positive spin on these events?

Various group members become involved and share their own faulty cognitions and how they have worked at changing them. Some members recommend, through their past experiences, that changing a negative mind-set to a positive one can be accomplished through the use of exercises. The patient makes a list of negative thoughts on one side of the paper and then on the direct opposite side of the paper, the patient counters his or her arguments with positive responses. For example:

Negative Thought	**Positive Thought**
Nobody ever likes me.	Scott and Ellen like me.
No one ever calls me.	Yesterday I got a call from Toby.

It is suggested that the patients begin this list in the group and then take it home as homework and work toward finding as many negative thoughts as possible and then find as many positive thoughts to counter these negative beliefs. By doing this, the group therapist can evaluate a number of areas in which the patient is "stuck" in his or her negative thought and belief system when he or she cannot find a positive response to the negative belief.

Conclusion

A geriatric group requires that the therapist be very flexible in conducting the group. Differences between supportive, insight-oriented, cognitive-behavioral and reminiscent intervention paradigms can create boundaries that are frequently blurred. Most patients in the group are socially isolated and interpersonally alienated, have limited interpersonal skills, and may have other difficulties such as some memory decline, hearing and vision decline, and gait disturbances. Regressive feelings related to dependency are seen in this type group and the group serves to help them feel connected and not isolated and alone. The group, which ultimately becomes the family in one's later life, helps the patient feel again connected and no longer alienated from the world at large.

Contraindications

This type of group therapy is contraindicated for patients who are suicidal, paranoid, and extremely aggressive. It is also contraindicated with patients who cannot attend to group process because of severe cognitive impairment, severe hearing loss, language difficulty, or for patients who constantly devalue others in an attempt to boost their own egos.

It is very important for the therapist to embrace the belief that older people can grow and make changes and to completely rid himself or herself of the negative belief, "You cannot teach an old dog new tricks." The therapist also needs to feel comfortable with geriatric patients and if the therapist is quite a bit younger than his or her patients, he or she must be consistently aware of countertransferential issues in which the group members may be turned either into parents or grandparents and not actually seen in reality.

References

Rush, A.J. (1983). Cognitive therapy of depression. *Journal of Psychiatric Clinical North America*, 6(1), 105–127.

Thompson, L.W., Gantz, F., & Florsheim, M. (1991). Cognitive-behavioral therapy in affective disorders in the elderly. In W.A. Myers (Ed.). *New Techniques in the Psychotherapy of Older Patients* (pp. 3–19). Washington, DC: American Psychiatric Press.

Ava J. Kotch, Psy.D., is in private practice in Miami Beach, Florida. Dr. Kotch does individual and group psychotherapy and works primarily with geriatrics. She is on staff at Mount Sinai and Miami Heart Hospital.

60 Using Dreams in Group Therapy

Robi Friedman

Differentiating Between Dreaming and Dreamtelling and Three Ways to Approach Dreams

A dream told in a group has a strong impact on its working culture, openness, trust, and deepens the understanding of individual and social unconscious processes. Although dreaming may be highly influenced by interpersonal stimuli, it is an autonomous, intra-psychic function. Dreamtelling is a social event, making it especially interesting in groups. Questions like: "To whom do we tell a dream and why? What is consciously and unconsciously expected from telling a dream and when?" may guide us to work with the difference between dreaming and dreamtelling (Friedman, 2002, 2004).

I use three approaches to a dream—the more familiar "informative" (Freud, 1965) and "formative" uses along with a new approach that focuses on its interpersonal and intersubjective aspects, which I call "transformative" of relations. A dream may interest us not only for its connection to its past or its personal or group meaning but also for its interpersonal and intersubjective impact on the future of the dreamer–audience relationship. Resonance and mirroring (Foulkes, 1965/1984) are considered by me as identifications with powerful contents (Bion, 1963) and communication.

Description of Population

This population included a group of nine late-age adolescents with the mean age of twenty years, consisting of three young men and six women. Most of them were in individual outpatient therapy for different periods of time. Basically, they were fairly well-functioning college students with different problems in relationships. I worked with a female cotherapist in her late twenties for about ten sessions.

Description of Intervention

Descriptive Example

On the second morning of the group, one of the clients, whom I will refer to as "A," the most introverted, shy and somber male participant in the group,

Using Dreams in Group Therapy 205

related a dream: "I'm part of a gang which consists of frightening strong men, who curse women."

Step 1

I suggested to the group that instead of interpreting the dream we could respond to the dream with our own experience, as if it was our own dream. This procedure, I said, included the dreamer.

Step 2

"A" says he often feels very attracted to this type of a gang and it is not his first dream about this particular topic, although in real life he has never experienced this situation.

Step 3

The first responses of the group came from client "M," a young and attractive woman, who told how she felt bullied in school. She felt so frightened that she refused to go to school for a while. Client "T," another young woman, described her loneliness. She could not really tell her mother how rejected she felt both in school and in her family, because she did not dare to be a burden on her. Client "U," a man who had made a beginning impression of being strong and spontaneous, started to describe his inhibitions with other people, especially with women. Whenever a woman is around he said he felt almost paralyzed, regardless if she is attractive to him or not. To him, every woman is attractive and frightening. Client "R," the third man, joined him by saying he felt very similar, only even more inhibited. He could never look someone in his or her eyes and he wished he was not so weak. He used to strengthen his body exercising but to no avail, as it did not help him to feel more open and secure. Client "A" related that he is often very angry at other people. The cotherapist asked him if he feels angry here in the group and he shouts and curses at us.

Step 4

Both the immediate and obvious responses to the dream as well as later communications, which are less evidently connected, are considered associations to its manifest and latent emotions. I make an effort to collect the responses, including my own, which was a feeling of sorrow and sympathy with the dreamer. I first summarize, aloud, some of the responses and conceptualize some of the contents for the group. I say something about being insecure and fearing the other sex. I describe how it must feel for a young frightened man to have to approach attractive women and how men often are threatening to women. This intervention, which conceptualizes the dream's ability to focus on the group's cross-gender occupation, goes on also in the next few sessions.

Step 5

This step involves the interpersonal use of the dream: at first I said that the dream had stimulated a lot of significant responses from everyone, and asked the dreamer if he felt understood by the responses. He said that he did not understand everything, but some responses were very close to what he felt. Then I asked if we had managed to set up a "Safe Space" for sharing dreams. They did not answer, but I felt my remark had opened another possibility for the group participants and was later corroborated by a second dream which was shared.

Next, I considered the relationships generated by the dream, between the dreamer and the group, and how its overt and hidden communications affected the sexes. My interventions concentrated on two processes in the group: (1) first the steps in A's emotional positions as a function of the development in the relationship in the group, moving from feeling aggression as a defense against loneliness, insecurity, and resentment toward threatening women to the uncovering of his pain; and (2) the process in the group relationship from his initial wish, conveyed through the dream, to frighten the female participants in the group with his potential violence and denial of their existence.

The women in the group actually responded anxiously to the dream's cursing communication, but soon enough they calmed down and their attitude changed to a less frightened, more compassionate one toward Client A and men in general. The strong feelings in both men and women initiated by the dream were used in the group to moderate and mature feelings toward the other sex.

Conclusion

In therapy I use a progressive interpretation technique that always begins with "dreamtelling" experientially. My interventions gradually shift from the content to the relationship created through the dream, trusting and using the group's significant reactions to it.

Contraindications

There are at least two *contraindications* to interpreting: the individual's situation and the group's maturity must be judged by the therapist as sufficiently mature to handle deep and frightening emotional content. I evaluate the situation using the dream's structure, my knowledge of the dreamer's psychic conditions, and his or her relationship with the group. If the dream is fragmented, indicating that both the dreamer's situation as well as the group's relationships may be in jeopardy, I tend to use a "formative" approach. Although the "informative" approach deepens the level of dialogue, the "transformative" use uncovers the relationships generated by dreams; a "formative" approach first acknowledges the need to structure dreams with noninterpretative means. It tries to form a safe-enough space to contain the difficulties without threatening the emotional existence of the dreamer or the group.

References

Bion, W. (1963). *Elements of Psycho-Analysis*. London: Jason Aronson.
Foulkes, S.H. (1965/1984). *Therapeutic Group Analysis*. London: Karnac.
Freud, S. (1965). *The Interpretation of Dreams*. New York: Avon Books.
Friedman, R. (2002). Dream-telling as a Request for Containment in Group Therapy—The Royal Road through the Other. In R. Friedman, C. Neri & M. Pines (Eds.). *Dreams in Group Psychotherapy*. (pp. 46–67). New York: JKP.
Friedman, R. (2004). Dreamtelling as a Request for Containment—Reconsidering the Group-Analytic Approach to the Work with Dreams. *Group Analysis*. Vol. 37(4): 508–524.

Robi Friedman (PhD) is a clinical psychologist and group analyst in private practice and an instructor at Haifa University. He is currently the President of the International Group Analytic Society and a co-founder of the Israel Institute for Group Analysis.

61 The Group Therapist as Storyteller

Marvin Kaphan

> Storytelling reveals meaning without committing the error of defining it.
> (Arendt, 1968)

Making Unconscious Ambivalence Conscious

In my view, one important function of the group is the education and acculturation of its members, in order to achieve a level of psychological sophistication where they can identify the psychodynamics of their fellow members and themselves. My own orientation is eclectic and psychodynamic. Like most of us, when I began training, 1 received a psychoanalytic background, which has been modified by my experiences with interpersonal theory, humanistic and existential psychology (Sullivan 1968; Jones 1957; Maslow 1968). One major goal of my work is making unconscious ambivalence conscious, so that patients are free to make conscious choices. This process makes use of interpretation. I believe, whenever possible, that there are significant advantages to making these interpretations through stories serving as parables (Crawford et al., 2004). One advantage of this approach is that the interpretation is not experienced as an ex cathedra authoritative pronouncement, but as an account of a discovery made by an "equal," from which the patient can draw the interpretation himself or herself.

Description of the Groups

All six of my groups were open-ended, having continued for over forty years, with patients entering and leaving based on their needs and growth. The groups are all heterogeneous psychodynamic groups, with, wherever possible, a family-like configuration of younger men, older men, younger women, and older women. Since these are all private patients, the groups all tend to be more or less high functioning, but each group seems to develop a personality of its own, which persists through the years.

Interventions

One of my goals in psychotherapy is to lead the patients' focus away from the "slings and arrows" the world seems to throw at them, and from patients' beliefs that they must be passive victims of the vicissitudes of life. Through making the unconscious conscious, patients have the opportunity to become aware of their own part or responsibility, however small that part might be, in creating those "slings and arrows." This consciousness can empower patients to become aware of and change those patterns, freeing them to make conscious choices. These interventions, as well as others, encourage the patients to examine subjective experience from a different viewpoint. In this exploration, it is essential that the patients be encouraged to avoid self-blame for unconscious forces of which they have been unaware.

As discussed, one of the interventions I have used with success is "storytelling." These poignant and often wise stories come from the self-disclosures of other patients over many years. Obviously, personal names are never used when relating the story nor are details given that could be used to identify another patient.

I have found the following story very useful when a group is dealing with patterns of disappointments: A woman in one of my groups came up with a very interesting observation. She said, "If the same thing happens to me in several situations, I have recognized that the only common factor is me."

- This can open a discussion of the many ways we can unconsciously determine the outcome of a situation, such as: tone of voice, body language, choice of a person to interact with, etc.

A similar device useful in a discussion of feelings of helplessness is as follows: A man in one of my groups said he feels like someone who carries around two steel bars that he holds in front of him wherever he looks, while shouting, "Let me out of this jail."

- This usually provokes laughter and recognition of similar dynamics in the group members themselves.

A longer story that I found useful in a discussion of truth as a panacea was: A man in one of my groups was a salesman. He had devoted his life to trying to tell people what they wanted to hear. His group frequently told him that he sounded "phony." For a long time, he didn't seem to understand what they were telling him. Finally, they got through to him. He said, "I see it. I've never said a true word in my life. I've been so busy trying to read other peoples' minds, and tell them what they want to hear; I don't even know what I think. From now on, I'm going to tell the truth."

He returned to group the next week very proud that he had told the truth. He had been out with a friend who was very sensitive about the size of his nose. In the middle of a conversation, he suddenly turned to his friend and said, "Gosh you've got a monstrous nose. I don't know how you can stand to look at it when you shave every day. If I had a nose like that, I'd run to a doctor and have it cut off as soon as possible." He sat back then and waited for the group to applaud.

Somehow, they weren't pleased. As they examined the situation, they agreed that he had been honest about what was going through his head, but the question was why that was going through his head.

As they explored, it was discovered that the "friend" had been his boss, and, he felt, had dealt unfairly with him. He returned to the man he had attacked and apologized, explaining that he had tried to hurt him because of various incidents in the past where he felt he was wronged. The other man told his side of the story, which hadn't been known to him. Eventually, they were able to become real friends.

- This story usually provokes thought and discussion involving recognizing that even truisms like "Truth is always good" are too simplistic to fit complex human interactions.

Perhaps, the most useful story I have used is an illustration of the tendency to resist an extremely pertinent interpretation by dissociation or "nodding off," not hearing, or not understanding a simple statement:

Once upon a time, a woman was describing to her group a compulsion which forced her to search through food she had prepared for her children, to make sure she hadn't accidentally dropped any needles or pins into it.

A man said (very gently):	"You know, sometimes a fear masks a wish."
The woman replied:	"I don't know what you're talking about."
The man said (still very carefully):	"I mean that perhaps somewhere in your unconscious, where you don't know about it and are not responsible for it, there's some little urge to harm your children, and this compulsion is a defense against that."
The woman said:	"Funny, I can understand each word you've said, but I can't make any sense out of what you're saying."
The man (making strangling motions, shouted):	"You want to kill your kids, you want to murder them."
The woman, sounding very confused, mumbled:	"Everything's getting foggy, I don't understand what's going on."

Typical Responses

Use of these and similar stories to illustrate points of interpretation have been very effective. In particular, the last one has had a lasting effect in the groups in which I have used it. Any time someone says, "I missed that" or "I don't understand" the other group members easily remind him or her of the story, the patient laughs, asks for a repetition, and listens very carefully.

Conclusion and Contraindications

These techniques of suggesting an interpretation through a story are quite easy to apply. If a therapist cannot find such illustrations in his or her own experience, it would be perfectly appropriate to adopt any of mine by adding the words, "I have heard of a person who . . ."

In relation to contraindications, when using any reference to actual patients, one must be careful that information is so vague or disguised that no one's confidentiality is ever compromised. It, too, is to be understood that whenever a therapist relates a story that it requires very delicate handling since the recipient of the story, whether an individual or the group as a whole, can easily perceive it as "blaming the victim." This can be avoided, if the necessary environment of safety and collegiality has been established.

References

Arendt, H. (1968). *Men in Dark Times.* New York: Harcourt, Brace & World.
Crawford, R., Brown, B., & Crawford, P. (2004). *Storytelling in Therapy.* Cheltenham, UK: Nelson Thornes, Ltd.
Jones, E. (1957). *Sigmund Freud: Life and Work.* London: Hogarth Press.
Maslow, A. H. (1968). *Toward a Psychology of Being* (Second edition.). Princeton, NJ: Van Nostrand.
Sullivan, H. S. (1968). *The Interpersonal Theory of Psychiatry.* New York: Norton.

Marvin Kaphan, MSW, LFAGPA, CGP, BCD, is a former president of the Group Psychotherapy Association of Southern California. He has engaged in the full-time private practice of psychotherapy since 1960. He has maintained six ongoing groups for over fifty years, and has given lectures and demonstrations throughout the United States and Canada, including two at the American Psychiatric Association.

62 Using Primary Language to Access Primary Affect

Jerrold Lee Shapiro

Back to Roots: An Intervention for Eliciting Greater Emotional Depth

I have, for years, worked in a multicultural, multiethnic practice. In such environments, it is common for English (at least standard English) to be a second language. As an existential therapist, it is always my process to join with my clients where they are emotionally, intellectually, and interpersonally. Personally, I am a monolingual English-speaking therapist.

Many authors (Santiago-Rivera, 1995; Santiago-Rivera & Altarriba, 2002) have argued that emotion may be language specific and that emotional depth is most tied to the primary language of individuals. In short, people do not feel something in one language and translate it to another easily. In fact, some emotions are tied to and locked into a personal cultural context.

Description of Population

I work almost exclusively with time-limited, closed, clinical, and growth groups. However, this technique should work equally well in an ongoing open-ended group. It is definitely a technique that lends itself best to adults.

I have used the technique with individuals who spoke Japanese, Hebrew, Farsi, Spanish, Russian, Korean, Thai, Urdu, French, several Chinese dialects, and pidgin English. In their lovely video demonstration, Gerald and Marianne Schneider Corey (2006) demonstrate this technique with a second generation Vietnamese woman.

A Five-Step Intervention

There are five steps to the intervention of this technique. Using standard descriptions of a four-phase group trajectory—Preparation, Transition, Working, Termination (Corey, 2008; Shapiro, Peltz, & Bernadett-Shapiro, 1998)—this procedure is one that is best suited to the third or Working (also known as Treatment or Therapy) phase. It is designed for an increase in intrapsychic depth, once the group trust is sufficiently strong to support such an increase in affect.

Step 1

Working in English with an individual at a level of emotional depth that becomes truncated or limited by language.

Step 2

Asking the individual if English is a secondary language (often this is very obvious) and if not what is the language of his or her childhood.

Step 3

Asking the individual if he or she would be willing to continue in his or her primary language. In my experience, this has never been refused. Provide the emotional space and time for them to shift into that language-related state of being (it often shows a marked change in demeanor or facial expression) and supportively allow them to continue with the issue, this time in whatever the language may be. It is important to tell the individual that it is okay if the group does not understand the language, only that he or she does.

Step 4

After the person does the work in his or her native tongue, ask him or her to debrief with the group in English.

Step 5

Asking the group members to describe what it felt like to be present while the individual was speaking another language.

In a recent growth-oriented, eight-hour marathon session with a population of mental health practitioners, one woman was struggling with two simultaneous issues: Feeling like an outsider in California, she was unable to communicate effectively her deeper feelings to her clients and her colleagues; being here with her husband and two children she was also quite homesick for her friends and extended family in Russia. She began to weep, but words were coming slowly and with difficulty.

I asked her (actually in Russian, but that is not mandatory) to repeat what she had said, only this time in Russian. Her countenance slowly became much more open and childlike. As she began talking about her pains of loneliness and fears that she would never make it in this country, she was able to also access a deep pool around issues of rejection and abandonment from her childhood. Although only one other group member understood what she was saying as she spoke in Russian, many of the other group members also had tears flowing.

During the debrief, she explained how she had been separated from her family for almost two years when she was a little girl and how she felt very alone during her medical training in the former Soviet Union. When she was done, the group topic shifted as several other members talked about their feelings as a minority and of loneliness.

Conclusion

This is a technique that extends another level of respect to clients, by telling them that their capacities are appreciated, albeit in a different form (language). It also reinforces the notion that cultural differences may be cherished in a group, rather than be reasons for exclusion.

There are at least two contraindications. First, the group must be sufficiently in the treatment phase to handle the level of affect the technique usually elicits. Second, the leader must be able to tolerate the ambiguity of not knowing what the person is saying for some time and rely on her or his ability to read culturally different tone and nonverbal cues.

References

Corey, G. (2008). *Theory and Practice of Group Counseling* (Seventh edition). Monterey, CA: Brooks/Cole.
Corey, G. & Corey, M. (2006). *Groups in Action: Evolution and Challenges DVD* (First edition). Monterey. CA: Brooks/Cole.
Santiago-Rivera, A. L. (1995). Developing a culturally sensitive treatment modality for bilingual Spanish-speaking clients: Incorporating language and culture in counseling. *Journal of Counseling and Development*, 74, 12–17.
Santiago-Rivera, A. L. & Altarriba, J. (2002). The role of language in therapy with Spanish–English bilingual client. *Professional Psychology: Research and Practice*, 33, 30–38.
Shapiro, J. L., Peltz, L. S. & Bernadett-Shapiro, S. T. (1998). *Brief Group Treatment: Practical Training for Therapists and Counselors*. Monterey, CA: Brooks/Cole.

Jerrold Lee Shapiro, Ph.D., is Professor of Counseling Psychology at Santa Clara University, a licensed Clinical Psychologist and a Fellow of the American Psychological Association. In addition to over 200 papers and journal publications, he has written 13 books, including, *Pragmatic existential counseling and psychotherapy: Intimacy, intuition and the search for meaning* (2016). He has been doing groups and teaching process group therapy since the mid-1960s.

63 "What's So Funny?"
The Group Leader's Use of Humor in Adolescent Groups

Sean Grover

They Can Talk About Almost Anything

It is nearly impossible to run an adolescent group without a sense of humor. For teenagers, a group leader without humor is just another authoritative, critical, or disapproving adult, the last thing any adolescent wants. Creating a lighthearted and playful spirit in an adolescent group is an art (Malekoff, 2004). A skilled leader encourages humorous banter, often initiating and exemplifying it. When problems are approached lightly with teenagers, they can talk about almost anything. Word play, puns, storytelling, jokes—these are important tools. If applied correctly, they soothe feelings of hurt and alienation that so often interfere with relationships and that play teenagers and adults against one another (Gadpaille et al., 1968). Too much seriousness often plagues teenagers' emotional, academic, and social life; a positive group experience can offer much-needed relief.

Am I a Hostage in This Group?

Unlike many adults who choose to be in therapy, many adolescents enter treatment as "hostages." They did not opt to be in a group, their parents or school psychologist made the decision for them. Once deposited into a group, they are almost certain to feel uncomfortable and to experience much anxiety and fear. Humor is especially important in the early phase of group. Our first task is to relieve anxiety and resolve resistances to participation, and for this humor is our most disarming instrument. After all, the ego of an adolescent has been weakened and made unstable by the massive psychological shifts and physiological maturation. As a result, adolescents confront feelings of uncertainty and insecurity daily. When they enter a group, these feelings often intensify and can easily develop into paranoia. At this stage, the leader employs humor to defuse their anxiety and tension.

Intervention

Interventions are best made in the spirit of good humor and playfulness. Humor is also your ideal resort for defusing hostility that could become disruptive. The best way to convey humor is to model it yourself by being good-tempered, relaxed, and at ease. Above all, use humor to avoid the "know it all" attitude that would create a totalitarian state in the room. Instead, assume a lighthearted and curious stance, even if it means making yourself the butt of your humor. In doing so, you demonstrate that you, like them, are not perfect and the group is a place to explore insecurities in a playful way—not a place for judgments or criticisms.

Examples of the Intervention

Example One: Humor Can be Used to Disarm Tension and Hostility

In an inner-city school, the decision is made to start a group in order to address the rising tensions between students and their teachers. The student population is composed of minority youths from low-income families; the school staff is nearly entirely Caucasian and from the middle class. At the start of the group, angry students are hatching a plan to harass a teacher and disrupt his class.

STUDENT: He hates us. He's evil.
LEADER: How do you know he's evil?
STUDENT: Because he is white.
LEADER: Oh, I know what you mean. My father was a white man.
STUDENT: So are you.
LEADER: Only on the outside.
STUDENT: You aren't black.
LEADER: You haven't seen my soul (laughter).

The students are perplexed. An adult joking while they lecture? As the banter continues some students begin to laugh along with the leader. The permissive atmosphere that ensues invites them all to talk and to put into words their feelings about racial and cultural differences.

The subject of racism is not an easy one. Without humor, serious tensions might have escalated and spilled out of the group into the school. Had this happened, the group may have done more harm than good.

The therapist's use of humor also helped the students to arrive at an important discovery: racial differences could be addressed in the school in a productive and non-threatening way.

Example Two: Remain Unflappable

Humor is also the ideal way for a therapist to cope with personal attacks. Every group leader is subject to verbal abuse and this is certainly true when you lead adolescent groups. You cannot possibly be popular with every teenager and many will transfer all their rage toward their parents or other adults onto you. When you are verbally attacked, never counterattack. Take it in stride; remain unflappable. In this way, you are modeling for the group members how they themselves can cope with hostility without becoming reactive.

In the following example, a group of teenagers addresses another loaded subject—homosexuality. Here the therapist uses humor to make it possible for the group members to discuss this taboo topic.

STUDENT: Are you gay or straight?
LEADER: I like to keep all my options open.
STUDENT: Well, are you?
LEADER: Am I what?
STUDENT: Gay or straight?
LEADER: I certainly could be.
STUDENT (exasperated): Why are you so strange?
LEADER: Why are you so normal?
STUDENT: I'm not normal!
LEADER: Finally something we can agree upon.

The student laughs and soon the group is on the way to a lively discussion, talking with much energy about a subject they previously approached in hushed tones or did not talk about at all.

Example Three: No Subject is Off Limits

Spring break is over—the group sits in sullen silence. The leader suddenly announces with mock seriousness:

LEADER: Okay, everyone look depressed. (Pause) Good job. You're doing great. (Pause) Tell you what; if you guys don't start talking I'm going to share the intimate details of my sex life.

(Several students laugh, while others cannot tell if the therapist is kidding.)

STUDENT (to the leader): You're probably still a virgin.
ANOTHER STUDENT: You mean like all of us?

A spirited debate begins about sexuality and soon energy flows into the room. The students begin to talk, not about the therapist's sex life, but about their own.

Conclusion

I have led adolescent groups in schools, clinics, and my private practice for over a decade and I continue to be enriched by the fun and playfulness that accompanies working with youth.

As Tennyson wrote, "Ever with a frolic welcome took the thunder and the rain," when a group leader adopts a stance of good humor he models how to approach life's challenges with ease and lightness (Tennyson, 1986). As group members internalize these qualities they become better equipped to handle anxiety and resolve conflicts.

Too many young people are surrounded by chronically stressed out adults for whom life seems a fundamentally unhappy enterprise, something to be endured rather than enjoyed. With humor we model a very different approach to living, one that teenagers can readily embrace: if life is a roller coaster, why not enjoy the ride?

Contraindications

Never use humor in anger or force humor in inappropriate moments. Teenagers are easily hurt. In addition, mocking or ridiculing a group member, by a leader or fellow member, is never acceptable and will destroy the spirit of your group. It may appear harmless but in time, attendance will taper off and the group will fall apart. I have seen this happen many times.

Keep it simple, stay light. Focus on connecting with teenagers and humor will flow quite naturally. Above all, be genuine. Do not use humor to win approval because teenagers in particular reject adults seeking to win praise or admiration.

And finally, never try to be funny; instead, work to create a playful and open atmosphere. Teenagers who feel accepted and warmed by a good-humored group leader are sure to look forward to group. More importantly, they will return willingly week after week. Soon you will find, as the teenagers are enriched by a positive group experience, you are well on your way to achieving your ultimate goal—awakening in them the hunger for more mature and satisfying relationships.

References

Gadpaille, W., Hawkins, M., Noshpitz, J., Rakoff, V., Settlage, C., & Wermer, H. (1968). *Normal Adolescence*. New York: Charles Scribner's Sons.
Malekoff, A. (2004). *Group Work with Adolescents* (Second edition). New York: Guilford Press.
Tennyson, A. (1986). *Ulysses*. In L. Simpson (ed.). *Introduction to Poetry* (Third edition) p. 248. New York: St. Martin's Press, Inc.

Sean Grover, L.C.S.W., is a columnist for the national Buddhist weekly, *The World Tribune*, in which he often explores the relationship between Buddhism and psychotherapy. His private practice is one of the largest child and adolescent group therapy practices in New York City.

64 Using Grammar to Increase Immediacy and Affect

Martha Gilmore

Distancing from Emotions

One of the common difficulties I face in my psychotherapy groups is the tendency for group members to intellectualize and distance themselves from emotions and from others through use of a polite and formal grammar. This often leads to confusion and boredom and keeps members stuck in their old patterns of relating. While grounded theoretically in a psychodynamic framework, I use a variety of techniques in my groups including many that stem from my early training in interpersonal Yalom-style (Yalom, 1995), gestalt (Polster & Polster, 1973), and redecision (Goulding & Goulding, 1979) group therapies. With these perspectives and a personal appreciation of language, I have found that close attention to subtle verbal interactions can often yield very fruitful results.

The Group Members

This technique works particularly well with well-educated professionals with highly developed verbal and intellectual skills. This population tends to rely heavily on their intellectual and verbal skills for both achievement and as a part of their psychological defenses. They have been regularly reinforced for communicating in an objective, remote manner and usually fail to notice the impact of this on their personal relationships.

Besides these intellectually inclined patients, this technique works well with people with trauma histories who show similar linguistic tendencies unrelated to their educational level. In these patients, I see that this style of language serves to distance them from affect and muddy the attribution of agency. Thus it becomes difficult to know who has done what to whom, how anyone is reacting, and to follow any sort of story line as the listener drowses off in a dissociative daze.

Intervention

The basic idea is to pay close attention to the verbal interactions of group members and to create norms of using immediate, emotional language that uses first-person pronouns and active verbs as much as possible. As I see this as an important group norm I address the issue early in the group in a psychoeducational way. Early in the group, however, it is important not to challenge the "we" or "the group" that indicates the growing formation of group cohesion and a group identity. This can be a delicate and important balancing act. Then, as the norm is fully established and the group matures, it becomes possible to address the defensive aspects of the verbal mannerisms more directly.

Early Group Stages

In this stage, give a cognitive explanation. Don't challenge "we" or "the group" at this point.

Example

Sarah continues to introduce herself to the group in the second session by saying, "You know, it's really scary to meet new people and wake up at night wondering what they thought of you."

THERAPIST: I imagine that you're speaking about your own experience after last week's group.
SARAH: Yes.
THERAPIST: Well, I want to point out that people will understand you better if you are really clear with what you say so that when you're talking about yourself, you use the word I.
SARAH: Well, I was really scared. In fact, I'm pretty shaky right now. (Others respond with resonating and empathetic comments.)

Middle Group Stages

In this stage, briefly point out verbiage.

Example

MARK: When Sarah said she was afraid of me, it felt frustrating—just like those times when my wife cringes away from me when I raise my voice.
THERAPIST: *It* doesn't feel anything—did *you* feel frustrated?
Mark (sounding more irritated): Yes, I felt frustrated. I feel like no one listens and tries to understand what I'm angry about in the first place.
THERAPIST: So look at Sarah and tell her about your experience. (Be ready to intervene so that first-person pronouns are used).

Advanced Group Stages

In this stage, be alert for one-word pointers, or, if pattern persists, ask client to look at his or her resistance.

Example

DIANE: You feel so bad you just don't want to get out of bed?
THERAPIST: Who?
DIANE: I feel so bad. It's hard for me to get anything done. It just feels better when you're lying there in bed and letting the world go by.
THERAPIST: I notice how you're choosing to be passive in the very way that you talk about your passivity. What do you make of that?
DIANE: It feels out of my control. The depression just takes over.
THERAPIST: I have a hunch that if you let yourself talk more directly about your experience you might have more feelings.
DIANE: I'm scared of feeling out of control!

Other Words to Watch for

- "You" (no pronoun/everyone/no one): Is there somebody feeling/ doing this? Who?
- "Make feel": Challenge this—can someone really make you feel something?
- "I think I felt": Why are they thinking/guessing about what they felt? Could they have a more immediate experience?
- Passive voice construction: e.g. "Yesterday there was a drinking binge." "The yelling got really out of control." Who drank? Who yelled?

Typical Responses

Usually group members initially respond to such interventions with compliance, laughter, and some embarrassment and without much processing. As the therapist continues to intervene, most members begin to see the impact of others changing their verbal habits and then they begin to enforce the norm on themselves and on others. Gradually, the negative impacts and defensive nature of this type of communication becomes clearer and is regularly challenged by group members.

In one open-ended group, "Mark" regularly complained about his wife's fear of him and minimized his own contribution to their dynamic. He would relate details of their fights using unclear pronouns so that the group became confused, frustrated, and eventually started to withdraw. My persistent pursuit of clearer language resulted in him gradually taking more ownership of his feelings and more directly expressing his frustration at group members for not understanding him. The group became able to quickly give him feedback when he was sounding quite angry and aggressive but seemed unaware of his affect. His awareness of his own anger and of the impact of his behavior and communication style increased.

Conclusions and Contraindications

I have found this to be a very useful technique for helping group members learn to clarify their communications, to have more immediate experience of themselves and others, and to increase intimacy. I have found it quite useful with a number of populations with varied language skills. However, careful consideration of cultural and language differences is necessary since there can be major differences in different cultures' understanding and valuing of individual responsibility and agency.

References

Goulding, M. M. & Goulding R. L. (1979). *Changing lives through redecision therapy.* New York: Brunner/Mazel.

Polster, E. & Polster, M. (1973). *Gestalt therapy integrated: Contours of theory and practice.* New York: Brunner/Mazel.

Yalom, I. D. (1995). *The theory and practice of group psychotherapy* (Fourth edition). New York: Basic Books.

Martha Gilmore, PhD, CGP, FAGPA, is a licensed psychologist and certified group psychotherapist with the Sacramento Center for Psychotherapy in Davis and Sacramento, California. She is a Fellow of the American Group Psychotherapy Association and Clinical Professor at the UC Davis Medical School, Department of Psychiatry.

65 Group as a Place to Practice New Behaviors

Myrna L. Frank

Introduction

The idea that the group is a microcosm of the world outside (Fehr, 1999, 2003; Yalom & Leszcz, 2005) leads us to explore how group members' behaviors and interactions in the group parallel their behaviors and interactions outside the group. It is proposed that the reverse is also true: that the group provides a place for new behaviors and interactions that can be paralleled in the outside world. The group thus can be experienced as a safe and secure environment within which its members can practice new behaviors before trying them out in their worlds outside. Although this intervention arose out of a psychodynamic-relational theoretical model (Greenberg & Mitchell, 1998; Rutan & Stone, 2001), it can also be conceptualized as a behavioral intervention and thus attests to the pragmatic value of an eclectic approach in group treatment (Fehr, 2003).

Client Population

This intervention is especially recommended in long-term therapy groups in which the process can unfold in a gradual step-wise fashion, and in which the group contract (Rutan & Stone, 2001) provides a safe structure within which to work. It may be somewhat less effective in a focused short-term group. It can be used with both adolescent and adult populations.

Intervention Guidelines

At the preparatory stage, when clients[1] are being prepared for group participation, the notion of the group as a place to practice new behaviors should be suggested to them. The therapist should start by offering a general explanation that group psychotherapy provides an opportunity to learn with and from other people and to understand the patterns of behavior of oneself and of others. Members learn about themselves in group as they typically interact in that setting in ways that parallel their interactions in their lives outside. The therapist should then listen for responses from the client so as to ensure that this concept is adequately grasped. The therapist then suggests that the inverse also occurs, and explains to the new member that group members are encouraged to practice new ways of engaging with others in the group, and that typically when a member feels safe with the group, she or he will take risks that would be avoided in his or her world outside. The therapist should then suggest that she or he might want to think about behaviors that the client needs or wants to change and that she or he could try out in the group. It is important to use the word "practice" as its provisional (temporary/transient) quality offers clients a sense of security in not committing to change behaviors for which they may not be ready, thus bypassing resistance. For example, the therapist could say: "You have reported that you have some difficulties talking openly with your friends; over time you may feel comfortable enough in the group to *practice* saying things to peers that you would not normally say to your friends." It is not necessary to add to this until the client is actually in the group.

How This Works and Client Responses

This intervention can work in many areas. I have found it useful especially in patients who have difficulties with (1) assertiveness, (2) impulsivity, and (3) trust.

Assertiveness

A patient with a history of vicarious trauma who abided by her mother's injunction to "be nice" lest chaos ensue, developed a disengaged style of relating to others in the group. After many months of group work she was able to practice alternative ways of engagement. Initially very tentative, she would preempt her response to her peers with: "I'm going to try something new as I want to practice saying what I think so please let me know if this is offensive," and proceeded to offer her thoughts or feelings regarding another group member. Inevitably, the group responded with very positive feedback and with reassurance that her remarks were perceptive and quite helpful.

Over time she became significantly more engaged and developed a bold and articulate, yet still "nice" way of being. In one instance she bravely shared her sense of discomfort about a peer's crass language and promiscuous behavior, saying that she believed that this young woman was destroying her much-stated desire for a relationship. The other group members were clearly relieved that someone had spoken up, but the following week the young woman announced that she had decided to terminate group treatment, and that this was the first of her last four group sessions.[2] Although this event could have been experienced as proof of the original injunction regarding the horrible risks of not being nice, the group framework provided the time for her and others to explore and clarify feelings, resulting in the young woman's increased self-awareness, her subsequent decision to stay in group, and the "practicing patient's" reassurance of the positive outcomes of her assertiveness. Her interactions with group peers have since extended to her world outside where she has asserted herself initially with family members and then with friends, resulting in a sense of increased self-worth.

Impulsivity

A patient with severe impulse control problems for which he has paid dearly in the workplace was adept at alienating group members with his hurtful comments about which he had little insight. Following about six months of careful work in which the patient's connection to the group was strengthened, he began to practice what he termed "postpone-postpone." The patient recruited the group in his diligent efforts to delay his reactions; in this effort they would encourage him to "hang in" with his feelings and thoughts despite his urges to react bitingly to others. This patient's relationships with group peers has shown marked improvements as was demonstrated when he successfully struggled with his powerful urge to "tell off" a new group member who was monopolizing the group session with constant and untimely advice giving. Although other group members may have been grateful had he done this dirty work for them, the group was left with the task of taking care of the new member's difficult behavior, and the "practicing patient" was left with a sense of increased self-control. Similar changes with this patient have begun to occur in his social relationships outside of group and are very gradually occurring in the workplace.

Trust

A female patient with a history of sexual abuse, after extensive individual work, felt ready to augment her treatment regimen with weekly group therapy. In the past she had participated in homogenous groups for women with similar issues. During the group preparation phase (Fehr, 1999, 2003) she expressed enormous anxiety that this therapist's groups were all mixed gender. The therapist was empathic about this concern but at the same time suggested that the patient had an opportunity to address this problem by using the group as a place to practice being trustful with men.

The patient was skeptical but felt encouraged by the safety of her own long-term relationship with this therapist. At her initial two sessions the patient was clearly anxious as she carefully watched the men's interactions in the group. At her third session she surprised herself by taking the risk of reporting her abuse history to the group, all the while eyeing the therapist who maintained a reassuring gaze. The male group members responded with genuine understanding and distress about her difficult history resulting in visible relief on the part of the patient. This interaction was experienced as profoundly reparative for her. It also had a significant impact on her previous knee-jerk stereotyping of men, and she repeatedly shares this "epiphany" with the group. This patient's practicing behaviors are followed up closely in her individual sessions where she is given ongoing encouragement about her successful efforts.

Contraindications

This intervention has few contraindications and the question is more one of how effective it is. It seems that its effectiveness lies in its timing and the readiness of the patient. A premature intervention would likely be experienced as behavior focused, and possibly superficial.

Notes

1 The terms "patient" and "client" are used interchangeably here: they are typically derived from traditional psychoanalytic and more contemporary Rogerian originated theories, respectively.
2 The group contract includes a commitment to attend four sessions following a decision to terminate group therapy.

References

Fehr, S. S. (1999). *Introduction to Group Therapy: A Practical Guide*. Binghamton, NY: The Haworth Press.
Fehr, S. S. (2003). *Introduction to Group Therapy: A Practical Guide* (Second edition). Binghamton, NY: The Haworth Press.
Greenberg, J. R. & Mitchell, S. A. (1983). *Object Relations in Psychoanalytic Theory*. Cambridge, MA: Harvard University Press.
Rutan, J. S. & Stone, W. N. (2001). *Psychodynamic Group Psychotherapy* (Third edition). New York: Guilford.
Yalom, I. D. & Leszcz, M. (2005). *The Theory and Practice of Group Psychotherapy* (Fifth edition). New York: Basic Books.

Myrna L. Frank, Ph.D., is an experienced clinical psychologist and a certified group therapist in private practice in Highland Park, NJ. She treats adolescents and adults with relationship issues, anxiety, abuse histories, depression and obesity.

66 Counterresistance
Its Manifestation and Impact on Group Intervention and Management

Carla Penna

Counterresistance

The concept of counterresistance was introduced by Racker (1958). Often in analytic work we do not communicate to the patient some of our observations and our understanding of the psychodynamic process. Sometimes this abstention seems appropriate given one's understanding of group technique; at other times, an emotive factor is at play, which is not conducive to an intervention, since one perceives the risk of setting in motion an undesirable process at that moment in the treatment. Resistances on the part of the psychotherapist, referred to as counterresistance, usually coincide with the patient's resistance to the same situation, highlighting the most important areas of conflict for the patient. In other words, counterresistance is defined as the expression of an identification on the part of the analyst with a resistance of the patient, even when, at the same time, it relates to the analyst's own areas of conflict. It differs and is distinct from countertransference, since as a concept, it specifically refers to the manifestations of resistance that occur during treatment.

According to Zimerman (1993), the phenomenon of counterresistance in groups becomes more complex, since the clinician can establish unconscious pacts with part or with the totality of the group. Generally, these resistive unconscious pacts emerge when the group leader avoids certain topics or manifestations of aggression or sexuality in the sessions while aiming to preserve some group equilibrium. The psychotherapeutic group can still make use of premature or pacifying interventions that would be at the service of a repressive act, preventing the free flowing course of group psychotherapy. In this way, the act of counterresistance on the part of the therapist can prevent group members from experiencing important group processes, thus not allowing fundamental empathic or reparatory experiences to occur within the group.

Utilizing the concept of counterresistance as a base, the author will attempt to describe, in a clinical vignette, how the perception of this phenomenon (by the therapist) and the accompanying clarifying intervention within the group can move the group process forward.

Description of the Group and Client Population

This kind of intervention is effective with both time-limited and ongoing process groups. The group leader pays attention to the phenomenon of counterresistance in all types of group psychotherapy. Nevertheless, in groups with regressed, aggressive, narcissistic, borderline patients, as well as patients with serious problems relating to others, then one should be doubly attentive. Greater difficulties can surface and one's careful interventions require more skill on the part of the therapist.

Resistance and Counterresistance in the Group Setting

A young-adult analytic group receives a new member, Lucy. After a while, two members leave the group almost at the same time and two new ones join the group. Lucy withdraws with the arrival of these two new members and when faced with experiences discussed in the group, Lucy deeply resents the situation, as she cannot identify with the problems brought in by the other members. She starts to miss sessions and her absence becomes the main topic of several sessions since other members take her no show personally, feel guilty about what is happening, and demand a more active role of the therapist in relation to her. She justifies her absences during long and tedious phone conversations that she utilizes as individual sessions over the phone. The therapist tries to set limits on this new development. Even after having identified the extent of the patient's difficulties within the treatment, in terms of her resistance to attend the sessions, the therapist is aware of the group setting and the group frame including the decision regarding Lucy's status in the group. Whether she would continue on or not is acted out due to the therapist's enormous difficulty in calling Lucy. The therapist struggles with her own counter-resistance to the patient's behaviors. Her countertransference is one of irritation with the patient's acting out, since after being warned, the patient behaves poorly, negatively impacting the functioning of the group. The patient resists showing up for group but does not leave the group, either. Her acting out and her resistance drains and depletes the work to such an extent that the group and therapist counterresist, responding in kind to her modus operandi. The group situation demands an urgent intervention given the risk of group dissolution.

Intervention

The counterresistance works exactly as a resistance on the part of the therapist: resistance to intervening, to interpreting, to creating meaning, since it opposes the recommended therapeutic attitude expected of the group leader. Ultimately, counterresistance leads to silence.

Step 1: Identifying Counterresistance

The therapist must examine what she or he is resisting/feeling in order to identify her or his counterresistances and to clearly understand what is happening in the group process. In the clinical vignette, various reasons were given (by the author/therapist) for postponing the telephone call to Lucy until I realized that my behavior, revealing extreme irritation along with an excessive zeal for the patient, indicated not only countertransference issues but also the obvious presence of the counterresistance phenomena.

Step 2: The Intervention

After understanding her or his counterresistance, the therapist must intervene, explaining firmly and as clearly as possible to the patient/group what is going on, aiming for the restoration of the attacked setting. In cases of deviation from the group contract, its reassurance must function as a compass for the maintenance of the group process. The denial of the frame indicates important resistances/counterresistances in action. In those situations, clarifying interventions are fundamental therapeutic tools. Lucy was informed, without subterfuges, that if she does not come to the next group session she would be excluded from the process.

Step 3: The Interpretation

The comprehension and interpretation of the multiple resistances and transferences between the members of the group and their relations with the therapist are fundamental. Somehow they reveal unconscious pacts that work against group cohesion and its development. Lucy shows up for the next session and presents her reasons behind her absence. At this moment she is confronted by the group, who explains how her ambivalent behavior affects the group, presenting the consequences of her actions. I intervene with a clarifying interpretation, telling Lucy that the group members including myself have experienced some of the angst Lucy feels in relation to herself. She was doing to the group what she does with her life. The group and therapist are in limbo, just as Lucy is. She manipulates the therapist by resisting the proposed therapeutic frame, not showing up, and pushing others to give up on her. Her acting out and her resistance were paralyzing the group.

The Renovated Group

After the intervention, the group can possibly move forward and understand that Lucy's absence and carelessness toward the group was eliciting ancient feelings of abandonment, anger, jealousy, rejection, and guilt for them. The members' ongoing questions regarding Lucy were revealing a genuine concern with the patient but also disclosing their subtle and veiled accusations toward me for not having effectively handled Lucy and adequately managed the group. The group could understand that they were also making use of Lucy's behavior to resist and to avoid working on other issues that need to be addressed. On the other side, I restored my own status within the group, which moved along the group process.

Conclusion and Counterindications

The group therapist's attention to the counterresistance phenomena (in addition to countertransference) is crucial when facilitating group psychotherapy with an analytic approach. When the group therapist detects the presence of these reactions in herself or himself, she or he should utilize them as a compass, which will direct interventions and interpretations. Counterresistance in group psychotherapy is much more common than many clinicians might think and is intimately linked to the patients' resistances in group situations, which interferes with group transferences in its various levels, in addition to the obvious countertransference issues.

Counterindications to this process are found in the group therapist. If the group therapist presents any resistance to the unfolding of the group process, the tendency of the entire group will be to identify with that resistance. Therefore, the therapist should be able to tolerate and contain different levels of anxiety, in addition to manifestations of an aggressive or sexual nature that may surface in the group. If the therapist is not aware of her or his own resistance, she or he will make a mistake in avoiding certain topics or not interpreting them adequately. In this case, the therapist's interventions will be premature or pacifying, functioning only to preserving her or him and the group. Subsequently, the therapist may prevent free-flowing reparatory and transformative interactions and experiences for the patients.

References

Racker, H. (1958). Counterresistance and Interpretation. *Journal of the American Psychoanalytic Association*. 6 (2), 215–21.

Zimerman, D. (1993). Fundamentos Básicos das Grupoterapias. Porto Alegre: Artes Médicas.

Carla Penna, Ph.D., is a psychoanalyst and group analyst from Rio de Janeiro. She is past president of the Brazilian Group Psychotherapy Association and Group Analytic Psychotherapy Society of the State of Rio de Janeiro. She is a member of the Group Analytic Society International and works in private practice.

67 "When Boundaries Breathe"

Richard Beck

The Frame or Boundary

We think of "the frame/boundary" in group therapy on many levels (Yalom, 1995). Most therapy groups are conducted in a regular clinical setting, be that in the practitioner's office, outpatient clinic, hospital, or agency setting. Establishing and maintaining this frame/boundary is crucial to the development of trust and safety in the group, regardless of the type of group, or the theoretical orientation of the group leader.

Disaster/trauma groups are unique in that these groups are rarely held in traditional settings and usually are led at or near the site of the disaster, be the disaster a natural occurrence such as a hurricane or tornado, or an act of terrorism.

The author was privileged to lead therapy groups for people impacted by the terrorist attacks on September 11, 2001, and the devastating hurricanes *Katrina*, *Wilma*, and *Rita*. The intervention to be discussed in this chapter took place in one of the trauma groups led in New York City after the terrorist attack on the World Trade Center.

Population

The group was composed of advertising personnel whose company had been based in the uppermost floors of Tower Two of the World Trade Center. In all, this company had lost over 250 employees, and the department whose membership comprised this group had lost over sixty of their friends and colleagues. The group met every Tuesday from 12 to 1:30 p.m. in their new temporary office location in Manhattan. I replaced the previous group leader of this group who had "burned out" after two months. The group location and composition was not of my choosing. Often we needed to hold the group in different rooms because business needed to be done in our group room, which took precedence over our "trauma/bereavement group." The membership of this group was mid- to upper-level managers in this advertising company, and attendance for this group was always voluntary. We had a core group of members who attended each session with me for the next three years, while other members could drop in and attend as they felt the need.

"Will You Do This for Us?": The Intervention

The group had been doing extraordinarily good work as we approached the first anniversary of the attack on September 11, 2001. The first anniversary in 2002 was on a Wednesday, and the group had been meeting every Tuesday since it began. It is impossible to describe the mood, not only in this company, who had lost so many employees, but also in New York City itself. The anxiety and tension in Manhattan alone was so palpable you could cut it with a knife. Nobody knew if another attack was planned for that day, but emotionally, it felt like every New Yorker expected something to happen. The week before the first anniversary, one of the group members asked me a question: "We have been meeting since 9/11 at 'Joe's Pub,' several times a week, which is where we truly mourn and grieve our lost friends and colleagues. We would like you to hold our trauma/bereavement group at Joe's Pub on the first anniversary, and we would like to invite other employees of this agency to come join us and grieve together. Will you do this for us?"

I was initially taken by surprise by this request, and told the group, "give me a moment to think this through, but either way, I am delighted that you invited me and included me in your anniversary ceremony." I thought about the "frame and boundary" issue again. Hold a group in a pub? Was I not stretching the boundaries enough by working in their office space during their working hours?

Short Description of the Response to the Intervention

I told the group that I would be delighted and honored to hold group in "their sacred space" and looked forward to meeting with them next week at Joe's Pub during the group time. The group met at Joe's Pub on Tuesday, September 10, 2002, and I had a beer with them, toasting the lives and memories of the dead in their department as well as all those who died in their company. It was a group experience that I will never forget.

Conclusion and Contraindication

This extraordinary group had taken me in and allowed me to share with them their grief in the place where their mourning took place. The members felt a greater connection to me; the leader, and the cohesion of the group became even more intensified. The group members felt well understood and accepted by the leader, who never judged how they mourned or the timing of their grieving process.

The contraindication in this intervention was in relation to me—the leader. In my decision to extend the physical boundaries of the group, I, however, felt a sense of shame about this choice to stretch the boundaries and meet in the pub. Yet when I discuss this scenario with distinguished colleagues across the country, the response has always been a resounding, "you did the right thing by holding the group in the pub," and that the group members would have been more wounded and felt more misunderstood had I rigidly stated the group boundaries. Boundaries, as Cecil Rice shared at an EGPS workshop in 2005, "had to breathe, otherwise under duress they became [sic] like chunks of hardened debris blocking therapy or in the words of my history, they became like clanging symbols, 'bereft of love'." So, too, were my feelings about the intervention of holding the anniversary group at Joe's Pub.

References

Rice, C. (2005, November). *A Master's Circle: Learning from the Changing Thinking of Senior Therapists*. Paper presented at an EGPS Annual Conference Workshop, New York.

Yalom, I. (1995). *The Theory and Practice of Group Psychotherapy* (Fourth edition). New York: Basic Books.

Richard Beck is a therapist specializing in psychological trauma and its treatment in group practice. Richard teaches at Columba University, and writes and lectures about trauma both nationally and internationally.

68 "What Do You Mean I Should Tell Her What I Think About Her?"

Psychoeducation About Interpersonal Processes

Anne M. Slocum McEneaney

A Teaching Tale

Although the interpersonal learning that can result from psychodynamic psychotherapy groups has been shown by both patients and therapists as among the most significant benefits they derive from group treatment (Yalom, 1995), many patients present for a group screening without having a clear understanding of how this learning will take place. Once it has been explained that this occurs by sharing one's own experience of being in the group, including one's impressions of and reactions to others, and by being as open as possible to hearing others' impressions of and reactions to themselves, most patients are intrigued, but wary. Many, even if interested in this idea, are unclear how being open might impact on themselves or others, and how exactly this would translate into learning something new about oneself that might change future behavior and the quality of one's relationships. This intervention provides an example of a "teaching tale" that can be used to illustrate an incident of conflict, which led to interpersonal learning and growth for both primary participants and for other group members. It is useful to educate patients about interpersonal process, to demystify group psychotherapy (Rutan & Stone, 1993), and to serve as a model of growth-producing group behavior.

Slow-Open and Time-Limited Group Populations

This intervention can be useful in any psychotherapy group in which members focus on their interpersonal interactions in the "here and now," so as to better understand and derive more from their relationships with others. It has been successfully used in both "slow-open" and time-limited groups, with both adults and teenagers.

A Psychoeducational Intervention Tale

Once group process has been explained in conceptual terms, the leader then says, "Let me give you an example of what I mean" and shares the following:

This happened many years ago, in a group of women with eating problems.[1] The members had met for five sessions and had bonded quickly around their similarities and the relief they felt at being understood and not judged. By this session, however, several had begun to wonder, "Where do we go from here? Can I talk about the things that I am not sure everyone does share and will understand? Is it safe to go deeper?"

Naturally, people became anxious as they had these thoughts, and there were two members in particular who had very different ways of trying to manage their anxiety. One became very quiet and withdrawn, sitting all the way back in her chair; she was clearly paying attention to what others were saying, but just as clearly did not want to engage with others. Another member, very outgoing, became focused on wanting to connect to the others. She began to ask a lot of questions of the person to whom she felt least connected—who was, of course, the very quiet person.

So began the interplay in which one member peppered the other with questions about everything the second had ever previously said in group. The second, at first, gave brief answers, then monosyllabic ones, then said "leave me alone." The interrogator would or could not, and the tension in the room rose, as these two became increasingly angry, and other members increasingly uncomfortable. After a few more minutes, I asked each of the primary participants to stop and tell the group what they had been experiencing, thinking, and feeling in this interchange.

Each said essentially the same thing: "I was anxious and when I get anxious, I get (quiet/try to connect). And I guess she doesn't like that, and I guess she doesn't like me, and I don't like her either." But, by hearing each other say this, each learned several significant things about themselves.

Responses to the Interpersonal Exchange

First, each realized that she had been assuming that the other was acting as she was because the other did not like her. By hearing this, they each "got it" that the other simply acts in this way when she is anxious, and it really had nothing to do with her personally.

Second, each was able to see and acknowledge that this way of dealing with anxiety had consequences that they did not necessarily like or want, and that it had led to negative consequences for each in the past. Each had had prior experiences of being left out of social groups they wanted to join because they became anxious and so withdrawn or intrusive that others chose to leave them out.

Last, each member returned the next week and spontaneously said that if she had left last week feeling the way she felt during that angry interaction, she would have acted out her feelings in eating-disordered behavior over the next several days. But, because each was able to talk about the feelings generated and gain this new understanding of herself and the other person, they had not felt the urge to use the eating disordered behavior. The feelings had been processed on the feeling level and did not need to be acted on behaviorally.

Other members talked about this experience as being powerful for them both in terms of vicarious learning and in helping them address their own fear and avoidance of conflict (also discussed in the group, after the primary participants had spoken)

Conclusion and Contraindications

This sort of psychoeducational modeling of interpersonal group process can be very useful to help potential group members who have the necessary skills in abstraction and introspection, but may not be familiar or comfortable with the (culturally incongruent) idea of sharing reactions and impressions (especially affective ones) with others, and may not understand the interpersonal benefit that may result from doing so in a psychotherapy group.

Such a therapy group may be contraindicated for people without these cognitive abilities. A person's inability to understand this story, and its interpersonal implications, may be useful in making such a determination.

Note

1. This example is relevant, however, to any psychodynamic psychotherapy group.

References

Rutan, J.S. & Stone, W. (1993). *Psychodynamic group psychotherapy* (Second edition). New York: The Guilford Press.

Yalom, I. (1995). *The theory and practice of group psychotherapy* (Fourth edition). New York: Basic Books.

Anne M. Slocum McEneaney, Ph.D., is a clinical psychologist who writes, lectures, supervises and leads workshops in the area of group psychotherapy, eating disorders, and the body in psychotherapy. She is a fellow of the American Group Psychotherapy Association.

69 Advice Giving

Russell Hopfenberg

What Should I Do?

"What should I do?" is a common question posed by patients to therapists. Experiencing an empathic connection with the patient, the therapist may then think to himself or herself "What should I do?" The inclination might be for the therapist to attempt to give advice. However, prescribing action ahead of gaining some level of understanding of the nature of the patient's difficulty may ultimately be unempathic. Advice often fails to mirror the patient's internal reality (Alonso & Rutan, 1996). Their difficulties may in fact serve an undiscovered purpose in their lives. Therefore, thoughtful assessment of a patient's experience will be more helpful than a therapist directly answering the question "What should I do?"

In group psychotherapy, the therapeutic agenda of exploring and uncovering the full nature of the individual group member's difficulties may seemingly be undermined by other group members' maneuvers to quell the anxiety inherent in the process. Among methods that group members employ is answering the question "What should I do?" or offering advice. At first blush, this might seem to corrupt the very purpose of therapy and lead some group therapists to discourage group members from giving advice. After all, many patients have first sought advice from family, friends, radio talk shows, and self-help books. Thoughtful and caring advice has been ineffective in helping the group member resolve his or her issues. However, member-to-member advice given in the context of a therapy group can be an essential vehicle for furthering self-exploration.

Patient Population

The intervention described as follows is used in a psychodynamically oriented therapy group. Patients treated in this modality characteristically have the cognitive ability to be introspective and integrate abstract concepts.

Case Example

Mr. A had been a member of an ongoing therapy group for about two years. He was divorced and had been embroiled in multiple legal battles with his ex-wife over custody and visitation of their teenage children. Mr. A had also been fired from his job but had some funds from savings and inheritance. He would ignore taking care of some of his household needs as well as attention to his career and social life. The group, and the group leader, viewed Mr. A as someone who passively, and sometimes actively, was destroying his life and all were concerned about the direction that he was taking.

Mr. B joined the group and presented with marital and career difficulties. He had many jobs over the years but would become anxious and angry if he received criticism. Yet, he also experienced heightened anxiety if he found himself to be succeeding. In either circumstance, Mr. B would quit his job and find another, which was usually less fulfilling and less financially rewarding. This behavior led to incidents of marital strife. Both Mr. A and Mr. B had experienced overtly critical fathers who were, at times, verbally abusive. They also experienced their mothers as loving yet passively demeaning.

Mr. A obtained and began working at a job that he thought would be personally rewarding. The group members were supportive and encouraging. Over time, it became clear that Mr. A was unwilling, or perhaps unable, to fulfill some of the basic job requirements and was at risk of being terminated. He spent a great deal of time working on administrative tasks with little or no attention to the more important responsibilities. Mr. A avoided changing his behavior or the perspective of his employer. The group was supportive and encouraged Mr. A to try to understand the pattern that he was enacting. Mr. B then stated: "Here's what you need to do. You're obviously avoiding being responsible about your work. You need to make a bodily effort to help yourself. I mean, stand up on your actual legs, take actual steps to walk over to your boss's office and diplomatically ask for help and feedback." To this, Mr. A responded "I've gotten that advice before and I still find it almost impossible."

Intervention

The basic flow of the intervention is as follows.

- Mr. A presents a difficulty.
- Mr. B offers advice.
- The group leader endorses the advice and indirectly recommends that Mr. B listen to himself.

In this vignette, Mr. B is presenting some sound advice but may be cutting off Mr. A's further exploration. Noting that Mr. B is presenting advice about a situation with which he himself struggles, the therapeutic intervention is, paradoxically, directed toward Mr. A. "Mr. A., this is important advice that Mr. B is giving and you should listen to what he is saying. And maybe, someday, Mr. B will listen to himself."

Patients' Responses to the Intervention

To continue with the example, Mr. B responded, "Yes, I know. I do the same thing. I guess that's why Mr. A's story gets to me. I've heard the same advice too and I find it hard to follow." Mr. B and Mr. A, as well as the other group members then examined the historical resonance of their difficulties.

Patients typically respond to this intervention by examining their behavioral patterns and history. With the revelation that the group member offering the advice has a similar difficulty and "knows what to do," it becomes clear that the causes of the presenting problems are not issues of competence or capability. The unconscious purpose of advice giving is to avoid feelings inherent in examining the meaning of patients' struggles. This intervention counters the unconscious purpose of advice giving and the result is a heightening of group members' curiosity about themselves and each other.

Conclusion and Contraindication

Therapeutic neutrality has often been defined by what it is not. One of these negative definitions is that neutrality "is not giving advice" (Alonso & Rutan, 1996). In a therapy group, although the group leader might not offer advice, it is difficult to prevent group members from doing so. Typically, a group member gives advice when the member offering advice resonates with the struggles of the member to whom the advice is offered. Using this intervention requires consideration of the group members' difficulties and historical issues. Although there are no specific contraindications, an indiscriminate application of the advice giving intervention can amount to group members experiencing the group therapist as being disingenuous. If the leader's assessment is that there is a mirroring of issues, the intervention described can open a dialog of rich exploration.

Reference

Alonso, A. & Rutan, J.S. (1996). Activity/Nonactivity and the Group Therapist: "Don't Just Do Something, Sit There." *Group*, 20, 43–55.

Russell Hopfenberg, Ph.D., CGP, FAGPA, is a Consulting Associate Faculty member in Medical Psychology at Duke University where he teaches courses in group psychotherapy. He is a past president of the Carolinas Group Psychotherapy Society, a past Board Member of AGPA, and maintains a private practice in Raleigh, NC.

70 Bridging as a Tool to Avoid Scapegoating

Melissa Black

A good scapegoat is nearly as welcomed as a solution to the problem.
(Author unknown)

The concept of scapegoating, a unified dislike or hatred of one member by the majority of the group, is often misunderstood as a phenomenon that is done "to" a member of a group rather than a collusion between a group and a member's defensive patterns (Gans, 1989). The role of the scapegoat is often placed upon a group member by the remainder of the group as a way to disavow negative thoughts, feelings, or behaviors that they may be experiencing. For the scapegoat, unconsciously eliciting this hostility may be in the service of avoiding positive connection and often is a replication of his or her family-of-origin negative relationship patterns. If the scapegoat is allowed to take all of this projected hostility, the group members will run the risk of becoming stuck in the split and not working with their own negative thoughts and feelings. The member who is scapegoated will often simply flee the group.

The technique of bridging in group psychotherapy has been described as "any technique designed to strengthen emotional connections between members, or to develop connections where they did not exist before" (Ormont, 1992). As group therapists, we know that the more we are able to stimulate interactions between members, the more we create potential for therapeutic work in the moment and in the future life of the group. Bridging is often used to move the focus from the leader to the members of the group. It is especially useful when a group is ready to move from its nascent stage of leader dependency into a more mature work group. But bridging is a technique that may be used throughout the developmental phases of the group. The following intervention demonstrates how bridging may be used to avoid a potentially destructive scapegoating situation during the later phases of group development.

Intervention

I inherited a group patient, Doug, from an associate of mine who, for a variety of reasons, was terminating an existing group. Doug had been in four previous therapy groups, always finding himself the target of anger and hostility in the group. Although he did not see the pattern, this phenomenon was always brought about as he cavalierly brandished the tale of his multiple marital infidelities, his excessive gambling with his inherited wealth, and his ultimate declaration that he truly loved his wife. Upon entering my ongoing weekly group, this attractive and very verbal man began, almost without invitation, to tell his "story." As I watched the group's reactions I could see the self-righteousness in the other married men and the hostility from the women. I quietly observed Doug's reaction to some of the initial comments of the group. Statements such as "I can't believe your wife has stayed with you. I would have left you" were made from one woman with the nodding agreement of the others. One man responded with a lengthy narrative on the "moral commitment of marriage" and was met with approval from the group. Doug immediately launched into an emotionally defensive speech, rationalizing his actions. I began to feel the scapegoating starting and knew that the patient would be both relieved and disappointed that we would end up being the fifth group to "fail" him if I did not find a way to successfully intervene.

I knew that he could easily maintain the scapegoat role if I made a direct intervention. He would dismiss the group as not understanding him and begin to split me from the group as I would be the only one who truly understood.

So I chose the woman with the most outwardly virulent response toward his story and addressed the following comment, "Barbara, you certainly have reasons from your own history to feel such anger and hatred toward Doug, but I wonder if there is anything else you think Doug is trying to accomplish tonight?"

Barbara was a beautiful, sensual woman in her early thirties who had often found herself in relationships where infidelity was present in her partner. The less obvious connection was the strong need that initially drove her into these relationships. Since her teens, she had used her beauty and sexuality to keep adoring men around her, flaunting them and playing with them to avoid the emptiness she felt inside. Men became expendable objects and relationships often had little reciprocity. The few occasions she engaged in what she believed would be "rescue-type Cinderella relationships," she was predictably met with infidelity. This would create yet another bout of loneliness, isolation, and despair and set into motion another assault on the hapless men in the city.

After my comment, she was quiet and reflective and then was able to say to Doug, "I know how scared and empty you must feel because when I fall back on my conquests, I am scared and alone. I hope this group can help you be brave enough to let us meet the real you sometime." This comment took the wind out of Doug's sails. He was speechless for the first time in the group. Another group member picked up the new theme and stated, "You have lived a soap opera—shallow, meaningless and always looking for the next ratings. That is incredibly sad for you."

The group let Doug be silent and absorb the abrupt change in the direction of the group. Many of the members joined in to talk about feeling scared to open up in group and scared to live their lives as themselves and even all the ways they had tried to make the group hate them or punish them. Eventually, Doug expressed his anxiety around not knowing what to do or say. This was met with approval from the group. The man who had been the most self-righteous and "moral" said, "Welcome to the real world, buddy."

Response to the Intervention

When this technique works, the typical response is to change the flow and tone of the emotional matrix of the group. It is most effective when there is too much dependency on the group leader or when an individual or subgroup is setting up to become a scapegoat. It is important to bridge between people or groups who you believe will be able to make an empathic connection, often based upon common defensive styles. Bridging can fall flat and actually increase the likelihood of scapegoating if the connection is rejected. In fact, in the intervention, had I chosen someone who had done less work on his own issues around intimacy and dependency, it may have increased the hostility in the group toward Doug. After all, who wants to join with someone who is admitting to such heinous behaviors and therefore, alluding to an implicit character flaw!

Possible Contraindications

It is important to pay attention to the stage of group development both when creating bridges in the group and in working with scapegoating. In an early group where anger, conflict, or other negative affect exists, unless you are attempting to bridge group members together in shared anger directed toward the leader, it is best to work directly with the negative affect and draw it toward yourself as leader. Members in a young group may not have the separation and autonomy from the group leader to support another member if it is perceived as emotionally risky.

A member of a new group who is setting himself or herself up as a potential scapegoat will certainly need an intervention by the leader to avoid being ostracized by the group. In an early stage of group development, this intervention will be most useful for the group if it is direct, and between the leader and the group, to limit the projections rather than exploring the collusive relationship within the group.

References

Gans, J. (1989). Hostility in Group Psychotherapy. *The International Journal of Group Psychotherapy*, 39(4), 499–516.

Ormont, L. (1992). *The Group Therapy Experience from Theory to Practice*. New York: St. Martin's Press.

Dr. Melissa Black is a licensed Clinical Psychologist and Certified Group Psychotherapist. She is in private practice as a member of the Group Analytic Practice of Dallas in Dallas, Texas, and is a Clinical Professor in Psychiatry at The University of Texas Southwestern Medical Center in Dallas, Texas.

71 The "I's" Have It!

Margaret M. Postlewaite

Heighten Awareness and Responsibility

I ask members of my groups to begin every sentence using "I." The goal of this intervention is to intensify the exchange between members and to heighten their awareness and responsibility for their thoughts, feelings, and actions. This can be an intervention, on both basic and more complex levels. It can be used in groups with great effectiveness.

In today's society, people often speak about how "the other makes me feel . . ." or "he or she made me . . . ." These "other-oriented" statements detract from directness. I want to encourage group members to own their role in formulating their thoughts, acknowledging their feelings, and determining their own responses or behaviors. Using "I" increases the immediacy of the interaction. According to Yalom (1995), this "here and now" focus offers the greatest opportunity for interpersonal learning. The "I's," as I call this intervention, specifically enhance the "here and now."

Multiple Populations

The "I" technique can be employed in all kinds of groups: process-oriented, therapy, training, workshop, communication skills, topic-focused, parenting, adolescent, parent-child, or family groups. This approach has the potential to be an incredibly powerful tool in a variety of situations, including individual, as well as couples' therapy and counseling. Although this can be implemented early in a group's existence, I have introduced it at a variety of times, particularly when I notice a prevalence of "you" statements between members. When a group or individual blames someone else in the group, I intervene with the "I's." When they begin to point a finger at a family member or friend not present, I can intervene with the "I's."

Intervention

In introducing this idea to groups, I present it as much larger than semantics. Rather than just altering the words, using "I" is a different way of communicating that can change the nature of the exchange between people. It makes for clearer, more straightforward communication.

I invite group members to practice phrasing every statement in the group (or for the next fifteen minutes) to begin with "I" rather than "you." As they struggle with this, I intervene to assist and help them rephrase. As time goes on and the group gets comfortable with this, my role diminishes enormously and the group can help each other with applying this idea.

Applying the Intervention

A variety of situations profit from this intervention. When members speak with strong emotion the therapist can model appropriate response:

GROUP MEMBER (to another member): You made me so uncomfortable with your angry shouting!
THERAPIST (modeling response): I become very uncomfortable when you raise your voice. I hear it as anger.

When members give feedback:

MEMBER: I think that you enjoy being the one in charge in here!
THERAPIST: I *feel* jealous when you speak with such authority.

When members want another member to change behavior:

MEMBER: Can't you stop smirking? Don't look at me like that!
THERAPIST: When you smile, *I* see it as a smirk and I feel diminished. I want to know more about what you are feeling toward me.
(The other member might respond): I'm smiling because I like you and I enjoy how you say things.

Later I might encourage the group members to explore their observations and feelings in response to this exchange, with the goal of members saying to themselves: "I'd like to understand more about what gets triggered inside me."

When individuals, speaking about their behavior, use "you" to describe what they themselves do:

MEMBER: When *you* get angry, *you* want to explode, but instead *you* keep your mouth shut. Why can't *you* speak up?
THERAPIST: Try changing the *"you's"* in your statement to *"I's."*
MEMBER: When *I* get angry, instead of exploding, *I* keep my mouth shut. I wonder if we might be alike.
(Therapist may ask group): Take a moment and hear how differently it sounds just by inserting I. What do you notice?

Over time, groups learn to listen for differences and respond with their own "I" statements. Because using "I" often feels less threatening to the other member, it provokes less resistance and increases the likelihood of members hearing one another Instead of asking questions of one another, the group uses the "I's" and carries on its dialogue.

Sometimes, groups need to be reminded that, if "you" is in the first four to five words, the statement rarely is an "I" statement. Usually, it is what Thomas Gordon (1975) describes as a "disguised-you message" (p. 121): "I think that you . . . I feel that you . . . You are . . . I wish you would . . ." Such statements as these need to be rephrased using "I" followed by a feeling, or closely by another "I": "I feel deeply touched by what you just said;" "I think that I just avoided your gaze by making a joke when I really felt uncomfortable."

Corollary Intervention

In conjunction with the "I's," another simple intervention that I use with groups instructs the members (including myself) to use statements rather than questions (Bernstein, personal communication, 1998; Roth, 1997). Behind every question there is a message. When members are asked to state the message in their question, this improves the openness, intensity, and clarity of communication between members. Using only statements, along with the "I's," reduces defensiveness and helps members become aware of their responsibility for their thoughts and feelings. By learning how one's behavior impacts others, and exploring together rather than inquiring, the group can achieve deeper understanding and joint problem solving. "I" statements, rather than questions, can allow for mutual exploration:

MEMBER: Why did you tell us that story about _____?
THERAPIST: When you were telling us about your past, I *felt* sad about what happened to you.

Both these techniques work well together. Using statements also helps group members stay away from hiding behind questions.

Contraindications and Recommendations

The "I's" can be used in all situations from group therapy to everyday communication. The more practice I as a therapist have in utilizing this technique in my life, the greater my skill in applying the concept in my group communication. With even more practice, in highly charged emotional moments, I can assist the group more effectively. Very quickly, as therapists, we can discover the shift in thinking and expression provided with this technique. As therapists develop proficiency with using the "I's," we begin to "hear" most conversations through this "ear." Greater practice ensures greater expertise. Although I have found no contraindications for this intervention, it is important for the therapist to be aware of the ego strength of the group members.

I have come to recognize how infrequently our society utilizes this important skill. In the various groups I run, therapy, supervision, and consultation, using the "I's" has enhanced the work done by the group. The "I's" have it!

References

Gordon, T. (1975). *P.E.T. Parent Effectiveness Training: The Tested New Way to Raise Responsible Children.* New York: New American Library.

Roth, B. (1997). Personal observation of demonstration group run at EGPS Annual Conference.

Yalom, I. D. (1995). *The Theory and Practice of Group Psychotherapy* (Fourth edition). New York: Basic Books.

Margaret M. Postlewaite, PhD, CGP, FAGPA, maintains a full-time private practice of individual and group psychotherapy, psychoanalysis and supervision in White Plains, NY. In addition to offering workshops and presentations at conferences, she consults on group and individual therapy for agencies and organizations.

72 Women's Empowerment Group Using Art Therapy

Tal Schwartz

An Emotional Journey

Art therapy treatment is an "experience" emotional journey, which puts emphasis on the process of doing, as a path toward the final product. The use of an "experience" projective tool in women's groups stems from the view that the goal is attainment of a "final product," in which women will grow to a better place in their lives. A place of self-awareness, and high self-image (in order to study or work), involves focusing on the process and the journey in the world of emotions, unconsciousness, metaphors, and symbols (Jung, 1978).

The treatment is based on the artistic doing (activity), using creative materials, and also the ability of the therapist to lead the patient to self-dialogue.

Art is a nonverbal means of communication. Using art, the group members contact and exchange their emotional inner world with the rest of the group, without the necessary verbal intermediation as a potential space (Winnicott, 1995).

Group Description

The women's groups range in age from thirty to fifty years of age. The average number of women participants in each group is fifteen. Each group therapy commitment consists of twenty-five sessions. The women's major occupation is house holding. They arrive with a feeling of unfulfillment, low self-image, and low self-assurance.

Due to their early age at time of marriage, they have not had the opportunity to build their own, independent careers. Their relationships with their husbands are characterized by economic and emotional dependency.

The intervention is appropriate for groups dealing with the narrative of a patient's life, to address and discover her creative and healthy parts. This type of group intervention can be prescribed to a general therapy group and is effective for both men and women.

Intervention

I use art and its symbols as a thread, which connects past, present, and future as a personal and group experience communication element (Bion, 1961).

Materials

At the beginning of the meetings I take care of supplying the art materials, such as colorful papers in different kinds and sizes. The women are asked to bring pictures of their childhoods. During the group, the women are asked to bring materials to present their life story with characterization and metaphors.

The process of the sessions is divided into three phases: past, present, and future.

Step 1

In this first stage, the women associate to their private name, draw their name and color it, according to the way they feel, on a sheet of paper. Issues such as: "Where did I put my name on the page?" and other issues, such as: the proportion of the name versus the page size, full versus empty space, the chosen colors, the materials attached to the name—all have the capacity to arouse thoughts and feelings which lead to personal "checking." An example of such would be, "Where am I with regard to my life and the rest of the group members?"

Step 2

In the second stage, women are asked to bring a picture of themselves as a child. I generally photocopy these pictures, magnify them, and make copies: one in black and white, and one in color. The magnification helps them watch and see the various details of that child observed in the picture. The different pictures invite them to use and contribute to the symbols in their life story.

Step 3

In addition to the pictures, I give each woman a poem as a starting point with the past and a connection to the present. The poems are about the forgotten things of childhood.

I look for poems that talk about memories and sights, with no specific mention of time or place, so as to let every participant make her own associations to the central issue of the poem as a stimulus which returns the woman to that forgotten childhood. You can also choose any song that talks about childhood that is relevant to the place or the culture of the patients.

Step 4

The women are asked to derive single words, or a related sentence, and create an emotional, conceptual integration between the words of the poem and the child in the picture. This step includes a group dialogue as well as a personal dialogue concerning the stories created from the association between the words and the picture. Issues such as: "What had the child left in her forgotten childhood? Who was she way back in the past? What were her dreams and expectations from herself? What was her place in her family of origin?" This part arouses nostalgia, smiles, and pain. In this part of the intervention it is important to check who among these women has social leadership skills, and what happened in her life's journey that made her leave all this behind, i.e., traumas, introjected, related family patterns.

Step 5

The link to the past touches the very intimate, delicate texture of the group, as well as personal lives. The women have to build a new lifeline—a rope, which connects the past with the present, a symbol of the "umbilical cord." This cord is translated to tastes, smells, prayers, and different textures that the women collect from their childhood environments and from their present. It is important to give this part a significant time space, as collections are created and presented as if in an exhibition. This part is especially exciting, since it involves a lot of effort, and confronts issues dealing with the reasons for the women's inability to carry out developmental tasks and progress.

Step 6

I use the term "curtain" to represent the situation of being stuck. This curtain stands between the self-fulfillment, i.e., between the desire, dream, and fantasy and their place in the present; a curtain, which they have to pass through in order to move to the other side.

The women have to metaphorically check and choose the various materials that make this curtain opaque, transparent, stiff, soft, etc. Different materials are then brought into the room: piercing thorns, nets with different density; the whole group contributes by looking at the unconcealed and into the hidden. At the end of this step, the women will have to go through the curtains and reveal their strength to cope with the past as a process of growing. They begin thinking about the future by searching for studying and working places, while still in the process of group therapy.

Typical Responses and Conclusion

The work technique and the various steps in the intervention create within the women a sense of responsibility, involvement, discovering the self and the existing forces, which facilitate looking into themselves with new views. There is no need to know how to draw or paint, but it is necessary to have the motivation to revive the concealed self. The multi-sensual experience is empowered by the group experience and thus creates revival, strength, and empowerment.

Contraindications

This process is viewed by the women as a positive, full of strengths and new discoveries about themselves and about the other group members. In fact, the only contraindication might be the new experience of using metaphoric language, and the world of symbols and imagination, but it appears that the women easily develop this ability with time and practice. For some of the women, their adult world had become concrete thus eliciting this initial difficulty of expressing their creativity but practice within this paradigm helps to remedy the transition from the concrete into the abstract.

References

Bion, W.R. (1961). *Experiences in Groups*. New York: Basic Books.
Jung, C.G. (1978). *Man and His Symbols*. London: Pan Books.
Winnicott, D.W. (1995). *Playing and Reality*. Tel Aviv: Am Oved Publishers, Ltd.

Dr. Tal Schwartz is a licensed Art therapist and Family and Couple Psychotherapist. She is in private practice and a professor at Ben-Gurion University where she teaches art therapy and group therapy in the Graduate School of the Center for Social Workers and Art Therapist Studies.

73 From Silence to Frenzy
Resistance in the Face of Shame
Steven L. Schklar

Seeking the "Corrective Emotional Experience"

The concept of the "corrective emotional experience" is to encourage a client to re-experience previously unfavorable circumstances which he or she could not effectively process in the past, then bring those conditions into the present in order to help set free the adverse influences of those circumstances. In the present, the client will be met with positive environmental and intrapsychic factors that were not present at the time of the traumatic experience (Alexander and French, 1946).

It is a courageous offering, on the part of a client, and the goal of my groups is to encourage group members to disclose previously inhibited strong burdensome feelings. One of these strong feelings is shame. Shame can burden an individual throughout his or her entire life, unless addressed. It is generally accepted in psychodynamic psychotherapies that feelings pave the road to discovery and that a "corrective emotional experience" can in effect change the original traumatic or painful experience a client previously had and provide in its place a new experience of acceptance and understanding. This new experience has the power to enhance personal growth and interpersonal relationships (Yalom, 1985).

Type of Group and Population

I lead weekly adult mixed-gender open groups (Yalom, 1985) in my private practice. In these groups I maintain the number of participants at a maximum of eight. When members leave they are replaced and the group continues. My clients are generally high functioning and I integrate various psychological theories, but most closely align my work with existential, relational, intersubjective, and self-psychological approaches. The overarching goal in my groups is to help participants relieve their suffering as they currently experience it. I assist them to articulate their thoughts and feelings in the "here and now," and help them focus on the interpersonal as well as intrapsychic experiences that occur during the group experience.

Intervention Rationale

The goal of encouraging strong feelings or highly charged emotional material, in a group, can elicit multifaceted resistance, of which the group therapist must be consistently aware.

This resistance may take a variety of forms. Frequently, the entire group will go dead silent. At other times there will be a frenzied attempt to fix or take care of the person experiencing the deep feelings of shame. Indeed both of these reactions can occur at the same time with part of the group going quiet, while other group members rush to help or rescue the individual who disclosed those feelings of shame.

When these polar reactions to shame persist, I take this as a signal that an intervention is appropriate (Rutan and Stone, 1993). Both the silence and the frenzied help can defeat the goals of a psychotherapy group. This can lead to the avoidance of further feeling through rationalizations (offering help and advice) or the shutting down of "here and now" emotional experience (silence).

For the member who had disclosed his or her feelings, silent or frenzied resistances (acting out) will likely be a reenactment of the original shame-inducing behavior. In the manifestation of the strong feelings of shame presented, other participants may behave in ways to avoid connecting either with the bearer or to their own emotional experience of shame. Exploration of each of these phenomena in the "here and now" can help to lessen the resistance and provide a "corrective emotional experience."

My goal is to continuously monitor my attunement (Rowe and Mac Isaac, 1991) to each member in the group as well as my own moment-to-moment thoughts and feelings, while at the same time remaining aware of the group process.

The following is a step-by-step example of how I have intervened to help the group members move out of their resistance. When this is accomplished the group can proceed toward a goal of increased self-awareness and a loosening of unhelpful patterns in their interpersonal relationships. The repetition of this type of interpersonal communication between members will increase group cohesion and safety to move deeper into emotional material.

Step-By-Step Guidelines

A Case Example

I have a friend who has stood by me in my times of illness and loss over the years. Now my friend is struggling with a life-threatening situation. She is quite alone and depressed. I can't stand to be with her, I can't take it; I make excuses for being absent. I'm weak, selfish and cruel. (client)

In this case, the client's voice trails off and her body sinks into her chair, head down. She appears to be waiting with trepidation. The group goes silent and remains that way for several minutes. Then several members begin very actively helping with their rationalizations about how she need not feel badly and how her behavior was not so awful. Their momentum builds and they begin a lively discussion of the reasons why the group member should not feel so ashamed. Some relate stories about how they had dealt with such feelings.

As the activity continues I notice the protagonist, though trying to listen and understand what is being offered, appears uncomfortable. Her face is blank, with a distant gaze in her eyes as if of shutting off from what is being offered. I become aware of the increasing energy in the group and my sense of their rush to avoid their own deeper feelings by focusing on her. In addition, I am aware that there are still two participants who remain silent and likely disconnected from the emotional content in the room.

Step 1

Step 1 involves making a group process comment to bring attention to the "here and now" response to the sharing and receiving of shameful feelings.

Therapist: There seems to be quite a lot happening in the group at the moment. Mary risked showing us some of her deep feelings of shame and right now the group seems to be having some strong reactions. What can we make of these reactions?

Step 2

Step 2 is working with the responses, either "silent" or "helpful," to assist individuals with their awareness of the feelings associated with their individual shame.

Therapist: Jim, as you relate your story you seemed to be very focused on details however I am not getting a clear understanding of the impact of this story on you.

Or,

Therapist: Samantha, you have not spoken since Mary's feelings were expressed. I am wondering what you are experiencing?

Or,

Therapist: Rudy, you seem to really want to help Mary. How do you feel you are doing in that regard?

Step 3

In this step ask the individual for her experience of risking to share her shameful feelings with the group.

Therapist: Mary, it has been a while since you risked being open and vulnerable in the group. I am interested in knowing how you are feeling right now and if you are willing to say, how the responses of the group impacted you?

Step 4

In Step 4, work with the group to explore the process and the "here and now" experience of what has just transpired.

Therapist: We have spent some time now exploring and experiencing how it is often difficult to express deep shame and to stay present with another's shame. We have also seen how various reactions impact on a vulnerable member. What are you now aware of?

Typical Responses

The most common response for the entire group is the realization of the group's ability to find its way to handle these "charged" events. To this end there is an increased sense of safety and closeness in the group for both the individual client and the entire group. Participants will often comment how important the session was or quite possibly the uniqueness and value of the group experience. Clients also disclose that they experience fear and vulnerability, at times, when there are "big" emotions in the room.

Frequently, the individual presenting the shameful feelings will first experience what seems like a reenactment of a childhood experience. This is ameliorated when others in the group validate him or her by connecting to their own shameful feelings thus providing the path for a corrective emotional experience to occur. The client no longer feels alone in his or her own thoughts and feelings and the process of guilt reduction begins to take effect.

Conclusion and Contraindications

This intervention can assist each group member to recognize his or her tendency to avoid (go silent) or attack (frenzied helping) when other group members present themselves as vulnerable and express deep feelings. It also demonstrates the possibility and the benefit of staying connected to others when they wished to express their own deeper feelings. This intervention is appropriate for process groups in outpatient facilities, inpatient facilities, or private practices that are dynamically oriented.

A contraindication of this intervention lies with the therapist. Eliciting deep feelings and providing a strong enough container for the affect and resistances takes energy and courage. If the group therapist is not yet ready for the intensity of possible affect, or he or she is uncomfortable with intense affect, it would be better that the therapist does not implement this intervention. The group leader who uses such interventions needs to understand the emotional challenges to him or her and the group members before moving into this realm.

References

Alexander, F. and French, T. (1946). *Psychoanalytic Therapy: Principles and Applications.* New York: Ronald Press.

Rowe, C.E. and Mac Isaac, D.S. (1991). *Empathic Attunement: The "Technique" of Psychoanalytic Self Psychology.* New Jersey: Jason Aronson.

Rutan, J. Scott and Stone, W. (1993). *Psychodynamic Group Psychotherapy* (Second edition). New York: The Guilford Press.

Yalom, I. (1985). *The Theory and Practice of Group Psychotherapy* (Third edition). New York: Basic Books.

Steven L. Schklar, B.A., CGP, is a Clinical Member and Past President of The Ontario Society of Psychotherapists. He is a Certified Group Psychotherapist in private practice in Toronto, Ontario. His group practice includes psychodynamic long term mixed gender groups. He also leads support and psychotherapy groups for The Artists' Health Center at Toronto Western Hospital.

74 "After the Group Has Ended"
Imagery to Vivify Termination

Miriam Iosupovici

> Endings are either too long or too short.
> (Miriam Polster, personal communication)

Ending Ritual

In all situations in which a group process has been established, the existentially imperfect process of termination may be one of the most important stages of an ethical group process, requiring considerable therapist skill (Mangione, Forti, & Iacuzzi, 2007; AGPA, 2007). To avoid colluding with avoidance of the feelings stirred up by ending in clients, and therapists, thoughtfully timed rituals may be useful.

Guided imagery, a form of trance, can vivify the actuality of ending prior to the event. Imagery, including directive suggestion, supports a more powerful group termination process. Functions such as prescribing the resistance, working through as yet unarticulated issues, and/or expression of gratitude and progress or their opposites, some of which might not have otherwise come to awareness sufficiently to be dealt within the group, can be accessed in this and the remaining sessions.

Population and Conditions

This intervention may be used, in both short- and long-term groups, when the entire group is terminating. It is important that the therapist be comfortable with the use of guided imagery and is able to explain the justifications for its use to group members. Moreover, imagery may create various levels of anxiety in some members and a permissive style is crucial: for example, no group member needs to close his or her eyes unless he or she is comfortable doing so and any member can choose not to actively participate. (Resources are suggested in the Bibliography for therapists who wish to explore imagery and trance further [Klipperstein, 1991; Yapko, 2003].) If unfamiliar with utilizing guided imagery or trance, it is suggested that the therapist write out the script and/or practice the intervention (including timing) prior to the group.

A Guided-Imagery Intervention

- Using your own language, introduce the imagery by explaining to group that as they will be ending in _____ weeks you would like to take them on a journey of imagination to a time after the group is actually over.
- Secure verbal permission and/or head nods to do so, after answering any questions that might come up about guided imagery. Give group a time frame for how long the imagery portion will last, usually about ten to fifteen minutes.
- Make certain that enough processing time is left in the therapy session, at least forty-five minutes but preferably an hour. You can refer back to the imagery in subsequent sessions.
- After utilizing an approximately five-minute induction of your own choosing (Yapko, 2003) create a scene one month following the end of the group; utilize all senses and incorporate seasonal information. Remember to speak slowly, softly, and distinctly. Leave pauses (see the following example) for members to develop their own imagery and access their memories.

Example

Allow yourself to imagine sitting on the beach on a beautiful, sunny day in July . . . It is warm but not too warm. . . . A breeze is gently blowing and you can feel the sun's rays on your skin. . . . You smell the tang of the salt air, the scent of sunscreen. . . . The sound of the waves gently washing onto the shore is like background music. . . . You watch the people playing in the water, enjoying their pleasure. . . . You sit comfortably, supported with the warm sand. There is nothing you have to do, nowhere you need to go, . . . you are comfortable, relaxed. . . . You notice, to your surprise . . . that the muted sound of the voices of other people on the beach brings you back to a vivid awareness of this group, like you were watching a video.

With that video playing in your head, you allow yourself to look carefully at each face in the group. . . . Allow yourself to be surprised at what you notice . . . for I do not know and you do not know just what this awareness might be for you. Be aware of who you wish to look at further, just like when you were in the group, perhaps noticing who you may find it easy . . . or difficult to look in their eyes. . . . Imagine each person looking at you . . . and because this video has sound, you can hear each member speaking. . . . You can allow your mind to drift deeper and focus on what is most important to you in these images. . . . Perhaps you are relieved that you did not avoid the ending of the group because it may be difficult to say goodbye or may have reminded you of other endings in your life. . . . Allow yourself to be fully aware of how you felt in the group with each of the members. . . . Who, if anyone, did you feel attracted to and who did you feel you needed to have distance from? Allow yourself to be aware of how that experience happened. . . . Did anyone in the group remind you of someone in your "real life" and did this affect how you interacted with them? You can gently notice if you told members of their impact on you, either positive or negative or in between? If not, how did you make that choice? . . . Who do you wish you had supported more? . . . Or confronted? . . . How did you make those choices to hold back? . . . Perhaps you kept yourself from getting more of what you wanted out of group? . . . Or, did you worry that you had asked for "too much"? . . . Allow yourself to imagine what might happen if you talk about these feelings. . . . As you continue this fantasy, be aware of any unfinished business. Imagine having attempted to work this through. . . . And, as this imagery begins to end: From whom did you learn? And what was that awareness? . . . and what have you learned from the group as a whole? What has been said, and experienced that you may wish to take with you into the rest of your life? Take a minute to review these experiences . . . allow yourself to hold them in your memory for the future . . . (leave a full minute of silence) . . . and now, come back to this room, with your awareness that our group is not yet over in reality and you have an opportunity to use this guided imagery experience to deeply utilize the rest of the time we have together . . .

Optional

Is there anything that the [use names/leaders] *did that helped you open up and use the group? Anything that the therapist did or said that led you to shut down?*

Note

After making sure all group members are fully awakened (counting backward from 5 to 1 works well), begin processing in your usual manner. Although there will usually be group members who have an easier time disclosing and may volunteer to begin, make sure to bridge to all members of the group if the participants do not do this for themselves. You can use the questions in the trance for prompts. It is also possible to refer back to the experience in subsequent groups.

Conclusion and Contraindication

In our underritualized culture, group therapy provides many opportunities for experiment and learning, including the processing of termination. Although caution may need to be exercised in groups of clients with high degrees of dissociative processes, utilizing well-timed and directive, guided imagery can significantly enhance this crucial last step of group life.

References

AGPA, Science to Service Task Force (2007). *Practice Guidelines for Group Psychotherapy.* www.agpa.org/guidelines/AGPA%20Practice%20Guidelines%202007-PDF.pdf.

Klipperstein, H. (1991). *Ericksonian Hypnotherapeutic Group Inductions.* New York: Brunner/Mazel.

Mangione, L., Forti, R., & Iacuzzi, C.M. (2007). Ethics and endings in group psychotherapy: Saying good-bye and saying it well. *International Journal of Group Psychotherapy*, 57, 25–40.

Yapko, M. (2003). *Trancework: An Introduction to the Practice of Clinical Hypnosis* (Third edition). New York: Brunner-Routledge.

Miriam Iosupovici, MSW, is in private practice with offices in Imperial Beach and San Diego, CA. She retired from UCSD (University of California, San Diego) where she coordinated the student Psychological & Counseling Services group program, developing and facilitating their APA-accredited internship group therapy training component.

75 Diminishing Dissociative Experiences for War Veterans in Group Therapy

Vivien Henderson

Theory

Dissociation is one mechanism that is used by the ego as a way to maintain its integrity for survival, and is a response to severe trauma (Gabbard, 1994). Research suggests that childhood physical abuse may be an antecedent to the development of combat-related post-traumatic stress disorder (PTSD) (Bremner, Southwick, Johnson, Yehuda and Charney, 1993). When doing group therapy with a veteran who is known to dissociate it can present a number of challenges for the group therapist. In particular, it is important for the therapist to be able to hold the patient's unbearable mental states of mind in mind for the patient (Hinshelwood, 1994). Having worked with war veterans for eight years, a case will be presented as a descriptor of the dissociative experience.

Freud's theory of repression and memory disturbance provides the therapist with valuable insights for working with these patients (Freud, 1896). In addition, Klein (1975) uses the clinical approach of working with the leading anxieties, and Bion's concept of "container" provides essential knowledge for this work (Bion, 1961). "Bion's *Experiences in Groups* served as a mandate to investigate primitive affects and object relations in groups" (Schermer, 1994, p. 15).

Description of the Group

In the earlier years, the groups were residential in the hospital for the first four weeks. The program was intense, providing psychoeducational groups, individual therapy, and group psychotherapy. Attendance was daily with home visitations for the weekends. After the four-week intensive phase, the men then came one day weekly for eight weeks.

Although the program has changed over time, with the shift being toward non-residential programs it still remains a time limited one of twelve weeks with a maximum number of eight members in the group.

Interventions

Brief Case Example with Concomitant Intervention Procedures

One day during the group process, there was a sudden loud banging noise in the ceiling and workmen shouting information to each other. This was a sudden unexpected event for all of us. Our dissociative patient leaped up from his chair, his eyes looking around wildly with terror; he could not decide whether to go up into the ceiling and attack the workers or run away. I took the entire group down the hallway to the kitchen where we continued with the work over a cup of tea, talking about the effects this sudden intrusion had upon all of them. By providing structure and containment (being in a smaller safer space with the whole group together) this man began to calm down and stayed until the group time came to an end.

Dissociative Patient as Barometer of Group Anxiety and Necessary Intervention

I use the patient who is clinically diagnosed with a dissociative disorder as a barometer for measuring the level of anxiety in the group.

To reduce the increased levels of anxiety, greater structure is implemented, through a number of options, within the group. The therapy moves according to the level of anxiety manifested by this patient. When the level of anxiety escalates to the degree that the risk of dissociation becomes prevalent with the concomitant possibility of a "flight or fight" response—structure needs to be implemented.

When the patient took "flight" out the door, I held him verbally, and took the group to the kitchen down the hall, on this occasion, to provide the necessary structure and containment and change away from the immediate environment.

Another measurement of anxiety with this man was the rate with which his memory began returning. Initially, he had almost no memory of things having occurred in his past. As his memory began to return, he described it as being like a board, with "pegs" popping up on it. This is exactly what we wish to occur. The reliving of the traumatic event(s) as a cathartic release for this patient's journey into recovery.

Clients' Responses to the Intervention

Following the traumatic intrusion into the group room, a state of chaos prevailed initially with a very high level of arousal amongst the group members. This was especially prevalent with the dissociative man in particular as being undecided whether to "fight" or "take flight." Although verbally "holding" the dissociative man, the group members began to calm down once a decision was made to move them all to the safe space of the kitchen down the corridor. They began to feel safe and relieved by the added structure and containment.

The dissociative patient managed to stay with the group. His level of anxiety was an excellent mirror of the group members' anxiety. Managing the anxiety level of this man and the anxiety of the group members was paramount. It also instilled a higher level of trust of the patients toward the therapist who was seen to be like an officer and able to cope with the unexpected in the "battlefield" and lead them to safety.

Conclusion and Contraindications

The dissociative patient can find a group program to be most helpful in the recovery process provided his level of anxiety is kept at a reasonable level. As a patient's memory begins to return he begins recalling events from many years gone by which increases his anxiety level. Prior to our program, this patient's memory was mostly a blank. It has also been demonstrated that when exposed to extremely stressful traumatic situations, containment for the reduction in anxiety through structure, and change of physical environment can contribute to maintaining the integrity of the patient's ego functioning in the "here and now." This provides the patient with the opportunity of multiple options in coping with sudden and unexpected trauma. It is hoped that upon repetitive experiences with these new options, the patient will be able to implement same when he begins to feel the increase in future anxieties during his road to recovery.

A salient contraindication is that it is not advisable to work in a group setting with such patients outside a hospital setting unless one is a very experienced clinician. The possibility of sudden decompensation and dissociation is not always predictable and could present considerable difficulties for the neophyte therapist.

References

Bion, W. (1961). *Experiences in Groups*. London: Tavistock.
Bremner, J.B., Southwick, S.M., Johnson, D.R., Yehuda, R. and Charney, D.S. (1993). Childhood physical abuse and combat-related posttraumatic stress disorder in Vietnam veterans. *American Journal of Psychiatry*, 150: 235–239.
Freud, S. (1896). Further remarks on the neuro-psychoses of defense. In James Strachey (Ed.). *The Standard Edition of the Complete Psychological Works of Sigmund Freud*, Vol. 3, London: Hogarth, 1953.
Gabbard, G. (1994). *Psychodynamic Psychiatry in Clinical Practice*. The DSM-IV Edition. Washington, DC: American Psychiatric Press Inc.
Hinshelwood, R.D. (1994). Attacks on the reflective space: Containing primitive emotional states. In V.L. Schermer and M. Pines (Eds.) *Ring of Fire* (pp. 86–106). London: Routledge.
Klein, M. (1975). *Envy and Gratitude*. London: Hogarth.

Schermer, V.L. (1994). Between theory and practice, light and heat on the use of theory in the Ring of Fire. In V.L. Schermer and M. Pines (Eds.) *Ring of Fire* (pp. 9–35). London: Routledge.

Vivien Henderson, BA, Grad Dip App. Psych., is a registered Psychologist and Individual and Group psychotherapist. She worked as a clinician in the Post Traumatic Stress Disorders Outpatient Unit with war veterans at the Austin Repatriation Hospital Heidleberg, Melbourne, Australia.

76 I Am Part of the Group Matrix
Ben Rippa

Theoretical Considerations

Foulkes (1964), the creator of group analysis, defines group matrix as the network of all communications in a group. It represents the conscious and unconscious expressions between the group members, including the conductor. Foulkes introduced the term *conductor* which compares the group therapist to the musical conductor, who is not the composer who wrote the music, but the interpreter of the music. The group analyst, or conductor, is part of the group and yet can observe it from the outside. Group matrix is a theoretical construct of the operative dynamic interaction in the group process. It is also possible to approach the group matrix as a creative building process of the web of communications. Like a colorful tapestry, each member participates with his or her special needle and thread color (Rippa, 1998). Emphasizing the creative quality of the matrix, Cortesao (1968) points out that in Latin, "matrix" means a mother, a womb, a place of origin and growth. The group matrix is intimately related to the attitude and contribution of the group analyst.

Understanding and Activating the Group

1. *Point out the "mirror" phenomenon.* The client sees himself or herself reflected in the interaction of other group members. He or she sees them reacting in a way similar to himself or herself or in contrast to his or her own behavior. He or she also gets to know himself or herself by the effect he or she has on others and the picture they form of him or her (Foulkes, 1964).
2. *Create awareness of "resonance" expressions.* Members of the group respond to a stimulating input with deep feelings discovered inside, so that the group as a whole, as a result of this input, may intensify a working-through process on the relevant issue (Roberts, 1984).
3. *Encourage the group to express insights and interpretations.* The group analyst does not adopt the role of unique expert. The analyst expresses his or her thoughts and feelings in a personal language, revealing himself or herself, within ethical principles (Foulkes & Anthony, 1989).

Description of Group and Client Population

This type of intervention is more efficient for clients who are capable of introspection and insight. Among those are therapeutic and training groups in clinics, therapeutic communities, institutes, and private practice. It is applicable for groups in organizations like groups of teachers or top managers. It is also effective for social issues such as addiction, probation, couples and family conflicts, and community problems.

It will not succeed with clients with poor ego strength and low internal resources. It is not recommended for very depressed clients or those in life-threatening conditions, or very isolated, or very antisocial clients.

Description of Interventions

When I am conducting a group, I sit on a chair similar to the other chairs in the room. I intervene verbally only after discussions or expressions of group clients and go along with the flow of interactions and respond with empathy to the points being discussed. I never impose an issue for discussion nor do I judge any disclosure(s) of group members.

I avoid summing up or presenting long interpretations and explanations. My aim is to avoid being the center of interaction. I respond to the group as a whole and, when necessary, I can work with individual problems. I watch for symptoms or expressions indicating a possible dangerous antigroup response (Nitsun, 1996). These antigroup responses may manifest themselves in behaviors such as scapegoating and acting out. I specifically am cognizant of the possibility and actualities of negative manifestations that can harm the group as a whole. My assumption is that the interactions will enrich, in a spiral movement, a deeper understanding of relevant repressed issues.

Case Examples

A Small Group of Students

Ada, a member of the training group, was very active from the beginning of the session. She shared a dream she had had the previous night, and continued focusing most of the attention on her unresolved problems with her parents, and cried from time to time. Close to the end of the session, Lily, a quiet client, made a personal remark saying that she (number eight of twelve children) feels sometimes neglected by her parents. Ada rejected abruptly Lily's intention to start a dialogue saying that there is no similarity. Lily, talking to Ada, said that she feels, again, a closed door and arrogance in Ada's attitude. Ada said that she doesn't know what Lily is talking about. At this moment I intervened asking Ada to try to look at Lily as a mirror that reflects what Lily sees. Three women participants continue to reflect to Ada what they see of her selfish and narcissistic attitude. Ada was astonished and remained silent until the end of the session.

A Small Group in an International Workshop

I conducted a small group of nine qualified European professionals, six women and three men. At the beginning of the second meeting, one female participant, Christine, a German psychologist, said that she remembers the end of an unpleasant dream. She was in a small airplane ready to land, but something went wrong and instead of landing, the plane began to shake and the passengers were anxious. When she woke up she was still afraid. Some colleagues tried to help her, unsuccessfully, to grasp the possible personal reasons for the anxious and insecure feelings. Goran, a Swedish psychiatrist, remembered a painful similar experience when flying, years ago, to London. The free associations continued, involving most of the group members who expressed their concerns to disclose personal issues that were aroused after Christine's dream. I said that I am also in this plane. I worry too, as the pilot, how to make a safe landing. I am a qualified "pilot," and I believe that in this trip everybody is involved. Claudia, an Italian participant, expressed her shame at her inability to speak because of her poor English, and I, the only one in the group who understood some Italian, translated her valuable interventions. In this friendly atmosphere, suddenly, Christine looked at me and said, "You know, my husband is from Israel. We are living in Heidelberg now, but he insists to go back and I don't know . . ." Other members opened new problems and discussed important conflicts. There was a readiness to share concerns. The group had a safe landing.

Typical Response to the Intervention

When clients are used to assuming a very dependent attitude, confusion and a sense of chaos often prevails during the first group sessions. A more direct intervention was expected from me. Many of the group members expressed their criticism openly and aggressively and I welcomed this behavior in order to show that it is possible to challenge authority and to be ready to confront frozen concepts about relationships and interpersonal communications. In future groups, the flow of interactions becomes easier, the silences shorter, and the silent participants less stubborn.

Conclusions and Contraindications

This type of intervention can be felt as leading to a "laissez-faire" group, that is, without any boundaries. It may appear so, but for me being part of the group matrix does not mean being an equal part. As the conductor, I watch the boundaries and hold the group together. I do not lead the group in a direction planned beforehand. I do not stand outside the group, but I help from the inside by interpreting and encouraging interpretations from clients in order to enhance their mutual understanding.

To be the conductor as part of the group matrix is a demanding task. I have to make certain that I am not crossing ethical boundaries and have to accept the uncertainty of not understanding everything. My emotional, sincere involvement in the flow of interpersonal communication may stimulate members of the group to attack me, pointing out aspects of my character that are sensitive for me. For example, when a client attacks me for being too mild or unassertive and stresses that this is why the group is stuck. A quick introspection on the countertransference situation brings me back to the role of conductor of the group. I have to rely on my own capability and experience and feel secure in my knowledge and be ready to be part of the continuous building process of the changing group matrix.

References

Cortesao, E. (1968). The Concept of Group Matrix. *Group Analysis–Group Psychotherapy Analytic Workshop*, 1(2) 35.

Foulkes, S.H. (1964). *Therapeutic Group Analysis*. New York: International Universities Press, Inc.

Foulkes, S.H. & Anthony, E.J. (1989). *Group Psychotherapy: The Psychoanalytic Approach* (Second edition). London: Karnac.

Nitsun, M. (1996). *The Anti-Group–Destructive Forces in the Group and Their Creative Potential*. New York: Routledge.

Rippa, B. (1998). Practical Aspects of the Group Matrix—A Theory in Practice Challenge for the Group Therapist. *Mikbatz, The Israeli Journal of Group Psychotherapy*, 4(1) 19–24.

Roberts, J.P. (1984). Resonance in Art Groups. *Group Analysis*, 17(3) 211–219.

Ben Rippa, born in 1930, received his PhD in 1982 from the University of Maryland, U.S.A. Ben is an honorary member of the IAGP, and an honorary member of the Israeli Institute of Group Analysis. In recent years his main interests include a client-oriented approach, applying aspects of Group Analysis to organizational consultancy and the junction of different practices to form effective intervention techniques.

77 To Err is Human
Turning Our Mistakes Into Useful Interventions
Dave M. Cooperberg

Therapist as Human

"You're my therapist and you forgot my name!" Some people in particular seem to need to see us as infallible—the One with the Answers. So what happens when we inevitably do make a mistake? This can be particularly difficult for the new group therapist whose sense of his or her own competency may not be as firm (Van Wagoner, 2000). How therapists handle their own, inevitable mistakes can define how well the group proceeds from there.

By mistakes, I am focusing on errors visible to the group that therapists make, not internal ones in our thinking, nor the ones the group members themselves will make. This could include anything from forgetting something significant about a member like their name, misinterpreting a member's expression or feeling, expressing a judgment that one or more members find hurtful, or even loudly passing gas. When a therapist makes a mistake that is obvious to the group, whether it reflects an objective or realistic countertransference to clients' personalities, or our own subjective transference to the client (Ormont, 1993), it still presents a useful opportunity if it can be worked in the group.

Therapists compound an error if they rush into putting it onto the members using verbiage such as, "And how do you feel about that?" without taking some personal responsibility. It is part of our job to help people be in touch with their feelings, but not when we use it as a defense. A public mistake creates an opportunity to role model healthy ways of dealing with errors and embarrassment, as well as revealing what issues are triggered for different members.

Group Clients

The groups I have worked with for the past thirty years have been outpatient, in-depth, ongoing, mostly process groups with members in the normal-neurotic range, and a few borderlines. My private practice has specialized in working with groups for gay-identified men. I believe working with visible therapist errors works well with a variety of therapy and support groups in this range of functioning.

The examples come from a small outpatient process group of six gay-identified men. Most have participated for over two years, one for two months, and one only three weeks. The newest member is aged twenty-eight, the rest are in their forties and fifties. The group starts with a brief check-in process, in which members express how they are feeling that evening as well as reporting anything significant that has happened during the prior week. Not having a waiting room, I put a sign out asking latecomers not to ring the bell, but wait until I get them.

Intervention

Mistakes happen. I am not suggesting intentionally doing something in order to elicit reactions from group members. In many ways this is about role modeling honesty, humility, and vulnerability as well as showing respect to members affected by the event. The ideal is to authentically take responsibility and use the event to help expose not only members' feelings in the moment, but any transferential expectations that were either re-enforced or contradicted by our behavior.

Step 1: Acknowledge Something Happened

One evening, soon after the initial check in, there was an interaction between long-term members Ralph and Ronald, which also served to avoid something upsetting one of the newer members had mentioned in check in. I started to comment on it and got their names reversed. Suddenly, I could see by their expressions that I had done something. An instant review made me realize that I had reversed their names, so I rolled my eyes in comedic recognition. Both started to laugh, followed by other group members. Taking the cue from their response, I continued by asking in a humorous way, how they felt now that I had exchanged their personalities.

This was both playful and serious. Ronald was clear there was no exchange of personalities, while acknowledging the pleasure he took in seeing my mistake. Ralph was typically less responsive, but also dismissed any difficulty with it, commenting on similar mistakes he had made. I then acknowledge, at times, showing some dyslexia, for some reason confusing their names—not their personalities—simply because both names start with an R. That helped Vince, another longtime group member, who is severely dyslexic, express how he feels when he makes such mistakes.

I had acknowledged the error, checked on responses, and could then have explored other issues such as embarrassment, any transferential emotions as well as the effects of the subgrouping of these two men. However, a new member had brought up a serious issue that was being skirted around. After acknowledging my mistake and checking immediate reactions, I chose to refocus back to what the group had been avoiding.

Step 2: Attend to the Transference and Other Projections

Members will have a variety of reactions. In taking responsibility for our actions, we do not want to inhibit members from recognizing and exploring their projections. In the following example, my error triggered basic feelings of inclusion/ exclusion in everyone, particularly in the person who was left waiting.

Peter was late for group, so I put the "Please Wait" sign out and the group began their check in. The last to check in was Juan, who had learned that morning that a friend had just died. Juan had joined the group two months earlier, three months after his mother's death, and one month after the end of a relationship. The group got involved in addressing his reactions, and I forgot to retrieve the sign. Unknown to me, Peter was waiting outside. Half an hour later, Peter rang the doorbell, reminding me to let him in.

Peter had been in the group for about nine months, working with major issues around intimacy and his feeling as if he did not really belong anywhere. I briefly apologized, and agreed when he asked, that it was my practice and responsibility to let people in after check in. He acknowledged some anger, but claimed it was about his issues, at first unwilling to directly address his anger to me.

After briefly checking in with Juan, I then turned to the group for reactions to what had happened to Peter. Members readily stated they would have felt very hurt, some more angry than hurt, if they had been forced to wait out there. A few added it would have been hard for them to ring the bell; after all, the sign had asked them not to do so.

Knowing that Peter had more feelings to express, I pointed out how I had reenacted one of Peter's worst fears. That freed him to more fully express his anger toward me, and relate more deeply what it triggered from his past. Other members empathized, discussing their own difficulties with feeling abandoned or rejected, as well as how difficult it was to confront an otherwise supportive authority. At the end I suggested to Peter that by ringing the bell, he not only avoided carrying his rage home by confronting me, but also asserted his membership in the group.

Response to Intervention

When I can acknowledge my mistakes the group responds positively in the following ways: (1) the group is more willing to process what my errors generate for them; (2) members feel more able to confront me as an authority, hence exploring more aspects of their transferences; (3) members feel more bonded with one another in dealing with me, making them more willing to hear one another rather than turn to me as the authority; and (4) members feel safer acknowledging their own mistakes to the group.

Conclusion

In terms of outpatient, higher-functioning groups, when, as therapists, we acknowledge our own mistakes as well as process the group's reactions to them we appear human and less mystical. This is dependent, of course, on the therapist's self-awareness and willingness to be transparent. In doing so, we turn our mistakes into rich opportunities to explore transferential and other issues, as well as role model how to accept interpersonal responsibilities.

Contraindications

No doubt there are individuals who are fragile in ways that they need to see us as strong and in control of all group dynamics, whereas seeing us stumble too soon could be frightening and destabilizing. Because of this, while it still can be appropriate, therapists need to be more cautious with visible mistakes when working with more dysfunctional populations.

References

Ormont, L. (1993). *The Group Therapy Experience—From Theory to Practice.* New York: St. Martin's Press.

Van Wagoner, S. (2000). Anger in Group Therapy. Countertransference and the Novice Group Therapist. In S. Fehr (Ed.). *Group Therapy In Private Practice* (pp. 63–75). Binghamton, NY: The Haworth Press.

Dave M. Cooperberg, MA, MFT, CGP, has been a member of AGPA since 1989. He has run workshops on the effectiveness of humor in psychotherapy and has been in private practice in San Francisco for the past thirty years. His specialty client population is gay-identified men.

78 The Ability to Verbalize One's Needs Clearly in a Geriatric Population

Toby Berman

Introduction

The ability to assert oneself appropriately is extremely important to good communication and leads to better mental health. The converse is true: individuals unable to assert themselves, clearly and appropriately, often suffer with poor mental health (Corey, 1995; Fehr, 2003; Yalom, 1985). Appropriate assertiveness can be taught in a group setting. Reasons verbalized for inability to assert oneself are excellent springboards for dynamic psychotherapeutic group work.

Description of Group

This particular group is open ended, having continued for over fifteen years with patients entering and leaving based on their own growth and particular needs. It is a geriatric group, with an age range of seventy to ninety-six years. All participants have had serious psychiatric illness such as major depression and bipolar disorder. There are no schizophrenics in the group. Most have been hospitalized for depression and about 25 percent have been treated with ECT. All are on psychotherapeutic medications.

The group fills multiple purposes: it offers a meeting place for very lonely people and allows them to feel connected. They feel cared about by me and other participants.

Patients' Statements Elicit the Type of Intervention

Most of my interventions are based on statements coming from the patients. One of my goals in the therapy is to lead the patients toward understanding the contributing factors that made them behave in inappropriate ways. I try to make these reasons conscious so that the patients can become more aware of their behaviors and change their behavioral patterns. I encourage the patients to reexamine underlying reasons for their behaviors.

Group Process

A patient has just come home from the hospital following treatment for major depression in a psychiatric unit after a radical mastectomy. She states:

I can't stand it in my home. Three nephews are there and there is a tent in the living room with two dogs and three cats. My cousin is there too and they have to move and we are waiting for checks to come in.

Therapist: Can you share with us why you are allowing this?
Patient: They are my family. I can't tell them it is too much for me.

Multiple questions are then asked by other group members. My focus is toward the inability, of the patient, to assert herself and get her needs met. Some questions that could be asked:

- How do you feel when you speak up?
- Are you afraid to hurt _____?
- Do you feel they won't love you?
- Are you able to speak up in other situations?
- What do you think would happen if you asserted yourself?
- As a child were you encouraged to speak up?
- Who in your family system encouraged you to assert yourself?
- Did anyone?
- What did your mother/father say if you spoke up?
- Did your family system value assertiveness or see it as selfish?
- What is self-love?

Various group members support the patient and her need to be able to assert herself. Inquire into the consequences of assertiveness and role-play:

- Will you feel good, bad, kind, unkind and to whom? Yourself or others?

Role-playing is done in the group with further exploration and explanation of feelings with the patient playing both sides in order to determine if the patient is projecting her personality onto others. This could be one of the inhibitory factors for the patient not disclosing to others how she is feeling. She may believe that on hearing what she feels, the other person would experience the same narcissistic injury the patient would experience if someone said that to her.

The discussion, after role-playing, considers how it feels to speak up, emphasizing self-love, self-care, appropriate assertiveness, and communication skills.

Conclusion

Geriatric groups are often bonded together by mutual caring and by advanced age, disability, and concerns regarding helping one another to avoid further decompensation, hospitalization, falls, and ultimate death.

There is a sense of hopefulness within the group; they pray for one another (for the forthcoming surgeries), recurring concerns, etc. In short, they have become a family and I am part of their family, sharing in and showing that the human condition is part of all of us and not just the patients. Most members come very regularly but some come only when they can get transportation. None of them come in their own car and all are dependent on other sources. Many never miss group and it is their most important outing and connection to people and the outside world.

Contraindications

Due to the nature of this particular patient population there is a very real contraindication, that is, the possibility of patient decompensation. Care and judgment should be utilized. During these events, patients are encouraged to avoid self-blame and are encouraged to use new behaviors and bring feelings and reassurances back to the group. Another serious contraindication, although obvious, is that the clinician must enjoy working with a much older population. If the clinician does not enjoy or feel comfortable with an older population, there is the possibility of therapist elder abuse.

References

Corey, G. (1995). *Theory and Practice of Group Counseling* (Fourth edition). Monterey, CA: Brooks/Cole.
Fehr, S. S. (2003). *Introduction to Group Therapy: A Practical Guide* (Second edition). Binghamton, NY: Haworth Press.
Yalom, I. (1985). *The Theory and Practice of Group Psychotherapy* (Third edition). New York: Basic Books.

Toby Berman, Psy.D., is on staff at Mount Sinai Hospital in Miami Beach, Florida. Dr. Berman practices group and individual psychotherapy as well as psychological testing. She has written chapters and articles in many books and journals.

79 Norm Repair

Joseph Shay

Theoretical Orientation

All groups have norms. But different groups develop very different norms. Norms, simply put, are the shared implicit and explicit rules of a group, and comprise a major ingredient of the culture of the group. They include the stated rules such as "you are expected to arrive on time," and more implicit rules such as "do not sit in the therapist's chair." Some norms are simple, such as "wait for someone to pause before you speak," while others can be more complex, for example, "do not express too much angry affect because the group gets frightened by it."

How do norms get established? Group members often carry into group therapy the norms of society, since norms are ubiquitous in society: "Social norms are the 'rules' that govern behavior within each society" (Agazarian & Peters, 1981, pp. 96–97). In this regard, new members to a group often expect to be welcomed as though they were entering a social situation as guests. If unprepared for the fact that this is not typically a group norm (especially in psychodynamic groups), they may feel rejected or mistreated.

Part of the therapist's task in group therapy is to initiate constructive norms and to recognize and modify disruptive or nontask-related norms, some of which are promoted by group members. Yalom and Leszcz (2005) write, "Norms of a group are constructed both from expectations of the members for their group and from the explicit and implicit directions of the leader and more influential members" (p. 122). Rutan, Stone, and Shay (2007, p. 36) state, "Since the therapist is a potent initiator of group norms, reinforcement through interest or noninterference serves to communicate and establish appropriate ways of interacting within the group." Ulman (2005) remarks, "I try from the outset to encourage the development of group norms that foster curiosity about everything that happens in group" (p. 94).

Norms can vary—some can evolve and change over time, while others become entrenched and difficult to modify. A particularly difficult situation arises when a norm is established inadvertently, and then ingrained, out of the conscious awareness of therapist or group members. These norms can be especially difficult to modify. The intervention described in the next section was developed to address one such situation.

Description of Groups

This intervention can be used in groups of all kinds since norms exist in all groups, and can go awry in any of the various group settings. In long-term groups, norms can, of course, become more entrenched and therefore harder to modify. The intervention was, however, used in a long-term open-ended co-ed group, with the intervention made about one year into the life of the group.

Intervention

In this long-term group of eight, five females and three males, aged thirty to fifty-two, members had developed a real facility for deep exploration of problematic or affect-laden situations, including situations in their daily lives as well as powerful experiences within the group itself. I viewed this group as an extremely high-functioning, successful one in which members routinely addressed core aspects of their lives, and worked hard to take responsibility for their thoughts, feelings, and behaviors. It was also a group in which members commonly got in touch with very painful dysphoric affects, with tears common in many sessions. Typically, after a member had begun to cry, other group members were attentively silent, with some of them tearing up as well in empathic support. The member who had been crying might then continue his or her discourse, and then respond to comments or associations from the other members. At times, however, when a member was experiencing acute emotional distress—sobbing or wailing, for example— the members remained silent, seemingly not knowing what to say. At such times, I often felt a need to be overtly supportive to the pained member, and would make one of several comments. These comments ranged from "take your time," suggesting there was no hurry to stop crying, to "how painful this is for you and perhaps for others in the group," to "when you are able, perhaps you can put your feelings into words." These interventions typically resulted in deepened emotional expression by the group member after which the member would begin to speak, and to elaborate on the experience.

Although I felt satisfied with these kinds of interventions, there were a few occasions where I thought that it would be better if the other group members intervened first, either with empathic statements, or questions, or their own associations. So, I let the silence linger. And it lingered, and lingered, and lingered—as the group waited for *me* to respond. I then realized that I had inadvertently shaped a complicated group norm: *when a group member is in deep distress, Dr. Shay will respond in a compassionate way. And I don't need to respond because he will.*

Recognizing this, and feeling uncomfortable with it, I decided to reshape the norm. At first, I tried outwaiting the group members as they were watching me and waiting for me, but this not only felt uncomfortable for me—because I was changing the norm without articulating this to them—but also uncomfortable for them, and more importantly might be experienced as abandonment by the acutely distressed member. I finally decided to use a more active intervention to reshape this norm.

At the start of a group, after the usual announcements about attendance and upcoming absences (another group norm), I said, "I want to begin by apologizing to the group for having made a mistake which I am now aware of. And I want to change this. As we saw last week, and in many previous groups, you all work very hard in this room and have developed a real ability to support each other, challenge one another, and feel deeply for other people in the group. When one of you becomes distressed in here—last week it was Ann, two weeks ago Bill, and last month Dave and Carol, but most of you have been there—I realize that I have often been the first one to speak when there is high emotion in the room. I think I have accidentally "trained" you to wait for me to be the first to speak, and I think that is my mistake because we now have this as a norm—wait for Dr. Shay to break the silence and then others can speak. This is a mistake on my part because I believe that you are capable as a group of being as supportive and helpful as I try to be, and in fact, my responding may have gotten in your way. So, I want to own responsibility for having shaped this norm, and now I'm owning responsibility for telling you that I'm going to try to change it. At first this might be uncomfortable for all of us, but I think this is for the best and I'm glad to hear any reactions."

Typical Responses

I have used this approach in various groups to modify other norms I have inadvertently shaped, e.g., too little attention to member lateness, members eating food during a session, so the responses to this situation above are typical in groups.

One member said, "Wow, Dr. Shay. You never say that much at one time." Another member followed, "I like it when you're the first to make a comment when someone is crying. I don't really know what to say." A third said, "I actually noticed how we always get quiet, but that was fine with me." And a fourth added, "I guess you think we can really do this." After a silence, I said, "I *do* think you can. And I think the group as a whole can find its own voice when someone is distressed, although it may feel awkward at first. If there are more reactions or feelings now, I'm glad to hear them, or even at a later point in the group when we see how it goes." A fifth group member then took the floor and spoke about how no one in his family even seemed to notice when he was upset, leading to a productive exploration for this member and for the group as well as they reacted to his story.

In subsequent group meetings—not in this one—group members did indeed respond to distraught group members, often after an initial silence, recognizing I trusted them to do so.

Conclusion

Group therapists are fundamentally responsible for shaping—and reshaping—group norms, although the group actively participates in this process, typically to support a norm but at times to sabotage it. The key for the therapist is to be consistently aware of the norms that have been and are being established, some intentional, some inadvertently, and decide what to do about those that work against optimal group functioning. At times, an indirect approach to reshaping a norm can work nicely, e.g., when the therapist simply draws attention to a particular area of concern, e.g., group lateness. At other times a more direct approach is called for.

Contraindication

There is one relative contraindication for the use of such a direct approach. When groups are in an extremely oppositional phase of the group's life, this may cause a direct approach to fail. With a solid therapeutic alliance, however, this contraindication is mitigated.

References

Agazarian, Y. M. & Gantt, S. (2005). The systems-centered approach to the group-as-a whole. *Group, 29,* 163–185.

Agazarian, Y. & Peters, R. (1981). *The visible and the invisible group.* London: Routledge & Kegan Paul.

Rutan, J. S., Stone, W. N., & Shay, J. J. (2007). *Psychodynamic group psychotherapy* (Fourth edition). New York: Guilford.

Ulman, K. H. (2005). Axis II had me spinning. In L. Motherwell & J. J. Shay (Eds.). *Complex dilemmas in group therapy: Pathways to resolution* (pp. 92–95). New York: Brunner-Routledge.

Yalom, I. D., & Leszcz, M. (2005). *The theory and practice of group psychotherapy* (Fifth edition). New York: Basic Books.

Joseph Shay, PhD, CGP, FAGPA, a psychologist in private practice in Cambridge, MA, has an affiliate position at the Harvard Medical School in the Department of Psychiatry, supervises at McLean and Massachusetts General Hospitals, and is on the faculty of the Psychoanalytic Couple and Family Institute of New England, the Northeastern Society for Group Psychotherapy, and the Massachusetts General Hospital Center for Psychodynamic Therapy and Research. Dr. Shay is the co-author of *Psychodynamic Group Psychotherapy* (4th and 5th editions) and the co-editor of *Odysseys in Psychotherapy* and *Complex Dilemmas in Group Therapy*.

80 Alchemy and Transformation
The Disturber in Group

Avraham Cohen

Expose the Gold

Most every group will have at least one person who is a "disturber," an individual who is pressing and persistent in ways that consistently disrupt the group, the process, and the leader. Such individuals are frequently the catalyst for much hair pulling, sweat, and anxiety for the leader. The tendency to diagnose and look for ways to suppress or remove such group members is very high. The DSM-IV (American Psychiatric Association, 2000) is full of labels that will find a home with these people. When I used to work with seriously disturbed adolescents in a residential treatment setting many years ago, oppositional defiant disorder was a very frequent and popular diagnosis. What this translated into is that the identified teen did not agree with staff on a frequent basis, and that this disagreement took a very disagreeable form. Although we have a whole new set of labels now, I believe we are still up against the same problem. We still have those who are disturbing in the world and in our educational and psychotherapy groups.

The idea that will be identified for this intervention is that the disturber is part of the alchemy of any group and to follow the metaphor a little further, has the potential to transform "base" material into gold. In other words, the disturber carries information that the group needs. The problem is that the signal that indicates the gold is not easily decoded. The individual who disturbs is the one that draws the tendency to shun, exclude, marginalize, and/or diagnose. The intervention that will be described is how to identify the disturber and how to "expose" the gold.

An Educational or Psychotherapy Group

This intervention is responsive to disturbance and perturbation that is initiated in the group by an individual. It has proven to be effective in both educational and psychotherapy groups. This intervention is beneficial for the individual who disturbs. It provides the opportunity to receive personal validation for the message that he or she carries. The disturbers feel included rather than their more usual experience of marginalization, and they gain some experience to convey their thoughts and feelings in a more skillful and effective way. An additional benefit for the whole group is to see the potential within "shadow" material and to learn about the process of transformation.

Description of Intervention

Example

A student in a counseling class complained consistently and constantly that the class was not "very real." She talked about the fact that everybody was being "too nice." She was so persistent with these comments that it was evident that other students were getting frustrated and not saying anything. They were avoiding her at breaks. I overheard comments and had some comments said to me directly about her being a "problem." One day she again began to talk about how unauthentic everyone was and how could we expect to be role models of real human beings if we were all so fake. She implicated me by saying that real leadership would not allow this phoniness to go on. I watched and saw eyeballs rolling, nervousness, and frustration. I felt that we were at critical mass.

I said to the group: "I am observing a lot of physical movement in the group. I wonder if anyone would care to put some words to their experience." There is silence. Finally, one student says, "I am really frustrated that we keep hearing the same complaining over and over." Another student said, "I wish you (looking toward me) would do something. I think there is too much time in this class devoted to people's problems and their feelings."

Inwardly I could feel a little tension mounting in me. Mutiny and rebellion seemed to be in the air. A number of other students spoke along similar lines; each with their own slightly different view of things. I said nothing about what was said. I did encourage students to speak with the odd word and with nonverbal cues. The disturber student finally spoke. She said, "I still don't hear any real honesty." The proverbial pin could have dropped at this point. I wondered if anyone would move to kill her. I turned to her and said, "Thank you for calling things as you see them. I would be very appreciative if you would be so kind as to demonstrate the kind of honesty that you are speaking about. I don't feel that even you are really saying what you really have to say."

Again silence, but this time a little briefer. Her eyes were darting here and there. She spoke again:

> I think that people are very mad at me and I also think that there are issues between people in the group. And, I think everybody is being nice to me or avoiding me, being nice to people with whom they are annoyed, and that we are all being fake. I want us to get real. If someone has something to say to me, I would like you to say it.

Now a very pregnant silence. I spoke:

> If anyone has something to say, I invite you to say it *and* (this next part is said in a tone that makes clear this is a conjunction and emotional safety reminder, and not an admonition to be silent) I want to remind you of the ground rules. No name calling. Speak for yourself. Speak to the person you are addressing directly. Take responsibility for your thoughts and feelings. If you have something to say to someone, check with him or her whether he or she is willing and able to hear it.

The room was thick with a mixture of anxiety and excitement. Clearly, something real was happening. I will not go into the details but a lot of students had a lot to say and not just to the disturber student. The atmosphere changed from what could be described as "as-if" to "as-it-actually is."

Format for Disturber Inclusion

- An atmosphere and culture is nurtured that encourages genuine openness and honesty.
- So-called problem students or disturbers are encouraged to express their thoughts and feelings rather than remove or suppress them.
- A culture must be established that provides a container within which an "other" person can be himself or herself.
  - This is done by the appropriate and authentic metadimensions (Cohen, 2002), expressions by the group leader along with the content of these expressions that explains that it is immanently acceptable to share in the group unpopular and potentially disturbing views and ideas.
  - The leader's modeling of acceptance is central to creating emotional safety and the culture of inclusion for group members, including the disturber.
- The group leader must watch for and jump on the earliest signs of a disturber, rather than the more common responses, which are to ignore, marginalize, and hope that she or he will not do "that" again.
- Early responses from the group leader send important signals to the group:
  - this group will be different than what most of you have experienced previously
  - safety will be attended to by acknowledging what is usually marginalized
  - individuals will be valued for their contributions, even when that contribution is in an unusual form
  - scapegoating will not be a part of the group, other than as material for the group's work.

Typical Response to the Intervention

The initial response to this intervention is surprise and even shock. For a leader who is new to this type of intervention, it is important to work with your own anxieties and feelings about the person who is disturbing and the group as a whole. You do not have to be perfect in your responses, but it is important to be aware of your experience and be ready to bring into the group as part of the intervention and for modeling purposes. I cannot emphasize too strongly the importance of demonstrating authenticity in our responses.

As the group begins to transform its culture to one of acceptance, curiosity, and interest in the disturbing, unusual, and previously marginalized, a new way of being and possibility appears. Group members report feeling empowered rather than helpless, angry, and victimized by those who are different and difficult for them.

Contraindications

Most contraindications can be attended to by skillful selection of group members. Selecting out individuals who are extreme in their responses, very fearful, and either unable to demonstrate self-awareness or incapable of making any use of the awareness that they do have will probably not be able to participate meaningfully even with this inclusive and supportive approach.

Occasions may present where it is important to identify disturbing expressions that must be dealt with intrapsychically prior to and sometimes along with the inclusive intervention. The contraindication here is that the skill of attending to all these dynamics simultaneously may be more than the leader is equipped to handle without further training and supervision in the use of this intervention.

Conclusion

This intervention depends on the leader's ability to work with a number of experiences simultaneously. Inclusion in this real way of so-called disturbers, promotes and teaches ideas of deep democracy (Cohen, 2004), which have implications beyond the classroom and therapy group. Such learning has a great potential for a *ripple effect* on those who are close to students and clients in the group and to those who are close to those who are affected by the ripple outside the group. The role of the teacher/group leader is central as facilitator and role model.

References

American Psychiatric Association. (2000). *Diagnostic and Statistical Manual of Mental Disorders* DSM-IV-TR (Text Revision). Washington, DC: American Psychiatric Publishing.

Cohen, A. (2002, April). The secret of effective psychotherapy: Metaskills. *The Private Practitioner Bulletin of the Canadian Counselling Association*, 1(4), 3–4.

Cohen, A. (2004). A process-directed approach to learning process directed counseling skills. *Canadian Journal of Counseling*, 38(3), 152–164.

Dr. Avraham Cohen, recipient of numerous academic and professional awards, is a Professor at City University of Seattle (Vancouver, Canada site) where he is also the director for the full-time Master in Counseling program. He has been in private practice as a psychotherapist for 28 years, has presented his work at national and international conferences, and is author and co-author of many publications.

81 Family Member Association

Carol Scott Drury

The Polite and the Not So Polite

I have the fortune or misfortune, depending on your perspective, to work with primarily very nice and gracious clients. However, that is not always an enviable position when trying to facilitate a group of highly passive and respectful adults in a psychodynamic psychotherapeutic group. The issues arise on how to encourage them to confront one another with honest feedback; how to ask for honest feedback and expect to get it; how to practice new behaviors like assertiveness or even some of their lifelong *forbidden* emotions like anger; or how to get them to become fully integrated personalities that encompass the polite and the not so polite.

This intervention is a safe way to start that process, especially for clients who are not comfortable with negative or hostile emotions. This will be particularly important as the group moves from the second stage to the third stage in the development of the group. According to Yalom (1995, p. 303) "the group embrace will seem ritualistic unless differentiation and conflict in the group are permitted . . . [and] . . . when all affects can be expressed and constructively worked through . . . does the group become a mature work group . . ."

Client Population

I work with open-ended process-oriented groups, as well as support groups, and couples groups. I have used this technique in my open-ended heterogeneous group, closed men's group, open-ended divorce support group, and closed couples group. All my clients are private-practice, self-pay, and fairly high functioning. I believe the technique is simple enough, however, to work with most populations in most types of groups.

Guidelines for the Intervention

There are several variations of this intervention, but use your imagination to come up with any number of others:

1. If someone in the group is having an issue with a relative (or coworker) I may ask them if anyone in the group reminds them of that person. I will then ask them if they would like to practice with the group member. We then process what it is about the group member that reminds them of the family member or coworker.
2. Sometimes when it is quiet in the group, I may say, *does anyone in the group remind you of a family member?* We then process what the similarities are, allowing both group members potential insight.
3. Ask members to reconstruct their family of origin with the other group members.
4. As part of a psychodrama exercise, I may ask a group member to select another group member who reminds them of a family member to play the role of the family member and then process the similarities after the psychodrama exercise. This allows both members potential insight.
5. For group members who do not have large immediate or extended families to draw from and may still have difficulty confronting directly I may ask them to relate to characters from history, movies, and literature rather than family members.

Typical Responses

A woman who had a very difficult time with confrontation wanted desperately to tell her critical brother-in-law to stop finding fault with everything she did, but was intimidated. I asked her who in the group most reminded her of her brother-in-law. She selected the group "grump" and was willing to practice on him, and he agreed, as well. What was interesting was not that she selected him, but the group discussion that followed. It was the first time the group had addressed the grumpiness and negativity of the grumpy member directly. It had always been there, but treated as a cute idiosyncrasy, when, in fact, it was obviously annoying to everyone.

During a quiet time in the group, I asked if there was another member who reminded them of a relative. One woman immediately raised her hand and said "Oh yes," as she pointed to the well-dressed and always in control professional young man sitting across from her. "You remind me of my arrogant uncle," she continued. He appeared to be stunned, as did the rest of the group for this was perhaps the first hint of negativity whispered within the confines of this group. As the group progressed, it became quickly apparent that the young man had no idea that he might be perceived this way, especially when other group members chimed in and supported the initial observation. It was an enormous risk for the first member, a huge step for the group, and it opened the door for further exploration on the young man's part on how his utter sense of control might be perceived by others.

Conclusion

I have never used a variation of this technique without a surprising response. I cannot predict exactly what the response will be, but it has never failed to move a member or the group forward—sometimes in small ways and sometimes in big ones. The intervention is easy to apply and could be used in various groups at any phase of the group, but I have found it most powerful in the transition from the second to third phase of the psychodynamic process-oriented group.

Contradiction

Like any intervention there is always the possibility that there might be a contraindication. In this particular one, the contraindication would be in the form of an inexperienced clinician. It takes experience to know when to use it and when to just sit and let the group do its own work, but I do not think this one can be harmful. At worst, it could be overused or it could seem inappropriate or trite if used at the wrong time.

Reference

Yalom, I.D. (1995). *The theory and practice of group psychotherapy* (Fourth edition). New York: Basic Books.

Carol Scott Drury, PhD, NCC, CRC, is in Private Practice in Maryland. Early in her career she trained in group work at the Psychodrama Institute in LA and currently uses the Imago Model of Relationships when working with couples. In addition, she addresses the mind/body connection by using guided imagery in her work with clients.

82 Building Self-Esteem Using Assertiveness Training and Props
Sheila Sazant

Equality in Human Relations

For many individuals, group therapy provides special skills to deal with problems in social situations. Among the difficulties experienced by clients is the inability to ask for acknowledgment of their personal rights and needs. The foundation of this problem may be a resistance to express both positive and negative feelings, a lack of confidence to be direct, and a judgment that their requests are unreasonable and unacceptable to others. Alberti and Emmons (1990) suggest that "Assertive behavior promotes equality in human relationships, enabling us to act in our own interests, and to stand up for ourselves without undue anxiety, to express honest feelings comfortably and to exercise personal rights without denying the rights of others" (p. 7).

The group experience provides for clients a forum for which they can reflect upon others' responses to their words and actions. It creates an opportunity to see themselves through the eyes of their group brethren and allows them to respond to their issues in ways that disclose their feelings and promote more direct responses. As a confidence builder, group therapy provides a safe environment wherein an insecure individual can practice intimidating interactions and learn various perspectives from others in similar situations. Support and reassurance from the group can be very empowering.

As a therapist now dealing with clients reluctant to advocate for their personal rights and feelings, I am reminded and often reflect on an intervention suggested to me while I was a member in group therapy many years ago.

Intervention: Attention! Attention! Now Hear This!

Joining a group was both a frightening and stimulating prospect. The group experience exposed me to a cross-section of society, which included professional men and women, married and unmarried, and parents living with and without children.

Among the most salient of challenges was my fear of venturing out of my "comfort zone" to self-actualize in an area outside my homemaking duties and find a job in the workplace. One of the difficulties of achieving and living a more psychologically healthy existence is the resistance of family members who prefer to remain unchanged by a new lifestyle of one of its pivotal members. Comments such as "I have not had a good meal in many weeks!" to "There is no orange juice" were expressed on a regular basis. Success in this arena meant my own acceptance and value of these achievements and my assertion that things have changed and that others in the household were now responsible for their daily living conditions. Being assertive at home and in the workplace required a skill that demanded practice and rehearsal, which the group experience supplied.

Exercise

My therapist suggested that I go around the group and tell each individual how I felt about him or her. The therapist instructed me to address each individual going around the group clockwise. The tendency to analyze, intellectualize, and give details was discouraged. For example, I would look directly at Bob and say, "Bob, I feel very safe and secure with you in group. I feel that I can trust you and value your input." "Cindy, it's difficult for me to take advice from you because you are very punitive and mean spirited." Their responses were not necessarily required, however should they want to respond they could do so after the exercise. Expressing myself released emotions and allowed me to address my discomfort and inhibition at dealing with unpleasant feelings. Avoiding redundancy and being sincere especially with negative feedback toward others was intimidating.

To embolden my position and help reduce the anxiety I felt at having to confront my issues with my family, it was suggested that I carry a megaphone, which was presented to me one night in group. Laughter is sometimes the best stress reliever! Armed with confidence, and a prop, I declared to my family that from now on "they were on their own!" Furthermore, the power of group involvement and support cannot be underestimated. Knowing that one has made a commitment to oneself and to group prevents the shirking of this responsibility. Coming back to group with a successful outcome, or at least a successful attempt at meeting the challenge, is self-affirming—a confidence builder on its own.

This Client's Response to the Intervention

In addition, our group leader consistently encouraged me to confront individuals with whom I had a strong transferences and stimulated interaction between those that had disagreements with me. Gradually I developed the ability to be more fluid in expressing issues and defending myself when challenged.

One's verbal ability is only part of the way in which to demonstrate assertiveness. Alberti and Emmons (1990) state that "the manner in which you express an assertive message is a good deal more important than the exact words you use" (p. 27).

Conclusion and Contraindications

The group's coaching provided support but self-efficacy is more achievable when the accomplishment is internalized and more likely to generalize outside of group. The theory of self-regulated behavior suggested by Bandura (1977), illustrates this: "[I]ntrinsic reinforcement that comes from self-evaluation is much more influential than the extrinsic reinforcement dispensed by others" (p. 333.)

Creating new patterns at home was an achievable goal provided consistency was maintained. The group experience provided positive and negative reinforcement when lapses in my behavior occurred. Donigan and Malnati (1987) suggest that assignments outside of the group help reinforce group behaviors, which were learned and practiced within the group.

In relation to contraindications for this exercise there are very few, if any, although it is important that the therapist be acutely aware of the ego strength and developmental stage of the client involved. The salient question posed to the therapist by himself or herself is "Is this client ready to take on this task in an environment where the client is now alone without the support of the group?" If the affirmative is decided, the client becomes aware that the therapist and the group have belief in his or her abilities to succeed with the task at hand, which is in itself a powerful reinforcement.

References

Alberti R.E. & Emmons, M.L. (1990). *Your Perfect Right: A Guide to Assertive Living* (Sixth edition). San Luis Obispo, CA: Impact.
Bandura, A. (1977). *Social Learning Theory.* Englewood Cliffs, NJ: Prentice Hall.
Donigan, J. & Malnati, R. (1987). *Critical Incidents in Group Therapy.* Monterey, CA: Brooks/Cole Publishing Company.

Sheila Sazant, M.S., is a Mental Health Counselor specializing in individual, group and family therapy.

83 Group Supervision Horseback Riding Workshop for Increasing Self-Awareness

Tal-Li Cohen

The Horse as a Powerful Therapeutic Modality

Yalom (1985) writes that the major impetus for learning is the therapy group. The structure of the group is a microcosm of the patient's cultural world. Through repeated experiences in the group, group members learn about interpersonal relations. Feedback from the group and observation allows interpersonal relations to reach higher levels. Through this process group members learn repeatedly that part of their former perception of themselves is distorted. Yalom (1985) holds the view that insight and transference have less therapeutic value than the "corrective emotional experience" of the authentic interpersonal reciprocal relations taking place in the group.

In this group supervision workshop, we use the horse as a powerful therapeutic modality. We use the unique characteristics that are experienced in the relation between the rider and the horse. Emotions directly influence the body and the horse senses the rider through the tension of his or her muscles, the posture of the rider, the way the hands hold the reins, and the overall communication the rider has with the horse. The horse interprets these multiple cues immediately and gives immediate feedback to the rider. This immediate response forces the rider to respond within a very short time, measured in seconds, in order to get what he or she wants from the horse. All this produces authentic behavior patterns on the part of the rider, and affects the issues of control, giving trust, and the capability of devotion.

During group work we make use of the sensitivity of the horse and the herd model "as a model for copying and communication by the members of the group who have closed ranks as a 'herd' around mutual aims" (Cohen & Lifshitz, 2005, p. 86). The "herd" elects a leader and acts in accordance with social codes that resemble to a great extent the communications between humans: they obey the leader, tend to play, attach importance to their private domain, communicate with the horses close to them, and when they are not answered they respond with threats and even with violence (Morris, 1991). These characteristics resemble what Bion (1992) wrote regarding human social relations.

The group experience is intensified via the relations between the individuals in the herd. The therapists are the leaders of the group and the herd. Since the horse is an animal that serves as prey it needs the protection of the herd; and it needs a leader as a shield and one who makes decisions for everyone. The individual rider represents for the horse both part of the herd and a personal leader. It expects the rider to lead it and is very dependent on the messages received from the rider.

The link created between the rider and the horse and between members of the group gives us a miniature picture of the interpersonal relations and provides insights into intrapersonal life.

The Professionals and the Group Participants

The group was directed by a clinical psychologist who is training to be a riding instructor, and aided by two riding instructors. The work was clearly divided between the professionals. The psychologist conducted the group utilizing therapeutic process and also developed the workshop working with horses; the riding instructors provided assistance at the technical level of learning how to ride.

In this particular group there were ten participants with an average age of thirty-five years. All of these participants are professionals in the mental health profession. The group had been meeting weekly in peer group supervision over a three-year period. The group members wanted to participate in an experiential process that would intensify feelings of self-awareness through horseback riding, and would help in the process of consolidation of the group and building its identity. Some of the participants had experience riding, most did not. The group met eight times, three hours each time.

The Goal of the Self-Awareness Intervention of the Group Supervision Workshop

The goal of the group supervision workshop is to enable group members to identify feelings experienced while riding and how these feelings impact and influence their inter-personal relations.

The group sessions took place at a ranch/riding school. All the horses were well-trained and were used to "working" with beginners. Each meeting was divided into two parts: the riding experience and a processing session utilizing group dynamics and expressive therapeutic tools.

First Stage: Familiarization

This stage involves familiarization with the facilitating environment (the work area) on the ranch, and with the horses. Group members are taught the horse's body language, and how to recognize how/when the horse reacts. Group members are taught the basics of "leading" and riding a horse. The initial direct contact with the horse produces anxiety in members and the fear that they might not succeed in mounting the horse, and that they might lose control. The success of some group members gives encouragement to the others to make the attempt. Some openly express their fears, while others experience this in an indirect manner, such as by asking: "Are you sure that I'm not too heavy for the horse?"

At this stage, a gradual process of familiarization takes place, with the unfolding of patterns of behavior relating to new situations. Group members are self-absorbed and their link with the group is weak. Only at the end of this stage is more attention paid to the group-as-a-whole, probably due to a greater feeling of confidence with the horse.

Second Stage: Developing an Interpersonal Relationship with the Horse

At this stage, riding is combined with handling and taking care of the horse. Riding lessons included galloping while standing up and sitting down, as well as maneuvering the horse around obstacles which demanded more precise handling of the horse. Handling and taking care of the horse included brushing and washing of the horse, and putting on the saddle. The group members also cleaned the stables. Greater emphasis was placed on group work, which involved "rubbing shoulders" with one another and addressing interpersonal situations. At this stage attention was paid to feelings of trust, readiness for devotion, and assertive behavior. Intimacy in the group increased and it appeared that this was facilitated by the decrease in the level of anxiety.

Third Stage: The Middle Phase of Group Processes

The riding process entered a "middle phase" in group process, where greater independence developed regarding the treatment of the horse and the interaction between and among the group members. In addition, learning new tasks and skills did not create anxiety regarding the potential responses of the others, and there was greater support among group members, through offering of advice based on experience.

Not always having the same horse enabled group members to experience riding horses with different personality characteristics. This enabled group members to have additional emotional and experiential experiences.

This stage was characterized by deeper personal and intimate interactions. Parallel to the confidence felt with the horses, group members also felt more comfortable toward one another, thus permitting greater risk taking with the possibility of helping one another.

An example of this was the sharing by one of the group members that she was suffering from cancer. This occurred shortly after the beginning of the technical aspects of the group. The issue arose around the strong somatic feelings she experienced during her "meeting" with the body of the horse. She felt her body responding strongly, which was in total contrast to her not experiencing her body during the initial course of her illness. The group was surprised by this new information, but was able to provide support, containment, and understanding.

Fourth Stage: Termination

This stage was the preparation for termination. The group planned (decision making) a field trip in order to provide a proper finish to the riding experience, which would permit them to reflect on the group process in both the fields of riding and of inter- and intrapersonal relationships.

Participant Responses to the Intervention

Some group members terminated by announcing that they intended to continue to take riding lessons. Others found difficulty in ending the process. One person said that she could not participate in the final meeting on the pretext of family commitments. However, after clarification and understanding of her difficulties, she did come to the final meeting.

Working with the horses enabled the group to relate to deep emotional issues that came out of the interface between body and soul. The group process developed from the stage of familiarization, through that of intimacy, to that of terminating. During the course of the group work the group members underwent personal experiences and learned about patterns of interpersonal systems, and also addressed intrapersonal issues.

Conclusion and Contraindications

The horse is an animal that is sensitive to others, and is a herd animal. These two elements were successfully utilized during work on the intensification of self-awareness regarding intrapersonal experiences that influence interpersonal relations. This method of working is suitable for all group process activities, with teenagers and with adults who are not necessarily professional therapists, but who wish to increase their personal awareness.

This type of group experience is contraindicated for participants who have severe psychological disturbances, as working with and around animals of this size requires a certain degree of awareness and the ability to communicate effectively both on a verbal and nonverbal level.

References

Cohen, T. & Lifshitz, S. (2005). "A Horse-Riding Group as Potential Space." *Mikhatz: Israel Journal of Group Psychotherapy*, 10, 83–99.
Bion, W.R. (1992). *Experiences in Groups*. Tel Aviv: Dvir.
Morris, D. (1991). *Horses and People*. Tel Aviv: Sifriat Ma'ariv.
Yalom, I.D. (1985). *The Theory and Practice of Group Psychotherapy* (Third edition). New York: Basic Books.

Tal-Li Cohen, M.A., is a clinical and educational psychologist, family therapist and riding instructor practicing in Israel. In the last year, she has developed a unique therapy approach using horses in her therapeutic paradigm.

84 Poetry as a Projective Technique and Springboard for Dialogue in Group Therapy

Scott Simon Fehr

And that has made all the difference.

(Frost, 1969)

The Language of Emotion

The language of emotion is often manifested in the words of poetry. It can be a natural resource for healing and, historically, its medicinal properties have been effectively used in every country and every language (Leedy, 1973). Poetry can be both a stimulus for eliciting emotion in one's group, which furthers dialogue, and a projective technique helping the group leader further understand, perhaps, the unspoken meaningful historical events in a client's life (Fehr, 1999, 2003). This intervention is especially effective for the novice group leader, the seasoned clinician who wishes to include group therapy into his or her practice and is anxious with initially promoting dialogue with group members, and the seasoned clinician who desires further and varied interventions in his or her work.

Process Oriented Groups

This intervention can be used with almost any type of group that is deemed process oriented. It too could be effectively used with groups where the intent is to demonstrate individual differences in order to reduce judgment and increase sensitivity. It does not matter if it is time limited or long term. The only two requirements are the person has to have the ability to read and the ability to have a certain potential to be introspective; its success is, in great part, dependent on the client having a subjective experience with the stimulus of the poem. It is not recommended for concrete-thinking clients or clients who have very loose associations.

Guidelines for Intervention

Materials

The materials for this intervention are quite simple. You will need to hand out pencils with erasers and a print-out of the poem for each group member.

If your groups are not around a table on which the clients can write you will need to give them a clipboard.

Selection of Poem

The selection of the poem that is to be used is of paramount importance. If the poem is to be effective, only one person truly will understand what it means and that is the author who wrote it. All other interpretations of the poem are projections on the part of the readers and in this case the clients. It must be an open-ended poem that does not lead the clients to a logical conclusion. In this case, a logical conclusion means that after reading the poem all the readers will relate similar themes or conclusions. An open-ended poem means that each person will relate entirely different scenarios including feelings and thoughts to the poem stimulus. Correlating the poem to classical music is of help to understanding the concept of open-ended. In classical music the listener is without boundaries to follow his or her own thoughts and feelings while listening to the music. In fact, the music is the stimulus to the inner world of the person listening and in group therapy the poem will be the stimulus for the inner world of the client as observed in the projections. An example of an open-ended poem is provided as follows. You may use this poem if you so choose. I have found it to elicit incredibly diverse and interesting responses.

> What is it that I feel?
> Is it new, is it real?
> Has it been with me before?
> Is it here to teach me more?
> What is it, it has a name?
> Inside of me, I'm not the same?

Instructions for Administration and Dialogue

Step 1: Handing Out Materials and Explanation

First and foremost it must be explained to the clients that this is not a test of intelligence nor is there any right or wrong answer to what is being requested of them.

Step 2: Actual Task

Ask them to read the poem, to themselves, and to write under the poem what they feel the author is feeling. After that ask them to write a title for the poem and also ask them to write whether they felt the author was male or female.

Step 3: Disclosure of Written Information

When all group members are finished writing ask them to individually disclose to the group what they had written. I think you will be quite surprised at the many varied responses.

Step 4: Initiating Dialogue Within the Group

After everyone has finished disclosing their information, you as the group leader can do further inquiry into the responses of the clients and, depending on your creative ability, can encourage dialogue within the group about each of the group members' contributions.

Step 5: Discussion of Individual Differences

It is here that the group therapist can explore the meaning of individual differences between people with exploration into the rainbow of responses from the poem. This can lead into a discussion of how dreary and dull the world would be if everyone was identical and predictable and these individual differences, in others, are not to be feared but rather embraced as they enhance one's life and relationship with the world.

Client Responses

Due to the fact that the clients often perceive this intervention as safe, they are usually quite receptive to taking on the task. Most have found the exercise to be interesting and enjoyable as they had the opportunity to learn about the other members of the group and about themselves. It is not uncommon, for me, to see in the following week's group clients bringing up information not only about themselves but also about the other group members, which obviously they have thought about during the week.

Contraindications

I have never found there to be any contraindications to this exercise with the clients. The only possible contraindication that might occur, could be found in the group leader and that contraindication would be that the group leader did not do anything therapeutic with the information projected onto the poem. Usually a wealth of information can be found in these projections. It needs to be explored in future groups when the group itself has become comfortable as a viable unit and the members' fear of rejection or being judged has been reduced due to their comfort level, with one another in their individual differences.

References

Fehr, S. (1999). *Introduction to Group Therapy: A Practical Guide*. Binghamton, NY: The Haworth Press.

Fehr, S. (2003). *Introduction to Group Therapy: A Practical Guide* (Second edition). Binghamton, NY: The Haworth Press.

Frost, R. (1969). The Road Not Taken. In E. Lathem (Ed.) *The Poetry of Robert Frost: The Collected Poems* (p. 105). New York: Henry Holt and Company.

Leedy, J. (1973). *Poetry the Healer*. Philadelphia, PA: J.B. Lippincott.

Dr. Scott Simon Fehr is a licensed Clinical Psychologist and a Certified Group Therapist. He is on the graduate faculty of Nova Southeastern University's School of Psychology. He has written and edited several books and has a son who is following in his professional footsteps.

85 Unexpected Consequences
Maintaining the Boundaries in a Therapy Group for Older Adults

George Max Saiger

Outside Contact in a Geriatric Psychiatry Group

Psychotherapy groups for older adults present the therapist with a dilemma—more exactly, with a contradiction. Older adults often suffer from social isolation; often they are attracted to group therapy because this is a modality, which relieves isolation (MacLennan, Saul & Weiner, 1988; Saiger, 2001; Leszcz, 1997). Juxtaposed against this reality is the position that group therapy is best conducted when the boundaries are firm; i.e., outside socialization is discouraged if not banned outright. There is good reason for this, even with older adult groups: outside contact allows for acting out rather than talking, partial resolution of issues that are then not brought back into group, and establishing subgroups that are shielded from therapeutic inquiry (Fehr, 2003; Rutan & Stone, 2001).

Members Must Be Over Sixty-Five Years of Age

For about a decade, I have conducted on open-ended, personal growth-oriented therapy group for seniors using an interpersonal model. Members must be over sixty-five years of age; in practice, almost all members have been seventy to eighty-five years old. The group meets weekly in my office. For some members, I am also the treating psychiatrist, providing medication and/or individual psychotherapy. Others are treated by outside providers with whom I stay in open contact. Most members remain for about two to three years. Inclusion criteria include that no two members have an outside relationship, and members are cautioned not to establish outside relationships with each other after joining the group.

The group continually wonders about, and challenges, "Dr. Saiger's rule" that there is to be no outside contact. There are often extended conversations in the parking lot after group, which the members will refer to in the group—sometimes with good-natured ribbing and sometimes with an air of serious challenge to my authority. To my knowledge, there have not been social or sexual assignations taking place at remote locations or at other times.

Case History

As often happens in groups for seniors, one of the members, Ms. A., was absent for two weeks due to surgery, in her case for cataracts. The surgery did not go well, and for some weeks thereafter, she was unable to drive. She could not reasonably afford cab fare to and from sessions (her fees are paid by state medical assistance) nor did she have available family. The group members frequently asked about her medical progress, and they grew uncomfortable with her extended absence. Why, they asked, could we not bend "Dr. Saiger's rule" this once and allow Ms. B., who lived near Ms. A., to drive her to and from group? Ms. B. promised not to discuss anything of importance during these rides. It seemed like a reasonable request to me, though I was distinctly uncomfortable with this weakening of agreed-upon boundaries. I consulted colleagues, including Ms. A.'s individual therapist, who was unequivocally in favor of the enterprise. Finally, still harboring qualms, I acquiesced. The group members were unanimous that this was the right decision.

At the next group meeting, the group members were pleased indeed to see Ms. A. again. Ms. C. hugged her warmly and enthusiastically. Ms. A. had brought a handmade quilt as a gift for her driver, and Ms. B. insisted that the gift be presented in the group, not in the car. It was, however, not mentioned nor did I notice the hand-off of the shopping bag containing it.

The group had other matters to discuss, of course. Foremost was that a new member, Ms. D., had made her debut. She introduced herself by complaining about the neglect she felt from the daughter she had moved here to be near. Her story prompted Ms. A. to talk about the neglect and disdain she had experienced earlier in her life from her own husband and mother when she had suffered a miscarriage. This represented a deeper sharing than she had done at any time prior to her absence.

At the next group, Ms. C. reported that, although this group is the social highlight of her week, the one place where she feels a sense of belonging and acceptance, she had left the previous week feeling alone and excluded. She had responded by phoning Ms. B., hoping for some reassurance! I had no idea that the two had ever exchanged numbers.

Ms. B. was not at home; when she heard the phone message she thought that the best thing to do would be to meet Ms. C. for lunch and shopping, but, remembering "Dr. Saiger's rule," she did not call back.

Ms. C. was still upset as she recounted this tale. It seemed to me most likely that the "special" relationship between Ms. A. and Ms. B. which was created by the ride-sharing experience led Ms. C. to feel excluded. I still think that this is true. Ms. C. thought otherwise. She recalled Ms. A.'s story of her miscarriage, and reported, with great emotion, how she had experienced the same constellation when she was a young, frightened, inexperienced bride. Those feelings of aloneness had been reawakened in the here and now.

The group ended with Mr. E. commenting that the whole issue of outside contact was so unimportant that we should not be wasting time on it. Then

Ms. D. asked if she could use my phone to call a cab. Ms. B. and Ms. C. quickly said, "Leave Dr. Saiger out of this. He doesn't need to know how we get you home!" And they bustled her out the door. Their sense of proud autonomy was palpable but the group boundary may have been weakened beyond repair.

Conclusion and Contraindication

Groups for older adults present a dilemma with no easy answers when it comes to the issue of outside socializing. In the case presented, there were clear benefits and equally clear costs to the intervention made. The therapist should not undertake it lightly, stopping to evaluate the group dynamic and the psychodynamics of the principles. But at some point, one must act. When one does, one must be ready for unexpected consequences.

References

Fehr, S.S. (2003). *Introduction to Group Therapy: A Practical Guide* (Second edition). Binghamton, NY: The Haworth Press.

Leszcz, M. (1997). Integrated group psychotherapy for the treatment of depression in the elderly. *Group* (21) 2.

MacLennan, B., Saul, S. & Weiner, M. (Eds.) (1988). *Group Psychotherapy with the Elderly*. New York: International Universities Press.

Rutan, J.S. & Stone, W. (2001). *Psychodynamic Group Psychotherapy* (Third edition). New York: Guilford Press.

Saiger, G. (2001). Group psychotherapy with older adults. *Psychiatry* 64 (2).

George Max Saiger, M.D., is Clinical Director of the Senior Intensive Outpatient Program at Montgomery General Hospital in Olney, MD., and was the founding director of the Center of Study of Psychotherapies for the Aging at the Washington School of Psychiatry in Washington DC. Dr. Saiger is a Fellow of the American Group Psychotherapy Association, and is affiliated with the National Group Psychotherapy Institute of the Washington School of Psychiatry.

86 Creative Use of the Group Contract in Long-Term Psychotherapy Groups

Melissa Black

The Group Contract

The group contract in a long-term psychodynamic therapy group is an explicit agreement between therapist and group members about the expectations and conduct for successful group membership (Fehr, 2003). It covers topics such as logistics of group meetings, fees for group therapy, confidentiality, and expectations about the minimal duration of group treatment as well as more intangible issues such as the necessity to explore the relationships within the group, particularly with the therapist. The contract also brings emotional issues, which are often difficult and avoided, such as money, sexual feelings, and anger, to a conscious space within the group member and highlights the importance of working with these issues as a vital part of the group experience. The idea that group is meant to be an avenue for *verbal* exploration of both intrapsychic and interpersonal conflicts is specifically spelled out in the contract. The directive to "put thoughts and feelings into words and not actions" is always an explicit part of my own group contract. Of particular importance in this intervention is the agreement that there is to be no contact between members outside of group.

Therapeutically, the group contract has several purposes. Initially, it provides a uniform set of expectations to each of the group members. Although there is nothing "democratic" about the contract, it is generally accepted as a benevolent directive from the group leader, which ultimately has the health of the group member at the heart of the document. Since the style of leadership in psychodynamically based group psychotherapy is less active than many other forms of group, the contract often provides the only structure for a beginning group. It is often the first shared experience of the group (Rutan & Stone, 1993). With group membership comes the inherent agreement that all will abide by the directives of the contract. The sense of predictability and safety these "rules" imbue in a new group can be a life raft for anxious new members.

Although the group contract feels predictable, safe, and comforting to a new group or even a new member in an open ended group, over time the group contract can take on many other meanings and purposes. The following intervention will illustrate one such manifestation of the therapeutic usefulness of the group contract in the later stage of an established group.

A Psychodynamic or Insight-Oriented Population

Although I believe that all types of groups need a contract, the content and use of the contract will vary according to the type of group and population. The following intervention is best suited for a psychodynamic or other insight-oriented group. Consistent with psychodynamic psychotherapy groups, the group members will have the capacity for self-reflection and insight and be seeking increased intrapsychic and interpersonal knowledge. The following group intervention occurred in a mixed, open-ended, long-term psychodynamic group that had been meeting once a week for approximately two years.

Intervention

Margie was a new member who had entered the group three sessions prior to the intervention. She was taking the place vacated by a very beloved member, Tina, who had terminated successfully after being a vital and passionate member of the group since its inception. Margie, like Tina, was an attractive, vivacious, and energizing woman. She was experiencing warmth, encouragement, and acceptance from the group members, with the exception of Doug, who was treating her with cool disdain. No matter how often Margie attempted to make genuine contact with Doug, she was rebuffed. During this particular session, Doug became especially hostile and finally shouted, "Who needs another beautiful woman in this group? I've written to Tina and I know she will e-mail back. All this group has ever done for me is keep me from experiencing love."

Doug had been sitting on his feelings of love and attraction for Tina throughout their shared time in the group. His inability to share them in real time with her had him acting out and unable to open himself to the possibility of another intensely sexual or loving relationship in the group. Much like the bitterness he carried forward from his fairly recent divorce, he was unable to love, but unable to let go. As the therapist, I was struck by the opportunity in the moment to help Doug and the rest of the group appreciate the difficulty and benefit in expressing the very real love that can be experienced safely in the group.

I had to think quickly through my intervention options. I could have quoted the contract and pointed out the "rule violation" and reinforced the need to put feelings into words and not actions. I could have made an interpretation for Doug relating to his life and relationships and hoped that others would pick up on it and generalize, but I decide to use the group contract to make this a group as a whole issue instead.

Questions for the Group

- Having a new member in the group is always a great time to think about how we are all using this group. This is an interesting situation.

- What do you all think about a relationship between Doug and Tina? Can anyone remember having a wish or fantasy to break the rules and talk or even get together with another group member outside of group?

The invitation for everyone to share their fantasies of a different kind of connection with group members led to a lively discussion of many of the group members' unspoken wishes to be Tina's lover or friend but with an awareness of the "contractual agreement" not to act on the feelings. Some members felt betrayed by Doug for breaking the boundary and contacting Tina, while others related to his anger at the restrictions that group placed on the ability to have "real" relationships with one another.

I then posed the following question.

- It seems like there were many possible suitors for Tina in this group. Could there be any current cases of undisclosed love or wishes for friendship between members of this group today?

This was the impetus needed for the group to start discussing wishes for pairings to play golf, go on a dinner date, watch a movie, vacation together, and even become lovers.

The final piece of my intervention:

- All of those ideas sound wonderful and exciting, but I wonder if anyone can explore what they might all have in common?

After a period of silence, it was Doug who responded, "We all want to love each other." Margie finally joined in saying, "It sounds like you already do." The group followed this path to finally accept that, even with the limitations of "real contact" or maybe because of the limitations, they were free to experience true feelings toward one another.

The Responses

The effective use of the group contract as more than a beginning frame for a therapy group is dependent upon the group's readiness for deeper interpretation of their behaviors. Like any premature interpretation, at best, it will fall flat and not be understood, but it can also result in hostility toward the leader for his or her perceived lack of understanding or even be seen as a punitive judgment by the leader. When this type of intervention is used correctly, it will easily move the group beyond the specific behaviors to an exploration of the emotional connections around the behavior choices.

Conclusion and Contraindications

In an established, long-term, psychodynamic group, the group contract can become a metaphorical member of the group. Rather than simply a set of rules to live by in group, over time it takes on a personality of its own. Each member has a relationship with the contract. How that relationship progresses will influence all of the other relationships in the group. Doug's acting out and awareness of not abiding by the contract foreclosed on his openness to forming other relationships in the group. Left unexplored, Doug would have eventually used his "misbehavior" with the contract to recreate the deep sense of shame that has been pervasive around vulnerable emotions in his life and likely lead to a premature termination of his group membership.

Using the group contract as a piece of the relational matrix of the group allows the therapist yet another set of relationships to explore and understand. It is important to note that there are times when even the deepest understanding of contract violations does not negate the damaging aspects of the behavior on the group. One example of such destructive behavior is a sexual liaison between group members. Obviously, this will require not only intense exploration, but it ultimately must lead to one or both members leaving the group if the outside relationship continues.

References

Fehr. S. (2003). *Introduction to Group Therapy* (Second edition). Binghamton, NY: The Haworth Press.

Rutan, S. & Stone, W. (1993). *Psychodynamic Group Psychotherapy*. New York: The Guilford Press.

Dr. Melissa Black is a licensed Clinical Psychologist and Certified Group Psychotherapist. She is in private practice as a member of the Group Analytic Practice of Dallas in Dallas, Texas, and is a Clinical Professor in Psychiatry at The University of Texas Southwestern Medical Center in Dallas, Texas.

87 An Angry Outburst
Responding to Aggression
Robert A. Berley

Introduction

Aggressive feelings are part of our human experience, and they are called into play whenever we feel frustrated or threatened. Early experiences, of course, will powerfully influence exactly what is felt. Even the "flight" part of the fight/flight response can become quite complicated, emerging more as a flight of mind that leaves the body frozen and quite vulnerable. For many, anger has become disconnected from data, such that the intensity of the response does not match the actual level of threat. Thus the conscious awareness and communication of aggressive feelings can contain elements of dissociated lack of awareness, anxious denial, fearful withdrawal, paralyzed inaction, various forms of modulated expression, as well as explosive activation accompanied by powerful impulses to act out.

Of course, individuals unable to manage feelings who are likely to explode require specific groups focused on self-control and should be carefully evaluated before being included in a therapy group with more diverse goals (Brabender, 2002). But because questions regarding appropriateness for group can be difficult to determine with any certainty, and because therapists are often loathe to reject a potential member without offering some opportunity to see if there might be a beneficial fit (Fehr, 2003), members with circumscribed concerns that could elicit such an outburst are often invited to participate.

Therapists are, of course, typically more comfortable with patients likely to exhibit too much self-control rather than too little. So it is essential to have some way to think about the more distressing situation in which a group member erupts, threatening another member or the group as a whole. Many therapists include a an agreement to "put feelings into words rather than actions" in their group contract (Rutan & Stone, 2001), so even though the threat may be explicitly not one of physical harm, the intensity of the expressed emotion may still be difficult to mange.

The Event

A (co-led) group for adults had been meeting for many years with a fairly stable membership. One of the two female leaders had left to have a baby, and a new therapist (myself) had recently come in to fill her role. Shortly thereafter, a new member was introduced into the group. This was Sara, a single woman, aged twenty-five with a drug and alcohol history whose mother had somewhat reluctantly agreed to help her daughter pay the group fee. Her first session was uneventful. At the second meeting, Francis, the longer-standing therapist, was absent and I conducted the group myself. The issue of disappointment in various caregivers arose, with the overt content centered on the ways members had been shortchanged by disinterested or self-absorbed parents. Sara remarked that she didn't think of her mother that way at all. In fact, she felt more the opposite: that her mother tended to be intrusive and overly concerned about her. Several members laughed at how they wished their parents had been that involved. Sara seemed to darken as though feeling unheard, and reiterated how her mother's oversight of her life was a burden. At this point, Jane, a longstanding member, became irritated and began needling Sara for being unappreciative of her mother's efforts on her behalf. Phrases like "What do *you* have to complain about?" and "You have it *so* easy!" were delivered with an increasingly forceful and demeaning tone of voice. Feebly, Sarah tried to defend herself and her feelings, while the other group members seemed to retreat into the background.

Feeling protective of a new member finding herself badgered by a more senior one who was also a generation older, I began to note Jane's seeming lack of self-observation and the probability that something was arising out of her internal world rather than anything actually about Sara. But, after just a few words from me, Jane turned toward Sara and exploded, furiously accusing her of being ungrateful, selfish, and self-centered. The group seemed shocked into frozen isolation, and Jane's disregard for my effort left me feeling momentarily irrelevant and impotent. After a breath, Jane continued to harangue Sara, whom I rapidly became concerned would be driven from the group.

Components of the Intervention

The initial challenge in these situations is to explore one's own internal experience and locate a stance or space from which thinking is possible. This is not an effort to suppress (countertransference) feelings, but to work with them in a creative and flexible way. It is thus not only essential as a therapist, but also good modeling for members. From that stance, a number of important considerations may be examined to help the therapist decide what might be going on and in what direction the group needs to move.

As usual, the overall trajectory we have in mind includes helping the individual and the group develop an increasing tolerance for affect, developing a capacity for empathy and mutuality, and eventually moving toward self-observation and reflection and thus here-and-now learning. This sequence can be facilitated if the therapist can:

1. *Lean in:* The first objective is to protect the group while attempting to link up with the affect expressed. Aggression is a signal of frustration

or threat, and here Sara is triggering something in Jane that is invisible as a source but terribly apparent as an effect. The therapist must "lean" toward Jane, identifying with her emotional state and providing an effective structuring (that is, empathic) response that conveys deep understanding and thus the capacity to tolerate the feeling evoked. In this case, I sat fully upright and moved physically forward toward both women, offering protection to Sara by getting into Jane's line of sight and containment for Jane by clearly being willing to engage with her no matter what her level of intensity.

2. *Make room and jump in:* As the most powerful individual and most important transference object in the group, I needed to be included in the situation and demand I be taken into account. Addressing Jane, I said very directly and forcefully: "Jane! I think right now you are having feelings about Sara that make you upset," a phrase that had to be repeated a second time in order to get Jane to address it and me. Her reply was a scornful "Well, yeah!" but it did force her to speak to me and I could now keep working at giving her something to think about. (This is a version of directing aggression toward the leader that others in this book have noted, but begins with affect rather than content.) Once I had Jane's attention, I could move on to saying "I think you are angry at Sara for her mother's interest because you're angry at Francis for bringing me into the group and paying no attention to your wishes." It is less relevant that this be insightful and accurate; it should carry the kind of emotional tension the member is expressing. Engaging and getting the patient's attention are the more basic objectives; accuracy will come later, when dialogue can be established. So, when Sara replied "That's stupid!" I did not take her retaliation personally but was ready to keep her mind engaged by saying "She not only left you and brought me in to cover for her, but she also brought a little sister into the family." There was a pause as she began to think, so I added "and you're upset with me because you're not getting enough from me, and it seems like Sara is getting so much from her caregiver." Again, accuracy is desirable, but affect matching or "pacing" is the true goal here.

3. *Titrate, but do not defuse!* The goal is to find a way for the entire group to remain engaged. Defenses will be aroused and titration may be necessary, but the whole group must work with the situation without anyone feeling their reaction is overwrought or meaningless. Too rapidly attempting an interpretation that moves away from the here-and-now of the interaction to archaic "explanations" tends to infantilize the group and implies the group is too immature to explore their own reactions. The experience of tolerating affect successfully helps develop what might be described as a tougher "skin" or insulation (Ormont, 1984), as well as increasing cohesion and trust in the group's ability to weather storms together. It should also be obvious that trying to defuse a situation by overpowering the angry member

(especially through shame or humiliation) is a poor choice and will lead to mistrust of the leader even if the situation is "successfully" deescalated. So once I had joined Jane and "paced" her affect, I noted how furious she was because "It makes you angry to see Sara get so much when you felt you got nothing," and then to the group "and I think everyone kept their hands off because they, too, were jealous of the one who seemed to get it all."
4. *Pursue meaning:* Following the expression of intense feeling, the central character as well as group members who pulled away may feel shame. Pursuing meaning thoughtfully and respectfully communicates a basic tolerance of and interest in emotional dynamics. One specific way to support the growth of "skin" is to investigate the affect (fear, anger, etc.), and see if members can imagine responding nonthreateningly in spite of it. Members who were "too scared to say anything" might be invited to imagine speaking anyway, despite their fear of retaliation.

There are many potential forms of meaning that could become available as members finally contemplate their experience together. In this case, members eventually admitted to fearing retaliation from Jane if they were to object to her treatment of Sara (or even note that she's acted this way before), and envy of Sara (e.g., identification with Jane), which made them collude to have Jane attack and demolish the "fortunate" new member.

Conclusion and Important Contraindications

Working with intense affect makes demands on both members and the leader, and the therapist must assess both the group's capacity to tolerate feelings and engage in thought as well as his or her own. Resistances are often discovered in the therapist (Billow, 2001), and it is part of professional training to seek consultation and perhaps further personal therapy to help resolve them. Assessing the group's capacity is not a black-or-white decision, however, as any group will become more cohesive and self-assured as the skills of emotional engagement are put into practice. Obviously, there will also be a limit, which must be respected by the leader, lest a traumatizing and possibly escalating process (fueled perhaps by scapegoating or unexpressed anger at the therapist) emerge.

Interventions or techniques are not, however, to be applied as though following a recipe. There is too much complexity in the intertwined feelings of leader and members, too much contributed by their shared history, and too much of the leader's own emotional constitution to thoughtlessly apply a formulaic response. Even something that comes recommended by a colleague must be carefully considered, assessing the situation and one's own therapeutic self for goodness of "fit." The reader is thus encouraged to consider the ways in which the proposed interventions might be adapted to a response that would feel organic to his or her own temperament and therapeutic stance.

References

Billow, R. (2001). The therapist's anxiety and resistance to group. *International Journal of Group Psychotherapy*, 51(2): 5–100.

Brabender, V. (2002). *Introduction to Group Therapy*. New York: John Wiley & Sons.

Fehr, S.S. (2003). *Introduction to Group Therapy: A Practical Guide* (Second edition). Binghamton, NY: The Haworth Press.

Ormont, L. (1984). The leader's role in dealing with aggression in groups. *International Journal of Group Psychotherapy*, 34(4): 553–572.

Rutan, S. & Stone, W. (2001). *Psychodynamic Group Psychotherapy* (Second edition). New York: Guilford Press.

Steinberg, P. & Duggal, S. (2004). Threats of violence in group-oriented day treatment. *International Journal of Group Psychotherapy*, 54(1) 5–22.

Robert A. Berley, Ph.D., C.G.P., is a psychologist in private practice in Seattle, Washington, and has taught group dynamics and group therapy at Seattle University and at the Washington School of Professional Psychology.

88 A Difficult Session

Marvin Kaphan

> The greater the difficulty, the more the glory in surmounting it.
> (O'Connor, 1993)

Inclusion

Virtually every authority will agree on the importance of careful screening and thoughtful selection of the members of a psychotherapy group (Rutan & Stone, 2000; Fehr, 2003). Yalom (1994) further suggests that the fate of a group can be sealed before the group begins due to the inclusion or exclusion of its members. Many years ago, when initiating my six groups, I found this relatively easy, since I drew the group members from my individual practice. I had worked with every participant for a considerable period of time, knew them quite well, and felt very comfortable placing each one in an appropriate group.

Group Descriptions and Inclusion

All of my groups are heterogeneous and psychodynamic. They are made up of private patients, on a continuum from moderate functionality to high functionality, and including diversity in age, gender, and diagnosis. Over the years, each group had developed a somewhat different personality, and I had become quite proud of the technique I had developed for placing patients in groups. This was a process of "fantasy." I would try to picture how a given patient would affect each of the other members of the group, how each of them would affect the patient, and what effect this patient might have on the functioning of the group as a whole. This method had worked so well that I had never been disappointed in the result, and the only surprises had been that patients would achieve more, progress more quickly, or reach more meaningful insights than I had expected.

As time went on, some of my groups' patients came from referrals from individual therapists who did not have groups, but felt that their patients could benefit from concurrent group therapy. Most group therapists require at least one screening interview before placing a referral into a group, but we still have to depend, to a certain extent, on the individual therapist's evaluation of the patient's readiness for group therapy.

On one particular occasion, I placed a referred patient into a rather high-functioning psychodynamic group after a single screening interview. Since the patient appeared to have trouble in social relationships, the therapist hoped that a group experience would give this individual some insight into how he was contributing to his problems. In rare instances, I have found that new patients, on entering a group, will begin to provoke the other members of the group. This becomes grist for the mill of group therapy, and with only minimal help from the group therapist, the group can explore the motivations and unconscious forces that drive such behavior. Usually, as a result of the "magic" of group process, everybody gains.

In this particular instance, it took a very different course. The new participant's attacks were particularly vicious, striking at each member's vulnerabilities, stimulating forceful retaliation from the group members. The provocateur's response to the retaliation seemed to be a rapid decompensation. His wild, frantic, and paranoid utterances seemed to be adding to the outrage of the group. I felt I was seeing a psychotic process in the making, and decided to direct the focus of the group away from the psychologically deteriorating new member.

Interventions

When group therapists feel the need to direct the attention of the group, they have a choice of only four directions in which to go. They can either incorporate all four directions, a combination of three directions, or utilize one direction as the intervention of choice. These four directions are as follows:

1. Draw the attention to the member making a comment.
2. Focus on the person responding to the comment.
3. Elicit the responses of another member of the group to the comment.
4. Involve the group as a whole in examining their feelings about the comment.

These four interventions are accomplished with therapist-posed questions. It is essential when such an intervention is used, that the group has been educated to the fact that the therapist will never use rhetorical questions. Most people in our society have been acculturated to expect that many questions are really commands. "Why did you do that?" often can be interpreted as "You should not do that." The therapist must emphasize repeatedly that his or her questions are real questions, aimed at exploring "reasons for behavior."

In this case, in order to protect the new patient, my interventions were meant to direct the group in only three of the four directions for the entire session:

1. Toward a group member subjected to an attack.
2. Toward another group member.
3. Toward the group as a whole.

When the target of an attack retaliated against the attacker, I turned the attention to the retaliator by asking, "If someone had used the words that you used to retaliate, what effect would it have had on you?" This question must be asked very carefully, because in spite of careful preparation for the meaning of questions, it is easy for the patient to experience the question as reproof thus the patient experiences a narcissistic injury. The patient's established trusting relationship with the therapist and the therapist's tone of voice forestalled that misinterpretation. That allowed the therapist to proceed to: "What do you think your purpose was?" and "How would the rest of you have experienced that remark?" This again has completely removed the focus from the new patient.

In directing or eliciting a response from a group member toward the victim of an attack, I used questions like, "How did that make you feel?" If I had wanted to direct attention toward the attacker, I could have asked if producing that emotion was his or her goal, but in this case, since I wanted to direct away from the attacker, I would follow this with, "When have you felt a feeling like this before?" From there it was easy to go to "How have you handled situations like this in the past?" which has completely removed the focus from the new patient. After that, I was able to involve other patients with questions like, "You have talked of similar experiences, how does the one just described compare to yours?" By this point, the group had once more been directed away from the attacker.

Finally, to direct the spotlight onto the group as a whole, I would ask such questions as: "What seems to be happening here?" and "How do you feel about it?" Gradually, as the center of attention was kept away from the deeply troubled patient, he could calm down somewhat. I needed only a brief session with him following the group to satisfy myself that he was sufficiently composed to return home safely. In a subsequent discussion with his individual therapist, it was decided that this kind of group experience was too dangerous for this patient, and no effort would be made to encourage him to return.

Typical Responses

The interventions that were used in this session are common devices to direct the focus of a group, although they are rarely repeated with this frequency and consistency. With moderate use of these techniques, even the most rebellious group members tend to react with benign compliance. Occasionally, a group member will protest with a comment like, "Wait, I want to hear more about . . .," but the delay in the transition does no harm, as a rule.

Conclusion and Contraindications

All the patients who enter my groups make a commitment to give a month's notice before leaving, but this patient left without notice. One of my concerns was that the group members might fear that other patients could be driven out of the group if they aroused disapproval, but after a lengthy discussion of the incident in the next session, I was convinced that they all accepted that this patient's decision to leave abruptly was in his best interest as well as the group's.

I cannot see any contraindications to the use of these interventions, except if they were regularly used with the demonstrated frequency and intensity during a single group session as they might strike some group members as overly authoritarian and overbearing on the part of the group therapist.

References

Fehr, S. S. (2003). *Introduction to Group Therapy: A Practical Guide* (Second edition). Binghamton, NY: The Haworth Press.

O'Connor, M. E. (1993). *The Essential Epicurus: Letters, Principal Doctrines, Vatican Sayings, and Fragments.* New York: Prometheus Books

Rutan, S. J. & Stone, N. W. (2000). *Psychodynamic Group Psychotherapy* (Third edition). New York: Guilford Press.

Yalom, I. D. (1994). *The Theory & Practice of Group Psychotherapy* (Fourth edition). New York: Basic Books.

Marvin Kaphan, MSW, LFAGPA, CGP, BCD, is a former president of the Group Psychotherapy Association of Southern California. He has engaged in the full-time private practice of psychotherapy since 1960. He has maintained six ongoing groups for over fifty years, and has given lectures and demonstrations throughout the United States and Canada, including two at the American Psychiatric Association.

89 The Nine Basic Steps for a Successful Group

Joshua M. Gross

Checklist for Starting a Group

The literature is ripe with information about how to conduct group psychotherapy. There are many approaches to this work and the interested reader has many choices for basic instruction of how to do this work (Berg, Landreth, & Fall, 2006; Bernard & MacKenzie, 1994; Fehr, 2003; Price, Hescheles, & Price 1999; Rutan & Stone, 1993; Trotzer, 2006). This intervention uses a checklist as a tool to determine if you are ready to have the first meeting of your new group. So often, therapy groups do not thrive and the literature is clear in describing a series of specific steps that are necessary to ensure that the group is ready to start. This intervention is for the leader(s) and is designed to assist them in determining if they have addressed the nine basic steps necessary for the initiation of a successful group.

Description

This is a generic intervention for group leaders and as such has application for many forms of group intervention including homogeneous or heterogeneous groups, a process or theme-based group, a time-limited or open-ended group, or any other category or theoretical approach to the work. The main point here is to ensure that the intervention is well planned, structured, prepared, and initiated.

Often, the beginning group therapist puts more emphasis on the procedures of leadership that take place in the first and subsequent meetings of the group. The main point of this intervention is the idea that the group work begins from the moment that the therapist has the idea that a therapeutic group is needed, which allows for a focus on the many details that require attention before the first group meeting. This checklist was designed with the idea that the beginning group therapist can benefit from having a tool which assures that all appropriate due diligence has been covered and that the group is in fact ready for the first meeting.

Checklist for Starting a Group

—— Clear statement of purpose for the group must include goals, objectives, membership criteria, time frame, and fee structure if appropriate.

— Well-reasoned plan for location, schedule, and clinical operations necessary to initiate the group.
— Distribution of a written announcement addressed to both referring colleagues and potential group members.
— Active development of referrals through presentations, outreach, discussion, posting of flyers, and direct solicitation.
— Discussion of prospective cases with colleagues to evaluate the goodness of fit for membership in the group.
— Scheduling of consultation session with prospective members to personally evaluate their readiness and to prepare them for their experience in the group.
— Orientation to group membership includes discussion of:

1. When the group will meet and start.
2. What to expect in the first meeting and those that follow.
3. Regular attendance.
4. Confidentiality.
5. Resolution of differences between members and leaders.
6. Acknowledgment of all contacts with members outside the group.
7. Clear description of fees if appropriate.

— Contact group members weekly to remind them of when and where the group will initiate as you are preparing the intervention.
— Initiate the first session with a review of the rules and some suggestions as to how the new group members can best start talking with one another productively.

References

Berg, R. C., Landreth, G. L. & Fall, K. A. (2006). *Group Counseling: Concepts and Procedures*. New York: Routledge.
Bernard, H. S. & MacKenzie, K. R. (Eds.). (1994). *Basics of Group Psychotherapy*. New York: Guilford.
Fehr, S. S. (2003). *Introduction to Group Psychotherapy: A Practical Guide* (Second edition). Binghamton, NY: The Haworth Press.
Price, J. R., Hescheles, D. R. & Price, A. R. (1999). *A Guide to Starting Psychotherapy Groups*. San Diego: Academic Press.
Rutan, J. S. & Stone, W. N. (1993). *Psychodynamic Group Psychotherapy*. New York: Guilford.
Trotzer, J. P. (2006). *The Counselor and the Group*. New York: Routledge.

Joshua M. Gross, Ph.D., ABPP, CGP, FAGPA, is Director of Group Programs at the University Counseling Center at Florida State University and practices as a Group and Family Psychologist. He is a licensed psychologist, Certified Group Psychotherapist, Fellow of The American Academy of Group Psychology, Fellow of The American Group Psychotherapy Association and serves as Member of the International Board for The Certification of Group Psychotherapy.

90 Stress Inoculation Training for Trauma and Stress-Related Disorders

Justin A. D'Arienzo

Stress Inoculation Training (SIT)

In 2004, Hurricane Ivan left its destructive wake through Florida's panhandle and the coastal regions of Alabama and Mississippi. Furthermore, due to the Global War on Terrorism operations and the storm's destruction of several military treatment facilities, I became the sole military psychologist providing psychosocial interventions for the region at Naval Hospital, Pensacola, Florida. To address the burgeoning and heterogeneous myriad of patients suffering from various anxiety disorders, I formed a closed process-oriented group utilizing Meichenbaum's Stress Inoculation Training (SIT) model (Meichenbaum, 1993, 1996, 2005).

SIT is a cognitive behavioral therapy (CBT), which enhances one's ability to cope with past, current, and future stressors through three phases of treatment. Patients first learn about the stress response. They are then exposed to anxiety-provoking experiences while acquiring the skills to mange their responses. Finally, patients learn to generalize their newly acquired skill sets to cope with increasingly demanding situations and return to the therapist for "tune ups" as needed. In this model, inoculation is similar to the physical immunity generated by exposure to less virulent forms of diseases. During SIT, exposure to minor stressors in therapy fosters psychological preparedness and promotes resilience.

Client Population

This particular group met weekly for twenty weeks and consisted of five women and three men. All were navy servicemen and servicewomen with the exception of one civilian. Ages ranged from twenty-one to fifty-three. Individual members suffered from combat-related post-traumatic stress disorder, hurricane-related acute stress disorder, sexual-assault-related post-traumatic stress disorder, panic disorder, and general adjustment problems with anxiety.

Intervention Guidelines

SIT is a flexible and individually tailored alliance-based intervention used with individuals, couples, and groups. Sessions are as short as twenty minutes and range in frequency from eight to forty sessions. SIT has been utilized successfully to prepare patients undergoing medical procedures (Meichenbaum, 2005) and with patients suffering from anxiety (Suinn, 1990), stress disorders, addictions (Meichenbaum, 2005), and anger control problems (Deffenbacher & McKay, 2000). The Joint Department of Defense and Veteran's Administration Clinical Practice Guidelines (2003) designates SIT as a "Class A" treatment for post-traumatic stress disorder (PTSD). Additionally, Meichenbaum (1993) found SIT to be useful for individuals adjusting to the military.

The objective of SIT is to strengthen the patients' coping repertoire (intrapersonal and interpersonal skills) and build their confidence to overcome the perceived demands of stressful situations. Moreover, the SIT model embraces the transactional view of stress described by Lazarus and Folkman (1984) where stress occurs because the perceived demands of a situation exceed the perceived resources to cope. In this view, stress is viewed as a dynamic relationship between the person and the environment. Similarly, SIT was influenced by the constructive narrative perspective (CNP) (Meichenbaum, 2005). In this view, individuals and groups are seen as "storytelling entities." Their stories are both personal and cultural. The nature and content of the stories that they tell themselves and others play a critical role in influencing the coping process (Meichenbaum, 2005; Brewin & Holmes, 2003; Ehlers & Clark, 2000).

The Three-Phase Stress Inoculation Training

1. Conceptual Education

Through Socratic discovery-based interviewing, the therapist assists the patients in identifying and then conceptualizing their symptoms and triggers. With greater knowledge and an understanding of the biopsychosocial underpinning of their responses, the group and therapist work collaboratively toward reconceptualizing each individual's presenting problem. The group then explores each member's established personal strengths, resources, and resiliencies to enhance personal control and mastery.

2. Skills Acquisition and Consolidation

In this phase each patient develops an action plan tailored to overcome his or her stressor. Interventions are problem focused and emotionally focused. Problem solving, rehearsal, in vivo exposure (in and out of group), and cognitive reframing may be used. Take advantage of the interpersonal interactions inherent in group therapy.

3. Application and Follow-through

During this final phase, patients are encouraged to practice their newly acquired coping skills across increasingly demanding levels of stressors utilizing the interventions described during the second phase. The objective is to achieve generalization and maintenance of changes. Use the group to develop individual relapse prevention plans especially targeting risky situations such as anniversaries, social pressures, or high and low emotional states. Reframe relapse as an opportunity for learning rather than a catastrophe destined to lead to further relapses. Lead patients to assume a consultative role for someone in the group or for a friend, and if appropriate, encourage group members to support one another beyond therapy sessions. Finally, provide a plan for future individual follow-up or booster sessions as needed.

Client Responses

The civilian in the group, a fifty-three-year-old woman, who had hurricane-related acute stress disorder, made significant progress. She entered group attributing her significant anxiety symptoms to fears and memories of dying during the storm. She had married later in life to a much older man, who during the storm, simply turned off his hearing aid and went to sleep, while his wife remained awake fearing for her life. During the course of therapy, she was transformed from a dependent and passive person to an action-oriented self-starter. The experience of the storm created a sense that she was alone and that her husband was unable to protect her. Over time and with the assistance of the group in reconceptualizing the meaning of the traumatic event, she transformed this memory of fear and vulnerability into motivation to become self-sufficient. By the end of therapy she had taken on the role of a consultant to her much younger counterparts, enrolled in college for the first time, and was producing a play in the local theater. It became evident that her passivity had diminished when she threatened to leave her job of ten years and demanded a substantial raise—she received the raise. Also, she no longer blamed her avoidance of social activities on her husband's laziness or obesity. With a new sense of confidence and a little persistence she persuaded her once-sedentary husband to break his symbiotic relationship with his La-Z-Boy chair, and assist his industrious wife with her theater production.

A combat veteran was referred to group after a domestic violence dispute. He benefited most from the psychoeducational component of SIT in understanding his hyperarousal and impulsive reactions to his wife's reactions during even the most benign arguments. The SIT group also assisted him in generating a strategy to evoke "more normal" reactions to stressors involving his wife. Another active duty service member, who had been sexually assaulted by a co-worker, acquired the anxiety management skills to cope with frequent interactions with the perpetrator and his friends during the investigation. The vulnerability experienced while discussing the event, several times in a group setting, desensitized her and promoted a healthier integration of her traumatic memory.

Conclusion and Contraindications

The goal of SIT is consistent with my objective of returning patients to optimal functioning in an expeditious manner with the aim of bolstering their coping skills and self-reliance.

There is, however, a general contraindication to this intervention. When dealing with anxiety and stress-related disorders, the resurfacing of traumatic memories is the rule rather than the exception. One can expect patients to react strongly to these memories and trauma-related fears and projections about the future. Therefore, it is imperative that those with significant personality dysfunction and poor affect regulatory abilities, be excluded from this type of group modality and be treated on an individual basis until they are more suitable for SIT.

References

Brewin, C. R., & Holmes, E. A. (2003). Psychological theories of posttraumatic stress disorder. *Clinical Psychology Review*, 23, 339–376.

Deffenbacher, J. L., & McKay, M. (2000). *Overcoming situations and general anger*. Oakland, CA: New Harbinger.

Department of Veterans Affairs and Department of Defense (2004). *VA/DoD clinical practice guideline, for the management of posttraumatic stress*. Washington, DC. Retrieved on 1 April 2007 from www.oqp.med.va.gov/cpg/PTSD/PTSDcpg/frameset.htm.

Ehlers, A., & Clark, D. M. (2000). A cognitive model of posttraumatic stress disorder. *Behaviour Research and Therapy*, 38, 319–345.

Lazarus, R. S., & Folkman, S. (1984). *Stress appraisal and coping*. New York: Springer-Verlag.

Meichenbaum, D. (1993). Stress inoculation training: A 20-year update. In R. L. Woolfolk & P. M. Lehrer (Eds.). *Principles and practices of stress management*. (pp. 373–406). New York: Guilford Press.

Meichenbaum, D. (1996). Stress inoculation training for coping with stressors. *The Clinical Psychologist*, 49, 4–7.

Meichenbaum, D. (2005). Stress inoculation training: A preventative and treatment approach. In P. M. Lehrer, R. L. Woolfolk & W. S. Sime (Eds.). *Principles and practice of stress management*. (Third edition). (pp. 203–219). New York: Guilford Press.

Suinn, R. M. (1990). *Anxiety management training*. New York: Plenum Press.

Dr. Justin A. D'Arienzo is a Board Certified Clinical Psychologist in private practice in Jacksonville, Florida, specializing in Clinical, Forensic, Business, and Military Psychology.

91 Using Metaphors and Stories to Resolve Impasses and Bridge Resistance

Jerrold Lee Shapiro

An Intervention for Eliciting Greater Emotional Depth and Creative Problem Solving

As an existential therapist, my own internal process informs much of my work during sessions. Often this "primary process" occurs in images, auditory memories, and fantasy. At certain times in group treatment, I am prone to expressing these images to clients: sometimes relatively unfiltered feelings and more commonly in story or metaphor.

Therapist storytelling has been used in a variety of theoretical approaches. Erickson (1980) and Erickson, Rossi, and Rossi (1976) for example, used stories to induce "informal" hypnotic states in clients. Techniques involved instigating a novel form of communication within therapy sessions. In the midst of the session, they altered their tone, word pacing, and often told a story that presumably had within it some clues for patient insight and/or behavior change.

Similarly, Honos-Webb, Sunwolf and Shapiro (2001, 2003) have indicated the salience of storytelling in therapy sessions in effecting alterations in behavior with or without an altered state on the part of the client. They define this healing power of stories in therapy as a method that may obviate some resistance by diverting clients' attention away from their anxiety and normative defense against any recommendations that promote change. Storytelling by a therapist has also been shown to help clients better handle crises (Pennebaker, 1997), i.e., increase their connection to unconscious process (Sturm, 2000) and expand their senses of the allowable. At the very least, therapist storytelling is useful in reducing client anxiety.

For existential therapists, there are two sources of anxiety: existential anxiety, which involves facing fears of the unknown and neurotic anxiety, which emerges from clients' attempts to avoid or defend against existential anxiety. In short, stories may help clients deal with existential anxiety by offering alternative expectations and projected outcomes and avoid neurotic anxiety by refocusing the clients' attention on the real challenge.

Description of Population

I work almost exclusively with time-limited, closed, clinical, and growth groups. However, this technique should work equally well in an ongoing open-ended group. It is definitely a technique that lends itself well to children, adolescents, and adults.

Description of Intervention

Unlike most techniques or exercises, this intervention is not distinct in appearance nor does it have a unique stage in group process. Instead, it occurs as if nothing different was occurring. At a critical juncture, the group leader may simply share a reflection that, on the surface, seems to be more there-and-then than here-and-now oriented. The reflection by the leader involves interceding in the discussion with a metaphor or with a *short* story that at some unconscious level is connected to the ongoing group process or as a response to an individual's personal sharing.

Using standard descriptions of a four-phase group trajectory: preparation, transition, working, and termination (Shapiro, Peltz & Bernadett-Shapiro, 1998), this procedure is one that is best suited to the third or working (also known as treatment or therapy) phase. It is designed to increase intrapsychic depth, once the group trust is sufficiently strong to support such enhanced levels of affect. However, it may be employed judiciously in the transition phase, while the group is testing the leadership, or in termination with a focus on transfer of training.

Step 1: Allow the normal group discussion to progress until something gets stuck.

Step 2: Focus on process including reflecting on the lack of movement, etc.

Step 3: Slip into a storytelling mode of speech and tell a short story or metaphor along with "therapeutic amazement" (i.e., *"I don't know why I would be thinking about this at this time"* or *"This reminds me of a fellow I once met"*).

Step 4: Allow the group members time to respond to the story, including any confusion they may experience.

Step 5: Continue as if nothing different or unusual had occurred.

Examples

During the treatment phase of a group of health care professionals, two members (Jake and Sally) were describing their "sandwich generation" dilemma, while other members of the group listened intently. Each of the members described feeling overburdened and trapped by simultaneous responsibilities to aging parents, school-aged children, and to their personal retirement. After sharing their experiences and feelings and hearing empathic feedback from other members, the group seemed to experience a lack of energy, described by Jake as a "sense that my own life is over."

Focusing on his experience of a loss of energy, I responded, to Jake, the forty-five-year-old male in the group. My initial response was empathy for his situation; then I began defocusing into a short story. *"Jake, your situation seems so difficult and you seem trapped by the very real responsibilities to your family."* Slowing my pace as if reminiscing, I said, *"I don't know why I am thinking of this, but as you were talking, I was hearing that little speech that accompanies every commercial airline flight. You know, the one that tells us if there's a drop in cabin pressure and the oxygen masks drop. If you are traveling with a minor child you are to put on your mask first."*

The client seemed confused by the story. As he began to respond slowly, he asked, "What does that have to do with how demanding my mother is?" I replied, "I am not sure. I was listening to you very closely and that is what came into my mind." At that point, Sally, the female "sandwicher" said, almost as if in a trance. "I think he means that we aren't stopping to breathe and need a break for some oxygen, or else our kids, parents and, yes, we will all fail." Jake said, "I do feel like I am almost out of breath, but I need to care for two aging parents and three children. There is no way out that I can see."

- I responded, *"I am not questioning your commitment or loyalty, I think I am focused on the other end of the equation—to look at how you will be able to care for them long term."*
- This led to a metaphor, *"Jake, Sally, I don't know about this but you both seem like sprinters and you are in a marathon. To run the best race, we need to figure out how you can best train and best conserve your strength. Nobody can sprint for twenty-six miles."*

Later in the same group as termination had begun, another member began to opine that she would "get my time when my children are grown." Other members began to argue with her that she would be close to sixty and that her parents might still need her. Several group members told her that she needed to have some time to herself while she was young enough to enjoy it. She claimed that her husband and kids all felt that she was too overprotective and stifled them. She replied that her husband and children told her that all the time. After about fifteen minutes of struggling with that, my co-leader turned to me and asked, "What are you thinking?" When I responded, *"Kenny's Cubs cap,"* all eyes in the group turned to me. After a pause, I continued,

- "I knew this guy, who, when he was a young boy wanted nothing as much as a brand new Chicago Cubs baseball cap. When he was nine, his older brother bought one for him. It was the greatest gift he could imagine. He held it, touched it, smelled it, put it on his dresser. He looked at it every night before he went to bed. However, he would never wear it for fear of losing it or getting it dirty. Regardless of his personal wish and his brother's encouragement that he wear it to school or to the ballpark, he was too afraid. That went on for five years. When he finally got to the point where he dared to wear it, he was fourteen and sadly it was too small."

A week later in the next session, she told the group that she had asked her husband to do the childcare on Wednesday nights, while she went to a dance class "just for me." She reported that he said yes without a second thought.

Clients' Experiences and Conclusion

This is a technique that increases for clients their ranges of expression and brings non-linear problem solving to the group. By approaching client issues in story or metaphor form, it suggests and encourages "out-of-the-box" solutions. It also has the great advantage of being somewhat transcultural.

There are at least two *contraindications*. First, the group must have sufficient ego strength to be able to handle the level of abstraction and not to be threatened by such a nonlinear intervention. The stories must be appropriate to the group's level of functioning and are best if they are either true or well-known fables or tales or in the pop culture. (i.e., *Aesop's Fables, Star Wars, Harry Potter*, children's stories).

Second, the leader must be able to trust her/his unconscious processing and be willing to share it in metaphor or story form. She or he must also be willing to appear less linear to group members.

References

Erickson, M. H. (1980). *The Collected Papers of Milton H. Erickson.* (E. L. Rossi (Ed.). New York: Irvington.

Erickson, M. H., Rossi, E. L. & Rossi, S. I. (1976). *Hypnotic Realities.* New York: Irvington

Honos-Webb, L., Sunwolf, & Shapiro, J. L. (2001). Toward the re-enchantment of psychotherapy: Stories as container. *The Humanistic Psychologist*, 29, 72–97.

Honos-Webb, L., Sunwolf, & Shapiro, J. L. (2003). The healing power of telling stories in psychotherapy. In J. D. Raskin & S. K. Bridges (Eds.) *Studies in Meaning 2.* New York: Pace University Press.

Pennebaker, J. W. (1997). Writing about emotional experiences as therapeutic process. *Psychological Science*, 8, 162–169.

Shapiro, J. L., Peltz, L. S., & Bernadett-Shapiro, S. T. (1998). *Brief Group Treatment: Practical Training for Therapists and Counselors.* Monterey, CA: Brooks/Cole.

Sturm, B. W. (2000). The "storylistening" trance experience. *Journal of American Folklore*, 113, 287–304.

Jerrold Lee Shapiro, Ph.D., is Professor of Counseling Psychology at Santa Clara University, a licensed Clinical Psychologist and a Fellow of the American Psychological Association. In addition to over 200 papers and journal publications, he has written 13 books, including, *Pragmatic existential counseling and psychotherapy: Intimacy, intuition and the search for meaning* (2016). He has been doing groups and teaching process group therapy since the mid-1960s.

92 Therapist Self-Disclosure as an Intervention Toward Normalizing and Eliciting Hope

Scott Simon Fehr

> Intervention: n. from (inter) between and (venire) to come, to come between. Interventionist: n. one who advocates or practices intervention.
> (McKechinie, 1963)

To Feel Alone

One of the profound benefits of group therapy is for clients to hear other clients speak about their particular problem and not feel so alone in their own intrapsychic world (Fehr, 1999, 2003). Yet at times, a client may present something that no one in the group can or is willing to identify as an issue salient to them. Thus the disclosure, of the client is met with group silence strengthening the possibility of future inhibitions where there is less probability that personal information will be divulged.

The concept of "therapist self-disclosure" is one that often elicits some form of professional discomfort for most of us (Fehr, 2003). Throughout our academics and training, self-disclosure is reinforced as a factor that creates boundary and ethical issues and needs to be avoided (Gutheil & Gabbard, 1993).

Specifically, there is the polarization of the orthodox Freudian stance of never disclosing as it demystifies the therapist and inhibits projections and transferential opportunities, whereas in the more humanistic, especially relational therapies, therapist self-disclosure is not as structurally implemented, (Jourard, 1964, 1971). Often, the catch phrase my colleagues use is "for whose benefit is the disclosure?" Obviously, the client has not come to us in group or individual therapy to hear about us nor are they here to help us with our interpersonal difficulties and conflicts (Corey, Corey & Callahan, 1998; Fehr, 2003; Weiner, 1983). But it is here, in fact, that therapist self-disclosure might be the intervention of choice for normalizing and giving hope to a client or clients in group therapy. This is especially true when the disclosure of the client reinforces existential aloneness. If no one in group identifies with the disclosure, the client may perceive his or her difficulty, as unique or bizarre.

Group Matrix

This particular intervention is effective with both time-limited and ongoing process groups. It is recommended solely for those clients who do not have difficulty with abstract thinking, as it requires the ability to be introspective. It is not recommended for those clients who fall at the lower end of the normal curve in intelligence or those clients who are so sadly disturbed that they cannot go beyond only seeing themselves and cannot make connections or identifications with other individuals.

An Intervention of the Therapist Self-Search

Therapist self-disclosure, if and only if it is in the interest of the client, may be the prescribed intervention. Over many years of running groups, I have found that there are very few interpersonal conflicts or experiences presented by clients with which I myself could not identify in varying degrees. In fact, I use the totality of my being in order to understand what a client is trying to relate in the hope of feeling what the client is feeling. This is similar to two tuning forks resonating on the same pitch (Fehr, 2003). In my mind, I run through my personal history and only disclose those factors that are salient to the issue at hand specifically if no one in the group identifies with the group member's disclosure. This self-disclosure is only presented if I have personally and successfully resolved the issue presented by the client as an intervention to help him or her not feel alone and to elicit hope that there can be a resolution although it might not be identical to mine.

The person of the therapist is the intervention as is the self-disclosure. Two very simple examples of the efficacy of this intervention are put forth: Example one is of a mixed-gender group, which I run. One client strongly confronted another berating him on the fact that he bites his nails. The client went on and on about how she would never date a person who bites his nails, that it looked disgusting. No one in the group either came to this man's aid with any form of identification, as he was truly embarrassed, nor did they come to his defense concerning her diatribe. Throughout my adolescence and early twenties, I too was a nail biter. I was not about to leave this client "hanging out to dry" and feel public humiliation and shame without aiding him. In order, for me, to normalize his behavior so he would not feel alone, and to give him hope that his compulsive behavior, nail biting, could be resolved, I disclosed an aspect of my history specifically related to his problem.

Analyzing the root of the symptomatology of the nail biting, I felt, would be of little help or value, at that moment. Normalizing and eliciting hope would be the most effective intervention. I disclosed that I had been a nail biter years before and found that becoming consciously aware of each time I brought my fingers to my mouth eventually helped me overcome this compulsive behavior. The relief seen in this man's face was quite remarkable. He thanked me profusely as he related that he felt so alone and so embarrassed throughout his life. His family and practically everyone in his interpersonal sphere had focused, at some point, on this behavior, which he felt was completely out of his control. Interestingly, two other group members disclosed, after my disclosure, that they too had been nail biters but were not about to disclose it after hearing the diatribe from the other group member. After helping to normalize the situation, other related issues came forth from the group-as-a-whole, which probably would not have taken place or may have taken place much further down the road in this group's history.

The second example is the case of a man who is about ten years younger than I am in. He was in his fifties. He had related that basically everything was going rather well in his life. His relationships with family and friends were good. Economically he was doing well but he felt lost and directionless and was not sure from where these feelings were coming.

The group worked effectively with him and he worked effectively with the group but could not find what might be the underlying issue that was stimulating this sense of loss of direction. I remembered how he would talk about the many times throughout his life that there were people he looked up to as guides in helping him navigate the capriciousness of life. I, personally, had heroes throughout my life but now for a number of years I had none. I thought about the opening line in the book *David Copperfield*, "Whether I shall turn out to be the hero of my own life or whether that station will be held by anyone else, these pages must show" (Dickens, 1991, p. 1). I disclosed, to this client and to the group, that I no longer had heroes in my own life to look up to for direction or to emulate their achievements and goals. I explained that upon this realization, which was about ten years earlier, I felt sad and lacked direction but realized that it was now my time to forge ahead on my own.

The client, upon hearing this disclosure, immediately said, "I think that's it." He related that over the past few months he had been feeling somewhat lost and directionless because there was no one whose footsteps he had wished to follow. He further disclosed that somewhere inside of himself he knew that a new direction of being was coming but could not figure it out. He smiled and said, "I guess it is time for me to be my own person and find my own direction" and like David Copperfield he became the hero in his own life. I wondered, at that time, after this man's insight if he would remain in therapy or leave but he stayed for another two years pursuing the self-search.

Typical Response

The typical response to this type of intervention has always been positive for me with respect to a client. It appears to normalize what he or she is experiencing and gives hope that another person, whom they theoretically respect, had a similar issue and worked it through. I also disclose to my clients that I am not Superman and feel, in many cases, that if I can do something I truly feel others can do it as well.

Contraindications

This intervention can be loaded with contraindications as boundary and ethical violations could easily be manifested. Because of this, keep in mind that the self-disclosure is for the client. Due to countertransference issues, many therapists are unaware of what they are doing and of the consequences of their self-disclosures. This often can take the form of competitiveness. The client discloses some issue and the therapist discloses a similar issue but with greater intensity, i.e., "If you think your divorce was difficult, you should have seen mine." For whose purpose is that type of disclosure as it is a complete negation of the client's feelings? That type of therapist self-disclosure is related to unresolved issues in the therapist's life that have been "set off" by the client's self-disclosure. To again reiterate, if you are considering disclosing personal information about your history, as an intervention, it must be an intervention and you must always remember, **"FOR WHOM IS THE DISCLOSURE DESIGNED?"** and what could be the possible consequences of demystifying your person in the eyes of your clients.

References

Corey, G., Corey M., and Callahan, P. (1998). *Issues and Ethics in the Helping Professions* (Fifth edition). Monterey, CA: Brooks/Cole.

Dickens, C. (1991). *David Copperfield*. New York: Alfred A. Knopf.

Fehr, S.S. (1999). *Introduction to Group Therapy: A Practical Guide*. Binghamton, NY: The Haworth Press.

Fehr, S.S. (2003). *Introduction to Group Therapy: A Practical Guide* (Second edition). Binghamton, NY: The Haworth Press.

Gutheil, T.G. & Gabbard, G.O. (1993). The concept of boundaries in clinical practice: Theoretical and risk-management dimensions. *American Journal of Psychiatry*, 150, 188–196.

Jourard, S.M. (1964). *The Transparent Self: Self-disclosure and Well-being*. New York: Van Nostrand Reinhold.

Jourard, S.M. (1971). *Self-disclosure: An Experimental Analysis of the Transparent Self*. New York: Wiley.

McKechinie, J. (Ed.). (1963). *Webster's New Twentieth Century Dictionary of the English Language* (Second edition). New York: The Publishers Guild.

Weiner, M.F. (1983). *The Use of Self in Psychotherapy* (Second edition). Baltimore, MA: University Park Press.

Dr. Scott Simon Fehr is a licensed Clinical Psychologist and a Certified Group Therapist. He is on the graduate faculty of Nova Southeastern University's School of Psychology. He has written and edited several books and has a son who is following in his professional footsteps.

93 Directed Eye Contact
Nonverbal Communication as a Group Strengthening Tool

Shari Baron

> Remembrance of past shames and fear of future shame become a straitjacket against spontaneity and knowledge of self-worth.
> (Goulding & Goulding, 1979)

Nonverbal Communication

Nonverbal communication includes the use of body posture (movement and position), tone and volume of voice, eye contact or avoidance and facial expression; we usually express our feelings about others through these nonverbal communications (Fehr, 2003). The way group members experience the nonverbal communications of one another is an important aspect of the group process that may be more powerful than the verbal (Perls, Hefferline, & Goodman, 1951; Fehr, 2003). The therapist can choose to direct a particular nonverbal structured exercise that strengthens the connections group members feel with one another. This intervention must be used judiciously—if it is used too frequently, it loses its potency and can become trite. However, when used on rare infrequent occasions, it can be a powerful tool that helps a depressed or shamed member feel safer in group and more joined with the other members.

Client Population

Yalom (1985) suggests that, in general, structured exercises are of more value in brief specialized groups than in long-term outpatient groups. However, this particular intervention has been used in the "working phase" of insight-oriented groups that focus on long-term relationship building and learning from the responses of and interactions with others. I have found it most useful when working with a client who has doubts about his or her membership in group, particularly when that doubt has grown out of a sense of shame or concern about rejection following "misbehavior" (in or outside of group) or revelation of what the client perceives as shameful historical material.

Guidelines for Intervention

Although this intervention requires an intuitive sense by the therapist of when it will be most beneficial, the technique is quite simple. The therapist asks a client, who has, in some way, been expressing doubt about his or her right to be included as a member of this group, to stop talking for a few minutes and sit quietly. The therapist directs him or her to "check out" what other group members think by silently looking around the room. All are requested to remain silent. The doubtful member looks from one person to the next, making eye contact. Without direct coaching by the therapist, the other members of the group gaze back with acceptance and reassurance. The doubtful member experiences the needed support of the group without the potential contamination that the addition of words might bring.

Examples

This intervention can be used when the shame or doubt originates with out-of-group behavior. Clara reported to group that she had spent the last few days in bed rather than going to work. She is angry with herself, feels worthless, and doubts that she will ever get better. She says that she is thinking about leaving group because "you must all be totally angry at me and disgusted with me." The therapist wonders aloud if the others in group actually do feel this way and suggests doubt that the group would reject her for her behavior (this plants the suggestion in the minds of the other members that they demonstrate acceptance of Clara despite her out-of-group behavior). The therapist directs Clara to stop for a few moments, close her eyes, and then open them and look silently around the room at her fellow members. As she moves her eyes around the room, each member in turn looks back at Clara with acceptance and compassion.

The intervention may also be used related to in-group behavior that leads to doubt and alienation. Jim had, for several weeks, been quite depressed and struggling with urges to cut or burn himself. He admits to the group that he has, just within the last few weeks, talked with his therapist about something that he had never discussed before; however, he is not ready to talk about this issue in group because it is too difficult and painful. Some group members express frustration because they cannot seem to reach Jim and want to help him. They feel he is distant and not participating fully in group. Jim withdraws further and says that maybe he should leave group if his participation is not good enough. The therapist wonders aloud if that is what the group is suggesting to him or if they might just be attempting to express their concern for Jim. The therapist directs Jim to sit with this thought for a few moments. She then asks him to look silently around the room at his fellow members. As he moves his eyes around the room, each member in turn looks back at Jim with reassurance and caring.

Typical Responses to This Intervention

Frequently, the results of this intervention are dramatic and emotional. The doubtful group member, who is usually feeling shame, isolation, and disconnection from the group, experiences the unconditional acceptance of the group as a whole and is able to believe that his or her membership in the group is valued. The other members also benefit from the sense of closeness and trust that lingers in the group following this exercise. There is rarely any interpretation or discussion about this reaction. I have found it more valuable to allow the insecure member and the group as a whole to experience the resulting sense of closeness nonverbally and without the contamination of analysis. The doubtful member is then encouraged to sit with his or her experience while someone else in the group works.

Conclusion and Contraindication

This tool is most useful in a group that is solidly in the working phase and whose members have the ability and experience to trust the responses of their fellow group members.

It would be contraindicated in a group where there are many new members or when there has been significant recent disruption in the group. Such disruption would undermine group trust and safety and this intervention could, in these circumstances, backfire and lead to further alienation.

References

Fehr, S. (2003). *Introduction to Group Therapy: A Practical Guide* (Second edition). Binghamton, NY: The Haworth Press.

Goulding, M. M. & Goulding, R. L. (1979). *Changing Lives Through Redecision Therapy.* New York: Grove Press.

Perls, F., Hefferline, R. F., & Goodman, P. (1951). *Gestalt Therapy: Excitement and Growth in the Human Personality.* New York: Dell Publishing.

Yalom, I. (1985). *The Theory and Practice of Group Psychotherapy* (Third edition). New York: Basic Books.

Shari Baron is a licensed Clinical Nurse Specialist and a Certified Group Psychotherapist who maintains a private psychotherapy practice in suburban Philadelphia. She also teaches group process and group therapy to psychiatric residents at the University of Pennsylvania.

94 "Remember Be Here Now"

Ellen J. Fehr
Gary L. Sandelier

Immediacy: Here and Now—Being in the Moment

The title of this contribution comes from Dr. Richard Alpert, a.k.a. Baba Ram Dass, author of the classic cult book of the early 1970s, *Remember Be Here Now*. The title encapsulates the essence of the following chapter in which different words are interchangeably used to identify a concept but the concept remains the same. That concept: the "present," which in psychology can be termed "immediacy, the here and now or being in the moment." They all represent the same thing and what they represent is an effective tool of intervention in interpersonal learning for clients in group therapy (Vinogradov & Yalom, 1989).

The need to keep the group and group members in the "present" can be a difficult undertaking for the group therapist as there often is a pull from the individual group members and the group-as-a-whole to verbally leave the room and return to anachronistic events in their lives. It would appear that most people exist in the past and future and due to this try to remain as such in group therapy (Fehr, 2003).

Obviously the past and future have their importance in psychotherapy but are best left to individual psychotherapy where individual time allows for their exploration. In group therapy, the "here and now" intervention is an effective opportunity for providing interpersonal learning that ultimately can reinforce personality change and restructuring.

Client Population and Types of Groups

This intervention is suggested for short- and long-term process groups that are designed for interpersonal learning. The underlying concept of interpersonal growth groups is focused on self-awareness or the self-search. This concept is simply stated as "How do others perceive me and how do I perceive myself in relation to others?" thus providing the opportunity for alterations in one's behavior and personality.

Interventional Goal and Technique

The goal of this intervention is quite simple in theory. The group therapist wants to keep the group members actively in the "present" disclosing their relationships to one another, their relationship to the person of the group therapist, and the relationship they are having with themselves in a particular moment in time—the "present" (Bernard & MacKenzie, 1994; Carroll & Wiggins, 1997; Fehr, 2003; Rutan & Stone, 1993). The group therapist does this by theoretically altering time. He or she brings the client from existing in either the past or the future into the "now" by creating interpersonal relationships thus providing opportunities for clients to become aware of their interpersonal style and relatedness, which is often the source of their interpersonal difficulties.

Although keeping the group in the "present," sounds rather simple, in actuality it is not. As previously stated, keeping the group-as-a-whole and group members in the moment can be, at times, a daunting task. Ormont (1992) suggested a rather simple tool, a question, labeled "bridging." This technique creates a bridge between the clients in group by asking them direct questions such as:

- "How do you feel about what John has said or John how do you feel about what Mary had said to you concerning your disclosure?"
- "Steve, how do you feel when Sally appears disgusted whenever one of the men speaks about his relationship with women?"

All of these questions are in the "present" and will bring the client, to whom they are directed, into the present with his or her response. These are direct questions to the client and the goal is for the client to be equally direct, at that moment, in his or her response.

Group-as-a-whole questions can be asked, such as:

- "How does the group feel each time Nico walks in late?"
- "Nico how do you feel toward the group each time you walk in late?"

There is no end to the many questions that can be directly asked to the individual group members or to the group-as-a-whole. It is very important that the client(s) do not answer you directly unless the question is about yourself. The meaning of this is that you feel there is something unspoken from the client to you and you inquire into what that may be.

If the question is not in relation to you, you want the client to directly express his or her answer to the object of the question such as:

- "Steve how do you feel about Gary?" Gary in this case is the object of the question posed. Very often clients, due to their anxiety, will begin to answer your question directly to you. This type of response will remain as such until they become more comfortable adapting to this focused type of relatedness. They, too, will have the opportunity of experiencing that they will not "fall apart" when speaking directly to another person and neither will the other person "fall apart."

This is a tremendous growth for the majority of clients who have rendered themselves passive to others throughout most of their lives and never truly expressed what they felt and thought about another individual.

Until the client becomes more comfortable speaking directly to others, you will probably repeat this phrase many times over and that is "please tell the other person." In the above case the other person is Gary and you would, of course, use the person's name.

Clients' Responses

In a newly formed group and, at times, in ongoing groups, it is quite common for members to express annoyance in attitude when they cannot turn group therapy into individual therapy and talk about their life experiences outside of the room. Spontaneously disclosing oneself in a room of other people or disclosing how one feels about another person is uncomfortable, especially if it is a relatedness style foreign to one's usual manner of self-expression. It is not uncommon to hear clients say that they do not want to hurt another person's feelings by telling him or her how they feel about what was said or how it was said. Nor is it unusual for clients to feel overwhelmed, rejected, and criticized when they hear others directly tell them how the others feel about what the client has disclosed and the manner in which the disclosure was presented.

This is not to suggest that all the client responses are negative to this intervention. The majority of the time, clients are grateful for the insight given them by the other group members. It provides them the opportunity to change how they relate to others and experience their lives and interpersonal relationships more effectively and with greater satisfaction. It, too, sends a very clear message and that is finally someone has listened when he or she has spoken.

Conclusion and Contraindications

This intervention attempts to create interpersonal relationships in an attenuated time span between people where an interpersonal relationship had not previously existed. There is a reality, which is everyone will move at his or her own pace but we can provide opportunities that clients had not previously had which could ultimately change a pace style. It is an awesome experience for the clients and the group therapist as both have the opportunity to gain insights into their behaviors with the concomitant opportunity to make behavioral changes in their personalities.

Perhaps, the most salient contraindication is to be found in the therapist's selection of the clients in the group. This group requires the client to have the ability to be introspective and to have the ego strength to allow direct interpersonal communications. These communications, at times, can be emotionally intense and not flattering. A fragile client would not be a good candidate for this type of group. This client would best be served and seen in a support group. After the support group, he or she could eventually be moved into a more interpersonal interactive group after developing the necessary ego strength. This particular ego strength is the buffer to hearing things about himself or herself that are not flattering at times, are not continuously experienced as a narcissistic injury by the client, but rather as observations that can be of tremendous help in resolving interpersonal difficulties.

References

Alpert, R. (1971). *Remember Be Here Now.* New Mexico: Lama Foundation.
Bernard, H. & MacKenzie, R. (1994). *Basics of Group Psychotherapy.* New York: The Guilford Press.
Carroll, M. & Wiggins, J. (1997). *Elements of Group Counseling* (Second edition). Denver, CO: Love Publishing Company.
Fehr, S. (2003). *Introduction to Group Therapy: A Practical Guide* (Second edition). Binghamton, NY: The Haworth Press.
Ormont, L. (1992). *The Group Therapy Experience: From Theory to Practice.* New York: St. Martin's Press.
Rutan, S. & Stone, W. (1993). *Psychodynamic Group Psychotherapy.* New York: The Guilford Press.
Vinogradov, S. & Yalom, I. (1989). *Group Psychotherapy.* Washington, DC: American Psychiatric Press.

Ellen Joan Fehr, M.S., is a Licensed Mental Health Counselor who specializes in running groups related to Women's Issues. She is also a published author.

Gary L. Sandelier, M.S., is a Licensed Mental Health counselor who runs Men's Groups that focus on interpersonal issues and personal growth.

95 Changing Chairs
Experiential Exercise for Exploration of Interpersonal Boundaries

Patricia Kyle Dennis

Whose Chair is This?

Soon after the formation of a new therapy group, the alert leader will hear members make references to chairs as they enter the group room. "Where am I supposed to sit?" "We always sit in the same places . . . guess we're in a rut!" "Maybe I'll sit in the leader's chair tonight!" (nervous laughter). People quickly choose places and the topic of discussion is dismissed as settled. However, a group event has already taken place that is rich with meaning and learning potential. This intervention is designed to tap that potential.

Although it is clear that there is a need to set and maintain appropriate boundaries in group therapy (Schoener & Luepker, 1996), it may not be immediately evident that there is therapeutic value to the struggle around boundaries in the group. This struggle may represent similar conflicts and difficulties outside the group room, past and present. The therapist can use this replication to help members learn more about their internal and interpersonal conflicts related to boundary issues.

Taking it one step further, the therapist may create a conflict through a group experiential exercise as a vehicle for learning. According to Hornyak and Baker (1989, p. 3) experiential treatment techniques are based on psychological principles, and are used for "increasing clients' present awareness of feelings, perceptions, cognitions, and sensations; that is, their in-the-moment experience. The method usually involves some degree of action on the clients' part, either physical or imagined."

In this intervention, the therapist asks group members to change chairs, and then discuss their reactions. The focus of the exercise is on interpersonal boundaries.

Description of the Group

A short-term psychoeducational group of six to eight members is the ideal setting for this activity. Since boundary issues are related to many presenting problems, the exercise may be included in various types of groups, such as those meant to address addictions, abuse, codependency, women's issues, men's issues, etc.

Changing Chairs: Experiential Exercise 337

The exercise is quite stimulating and will require plenty of time to process. The length of the group should be eight to ten sessions or more. One entire group session should be dedicated to the intervention, and the therapist should expect that members will refer back to the experience in subsequent sessions.

This intervention requires a group with closed membership, which facilitates the establishment of relationships and familiar patterns of interaction.

Intervention

Some time in the middle of the group, after members have had some time to establish their "place" in the group, but well before the group ends, to leave time for discussion, a session should be dedicated to the experiential exercise of changing chairs. It is important not to give clues about the activity in advance, or its effectiveness will be destroyed. The session title may include a reference to boundaries or limit setting, but the content of the session should be left up to the imagination.

- Listen closely to comments about seating and chairs as members enter the room, during all sessions leading up to this exercise. These will be useful for discussion. Take extra time allowing people to get seated, with their drinks, coats, etc., stashed in their favorite places. Be sure that latecomers have had time to arrive. Promote small talk and settling in.
- Carefully note where each person is sitting. Form a plan to reseat each individual in a chair that is most unlike the one he or she chose. Those who sit close to you, will be moved far away. Those who like to sit on the couch, will be moved to individual chairs. Plan to fill the couch completely with people who chose individual chairs.
- Once everyone is settled in, announce that the activity planned for this session will require a new seating arrangement. This matter-of-fact approach makes it seem as if the rearrangement is an insignificant detail. This will prevent members from trying to second guess your intent, which would keep the experience from being spontaneous and characteristic of their usual behaviors.
- Ask each member by name to move to his or her new chair. Take note of the many comments, questions, and reactions that your intervention will engender for later discussion, but encourage everyone to postpone discussion until later. After group members have taken their reassigned places, ask the group to close their eyes, relax, and think about their answers to the following questions, leaving time in between for members to reflect.
- Ask: How do you feel about your new chair? Do you prefer having someone next to you, or do you like having your own space? How did you feel when I moved you? Where would you most like to sit? What

would you need to do now to get the chair that you want? How hard would it be for you to do that?
- Ask the group members to open their eyes. Before they have a chance to talk, say "Now I would like you to go and get the chair that you want, without touching anybody." Again, pay close attention to all the ensuing interactions, verbal and nonverbal.
- As soon as it appears that there will be no more change, ask the group members to report on their experience of the exercise, drawing on the questions that you asked while their eyes were closed. Use the rest of the group time to process their thoughts, feelings, and nonverbal experiences, taking the opportunity to use what they say to teach what you want them to know about interpersonal boundaries. It is likely that they will learn as much or more from one another than from you in this process, so encourage discussion and feedback among the group members. It can be particularly helpful to ask members if they have similar experiences outside of the group or in their families of origin.

Intervention Responses

After conducting this exercise more than seventy-five times, the author has found that there is a very wide range of responses to the experience. Hundreds of meanings and insights have been uncovered in this way. Group members almost always report a heightened understanding of their experience with personal boundaries, intrusiveness, abandonment, competition, and conflict resolution. Connections may be made to family experiences of unwanted touching, interrupting, projective processes, competition, over-control, lack of privacy, difficulty saying "no," not being taught to negotiate, and many others.

Often group members will not realize that although it is not OK to touch while they go after their desired chairs, *talking* has not been prohibited. The healthier members may try to negotiate. Many will make a run for their new spot, or stay put in order to avoid conflict. Sometimes there is a great deal of laughter and good-humored self-consciousness. Other times, the anxiety level goes up to a point where people become confused, flustered, or confrontational.

The therapist should take care to be sure that each individual group member has the chance to debrief, learn from his or her experience, ask questions, and get suggestions. It will take active listening and questioning to help people talk about any conflicts that arose, how they dealt with them, and what makes it difficult to get the chair, or anything else, that they need or want. Those who avoided conflict must not be lost in the process, as they may have the most difficulty of all.

Conclusion and Contraindication

There are some contraindications to conducting this intervention. It may be very challenging for people who were not allowed to say *no* as children.

People with borderline personality disorder or those with other severe interpersonal deficits may have a great deal of difficulty managing their feelings and interactions during the event. The therapist should increase supportive comments when this occurs. It is important to have an alternate agenda if the exercise appears to be too challenging for one or more group members.

Empathic, nonjudgmental, and supportive processing of this experiential exercise is usually beneficial to the group members and can be a highlight of the group experience, clearly remembered and referred to often when a group member continues in therapy. Generally, people take their new places and are able to engage in a rich exploration of the event, learning about their difficulties and needs. The event usually results in a deepening of the attachments in the group, the level of self-disclosure, and dedication to the group process. Members almost always try out and discuss new behaviors while finding their seats in subsequent group sessions.

References

Hornyak, L. M., & Baker, E. K. (Eds.) (1989). *Experiential therapies for eating disorders*. New York: The Guilford Press.

Schoener, G. R., & Luepker, E. T. (1996). Boundaries in group therapy: Ethical and practice issues. In B. DeChant (Ed.). *Women and group psychotherapy: Theory and practice* (pp. 373–399). New York: The Guilford Press.

Dr. Patricia Kyle Dennis, LCSW, CGP, specializes in eating disorders in private practice. She leads psychotherapy groups for women who present with the problems of overeating and gaining weight.

96 Surfing an Unexpected Group's Tide

Uri Amit

Dispel a Belief

Since most adults possess the capacity to anticipate shame, some personal fantasies of psychical significance may remain suppressed and adversely impact the individual's affective agility. The energy spent on containing these fantasies may result not only in emotional rigidity, but also in self-alienation. It may also result in unrewarding interpersonal relationships and stifle creativity. In short, the fear of being discovered robs the scared of the momentary joys life presents.

Group therapy affords participants the opportunities to dispel the belief that one must remain all alone in his or her internal world (Fehr, 1999, 2003) and endure a torturous, lingering process of self-shaming and inadvertently self-deprivation.

Sex Offender Client Population

This particular intervention is appropriate for sex offenders who (1) do not display delusional processes, (2) use language indicative of sex and aggression inextricably intertwined, and (3) have been working together for one or more years in a contained environment.

Intervention

Brief Case Example

"Guy" is a Euro-Asian, lanky man who was assigned to a ten-man therapy group that met twice weekly for a total of three hours. Guy was always the first to arrive for sessions and occupy a chair placed in one of the corners. We were both easily visible to each other. After about a month in group and on occasions outside the hour, Guy used to engage me in chats about sports and movies, inform me of movies to be shown on television on certain evenings, and make it a point to see me on a subsequent day to ask if I saw this or that movie.

During his first month in group, I noticed Guy's propensity to be a silent participant. Consequently, I started to progressively contact him more in each session. So as not to "blow him away," I used to ask him if he concurred with my hunches about the affect reflected in the men's presentations. His replies were terse summaries of the presented and devoid of feelings. I also observed that he writhed in the chair when offenses were described. On one occasion several months down the road, I asked Ben, a group member with an uncanny ability to intuit, to speculate on Guy's seeming discomfort when offenses are described. Ben replied: "He is dying to describe his offenses, but is afraid." Guy nodded his head in agreement and added, "I'm not ready."

Aware of Guy's sexual crimes and appreciating his reluctance to describe his sexual sadism as was reflected in his governing offense, I asked him on this occasion: "Would you agree to go to a movie with me?" He looked at me with surprise written all over his face and said: "You're messing with me, Doc." I said, "No, I shit you not." He then asked: "You mean outa here?" I replied, "No, right in this room, right at this moment."

With that, I got off my chair, asked the group to create three rows of three chairs in each behind the two chairs that I placed next to each other. I sat in one of the chairs and asked Guy to join me. Ben was asked to turn off the light (the large window in the room did not allow for darkness). I invited Guy to project on the wall we faced the movie he created in the mid-1980s and for which he was civilly committed for treatment. He hesitated. I, then, said to him provocatively, "Nothing sexual in this world would be shocking, arousing, perhaps." This was said in order to lessen Guy's anticipatory shame and fear of being judged by the others.

As Guy proceeded to describe subduing the then eight-year-old boy and anally penetrating him; Ben, seated behind Guy, cried out, "This is how I was raped at summer camp," and proceeded to sob uncontrollably. Thick silence befell the room. I turned my chair around to face Ben and asked Guy to do the same. Placing my hands on their shoulders, I encouraged them to look at each other and give voice to all that emerged between two perpetrators of whom one chose to remind himself of his own victimization.

Responses

After the initial exchange between a perpetrator (Guy) and a victim (Ben), I felt compelled to interrupt and remind Ben that while himself a victim of sexual abuse, he assaulted a prepubescent female in the same manner as Guy. During the remainder of the session and for the two that followed, both Guy and Ben disclosed the nature of their offenses in manners consistent with the victims' statements.

Conclusion and Contraindication

What started as an attempt to move one man (Guy) from a silent group participant to a verbally active one resulted in an unexpected outcome. The familiarity of the two involved men's histories prevented the session from turning into a "How could you?" salvo by Ben. At that point, the journey began on the long and bumpy road to understanding the respective psychologies reflected in these men's offenses.

It is strongly recommended, especially with this particular population, that having knowledge of clinical theories is necessary but insufficient to working with a felonious group—one that displays disregard for the personal boundaries of others. Personal contact via the seemingly mundane, e.g., the chats about sports and movies, is important as is the sense of timing, and the readiness to take a clinical risk; the insistence to connect often reflects care that this particular population appreciates. In this respect, these individuals are willing to try out recommendations made by the therapist.

In relation to contraindications with this particular population, a group therapist must be able to free herself or himself from judgment and outrage at the acts committed by these individuals, and keep moral opinions in abeyance. One must feel comfortable with her or his own oddities and, above all, believe that light can be found in darkness' depth.

References

Fehr, S.S. (1999). *Introduction to Group Therapy: A Practical Guide*. Binghamton, NY: The Haworth Press.

Fehr, S.S. (2003). *Introduction to Group Therapy: A Practical Guide* (2nd ed.). Binghamton, NY: The Haworth Press.

Dr. Uri Amit has held senior clinical positions in forensic facilities for over thirty years, is a psychology faculty member at a large public research university and is a private practitioner. He is affiliated with a psychoanalytical institute in a metropolitan city, a Diplomate of the American College of Forensic Examiners and a Certified Group Psychotherapist by the American Group Psychotherapy Association.

97 Mindfulness in Group Therapy

Mark A. Cohen
David Cantor

> Mindfulness is the awareness of present experience with acceptance.
> (Germer, 2005)

A Mindful Individual

Most times, when people enter psychotherapy, they are not mindful of themselves or of others. They often enter therapy unaware of what they feel, why they feel as they do, and in what context these feelings are likely to be elicited. There also tends to be an unawareness of the feelings and motivations of others. Many use projection rather than mindful awareness when trying to understand what another person is feeling. This of course leads to difficulties in relationships.

In addition, people tend to use what they have been told about themselves by others instead of being mindful of who they are and instead of being aware of how they feel. People also tend to use the standards of society in trying to figure out how they should be and feel. Instead of looking inward and being aware of what they feel, they replace this introspection with a focus on how society says they should be and feel.

There are negative consequences to living a mindless life. Tart (1994) writes that without mindfulness we live in a state of distorted perceptions and fantasies, acting inappropriately with reference to our own true nature and the reality of the immediate situation, consequently creating stupid and useless suffering. There are positive consequences to living a mindful life. Surrey (2005) writes that mindfulness is a practice or skill, which opens and deepens our capacity for connection and for relational as well as spiritual renewal.

Group psychotherapy is about building connections between people and building bridges between their self-awareness and those aspects of themselves, which have been disavowed. Group psychotherapy helps the patient do this in a number of ways including providing an arena for interpersonal exploration, a focus on interpersonal interactions, and most importantly a focus or mindfulness on what the patient is experiencing in the moment both with himself or herself and in relation to the other group members. Ormont (1992) writes that the primary task in making our group function effectively is to use any technique which evokes meaningful talk between group members and to develop emotional connections where they did not exist before. He calls this process bridging, and for it to occur the members must use mindfulness.

Short- and Long-Term Group Populations

The intervention of using mindfulness in group psychotherapy is effective with most patients both in short-term and longer-term groups. In a short-term group, this intervention is best limited to building mindfulness of feelings and bodily sensations which are already close to awareness. In a long-term group this intervention can be used to teach them to be mindful of feelings and bodily sensations which are less congruent with how they want to perceive themselves.

This intervention is best used with patients who fall within the normal range of intelligence and who have the ability to step back from themselves and observe their feelings and their behaviors. It is also most effective with patients who are able to receive feedback from others without being unduly hurt. It is least effective with those patients who tend to be overly concrete and who lack the ability to suspend projection of their own mental contents onto others.

This intervention can be used by therapists from different theoretical orientations including psychodynamic, cognitive, and behavioral. The psychodynamically oriented therapist can also use this intervention in terms of the patient being mindful of transference issues with the therapist, each group member, and the group as a whole. The cognitively oriented therapist can use this intervention while perhaps focusing more on the patient's thoughts and schemas. The behaviorally oriented therapist would tend to focus more on mindfulness as a behavior rather than as a mental process.

Guidelines for Intervention

The key to promoting mindfulness in group is based upon helping the individual to become more in touch with what he or she is feeling and thinking in the moment. These interventions can be applied to the group as a whole, such as asking all group members to try the technique. They can also be directed at individual group members who may need assistance with becoming more in touch with the moment. The group therapist can also use this intervention to enhance his or her own personal mindfulness in group.

Identification of Body Language

Using this technique, the individual group member is instructed to become aware of both his or her own body language and that of other group members, and also how they feel in regard to the body language. Examples of this include how one is sitting, one's gestures, and one's facial expressions. By looking at one's own body language one can become more in touch with how one is feeling. Likewise, looking at another individual's body language can help put the patient in touch with how he or she may be feeling.

Mindfulness Toward Behavior

Our behavior in group tells us a great deal about how we are feeling and what we are thinking, even at an unconscious level. Examples of things group members can try to be aware of are where one sits (near the therapist, near the door, near the restroom, etc.), whom one sits next to, how one dresses, whether one arrives early, on time, or late for group, whom one chats with before and after group, etc.

Closing Our Eyes

The therapist can ask one group member or the whole group to close their eyes while they listen to the other group members speak. This simple but powerful intervention gets one past the superficial exterior and more in touch with how one feels about the other and how the other speaks. This helps people to focus more on tone of voice and affect—that is, how one is saying things, rather than the actual words. Many group members have been surprised how doing this can help to immediately put them in touch with feelings about the speaker that they were not aware of. This is also an effective intervention for the seasoned clinician to help get in touch with his or her feelings about a specific group member or the group as a whole.

Mindfulness of Physical Sensations

There are many physical sensations therapists and group members have that can help us get in touch with the moment and our feelings. Being aware of one's heart rate, respirations, perspiration level, and level of muscle tension helps one to be more mindful of feelings and even reactions on a subconscious level. For example, because the body reacts so quickly in the fight-or-flight mechanism, one might start to get hot, perspire, or feel his or her heart start to pound before becoming aware of feeling anxious or scared.

Mindfulness of Thoughts in the Moment

Often, a group member might have passing, fleeting thoughts that flash in and out of his or her mind, might have a quick mental or visual association, or may have a verse from a song pop in and out of his or her head. These are all short events that, if one is trying to be mindful, will help an individual become more in touch with what he or she is feeling and thinking in the moment.

Client Responses

When group members apply self-motivated interventions into their personal experiences to help with mindfulness they are surprised at how well and how quickly the intervention works toward becoming more aware. These are not interventions that require a lot of practice and training, and individuals trying them for the first time can have great success, which ultimately reinforces its continued application. Individuals become astonished sometimes at how much nonverbal communication occurs in a group or at how much of their own thoughts and feelings they were not aware of before practicing mindfulness in their daily living.

Contraindication

It has been our experience that there is no population for which these interventions are contraindicated although individuals must have some introspective ability. If one has the ego strength to be in a process-oriented group therapy setting, then working on mindfulness will enhance the group process. These interventions can be applied to individuals, the group, and the therapist to enhance mindfulness in the group setting.

References

Germer, C. K., (2005). Mindfulness: What is it? What Does it Matter? In C. K. Germer, R. Siegel, & P. Fulton (Eds.). *Mindfulness and Psychotherapy* (pp. 3–27). New York: The Guilford Press.

Ormont, L. R. (1992). *The Group Therapy Experience: From Theory to Practice.* New York: St. Martin's Press.

Surrey, J. L. (2005). Relational Psychotherapy, Relational Mindfulness. In C. K. Germer, R. Siegel, & P. Fulton (Eds.). *Mindfulness and Psychotherapy* (pp. 91–110). New York: The Guilford Press.

Tart, C. T. (1994). *Living the Mindful Life: A Handbook For Living In The Present Moment.* Boston, MA: Shambhala Publications, Inc.

Mark A. Cohen, Psy.D., received his doctorate degree in Clinical Psychology from Nova Southeastern University and practiced in Cleveland, Ohio. He had a diverse practice consisting of therapy, evaluations, and testing of adults, children, and geriatrics.

Dr. David Cantor is a licensed clinical psychologist in private practice and has led over 2000 hours of group psychotherapy. He has previously taught several classes as an adjunct faculty at East Tennessee State University.

98 Trauma Therapy as a Community Enterprise

Norman Claringbull

The Most Traumatized are the Victims of Minor Events

Although the major disasters hit the headlines, the fact remains that most traumatized persons are the victims of *"minor"* events (at least in terms of their newsworthiness). Put simply, there are far more armed-robbery victims, assault victims, car crash survivors or people encountering random/unexpected, violent, or otherwise traumatic, events than there are victims of tsunamis, war, or terrorism. Most people's everyday experiences of trauma happen on the street corner, in the workplace, in the home, as part of everyday life and usually involve a very small number of participants, often less than three or four, including the perpetrator.

Nevertheless, whether the traumatic event is affecting large groups or small, it has traditionally been the case that responding to the needs of the potentially traumatized is the province of the specialist, the "Expert Trauma Therapist." However, the U.K. National Institute for Health and Clinical Excellence (2005) warns us that trauma therapy *"should only be offered if it is actually necessary"* and argues that there are many cases when clinical inaction is the treatment of choice. This proposition raises the possibility that trauma therapists may not necessarily be best deployed if they are primarily seen as *"frontline troops."*

A recent literature review (Rutter, 2007) strongly suggests that many, if not most, victims much prefer the help of friends and colleagues to the services of the allegedly expert therapist. These observations are powerfully reinforced by Ørner et al. (2003), who found that employees in high-risk occupations responded best to the flexible and informal help routinely offered to them by their workmates. It seems that trauma victims often prefer to turn for help to their own local communities, (workplace, social, familial, etc.), than to therapists. Therefore, is trauma therapy best delivered when it is embedded as part of a community enterprise?

Description of The Client Population

The client population is, literally, anybody, anywhere, any place, any time, any circumstances. It really is *"a small world"*!

Interventions

Example 1

Christmas 2004 simply did not happen for me. I spent it as a member of a dedicated "Reception Team" helping the survivors of the Indian Ocean tsunami who were arriving at London Gatwick. A special receiving area had been set up at the airport where, as they got off the plane, the returnees passed through an organized and orderly reception process that involved medical teams, social welfare teams, clothing and refreshment providers, showers, rest areas, access to phones/e-mail and the help of transport specialists who organized their onward journeys. Of course, as this was the United Kingdom, at all stages there were copious amounts of tea available!

The interesting thing about working with these people was this: There were probably about thirty to forty experienced "service providers" present, including doctors, nurses, paramedics, social workers, police, NGO "experts" and so on. However, as soon as any of the "customers" showed any form of overt emotion whatsoever, the cry went up, "get the therapists!" Why? What was everyone scared of? In the immediate aftermath of the disaster, before any proper organization got going, these victims had been simply scooped up off the beaches and from the wrecked resorts, packed into the first available plane to anywhere and sent off. It was not uncommon to see people arriving still wearing their swimsuits and with no other luggage. One woman turned up wearing only her bikini bottom! Naturally, as soon as they got home to the United Kingdom, and could at last feel safe, these people immediately began to react emotionally in very overt and initially inconsolable ways.

My deliberate response to this obvious psychological discomfort amongst the team was to take my co-workers to one side and quietly explain this very normal emotional healing process to them. I wanted to get it established and accepted that it was more than just okay to weep, but actually quite a common human event and even a desirable one. Therefore the most helpful thing that they could do was simply to allow this natural healing progress to occur without pathologizing either the returnees or their psychological reactions. What was I doing? Was I giving my co-workers "therapy," "psycho-education," "normalization/permission" or whatever? I don't know, but I do know that it worked and it was probably the most effective therapeutic intervention that I offered over the entire ten days that we spent meeting the survivors. I know this because I could see the obvious benefits to the survivors and the positive changes in the team's attitudes. Would I do it again? I have no idea—it just seemed right at the time!

Example 2

In the Gulf War, a well-known, international petrochemical company who was concerned about terrorist activity, briefed me to run coping-strategy training courses for their European staff whose colleagues might suffer psychologically from terrorism-generated trauma. The plan was to help the workers to help themselves. Most employees were keen to get involved but they mostly shared a general feeling of potential incompetence and impotence when faced with, what to them was, the apparently impossible, or even overwhelming, task of dealing with overt human emotion. They were scared of being scared! The following two exchanges show how I tried to respond to their problems and you can judge if (and perhaps how) you might have done things differently.

Employee A

> *I was involved in a bad traffic accident. Although not hurt myself, several people were and the paramedics asked me to sit with one young chap who was quite badly injured and awaiting transfer to hospital. I suppose that I was with him at the roadside for about twenty minutes—it seemed like hours at the time. We chatted idly and then he asked me to ride in the ambulance with him. Altogether I was with him for about an hour. I've never felt so useless in my life! He needed urgent medical help and there was just nothing that I could do for him. I keep having nightmares about all this.*

In technical terms, my intervention could be described as psychoeducational. In reality, all I did was to explain that the victim was simply asking for the immediate comfort of human contact. Therefore their "idle chatter" was exactly the sort of emotional help that he needed at that time. Far from being "useless," what Employee A was doing was essential and skillful work in helping the victim cope with his fears and make some sense of his shattered world. My input apparently helped because at a subsequent meeting Employee A told me that the nightmares had stopped.

Employee B

> *My neighbor was robbed at gunpoint and afterwards she became a changed woman. She was a different person; someone I didn't know. She had huge mood swings; she lost all of her sparkiness and was quite aggressive to everybody. One day she told me that she was terrified that that she might be going crazy and I just didn't know what to say to her because I didn't want to make her worse.*

This fear of insanity seems to be quite common in trauma victims who, at least in the short-term, find that their lives and their emotions have been distorted by their psychologically disruptive experiences. My usual intervention is to simply tell them that they are actually quite okay and that it is normal to react abnormally to an abnormal situation. I explained to Employee B that we all get crazy in crazy circumstances and that it usually helps trauma victims if we all openly acknowledge this. There was an immediate alteration in his body language. I could see the changes take place. It seems that learning this simple fact made him feel much better about himself and he later told me that he now felt more confident about dealing with similar situations in the future if he had to.

In both the first and the second examples, at no time was I presenting as an expert trauma therapist. I was just doing a bit of psychological handholding and I was not doing anything that any reasonably informed, concerned person could not do. All that I was doing was helping, or encouraging, the members of the community to respond more confidently and more effectively to the needs of trauma survivors. In effect, I was helping to promote the concept of trauma therapy as being a community enterprise. So, if this means that sometimes I find myself making the sandwiches just to show that the response team cares enough about the survivors to worry about feeding them, then so be it. It is often claimed, although unfortunately never substantiated, that Freud once told a group of students that, "sometimes a cigar is just a cigar." True or not, it is a great story, so if our traumatized clients tell us that they only "need a smoke" then perhaps we should leave worrying about transferential analyses, core conditions, object relations, or any of our therapeutic whatevers until another time. Or, better still, perhaps—sometimes even forget about therapy altogether!

A Redefining Conclusion

There are already a number of community-based approaches to trauma relief in current use. Here are two popular examples:

The first example can be found in a process commonly known as "Critical Incident Defusing" (Mitchell & Everly, 2001). This is basically an emotional recovery process, which is usually most effective if those involved in a traumatic incident carry it out for themselves. This is because defusing is essentially a peer-supported normative process and so bringing in outside "experts" might unnecessarily exacerbate the situation. Defusing is a method of focusing post-incident conversation and social interactions so as to ensure that everybody who was involved, or is otherwise affected, feels able to acknowledge and, if necessary, express their thoughts and feelings. In other words, defusing is a process that acts as an emotional pressure-relief valve that reduces immediate psychological tensions and prevents accumulative stresses from building up.

The second example of trauma intervention as a client-led, community-centered process can be found in the Psychological First Aid (PFA) protocols, developed jointly by the U.S. National Child Traumatic Stress Network & National Center for PTSD (2006).

- Contacting and engaging the victims
- Helping the victims find safety and comfort
- Emotional stabilization
- Finding out just what the victims really need *(everything and anything)*

- Organizing practical assistance
- Connecting victims with own/local social support systems
- Providing the victims with information about what has happened to them, how it might affect them (including psychological/emotional affects), and how to cope
- Developing links with welfare and health services in case of subsequent need.

In sum, it should be noted that most, possibly all, of the components of both defusing and PFA are not essentially psychotherapeutic in nature but focus on meeting basic needs (e.g., physical safety, interpersonal connectedness, support, normalization, encouraging postevent functioning, etc.). These services must be flexibly delivered, using strategies that meet the specific needs of the victims. As McNally, Bryant, and Ehlers (2003, p. 68) note, "the bottom line is that in the immediate aftermath of trauma, professionals should take their lead from the survivors and provide the help they want, rather than tell survivors how they will get better." So, given that there is a strong case for taking the supposedly expert trauma therapist out of the posttrauma scenario, does psychotherapy still have a part to play in the general care of the traumatized? Can therapists still be of use? Perhaps we might have to retarget our professional intentions and remodel our therapeutic activities. The sample interventions, which I have described in this chapter, suggest that this very task-focused therapeutic evolution might well be achievable and possibly even desirable.

Contraindications

A major weakness of the community-based approach to trauma therapy lies in ensuring that the needs of the genuinely emotionally pathologized survivor are identified. Relying on laypersons to normalize the abnormal is fine providing that the needs of the seriously disturbed are not overlooked. This is why I argue that is essential that therapists form part of immediate response teams. I do not suggest that they have to be there to overtly therapize but, as they generally help out in any capacity, they can be watching what is going on and sometimes, quietly, unobtrusively and, above all, respectfully they might identify someone who appears to be a more acutely affected victim, (this includes team members as well as the trauma survivors). In such cases the watchers can become overt therapists once again, even if only temporarily, and use their professional skills to start to address the needs of the more deeply troubled people at a different level, perhaps even at a psychotherapeutic one.

The question we have to ask ourselves as therapists, is, can we find the humility in ourselves to believe that sweeping up at the reception center is as vital a therapeutic task as is being an expert trauma therapist? What is more important—making deeply insightful psychotherapeutic comments or making the tea?

References

McNally, R., Bryant, R. & Ehlers, A. (2003). Does early psychological intervention promote recovery from posttraumatic stress? *Psychological Science in the Public Interest*, 4, 45–47.

Mitchell, T. & Everly, G. (2001). *Critical Incident Stress Debriefing: An Operations Manual for CISD, Defusing and Other Group Crisis Intervention Services*. New York: Chevron Publishing Corp.

National Institute for Health & Clinical Excellence. (2005). *Clinical Guideline 26—Posttraumatic Stress Disorder.* NICE Guidelines London: Royal College of Psychiatrists; Leicester: British Psychological Society.

Ørner, R., King, S., Avery, A., Bretherton, R., Stolz, P. & Omerond, J. (2003). Coping and adjustment strategies used by emergency staff after traumatic incidents. *The Australasian Journal of Disaster and Trauma Studies*, 1.

Rutter, M. (2007). From sympathy to empathy—organizations learn to respond to trauma. *Journal of Counselling at Work*, (55), 9–11.

U.S. National Child Traumatic Stress Network & National Center for PTSD (2006). *Psychological First Aid: Field Operations Guide* (Second edition). Washington, DC: U.S. Dept. of Veterans Affairs.

Dr Norman Claringbull is a UK Senior Accredited Psychotherapist and Licensed Trauma Therapist. Formerly the Head of Counselling and Psychotherapy Studies at the University of Southampton, he currently maintains an extensive private consultancy practice.

99 Dealing With Anger in Two Different Phases of Group Psychotherapy

Michael P. Frank

Encourage a Win/Win Outcome

Dealing with conflict is an important aspect of life. Dealing with it in a way that encourages a win/win, positive outcome is important to good relationships. A therapy group provides an environment in which conflict can naturally occur and, if properly handled, can have a positive outcome for everyone in the group (Fehr, 2003; Rutan & Stone, 2001).

Since groups change and develop over time, the best ways to intervene can also be different depending on the phase of development the group is in. There are times in a group's life in which conflict can be well tolerated, and times in which it has greater potential for adverse outcomes for individual group members or for the group as a whole. Once a group is well under way, either of these conditions can occur at any time. Typically, however, the group is less able to deal with conflict early on in its life (Fehr, 2003; Rutan, Stone, & Shay, 2007), or when there are significant changes in its state (turnover, environmental changes, etc.). It is better able to deal with conflict after it has achieved a good measure of cohesion.

Description of Group and Client Population

I work mainly with long-term, mid- to high-functioning outpatient groups. These groups are interpersonal/psychodynamic with goals of increased insight, relief of symptoms, improved relationship skills, and general personal growth. Just because someone functions well in general, however, does not automatically mean the person will do well with any particular issue. Conflict, in particular, is something that many people have difficulty experiencing. The difficulty can manifest in many ways, from overaggressiveness, to avoidance, to passive-aggressiveness. The interventions in this chapter can be useful in a wide variety of clinical situations, with various populations.

Early in the Group's Life

When a group is forming there is a lot of anxiety about whether the group is a safe place (Tuckman, 1965). Among the fears each member brings with him or her are those that have to do with what could happen if there is conflict. Will I be damaged? Will I damage someone else? Will it just be too scary or uncomfortable? Will the group fall apart? The therapist will share in this experience.

Since we each learn about conflict early in our lives, mostly in our original families, that is the experience we bring into the group. If we grew up in a painfully conflictual environment, this is what we will anticipate when conflict arises in the group. If we grew up in a conflict-avoidant environment we received two messages: conflict is scary and/or useless, and we are better off not dealing with it. Often, in the family of origin, when there was conflict there was always a "winner" and a "loser" with no experience of a mutually beneficial result. Regardless of the dysfunctional style, when these families were in conflict they were incapable of being nurturing and secure.

Major questions then arise about the group itself. When there is conflict, how durable is the group—will it survive? How safe is the group—can I survive? How durable is the leader—will he or she be okay enough to take care of me?

The first step in establishing the safety, security, and efficacy of a group is the experience of the therapist as being durable and safe. In dealing with a confrontation will he or she retaliate? Punish? Fall apart? Avoid the issue? Or will he or she deal with the conflict non-defensively and in a way that leads to understanding and growth?

So at this stage, the therapist must be ready to hold each member individually as needed. When there is conflict, one way to do this is to redirect the anger away from the group member and onto the therapist.

Description of Intervention

Example 1

Jane becomes angry with Andrew for coming late and "forcing" her to repeat her story. Andrew responds with increasingly uncomfortable mumbled apologies and excuses. Jane only becomes angrier. Neither seems able to effectively engage with each other. There is a real risk of either or both of them becoming an early group casualty.

- At this point, the therapist can intervene by redirecting both of them to himself/herself. To Jane, the therapist may say, "I can understand how you might feel about Andrew's lateness, but I think you also have some feelings about whether I'm doing a good job of establishing the group's boundaries." To Andrew, he/she may say, "I can see this is difficult for you. Maybe you are somewhat angry at me for allowing you to be criticized."

JANE: Yeah, Doc, how can you allow this? You have no idea how irritating this is for me. If you can't get *your* act together how are the rest of us supposed to?

THERAPIST: You're angry at me for not making sure you can get your needs met in here?
JANE: That's right.
THERAPIST: So what is this like for you?

Example 2

ANDREW: I thought this was supposed to be a safe place. I guess I was wrong.
THERAPIST: You feel you were unfairly criticized for something that wasn't your fault and I didn't do anything to prevent it.
ANDREW: You just sat there and let it happen. You didn't do a damned thing about it!
THERAPIST: What's it like for you to be angry at me about this?

Typical Response

There will be a sense of relief on the part of both principals, as well as the rest of the group. The confrontation did not escalate out of control (nobody "died"). Both of them were able to express some anger at a safe and receptive target (the therapist). In addition, the therapist provided a model for nondefensively handling negative feelings. Both principals were also invited to explore and express their own experience of the encounters, thus helping to establish an important therapeutic norm. Other members of the group should also be invited to share what it was like for them. This will open up further disclosures about their outside current and past relationships, fostering more sharing and greater cohesiveness.

Later in the Group's Life: The Working Phase

As the group develops over time, the individual members are more able to tolerate and respond to one another's feelings. There is a greater sense of safety and common purpose: whatever happens, we are here to help one another. The therapist can allow exchanges to play themselves out for longer periods of time intervening later on with questions, observations, or interpretations that foster further insight and growth.

Now, when a confrontation occurs, the therapist can sit back and observe, knowing that the group has experienced this before and knows that he or she will intervene if the therapist thinks it's necessary. Otherwise, as uncomfortable as it may get, it feels safe enough. After a time, the therapist has a choice of interventions, depending on the therapist's theoretical orientation.

Description of Interventions

Once again, Jane confronts Andrew with his lateness to group. Andrew makes excuses and Jane gets angrier. This time, however, the therapist allows it to continue. After a time, Andrew starts to fight back.

ANDREW: I'm not the only one who's ever late, you know. How come you always get mad at me?
JANE: I don't know. There's just something about how you're always so apologetic but you never really take responsibility.
ANDREW: And you always look to blame first and understand later. Or never?
THERAPIST: I know that you two have had this issue before, but this time it feels a little different?

The therapist can address the interchange with the principals and the rest of the group in many ways:

The here and now: "What are you each feeling right now?", "What was it like for you all to witness this?"

Family-of-origin or transference work: "Did this experience feel familiar to you?", "How did something like this play out in your own family?", "Jane, how you are feeling about Andrew right now sounds an awful lot like what you've told us your relationship with your mother was like."

Relationship work: "How did you participate in creating this conflict? In resolving it?", "Is there something you would want to do differently?", "Andrew, when you and your partner get into an argument, is this how it goes?"

Each of these interventions opens a door for further work for everyone in the group, turning a "negative" group event into something richly therapeutic.

Conclusion and Contraindication

Anger and conflict in the group can threaten therapeutic outcomes and even the existence of the group itself. If well handled by the therapist, however, these emotions can also be openings of great therapeutic power and effectiveness. Knowing how, and when, to intervene is part of the art of group therapy.

The contraindication of this intervention often lies with the therapist's lack of skill and experience. It too depends on the therapist's ability to comfortably experience anger in his or her groups, and the therapist's psychological sophistication. It is important to know where your group is in its development. Early on in the life of the group, and at times later on, interventions in conflictual situations must protect the integrity and safety of the group first, with the goal being the establishment of cohesion and therapeutic group norms. After the group has become more established the therapist has a much greater range of possible interventions, including the most powerful intervention of all: sitting back and allowing the group to work it out for themselves.

References

Fehr, S.S. (2003). *Introduction to group therapy: A practical guide* (Second edition). Binghamton, NY: The Haworth Press.

Rutan, J. S. & Stone, W. N. (2001). *Psychodynamic group psychotherapy* (Third edition). New York: Guilford.

Rutan, J. S., Stone, W. N., & Shay, J. J. (2007). *Psychodynamic group psychotherapy* (Fourth edition). New York: Guilford.

Tuckman, B. W. (1965) Developmental sequence in small groups. *Psychological Bulletin*, 63, 384–399.

Michael P. Frank is a licensed Marriage and Family Therapist, a Certified Group Psychotherapist, and a Life Fellow of the American Group Psychotherapy Association. He maintains a private practice in Los Angeles, and is the Clinical Supervisor and Coordinator of the Group Therapy Program at the Maple Counseling Center in Beverly Hills, California.

100 The Fee
A Clinical Tool in Group Therapy
Shoshana Ben-Noam

Money: A Taboo Topic

Money is transactional, interpersonal, and symbolic. It is a taboo topic in many cultures. Talking about it often evokes powerful feelings and impacts our significant relationships. Its symbolic meanings, often unconscious, are shaped by cultural, religious, and familial attitudes and beliefs.

In therapy groups, setting and collecting fees may trigger, among other feelings, anger, shame, jealousy, and greed both in the members and leaders. To gain insight into these feelings and understand their interpersonal meanings, the money taboo has to be lifted.

To this end, money matters need to be normalized and openly discussed in the group. A clear fee and billing policy has to be presented so that members know what to expect, and policy violations can be therapeutically explored (Gans, 1992; Fehr, 2003; Rutan & Stone, 2001). To effectively do so, therapists need to work through any discomfort about discussing money matters, and resolve conflicting feelings about a therapy practice being a "business" (Ben-Noam, 2004).

A Self-Reflective Group Population

Psychodynamic groups in private practice are most suitable for acquiring insight into negative feelings and/or conflicts triggered by fee payments. To explore the money transaction between therapist and patient, members need to be adults who self pay or use third-party payments. Adolescent and children's groups need to be excluded. Members need to be self-reflective and insightful. The more insightful patients will gain the most out of these explorations. The less insightful ones may also obtain some understanding regarding money exchanges/matters.

Interventions

There are two prerequisites to using fee as a clinical tool in group therapy: First, the leader needs to feel "entitled" to his or her earnings and free to lift the money taboo in the group. Second, a fee and billing policy has to be presented to and accepted by prospective members in the pregroup interviews: members are responsible for paying the bill. Those using third-party payments should pay the therapist directly, if possible, and get reimbursed by the insurance company.

Bills will be handed out in the first session of the month and members are expected to pay in full prior to the end of the month (or any other consistent agreement). All financial matters will be discussed in the group, including overdue payments.

Members missing sessions will be charged. Some therapists agree to a number of missed sessions per year (it has to be clarified that third-party payers do not reimburse for missed sessions).

The policy needs to be revisited in the initial sessions or when a new member joins the group. Contract violations, however, are inevitable.

Clinical interventions when the contract is violated: Mike stayed in the group room until all the other members left. He seemed nervous as he told me he could not pay the bill that month because he lost his job. I responded: "it is important we discuss it next week in the group?" The following session, I announced in the beginning of the session that some members were late with their payments. Mike was quiet until Joe said to him: "You look distracted." He then shared: "I lost my job two months ago. I can't pay my bills." Joe turned to me and asked if I can postpone Mike's payment this month. Mike's voice broke as he said: "I was ashamed to share it with the group, I feel like a failure. My brothers have high-powered positions. I couldn't tell them I lost my job." I asked the group how I should handle Mike's fee for that month. Several members asked me to postpone the payment and I agreed.

Following this session, Mike reported feeling more confident in his job search and told his brothers he lost his job. To his surprise, they offered him a loan. By initially not sharing his job loss with the group, he enacted his fear of being humiliated by his brothers (this was later discussed in the group). My adhering to the policy that financial matters will be discussed in the group, and the group's supportive and nonjudgmental responses, empowered Mike to discuss the job loss with his brothers and pursue the job search assertively.

David announces in one of the group meetings he will miss one of the group sessions the following month since he will be on his honeymoon. He then turned to me and said: "I am giving you five weeks' notice so you won't charge me for the session." The whole group was looking at me. I had mixed feelings. On one hand, I felt happy for David who was getting married after searching for a mate for a long time and wanted to do something special for him. On the other, I wanted to enforce the agreement that I charge for missed sessions. I kept quiet. David then asked me: "Is this okay with you?" I then responded: "Our contract is that all members pay for missed sessions." David and two other members were enraged with me. Mark said: "That's his honeymoon, how can you do it?" Sara then said: "So since I am not married I can't get special privileges?" David then shouted: "My brother was always special. He got the awards at school, he played the violin, the girls loved him, my mother loved him. I always thought I was adopted. I never did anything right!" Sara responded: "I love you. I am happy for you that you are getting married, but I think you need to pay for the session."

This was the first time David expressed the transferential wish to be special and the intense anger toward his mother. In following sessions he expressed warm feelings toward Sara, apologized for shouting at me, and paid for the missed session.

Conclusion

Fee-related interventions open up a host of interpersonal learning opportunities. In reaction to these interventions, pent-up feelings of rage, pain, or humiliation toward significant others may be released, discussed, and better or differently understood.

Conflicts regarding money matters in the group or in life may be resolved.

Contraindications

These interventions are contraindicated for highly narcissistic and borderline patients who will not be able to tolerate and metabolize the intense feelings evoked. Also, leaders who have difficulties in addressing money matters freely and containing negative feelings may not be successful in using the fee as a clinical tool.

References

Ben-Noam, S. (2004). Money doesn't grow on trees, or does it? *The Group Solution.* The Newsletter of the National Registry of Certified Group Psychotherapists. February/March issue.

Fehr, S.S. (2003). *Introduction to Group Therapy: A practical guide* (Second edition). Binghamton, NY: The Haworth Press.

Gans, J.S. (1992). Money and psychodynamic group psychotherapy. *International Journal of Group Psychotherapy*, 42 (1), 133–152.

Rutan, J.S. & Stone, W.N. (2001). *Psychodynamic Group Psychotherapy* (Third edition). New York: The Guilford Press.

Shoshana Ben-Noam, PsyD, is a Clinical Psychologist, Certified Group Psychotherapist and a Life Fellow of the American Group Psychotherapy Association. She is also an Adjunct Professor at Pace University Doctoral Psychology Program and maintains a private practice in New York City.

101 Installation of Hope in Bereavement Groups for the Elderly

Mark A. Cohen

The Profundity in a Word

Death. No one word in the English language may stir so many strong emotions. Now imagine yourself being older, elderly. Your spouse, your partner in life, your best friend and confidant, dies. You are alone. The scene is a large room in a senior citizens' activity center. The empty chairs start to fill with elderly people. They have all lost a spouse. They are alone. Anxious. Bereaved. Hopeless. Scared. They are attending a bereavement group for the first time. The session starts.

Based on my work in group therapy with the elderly, I have observed a number of healing and curative factors. These curative factors are: the installation of hope, acceptance, a decrease in social isolation, finding of a new identity and meaning in life, support, catharsis, amelioration of fears, education, assistance in processing and dealing with painful or intense feelings, and an opportunity to help others (Cohen, 2000). Individuals who have lost a spouse often feel hopeless that they can return to a life of happiness and joy. They may even feel hopeless that they will ever just stop feeling sad all the time. We will look at specific interventions in bereavement groups that exemplify the installation of hope.

The Loss of a Spouse

The population for this group was elderly individuals in the community who had all lost a spouse. These techniques could also be extended to younger bereaved spouses and perhaps other bereaved groups.

A Population Within an Ongoing Group

Mix the more recently bereaved with individuals who are further along in the bereavement process.
One particularly effective intervention in the installation of hope is to have bereavement groups that are mixed among people who are more recently bereaved and those who are further along in the bereavement process (Roy & Sumpter, 1983). Those who are more recently bereaved can see how those further along are finding happiness and joy again in life. They can

also see how those further along are able to talk about the death and their loved one without the intense overwhelming emotions that are often present in the earlier stages of bereavement. Asking specific guided questions of those further along can highlight the possibility of hope to those less further along.

Identify by group members who are further along in the bereavement process with those more recently bereaved.
It is quite helpful to encourage group members who are further along in the bereavement process to disclose and identify how they can relate to what an individual who is more recently bereaved is experiencing. They can be encouraged to explain how they used to act/feel the same way, but through time and the help of the group they have come to learn to accept and effectively interact with the vicissitudes of life and find happiness and joy again. It also is of great help to hear that the intense feelings of sadness will dissipate with time. This intervention process can also be an effective intervention for those who are further along, by helping them to see how far they have gone in the bereavement process and giving them hope that they can still go further.

Use stories and poems that encourage hope and a new future.
Having group members bring in stories and poems they have read or to write stories about hope and a new future can help to install hope in other members. One such poem, whose author is unknown, follows (in edited format):

> I'm tired of gloom;
> I'm tired of pain;
> I want to rejoin
> The world again.
>
> Today I will try
> To smile once more.
> Death disappeared
> And left my door.
>
> I'll pick myself up
> And try again;
> I'll make the effort
> To function again.
>
> It won't be easy
> As I well know,
> But I won't give up
> The change made me grow.

The pain in my heart
Will remain for a while
But yesterday's gone
Today I will smile.

Learn new tasks, things a spouse did, or engage in new behaviors.
Asking the individual questions, such as what he or she always wanted to do but never had time for, or what he or she wanted to do but were never able to do because of his or her situation/spouse, can help the individual to look at ways to find new things in life.

Having group members encourage individuals to try new things that may be scary or different can be quite beneficial. It is not uncommon to find that group members may benefit from trying new behaviors together. For example, two bereaved women decided to take a cruise together because each was too fearful to go alone.

Asking a bereaved group member to explain some things his or her spouse used to always do that they would like to learn leads to a detailed explanation. This can then help them to see that they learned how to do the task just by observing their spouse do it so many times.

Visualize a new and hopeful future.
Another effective exercise is to ask group members to close their eyes and visualize themselves doing something enjoyable in the future and being happy. Using this visualization may help the members get in touch with something that can still bring them joy and provide hope that that they can still enjoy life again.

The Clients Respond

These interventions can evoke a variety of client responses. Frequently, for the more newly bereaved individuals, there may be doubt in their mind that there is hope for a better future. However, with repeated exposure to these interventions that doubt can change. Some may start to feel hopeful about the future but then experience guilt that they are feeling better while their spouse is deceased. This is an issue that can then be effectively worked through within the group.

Contraindications

Due to the very serious and profoundly upsetting experience of spousal loss with its concomitant lifestyle change, this intervention would be contraindicated for individuals who are newly bereaved and still in the midst of intense mourning and hopelessness. The installation of hope, which may take time and patience, is a secondary intervention. The primary intervention is the acknowledgement of and the compassion toward the patient's loss. Jumping to the secondary intervention of trying to give hope is not only useless but indicates insensitivity, impatience, and possible discomfort with loss in the group therapist.

Moving an individual from hopelessness to hope and the possibility of a future takes patience, sensitivity, and skill on the part of the group therapist. Its essence is like the phoenix rising out of the ashes. In words beautifully written by Dickinson (1960) "hope is a thing with feathers that perches in the soul" (p. 68). Reaching what has become, for many, a dormant hope is the goal of the bereavement group therapist.

References

Cohen, M. (2000). Bereavement groups with the elderly. In S. Fehr (Ed.). *Group Therapy in Independent Practice* (pp. 33–41). Binghamton, NY: The Haworth Press.

Dickinson, E. (1960). Hope is a thing with feathers. In T. H. Johnson (Ed.). *The Complete Poems of Emily Dickinson*. New York: Little, Brown and Company.

Roy, P. & Sumpter, H. (1983). Group support for the recently bereaved. *Health and Social Work*, 8(3), 230–232.

Mark A. Cohen, Psy.D., received his doctorate degree in Clinical Psychology from Nova Southeastern University and practiced in Cleveland, Ohio. He had a diverse practice consisting of therapy, evaluations, and testing of adults, children, and geriatrics.

Index

Acceptance and Commitment Therapy (ACT) 106
action
  group centered 68
  group structure/format and types of 68
  purposeful 68
  self-initiated 68
  spontaneous here and now 68
Action Theory 29–32
  conclusion 31
  contraindications 31–2
  intervention 29–30
  population 29
  responses to intervention 31
active listening, dying group members 192
addiction 36
  and Fireball game 173–5
adjourning 195
adolescents
  and dreams 204–7
  and humor 215–18
  and identity formation 180
  and masks 180–2
advice giving 237–9
  case example 237–8
  conclusion 239
  contraindication 239
  intervention 238
  population 237
  responses to intervention 239
  'what should I do?' question 237
African-Americans
  and racism 19, 20
  use of primal scream to facilitate release in male 19–21
ageing see geriatrics
aggression, responding to 306–10

conclusion 309
contraindications 309
the event 306–7
intervention 307–9
pursuing meaning 309
titration 308
Akhtar, Salman 58
Alberti, R.E. 288, 289
Alcoholics Anonymous 12-Step program 173
Alien (movie) 36
Alpert, Dr. Richard 332
American Group Psychotherapy Association 39
anger
  awareness of 33–5
    conclusions 35
    contraindications 35
    intervention 34
    population 33–4
    responses to intervention 34
  dealing with 353–7
    conclusion 356
    contraindication 356
    early in the group's life intervention 353–5
    later in the group's life intervention 355–6
    population 353
    responses to intervention 355
    win/win outcome 353
  responding to aggression 306–10
animal assisted therapy 183–5
  chinchillas 184, 185
  contraindications 185
  intervention 184–5
  peer group culture 184–5
  population 183
  responses to intervention 185

anxiety
    and depression 117–20
    dissociative patient as barometer of group 262
    and phobia 94–6
    reducing of through storytelling 321
anxiety-response ladder 95
apology 26–8
    conclusion 27
    contraindications 27
    dialogue intervention 26–7
    population 26
    responses to interventions 27
    unforgotten hurt 26
art material, use of in failure 125–6
art therapy
    applying of within group therapy 102–5
        case examples 104
        conclusion 104
        intervention 102–4
        population 102
        squiggling 102, 103
    and women's empowerment group 248–51
        conclusion 250–1
        contraindications 251
        emotional journey 248
        intervention 249–50
        materials 249
        population 248
        responses to intervention 250–1
assertiveness 224–5
    and geriatric population 273–5
        conclusion 274–5
        contraindications 275
        group description 273
        intervention 273–4
        role playing 274
    training for self-esteem 288–90
        conclusion 290
        contraindications 290
        equality in human relations 288
        intervention 288–9
        responses to intervention 289
Association for University and College Counseling Center Directors (AUCCCD), Annual Survey (2013–14) 22
attachment behaviors 72
Automatic Thought Record (ATR) 29, 30, 31
automatic thoughts (ATs) 30

awareness
    heightening of by 'I' intervention 244–7
    increasing 53–6

Back to the Future (film) 61, 63
Baker, E.K. 336
Bandura, A. 290
Bartels, D. 110
'battling the Alien' 36–8
Beck Anxiety Inventory 30
Beck Depression Inventory-II 30
Beck, J.S. 29, 31
beginning a group *see* starting a group
behaviors
    group as place to practice new 223–6
        assertiveness 224–5
        contraindications 226
        impulsivity 225
        intervention 223–5
        mindfulness toward 345
        population 223
        responses to intervention 224–5
        trust 225
belief, sex offenders and dispelling a 340–2
bereavement groups for the elderly 361–4
    contraindications 363–4
    intervention 361–3
    learning new tasks 363
    loss of spouse 361
    population 361
    responses to intervention 363
    stories and poems 362–3
    visualizing new future 363
billing policy 358–60
Bion, W. 261
bodily sensations, and grounding 77–9
body language, and mindfulness 344–5
bond-building 53, 55
borning 195
boundaries 231–3
    changing chairs and interpersonal 336–9
        conclusion 338–9
        contraindication 338–9
        group description 336–7
        intervention 337–8
        responses to intervention 338
    and disaster/trauma groups 231–3
        breathing of 233
        conclusion 232–3

contraindication 232–3
  intervention 232
  population 231
  responses to intervention 232
 maintaining for older adults
    299–301
  case history 300–1
  conclusion 301
  contraindication 301
  discouraging outside
    socialization 299
  population 299
Brabender, V.A. 176
breathing 55
breathing buddy exercise 92
bridging 72–3
  avoid scapegoating 240–3
  definition 240
  and keeping the group in the
    present 333
  of resistance 321–4
bubble meditation 91
Bugental, J.F.T. 86–7
Burdick, D. 90
Burke, C.A. 90

'calm place' intervention 92
cancer sufferers 191–4
case conceptualization 31
CBT (cognitive behavioral therapy)
  and depression 201–3
  integrating Action Theory and
    29–32
  and phobia treatment 94–7
  and post-traumatic stress disorder
    80–2
  and psychodrama 30–1
    automatic thoughts 30
    case conceptualization 31
    downward arrow technique
      30
    stress inoculation training (SIT)
      317–20
chair arrangement 176–9
  conclusion 178–9
  contraindications 178–9
  group description 178
  and interpersonal boundaries
    336–9
  intervention 178
  responses to intervention 178
  theoretical considerations 176–8
checklist for starting a group 315
children
  and mindfulness practice 90–3

closure 135–7
  conclusion 137
  and fantasies 136
  and feedback 136–7
  intervention 136–7
  population 135
  responses to intervention 137
cognitive behavioural techniques
  see CBT
cognitive insight (in organizations)
  conclusion 116
  contraindications 116
  and expressive therapies 114–16
  intervention 114–16
  population 114
  responses to intervention 116
collateral damage 4–7
  conclusion 6
  contraindications 6
  group description 5
  intervention 5–6
  responses to intervention 6
  theoretical considerations 4–5
combat veterans see war veterans
communication
  grammar 219–22
  language see language
  nonverbal 329–31
  promoting amongst Sub-Saharan
    Africa immigrant women
    131–4
  talk therapy 19
  see also dialogue
community enterprise
  and trauma therapy 347–52
    conclusion 350–1
    contraindications 351
    critical incident defusing 350
    interventions 348–50
    minor events 347
    population 347
    Psychological First Aid (PFA)
      350–1
    terrorism coping strategy 348–9
    tsunami disaster 348
confidentiality, and dying group
  members 192
connection 53–6
  conclusion 55
  contraindications 55
  intervention 54
  population 53
  responses to intervention 54–5
consciousness, making the unconscious
  conscious 208, 209

Index

constructive narrative perspective (CNP) 318
container, Bion's concept of 261
continuous reinforcement 11
corollary intervention, and 'I' technique 246
corrective emotional experience 252, 253, 291
corrective experiences 141–3
  conclusion 142
  contraindications 142
  intervention 141–2
  population 141
  responses to intervention 142
Corsini, R.J. 27
Cortesao, E. 265
counterresistance 227–30
  concept and definition of 227
  conclusion 230
  counterindications 230
  in the group setting 228
  identifying 228–9
  interpretation 229
  intervention 228–9
  population 228
  renovated group 229
  and unconscious pacts 227
countertransference 38
  in severely ill inpatient groups 15–18
  and therapists' self-disclosure 328
critical incident defusing 350, 351
cultural influences 14
cultural shock, and immigrants 57, 58
culture *see* group culture development

daughters, relationship with mothers *see* mother–daughter relationship
David Copperfield 327
de Beauvoir 157
death and dying 191–4
  active listening 192
  conclusion 193
  and confidentiality 192
  contraindications 193
  fear of 15, 17
  four-stage intervention 191–2
  hope in bereavement groups for the elderly 361–4
  medical comfort and needs 191–2
  population 191
  responses 192
  talking about 17

decision-making 64–6
  conclusion 65
  contraindications 65
  intervention 65
  responses to intervention 65
defusing, and trauma therapy 350, 351
democracy, deep 283
depression 117–20
  and anxiety 117–20
  case examples 118–19
  and cognitive behavioural therapy 201–3
    conclusion 203
    contraindications 203
    intervention 201–3
    population 201
    verbatim patient disclosure 202–3
  conclusion 119–20
  contraindication 119–20
  intervention 117–19
  population 117
  responses to intervention 119
detrimental family loyalties *see* family loyalties, detrimental
dialogue
  Group Sandwich Model and international conflict 83–5
  internal 148, 149, 150
  poetry as a springboard for 295–8
  unforgotten hurt and intervention of 26–7
differences, individual 1–3
difficult sessions 311–14
  conclusion 314
  contraindications 314
  group descriptions 311–12
  inclusion 311
  interventions 312–13
  responses to intervention 313
disaster groups, and boundaries 231–3
dissociation 261
  diminishing of for war veterans 261–4
    conclusion 263
    container concept 261
    contraindications 263
    group description 261
    interventions 262
    responses to intervention 262–3
disturber 280–4
  conclusion 283
  contraindications 283
  exposing the gold 280

format for inclusion of 282
  intervention 281–2
  population 280–1
  responses to intervention 283
  ripple effect 283
Donigan, J. 290
downward arrow technique 30
dreams 204–7
  approaches to 204
  contraindication 206–7
  and dreamtelling 204, 206
  formative approach 204, 206–7
  informative approach 204, 207
  intervention 204–6
  population 204
  progressive interpretation technique 206
  transformative approach 204, 207
dually diagnosed clients 166–9
  conclusion 168–9
  contraindications 168–9
  creating insight about sources of distress 166
  intervention 166–8
  population 166
  responses to intervention 168
dying see death and dying

elderly see geriatrics
Emmons, M.L. 288, 289
emotional blocks/blocking 148, 149
emotional processing 148–50
  conclusion 150
  contraindication 150
  internal dialogue 148, 149, 150
  intervention 149
  population 148–9
  responses to intervention 150
emotion(s)
  grammar and distancing from 219
  poetry and language of 295
  and primary language 212
empathy 27
empowerment for women see women's empowerment
engagement, increasing 53–6
Erickson, M.H. 94, 321
existential anxiety 321
experiential treatment techniques 336
expressive therapies, and cognitive insight 114–16
eye contact 329–31
  conclusion 331
  contraindication 331
  intervention 330

population 329
  responses to intervention 331

failure 124–7
  conclusion 126–7
  contraindications 126–7
  intervention 124–6
  and Kintsugi philosophy 124
  use of art material and pottery 125–6
family loyalties, detrimental 61–3
  contraindications 63
  intervention 61–3
  patient population 61
  stuck in the past 61
family member association 285–7
  conclusion 287
  contraindication 287
  intervention 285–6
  politeness 285
  population 285
  responses to intervention 286
family role models
  and gender roles 187–90
  conclusion 189
  contraindications 189
  four-stage intervention 187–8
  group participants 187
  responses to intervention 188–9
fee payment
  as clinical tool in group therapy 358–60
  conclusion 360
  contraindications 360
  interventions 358–60
  population 358
feedback
  and closure 136–7
  and corrective experiences 141
Fehr, S.S. 176
fight/flight response 306
Fireball 173–5
  conclusion 175
  contraindications 175
  intervention 173–4
  population 173
  responses to intervention 174–5
Folkman, S. 318
Fosha, Diana 53
Foulkes, S.H. 102, 265
Frank, A. 193
Freud, Sigmund 183, 261, 325
Functional Group Model 67
'Funeral' ritual 40

370 Index

future self 110–13
  conclusion 111–12
  contraindications 112
  intervention 111
  population 110
  responses to intervention 111

gay group therapy 160–2
  childhood 160–1
  conclusion 162
  contraindications 162
  intervention 161
  negative sentiments towards 160
  population 161
  responses to intervention 162
gay men
  transition to older age 121–3
    conclusion 123
    and continuous
      reinforcement 121
    contraindications 123
    intervention 122–3
    loss and gain 122–3
    population 122
Gaye, Marvin 19
gender roles, and family role
    models 187–90
geriatric population
  assertiveness 273–5
    conclusion 274–5
    contraindications 275
    group description 273
    intervention 273
    role-playing 274
  hope in bereavement groups
    361–4
    contraindications 363–4
    intervention 361–3
    learning new tasks 363
    loss of spouse 361
    population 361
    responses to intervention 363
    stories and poems 362–3
    visualizing new future 363
  maintaining boundaries 299–301
    case history 300–1
    conclusion 301
    contraindication 301
    discouraging of outside
      socialization 299
    population 299
Germer, C.K. 343
Gladding, S.T. 138
glass, refilling and repairing your
    166–9

goals
  assessing of by Hot Air Balloon
    exercise 154–6
  breaking of into small attainable
    steps 98–100
goodbye, saying 86, 88
Gordon, Thomas 246
Goulding, M.M. 329
Goulding, R. 329
grammar 219–22
  conclusions 222
  contraindications 222
  distancing from emotions 219
  group members 219
  intervention 219–21
  responses to intervention 221
Grier, William and Cobbs, Price M.
  Black Rage 19
grieving 8
grounding 77–9
  conclusion 79
  contraindications 79
  intervention 77–8
  population 77
  responses to intervention 78–9
  and Somatic Experiencing (SE) 77,
    78–9
  and standing up 79
Group Agreement 40
group cognitive action therapy
    (GCAT) 29–32
  applying CBT interventions/
    techniques to psychodrama
    30–1
  automatic thoughts (ATs) 30
  case conceptualization 31
  client/patient population 29
  conclusion 31
  contraindications 31–2
  downward arrow technique 30
  guidelines and intervention 29–30
  responses to intervention 31
group cohesion facilitation 67–70
  action components of a functional
    group 68
  conclusion 69
  contraindications 69
  and Functional Group Model 67
  and group structure/format 67–70
  intervention 68
  population 67
  responses to intervention 69
group contract 302–5
  definition 302
  intervention 303–4

population 303
purposes 302
group coordinator, hiring of 22–5
 conclusion 23–4
 contraindications 24
 intervention 22–3
 responses to coordinator 23
group culture development 43–5
 conclusion 45
 contraindications 45
 intervention 43–5
 population 43
 responses to intervention 45
group developmental stage theory 195
group format, and group cohesion facilitation 67–70
group identity, and trauma 46–8
group leader, and group culture development 43–5
group matrix 102–5, 265–8
 case examples 104, 266–7
 conclusions 104, 267–8
 contraindications 267–8
 creative quality of 265
 definition 102, 265
 expressing insights and interpretations 265
 interventions 102–4, 266
 mirror phenomenon 265
 population 102, 266
 resonance expressions 265
 responses to intervention 267
 squiggling technique 102–4
 theoretical considerations 265–6
group member introductions 138–40
 conclusions 139
 contraindications 139
 intervention 138–9
 population 138
 responses to intervention 139
Group Sandwich Model 83–5
 conclusion 85
 contraindications 85
 and international conflict dialog 83–5
 intervention 84
 population 84
 responses to intervention 85
group structure/format
 action components of a functional group 68
 and Functional Group Model 67

and group cohesion facilitation 67–70
guided imagery *see* imagery
guilt, and gay men 160
Gulf War, trauma therapy 348–50
gut, trusting your 75

Henderson, J.L. 198
herd model 291–2
here and now 253, 254, 263, 332–5
 conclusion 334–5
 contraindications 334–5
 intervention 332–4
 population 332
 responses to intervention 334
Hershfield, H.E. 110
HIV patients 106–9
 conclusions 108–9
 contraindications 108–9
 'I Am Me' poem 107–8
 intervention 107–8
 living with dying 191–4
 population 107
 responses 108
 rewriting your story 106–7
Holmes, L. 157
Honos-Webb, L. 321
hope
 in bereavement groups for the elderly 361–4
 contraindications 363–4
 intervention 361–3
 learning new tasks 363
 loss of spouse 361
 population 361
 responses to intervention 363
 stories and poems 362–3
 visualizing new future 363
Hornyak, L.M. 336
horseback riding workshop 291–4
 conclusion 294
 contraindications 294
 herd model 291–2
 horse as a powerful therapeutic modality 291–2
 intervention 292–4
 population 292
 responses to intervention 294
Hot Air Balloon 154–6
 conclusion 156
 contraindications 156
 intervention 154–6
 population 154
 responses to intervention 156

humor
   and adolescents 215–18
      conclusion 217–18
      contraindications 218
      coping with personal attacks by therapist 216–17
      disarming tension and hostility 216
      intervention 215–17
      talking about anything 215
Hurricane Ivan (2004) 317
hybrid identity, and immigration 58

'I' technique 244–7
   contraindications 246–7
   and corollary intervention 246
   intervention 244–6
   populations 244
   recommendations 246–7
identity
   immigration and hybrid 58
   and masks 180–2
   multi-faceted 59
imagery, used to vivify termination 257–60
immediacy 332–5
immigrants/immigration
   and hybrid identity 58
   and intercultural group therapy 57–60
   promoting communication in Sub-Saharan African women 131–4
   stressors 57
   as third individuation phase 58
impulsivity 225
incarcerated male population 49–51
   conclusion 51
   contraindications 51
   interventions 50–1
   population 49–50
inclusion 311
Indian Ocean tsunami survivors 348
integrity, increasing of and Fireball game 173–5
Intensive Outpatient/Partial Hospital program (IOP/PHP), and anger 33–5
intercultural group therapy 57–60
   client population 57
   conclusion 59
   contraindications 60
   cultural shock 57
   intervention 58–9
   responses to intervention 59
   situation before intervention 58
   third individuation process 58
intergenerational women's psychotherapy groups 157–9
   conclusion 159
   contraindication 159
   intervention 159
   population and client histories 157–9
internal dialogue 148, 149, 150
International Association of Group Psychotherapy and Group Processes, Task Force for Disaster/Trauma Management 46
international conflict dialog, and Group Sandwich Model 83–5
interpersonal learning 234–6
   conclusion 236
   contraindications 236
   and here and now 332–5
   intervention 234–5
   population 234
   responses to intervention 235–6
   teaching tale 234
introductions see group member introductions
introjected bad object 36–7, 38

Janov, Arthur 19

Kintsugi philosophy 124
Klein, M. 261
Kress, V.E. 110, 112

language
   and accessing primary affect 212–14
   body 344–5
   using grammar to increase immediacy and affect 219–22
Lazarus, R.S. 318
learning, interpersonal see interpersonal learning
Lee, J. 90
lesbians
   conclusion 10
   contraindications 10
   identifying and grieving losses incurred by 'coming out' 8–11
   intervention 8–9
   population 8
   responses to intervention 9–10
Leszcz, M. 276
'letting go', and closure 136, 137

Levine, P. 79
Levinson, Boris 183
'listening to the bell' 90–1
loneliness 46–8
  conclusion 48
  responses 48
  suggestions from international colleagues 46–8
long-term groups, and group contract 302–5
loss totem, creating of by lesbians 8–11

Machado, Antonio 124
McNally, R. 351
Malnati, R. 290
masks 180–2
  contraindications 182
  intervention 180–2
  population 180
  responses to intervention 181–2
  using the concept of 180
matrix, group *see* group matrix
meditation, bubble 91
Meichenbaum, D. 317
memory disturbance 261
metaphors, and bridging resistance 321–4
micro-expressions, attuning to 71–3
  conclusions 73
  contraindications 73
  group members/population 71
  intervention 71–3
  responses to intervention 73
mindfulness 343–6
  and body language 344–5
  and children 90–3
    breathing buddy exercise 92
    bubble meditation 91
    'calm place' intervention 92
    conclusion 92
    contraindication 92
    definition 90
    interventions 90–2
    'listening to the bell' 90–1
    population 90
    responses to intervention 92
    sitting still like a frog 91
    smell and tell 92
  closing our eyes 345
  contraindication 346
  definition 343
  intervention 344–5
  physical sensations 345
  population 344

positive consequences 343
  responses to intervention 346
  of thoughts in the moment 345
  toward behavior 345
mirror phenomenon 265
mirroring 141–2
mistakes
  making by therapists 128–30
  turning into useful interventions by therapists 269–72
money
  and fee as clinical tool in group therapy 358–60
  as taboo topic 358
mother blaming 144, 145, 146
mother–daughter relationship 144–7
  ambivalent relationship 144
  conclusion 146
  contraindications 146
  interventions 144–6
  mother blaming 144, 145, 146
  population 144
  and separation/individuation 187–90
multi-faceted identity 59

nail biting 326–7
National Institute for Health and Clinical Excellence 347
neutrality, therapeutic 239
new group members 195–7
  contraindications 197
  and group developmental stage theory 195
  intervention 196–7
  population 195
niceness, women and culture of 12–14
non-verbal communication 55
  attuning to micro-expressions 71–3
  and eye contact 329–31
norm repair 276–9
  conclusion 279
  contraindication 279
  group description 277
  intervention 277–8
  responses to intervention 278
  theoretical orientation 276
norming 195
norms
  definition 276
  social 133, 276

O'Connor, M.E. 311
Ørner, R. 347
Ormont, L. 72, 333, 343–4

pain
  experiencing of in group interactions 4–6
  racism and repressed 19–21
Parfit, Derek 110
perception, different levels of 1–3
  conclusion 3
  contraindications 3
  intervention 1–2
  responses to intervention 2–3
pet therapy 183
phobia treatment 94–7
  conclusion 96
  contraindications 96–7
  intervention 94–6
  population 94
  and relaxation therapy (RT) 94–7
  responses to intervention 96
  theoretical considerations 94
PHQ-9 and Anxiety Inventory 30
poetry
  as a projective technique 295–8
  contraindications 297
  intervention 295–7
  language of emotion 295
  poem selection 296
  population 295
  responses to intervention 297
  use of in bereavement group for the elderly 362–3
  use of in women's empowerment groups 249–50
post-traumatic stress disorder (PTSD) 261
  combat veterans 80–2
  and cognitive behavioural therapy (CBT) 80–2
  conclusion 82
  contraindications 82
  intervention 81
  population 80
  responses to intervention 81–2
  and stress inoculation training (SIT) 318
pottery, use of in failure 125–6
Practice Guidelines for Group Psychotherapy 24, 39
present time 332–5
  being in the moment 332
  bridging 333
  conclusion 334–5
  contraindications 334–5
  group-as-a-whole question 333
  intervention 332–4

population 332
  responses to intervention 334
primal scream 19–21
  conclusion 21
  contraindications 21
  intervention 20–1
  population 20
  responses to intervention 21
Primal Therapy 19
primary language 212–14
  conclusion 214
  contraindications 214
  and emotions 212
  five-step intervention 212–14
  population 212
progressive interpretation technique, dreams 206
psychoanalytic object relations theory 36–7
psychoeducation, and interpersonal process 234–6
psychological connectedness 110
Psychological First Aid (PFA) protocols 350–1
psychodrama, applying CBT techniques within context of 29–31
PTSD *see* post-traumatic stress disorder

racism, and repressed pain in African-Americans 19–21
Racker, H. 227
Red Cross 131, 132
regression 195
Reik, Theodore, *The Need to be Loved* 121–2
relatedness, increasing 53–6
relational technique, and micro-expressions 71–3
relationships, and Hot Air Balloon exercise 154–6
relaxation 55
  and PTSD 81
relaxation therapy (RT), and phobia treatment 94–7
'remember be here now' 332–5
  being in the moment 332
  bridging 333
  conclusion 334–5
  contraindications 334–5
  groups-as-a-whole question 333
  intervention 332–4
  population 332
  responses to intervention 334

resistance
  in the face of shame 252–6
    case example 253–5
    conclusion 255–6
    contraindications 255–6
    corrective emotional
      experience 252
    intervention 253–5
    population 252
    responses to intervention 255
  in the group setting 228
  use of metaphors and stories to
      bridge 321–4
    conclusion 324
    contraindications 324
    intervention 322–4
    reducing of anxiety 321
  see also counterresistance
responsibility 151–3
  conclusion 153
  contraindications 153
  heightening of by 'I' intervention
      244–7
  intervention 152
  population 151–2
  responses to intervention 152
Rice, Cecil 233
rituals 68
  as rite of passage 39
  for termination 39–41
role-playing, and assertiveness in
    geriatric group 274
Rosenberg, B. 221
Rossi, E.L. 321
Rossi, S.I. 321
Rutan, J.S. 35, 176–7, 276

Sandwich Model see Group
    Sandwich Model
scapegoating
  bridging as a tool to avoid 240–3
    conclusion 242
    contraindications 242
    definition 240
    intervention 240–2
    responses to intervention 242
schizoid-paranoid spectrum
    49–51
screening of group members 311
selection of group members 311
self-awareness 53–5
  family role models 187–90
  increasing of through horseback
      riding workshop 291–4
self-disclosure of therapists 325–8

  aloneness 325
  contraindications 328
  and cranking up a new group
      171–2
  group matrix 226
  intervention 326–7
  responses to intervention 327
self-esteem
  assertiveness training 288–90
    conclusion 290
    contraindications 290
    equality in human relations 288
    intervention 288–9
    responses to intervention 289
self-hatred 36–8
  conclusion 37–8
  contraindications 38
  intervention 36–7
  and introjected bad object 36–7, 38
  population 36
  responses to intervention 37
self-regulated behaviour, theory
    of 290
Semple, R.J. 90
September 11th (2001) 231–3
severely ill inpatients
  conclusions 17
  contraindications 17
  countertransference in groups for
      15–18
  defrosting feelings 16–17
  group and client description 16
  structure and attendance 16
  talking about death 17
sex offenders
  dispelling a belief 340–2
    case example 340–1
    conclusion 341–2
    contraindication 341–2
    intervention 340–1
    responses to intervention 341
Shadow concept 104
Shakespeare, William 180, 181
shame
  and gay men 160
  resistance in the face of 252–6
shielded name tent 138–40
silence 253
  from silence to frenzy 252–6
  norm repair 277–8
  and trauma 46
'Silence' (poem) 48
sitting still like a frog activity 91
smell and tell activity 92
Social Network Inventory 30

376 Index

social norms 133, 276
Socratic questioning 29
Somatic Experiencing training 77
spousal loss 361–4
squiggle drawing 102–4
starting a group, checklist for 315–16
Stone, W.N. 35, 176–7
stories/storytelling
   and bridging resistance 321–4
      conclusion 324
      contraindications 324
      intervention 322–4
      population 321–2
      reducing of anxiety 321
   and group therapist 208–11
      conclusion 211
      contraindications 211
      interventions 208–10
      making unconscious ambivalence conscious 208
      population 208
      responses to intervention 210
   use of in bereavement group for the elderly 362–3
storming 195
stress, transactional view of 318
stress inoculation training (SIT) 317–20
   application and follow-through 318–19
   conceptual education 318
   conclusion 320
   contraindications 320
   intervention 317–19
   objective and goal of 318, 320
   population 317
   responses to intervention 319
   skills acquisition and consolidation 318
stressors, immigrant 57
structure, group *see* group structure/format
Sub-Saharan Africa immigrant women
   conclusion 133–4
   contraindications 133–4
   intervention 132–3
   population 131–2
   promoting communication 131–4
   responses to intervention 133
substance abuse, and refilling and repairing your glass exercise 166–9
success, building a pathway to 98–101
   breaking down goals into small attainable steps 98
   conclusion 100
   contraindications 100
   goals 98, 99
   intervention 99–100
   population 98–9
   questions to ask 99–100
   responses to intervention 100
successful group, nine basic steps for a 315–16
supervisors, and trainee therapists 75–6
Surrey, J.L. 343

talk therapy 19
Tart, C.T. 343
teaching tale, interpersonal learning 234
Tennyson, A. 217
termination 197
   five-stage technique 86–9
      conclusions 88
      contraindications 88–9
      intervention 87–8
      obstacles to effective 86
      population 87
      saying goodbye 86, 88
      transfer of training 86–7, 88
   as group development stage 195
   imagery to vivify 257–60
      conclusion 259
      contraindication 259
      intervention 258–9
      population and conditions 257
rituals 29–41
   conclusions 41
   contraindications 41
   'Funeral' ritual 40–1
   goals for 39
   Group Agreement 40
   group description 40
   intervention 40
   responses to intervention 40–1
therapeutic letter writing 110
therapists
   cranking up a new group 170–2
      conclusion 171–2
      contraindications 171–2
      intervention 171
      population 170–1
      responses to intervention 171
      self-disclosures 171–2
   group therapy for 163–5
      conclusion 164–5
      contraindications 165
      intervention 164

population 163–4
responses to intervention 164
in the making 74–6
  be yourself 75
  conclusion 76
  contraindications 76
  get out of your head 75
  inner dialogue 74
  intervention 75–6
  population 74
  responses to intervention 76
  say what you feel and think 75
  trust your gut 75
making mistakes 128–30, 269–72
  acknowledging of 270
  conclusion 130, 271–2
  contraindications 130, 272
  interventions 129–30, 270–1
  population 128, 269–70
  responses to intervention
    130, 271
  transference and other
    projections 271
self-disclosure 325–8
  and aloneness 325
  contraindications 328
  group matrix 326
  intervention 326–7
  responses to intervention 327
as storyteller 208–11
use of humor to cope with personal
  attacks 216–17
therapy, reasons for people coming
  to 141
titration of anger 308
totem, loss 8–11
transfer of training 86–7, 88
transference 159
transitional objects 198–200
  conclusions 200
  contraindications 200
  intervention 198–9
  population 198
  responses to intervention 199–200
trauma
  and boundaries 231–3
  and group identity 46–8
    client responses 48
    conclusion 48
    international colleagues
      suggestions 46–7
    loneliness 46–8
    'Silence' poem 48
  stress inoculation training for
    317–20

see also post-traumatic stress
  syndrome
trauma therapy
  community-based approach 347–52
    conclusion 350–1
    contraindications 351
    critical incident defusing 350
    interventions 348–50
    minor events 347
    population 347
    Psychological First Aid (PFA)
      protocols 350–1
    terrorism coping strategy 349
    tsunami disaster 348–9
trust 225
trust boost, and termination 87–8
Tuckman, B.W. 195
Tuttman, S. 37–8
Twain, Mark, *The Adventures
  of Tom Sawyer* 39

Ulman, K.H. 276
unconscious ambivalence, making
  conscious 208, 209
unforgotten hurt 26–7
  conclusion 27
  contraindication 27
  intervention of dialogue 26–7
  population 26
  responses to intervention 27
universalization 27
'unthought known' 71
Urminsky, O. 110

Van Gelder, J.L. 110

Wallin, D.J. 71
war veterans
  diminishing dissociative experiences
    for 261–4
    conclusion 263
    container concept 261
    contraindications 263
    group description 261
    intervention 262
    responses to intervention 262–3
  and PTSD 80–2
    and CBT 80–2
    conclusion 82
    contraindications 82
    intervention 81
    population 80
    responses to intervention 81–2
'what should I do?' question 237
Winnicott, D. 102

women
  and culture of niceness 12–14
    conclusion 13
    contraindications 13–14
    intervention 12–13
    population 12
    responses to intervention 13
  empowerment using art therapy 248–51
    conclusion 250–1
    contraindications 251
    emotional journey 248
    intervention 249–50
    materials 249
    population 248
    responses to intervention 250–1
  intergenerational psychotherapy groups 157–9
  promoting communication/interaction in Sub-Saharan African 131–4
working through process 35

Yalom, I. 176, 198, 244, 276, 285, 291, 311, 329
young children
  and animal assisted therapy 183–5
  and mindfulness practice 90–3
Young, J.E. 30

Zimerman, D. 227